Changing Perspectives on International Education

Changing Perspectives
on International Education

Edited by **Patrick O'Meara,**
Howard D. Mehlinger,
and Roxana Ma Newman

INDIANA UNIVERSITY PRESS
BLOOMINGTON AND INDIANAPOLIS

This book is a publication of
Indiana University Press
601 North Morton Street
Bloomington, IN 47404-3797 USA

http://www.indiana.edu/~iupress

Telephone orders   800-842-6796
Fax orders   812-855-7931
Orders by e-mail   iuporder@indiana.edu

© 2001 by Indiana University Press
All rights reserved

No part of this book may be reproduced or utilized in any form or
by any means, electronic or mechanical, including photocopying
and recording, or by any information storage and retrieval
system, without permission in writing from the publisher. The
Association of American University Presses' Resolution on Permissions
constitutes the only exception to this prohibition.

The paper used in this publication meets the minimum requirements
of American National Standard for Information Sciences—
Permanence of Paper for Printed Library Materials, ANSI
Z39.48-1984.

MANUFACTURED IN THE UNITED STATES OF AMERICA

Library of Congress Cataloging-in-Publication Data

Changing perspectives on international education / edited by Patrick O'Meara,
Howard D. Mehlinger, and Roxana Ma Newman.
     p.   cm.
  Includes bibliographical references and index.
  ISBN 0-253-33816-6 (cloth : alk. paper)
  1. International education—United States—Congresses. 2. Education, Higher
—United States—Congresses. I. O'Meara, Patrick.   II. Mehlinger, Howard
D.   III. Newman, Roxana Ma.

LC1090 .C46 2000
378'.016'0973—dc21

                                                                00-038876

1 2 3 4 5   05 04 03 02 01 00

CONTENTS

PREFACE

This book is one of two volumes resulting from a national conference, "International Education in American Colleges and Universities: Prospect and Retrospect," held in Washington, D.C., in April 1998, to celebrate the fortieth anniversary of Title VI of the Higher Education Act (formerly Title VI of the National Defense Education Act). In a special message read at the opening of the conference, President Bill Clinton recognized the important contribution of Title VI in encouraging the free exchange of ideas and knowledge and in promoting international understanding and world peace. U.S. Secretary of Education Richard Riley's letter addressed to the conference participants praised Title VI's successful partnership between the federal government and American colleges and universities.

Indiana University received support from the United States Department of Education, International Education and Graduate Programs Service, to conduct the conference and to publish related materials. The first volume, *Globalization and the Challenges of a New Century: A Reader,* edited by Patrick O'Meara, Howard D. Mehlinger, and Matthew Krain (Indiana University Press, 2000), is intended for university classroom use. We hope that this companion volume, *Changing Perspectives on International Education,* will provide university administrators, policymakers, and educational planners with a historical perspective on the accomplishments of Title VI programs and new insights into the directions currently affecting international studies.

ACKNOWLEDGMENTS

Grateful acknowledgment is made to the following authors and sources for permission to include or reprint material in this anthology:

"The Future of Area Studies," by David E. Albright, was presented at the Title VI 40th Anniversary Conference, "International Education in American Colleges and Universities: Prospect and Retrospect," held in Washington, D.C., April 16–17, 1998.

"Higher Education's Role in Developing Human Resources" and "The Stakeholders: An Agenda for Action" (in Part 5's final chapter, "Educating for Global Competence") are Chapter 2 and Chapter 3, respectively, of the American Council on Education's Commission on International Education report *Educating for Global Competence*. Copyright © 1997 by the American Council on Education. Reprinted with permission.

"Area Studies and the Discipline: A Useful Controversy?" by Robert H. Bates, from *PS: Political Science & Politics,* vol. 30, no. 2 (June). Copyright © 1997 by Robert H. Bates. Reprinted with permission of the author and the American Political Science Association.

"National Language Needs and Capacities: A Recommendation for Action," by Richard D. Brecht and A. Ronald Walton, from *International Education in the New Global Era: Proceedings of a National Policy Conference on the Higher Education Act, Title VI, and Fulbright-Hays Programs,* ed. John N. Hawkins et al. (Los Angeles: International Studies and Overseas Programs, UCLA). Copyright © 1998 by the Regents of the University of California. Reprinted with permission.

"Study Abroad and Foreign Language Programs," by Barbara B. Burn, from *International Education Forum,* vol. 16, no. 1 (Spring). Copyright © 1996 by the Association of International Education Administrators and Washington State University Press. Reprinted with permission.

"Guidelines for Global and International Studies Education: Challenges, Cultures, and Connections," by H. Thomas Collins, Frederick R. Czarra, and Andrew

F. Smith, from *Social Education,* vol. 62, no. 5 (September). Copyright © 1998 by the National Council for the Social Sciences. Reprinted by permission of the authors and the publisher.

"Guide to Selected International Resources," by Robert Goehlert and Anthony Stamatoplos, is excerpted from the booklet *International and Area Studies Resources: A Selected Guide,* prepared, with the assistance of Roberta Astroff, for the Title VI 40th Anniversary Conference, "International Education in American Colleges and Universities: Prospect and Retrospect," held in Washington, D.C., April 16–17, 1998. Copyright © 1998 by Indiana University. Reproduced with permission of the Office of International Programs, Indiana University.

"Globalization and Area Studies: When Is Too Broad Too Narrow?" by Peter A. Hall and Sidney Tarrow, from *The Chronicle of Higher Education,* January 23. Copyright © 1998 by Peter A. Hall and Sidney Tarrow. Reprinted with permission of the authors.

"An Attainable Global Perspective," by Robert G. Hanvey, from the theme issue on "Global Education" of *Theory Into Practice,* vol. 21, no. 3. Copyright © 1982 by the College of Education, The Ohio State University. Reprinted with permission of the publisher.

"An Overview of Title VI," by Ralph Hines. Paper presented at the Title VI 40th Anniversary Conference, "International Education in American Colleges and Universities: Prospect and Retrospect," held in Washington, D.C., April 16–17, 1998.

"Preconception vs. Observation, or the Contributions of Rational Choice Theory and Area Studies to Contemporary Political Science," by Chalmers Johnson, from *PS: Political Science & Politics,* vol. 30, no. 2 (June). Copyright © 1997 by the American Political Science Association. Reprinted with permission of the author and the publisher.

"Domains and Issues in International Studies," by Richard D. Lambert, from *International Education Forum,* vol. 16, no. 1 (Spring). Copyright © 1996 by the Association of International Education Administrators and Washington State University Press. Reprinted with permission.

"Pedagogy for Global Perspectives in Education: Studies of Teachers' Thinking and Practice," by Merry M. Merryfield, from *Theory and Research in Social Education,* vol. 26, no. 3 (Summer). Copyright © 1998 by the National Council for the Social Sciences. Reprinted by permission of the author and the publisher.

"International Outreach for the New Millennium," by John D. Metzler, from *International Education in the New Global Era: Proceedings of a National Policy Conference on the Higher Education Act, Title VI, and Fulbright-Hays Programs,* ed. John N. Hawkins et al. (Los Angeles: International Studies and Overseas Programs, UCLA). Copyright © 1998 by the Regents of the University of California. Reprinted with permission. This is a slightly revised version.

"Keynote Address," by Walter F. Mondale. Excerpted, with permission, from a speech presented at the Title VI 40th Anniversary Conference, "International Education in American Colleges and Universities: Prospect and Retrospect," held in Washington, D.C., April 16–17, 1998, by arrangement with the Greater Talent Network, Inc., New York.

"Changing U.S. Business Needs for International Expertise," by Richard W. Moxon, Elizabeth A. C. O'Shea, Mollie Brown, and Christoffer M. Escher, from *International Education in the New Global Era: Proceedings of a National Policy Conference on the Higher Education Act, Title VI, and Fulbright-Hays Programs,* ed. John N. Hawkins et al. (Los Angeles: International Studies and Overseas Programs, UCLA). Copyright © 1998 by the Regents of the University of California. Reprinted with permission.

"The Future of International Research," by Kenneth Prewitt, is the President's Report in *Social Science Research Council Biennial Report, 1996–98.* Copyright © 1999 by the Social Science Research Council. Reprinted with permission of the author and the publisher.

"Redefining International Scholarship," by Kenneth Prewitt, from *Items,* vol. 50, no.1 (March), and vol. 50, nos. 2/3 (June/September). Copyright © 1996 by the Social Science Research Council. Reprinted with permission of the author and the publisher.

"Campus Developments in Response to the Challenges of Internationalization: The Case of Ramapo College of New Jersey (U.S.A.)," by Robert A. Scott, from *Higher Education Management,* vol. 6 (March). Copyright © 1994 by the Organisation for Economic Co-operation and Development. Reprinted with the permission of OECD.

"The Internationalization of Higher Education: Policy and Program Issues," by Seth Spaulding, James Mauch, and Lin Lin, is an updated version of the original article, "The Internationalization of Higher Education: Who Should be Taught What and How," by James Mauch and Seth Spaulding, from *Journal of General Education* vol. 41. Copyright © 1992 by The Pennsylvania State University. Reprinted by permission of the Pennsylvania State University Press.

"Introduction: The Area Studies Controversy," by Mark Tessler, Jodi Nachtwey, and Anne Banda, is the first half of the introduction from *Area Studies and Social Science: Strategies for Understanding Middle East Politics,* ed. Mark Tessler, with Jodi Nachtwey and Anne Banda (Bloomington: Indiana University Press). Copyright © 1999 by Indiana University Press. Reprinted with permission of the publisher.

"The Future of International Studies," by David M. Trubek, in *Proud Traditions and Future Challenges: The University of Wisconsin–Madison Celebrates 150 Years,* ed. David Ward (Madison, WI: Office of University Publications, University of Wisconsin–Madison). Copyright © 1999 by University of Wisconsin–

Madison. Reprinted with permission by the Office of the Chancellor, University of Wisconsin–Madison.

"Crossing Borders: The Case for Area Studies," by Toby Alice Volkman, from *Ford Foundation Report,* vol. 21, no. 1 (Winter). Copyright © 1998 by the Ford Foundation. Reprinted with permission of the publisher.

"Forty Years of the Title VI and Fulbright-Hays International Education Programs: Building the Nation's International Expertise for a Global Future," by David Wiley, was presented at the Title VI 40th Anniversary Conference, "International Education in American Colleges and Universities: Prospect and Retrospect," held in Washington, D.C., April 16–17, 1998.

INTRODUCTION

More than forty years ago, there was a compelling need for Americans to become better educated about other languages and cultures if the United States was to maintain its position as a major world power. Recognizing that higher education would need to take the responsibility for that task, the U.S. government passed the National Defense Education Act (NDEA). Title VI of NDEA provided extensive aid for foreign languages and area studies development. This priority finds its modern expression in the foreign language, area, and international studies programs authorized by Title VI of the Higher Education Act. As a result, millions of Americans acquired knowledge about parts of the world that otherwise would have remained unknown to them.

Today there are new issues, demands, and perspectives. The world in which we live and our academic institutions are different places from what they were forty years ago. More people are traveling and living abroad, and more businesses are involved in global transactions. On the interpersonal level, Americans are more likely than ever before to encounter different cultures, ideologies, and ways of living. Furthermore, as perhaps the world's last remaining superpower, the United States is increasingly called upon to intervene or mediate in regional and local crises beyond its borders.

Because of these changes, there is a growing awareness on our campuses that we must teach our students more about the larger world in which they will live and work. Our educational institutions should provide the knowledge necessary for them to have informed opinions about complex international problems and issues that will affect them. The classroom is the place to begin sensitizing and educating young people about such issues as freedom and respect for human life, and to provide them with the necessary tools for critical thinking about the world and working in that world.

The 40th Anniversary Conference celebrating Title VI, "International Education in American Colleges and Universities: Prospect and Retrospect," was a good occasion to do some stocktaking about the achievements of the past and to consider new perspectives for the future. This volume includes some of the conference papers that acknowledge those achievements and that recognize the ways in which Title VI will continue to address the international education needs of the

United States. Other papers in this volume are drawn from the recently published literature on international education.

In considering the future, we appreciate that there are conflicting theories, practices, and strategies in how to approach international studies, and we have therefore included papers that are representative of the current debates. Other articles are concerned with how U.S. universities and colleges can effectively commit scarce resources to the study of different cultures and societies and how to productively serve such diverse interests as teaching, research, business, and outreach.

The formative impact of international education on K–12 through the graduate level is extremely important, and some of the authors deal in detail with precollegiate education. They raise questions about the content of global curricula in the schools and outline the background and training necessary to equip teachers for the task of exposing their students to a wider world.

We believe that international teaching, research, and service are fundamental to American education. In the future, students and scholars will have even greater opportunities to exchange ideas and jointly pursue new knowledge. But preparing people to cope with international challenges and opportunities is not a rarified or elitist mission; it must be inclusive, encompassing universities, colleges, elementary through high schools, governments, businesses, and community groups. We hope that some of the ideas expressed in this collection of papers will be useful in guiding those whose decisions today will affect the future.

Patrick O'Meara
Howard D. Mehlinger
Roxana Ma Newman
Indiana University

Changing Perspectives on International Education

Title VI and International Studies in the United States: An Overview

During the Cold War, Title VI support enabled universities and colleges to develop vital resources on various world regions and, by so doing, serve the strategic needs of the United States for international expertise. Today, the relevance of Title VI in a multipolar world of competing interests is even more crucial. Regional and local conflicts, worldwide environmental problems, and economic competitiveness on a global scale all demand wider perspectives, more specialized knowledge, and broader educational training if new solutions to these problems are to be found.

The keynote address presented at the Title VI anniversary conference by Vice President Walter F. Mondale reaffirms the vital importance of international research and teaching to the interests of the United States and its citizens, who must be able to function in an increasingly interdependent world. A distinguished practitioner and public servant, Mondale reflects on his experiences as former Vice President of the United States and as U.S. Ambassador to Japan. As ambassador, he was highly dependent on a proficient diplomatic staff with international knowledge and training.

Ralph Hines, director of the International Education and Graduate Programs Service of the U.S. Department of Education, and David Wiley, director of the African Studies Program at Michigan State University, both reflect on the origins and impact of Title VI support for international education in the United States. Their two papers record the accomplishments of this uniquely American partnership between the federal government and the higher education community. Hines maintains that many of the programs focusing on less commonly taught languages and related area studies could not have developed and survived without the government's pivotal support. Wiley emphasizes that the expertise in human resources and scholarship generated by Title VI centers and programs continues to profoundly influence and inform U.S. government agencies, the World Bank, a host of international organizations, the private sector, and the general citizenry. He reiterates the continuing need for the United States to maintain its international expertise, in the face of declining resources, changes in university priorities, and rising costs, through innovative practices such as new collaborative and exchange partners, greater outreach efforts, and the use of new technologies.

Richard D. Lambert presents a comprehensive survey of the many dimensions that constitute international education in the United States, and hopes that these can become more interrelated and integrated. He examines such important topics as funding for area programs, the need for interaction with scholars abroad, the emergence of "transnational" studies, foreign language instruction, study abroad, and the impact of foreign students on U.S. campuses. All of these are themes that recur throughout subsequent parts of this book.

Keynote Address

Walter F. Mondale

I have always believed in what Title VI is doing in training Americans to use and understand other languages of the world. We are a tongue-tied nation, which is dangerous to our future, to our economic health, to our national security and diplomacy, and to our relationship with other peoples in the world. Teaching languages with the support of Title VI has been absolutely crucial. Languages are essential to begin with, but I think much more is required. We need to understand, in the deepest sense possible, how other societies work, and this is not simple. It requires thoughtful scholarship, education, friendships, time, and all that goes into moving from an initial understanding to wisdom, depth, appreciation, and respect. The passage to mature relationships with different peoples is the basis for peace and stability.

When I went to Japan, one of the first things I discovered was how dependent I was upon people who were trained in the skills that you are teaching your students. If it were not for the career officers who assisted me in the embassy and in the U.S. consulates in Japan, I could not have been the ambassador. Their facility and ease in Japanese—a difficult language—their institutional wisdom, understanding, experience and learning, were vital. Every hour of every day, their background and training were absolutely essential to the national interests of our coun-

Excerpted, with permission, from the "Keynote Address" presented at the Title VI 40th Anniversary Conference, "International Education in American Colleges and Universities: Prospect and Retrospect," Washington, D.C., April 1998, by arrangement with the Greater Talent Network, Inc., New York.

try. The career officers in the embassy, the cultural affairs officers, the military personnel, all served the national security interests of our country and the needs of the business community through their indispensable skills. I am sure that this is repeated wherever the United States is represented throughout the world.

During the four years that I was in Japan, I was impressed with the economic dynamism which was transforming the countries of Asia. I was impressed by the richness, the complexity, and the depth of the cultures and the growing economic and political power evolving in Asia. Despite the current problems, I think that over the long run, the dynamic growth of these nations will continue. Our increasing interdependence with the region means that we have an ever greater need for deeper understanding of the history, societies, languages, and cultures of these nations, and this calls for more interdisciplinary study.

The stakes are huge: the history of our involvement in Asia is considerable. In my lifetime, three wars have broken out there. We have had more than our fair share of misunderstandings, mistaken assumptions, ignorance, arrogance, and tragic wars. Even today, it is still all too easy to get trapped into accepting and using stock images and perceptions of these very complex societies. More than ever, we need to develop a deeper, more nuanced understanding based on real experience and knowledge, not on caricatures and stereotypes. Unfortunately, the level of knowledge that we have about these societies continues to lag behind the growing importance of our relationships with Asia. We are still an insular nation, and to understand the rest of the world will take effort for most Americans.

I know that most of you have been working very hard for a very long time to help close this gap, but the challenge remains for all of us. This is why good scholarship and education are essential. Diplomacy is concerned with compelling current problems which often distract attention away from planning for the long term. People like me, who have spent their lives on politics and diplomacy, work with the world as it is. Most of our lives are spent dealing with problems that are on our desks on a particular day. In a sense, our power is limited to moving papers around the desk. We can do very little to change the direction of the ship. But scholars and students have the potential to change the direction in which the ship is steered. You can truly move our relationship with Asia to a stronger and more secure foundation.

Long-term success in our relationship across the Pacific requires more human ties and interaction. In particular, student exchanges are an investment in the future. High school or college students who go to another country and live with families really learn to function in another society. But to be successful takes effort. Language is not enough, since our cultures are so different. It is when individuals are finally able to bridge differences and deal with one another that they can build something new and better.

I left Japan with different views about international education from those I had when I first arrived. The core of skilled and language-proficient officers at the embassy and consulates are utterly crucial to our nation. I wonder how many Americans realize how crucial they are and how thin are their ranks. I am convinced that increased resources for all aspects of international education are needed. I would often ask some of my most gifted advisers, as well as skilled reporters and business leaders, how they became interested in Japan. And a remarkable number of them became involved in Japan when they were in high school or in college. Some had been part of a student exchange program or had grown up in Japan when their parents were there in the military, in business, or as missionaries. Their experiences profoundly changed their lives, and hence their professional careers centered on Japan.

I have become a strong advocate of student exchanges starting in the high school years, especially where these involve living with a host family. I think we need much more. Nearly half a million international students attend U.S. colleges and universities; by contrast, just over 100,000 American students study abroad each year. This is especially striking given the fact that almost 60% of all international students are from Asia, especially from Japan and China. In fact, Asia accounts for nine of the top ten nations of origin for international students. The problem, of course, is that fewer than 6,000 American students go abroad to Asia each year, just one-tenth of the number we send to Europe. I was glad to learn, when I was in Japan, that there is a growing interest on the part of American and Japanese businesses in hiring young liberal arts students with some language training and multicultural experience.

Your work is absolutely crucial. When you think of how important different nations are to us, and you look at the very thin veneer of people that are actually involved in understanding and speaking their languages and working with them, the situation is dangerous. These relationships are so critical that we need a much broader underpinning of connections than we currently have today. And that is what *you* do. I am proud of your work; congratulations!

An Overview of Title VI

Ralph Hines

This paper discusses the history of Title VI and its impact on the development of international studies in the United States. It also references other legislation and developments that helped shape the character and administration of the programs authorized under Title VI. Finally, it discusses the current activities supported under this legislation and the contributions Title VI and Fulbright-Hays have made toward developing the nation's international expertise.

In the Beginning: 1958

In August 1958, largely as a response to the Russian launching of *Sputnik,* Congress enacted the National Defense Education Act (NDEA). At that time, its objective was narrow and clearly articulated: "to insure trained manpower of sufficient quality and quantity to meet the national defense needs of the United States." Under that rubric, the federal government supported the education of specialists in various disciplines, among them foreign language and area studies. Title VI was entitled "Language Development."

Prior to the passage of the act, few of the languages spoken by more than three-fourths of the world's population were being offered in the United States, and not enough scholars were available to perform research in such languages or to teach them. These uncommon, neglected languages, when they were taught, were offered irregularly, and usually to only a handful of students. Hindi, for example, was being studied by only twenty-three students in the United States in 1958. Even the common languages, those usually found in the curriculum, were

This paper was presented at the Title VI 40th Anniversary Conference, "International Education in American Colleges and Universities: Prospect and Retrospect," Washington, D.C., April 1998.

taught by methods and materials largely inadequate to provide speaking and listening skills, and with little reference to research in language learning and other fields. To help remedy this situation, several interlocking programs were authorized under Title VI:

> *Language and Area Centers* for expansion of instruction in higher education of the uncommon languages and related subjects;

> *Modern Foreign Language Fellowships* to assist qualified advanced students in the study of the uncommon languages;

> *Research and Studies* to support research in language learning methodology and specialized teaching materials in both the common and uncommon languages; and

> *Language Institutes* to provide advanced language training, particularly in the use of new teaching materials and methods, for elementary and secondary school teachers.

In the first year of the program, 19 centers, 171 fellowships, and 20 research projects were funded, at a cost of $3.5 million. That same year, 16 language institutes were conducted, totaling $1.5 million. By the end of the fourth year of operation, Title VI was supporting 55 centers, 904 fellowships, 33 research and studies projects, and 83 language institutes. Since the original concern driving the passage of Title VI was the lack of expertise in the uncommon languages, it is easy to understand why the bulk of the early appropriations went to the preparation of foreign language teachers and research and studies related to language learning. In 1963, language institutes received $7.25 million and the other three programs a total of $7.97 million.

While Title VI was evolving and expanding its original mandate, Senator J. William Fulbright was successful in getting Congress to pass the Mutual Educational and Cultural Exchange Act of l961 (Fulbright-Hays Act). This act grew out of the conviction that intellectual and cultural exchange between nations contributes to increased awareness of intercultural similarities and differences, and thus contributes to mutual understanding and increases the opportunities for peaceful resolution of conflict. Because of its emphasis on strengthening American education, Section 102(b)(6) of this act was ultimately assigned to the Department of Health, Education, and Welfare through an Executive Order issued by President Kennedy. Although there were no specific programs designated by this legislation, it did provide for visits and study in foreign countries by American teachers and prospective teachers. Therefore, under the authority of this section, four programs were established: Doctoral Dissertation Research Abroad (DDRA); Faculty Research Abroad (FRA); Group Projects Abroad (GPA); and Foreign Curriculum Consultants (FCC). Three of these programs continue to be administered by the Department of Education. They provide an essential overseas complement to the activities authorized under Title VI.

Another important piece of legislation that helped define the federal role in international education was the International Education Act (IEA). It was passed by the Congress in 1966 and signed into law by President Johnson. Though funds were never appropriated to support this visionary statute, it made an impact on future iterations of Title VI and on the way the federal role in international education was viewed. Many of its provisions would find expression in new programs and expansion of activities in existing programs in the early 1970s and beyond. IEA assumed that the federal government had an obligation to provide broad-based institutional support for international education, that federal funds should be used to enrich the general curriculum, and not be limited to advanced training in languages and area studies. IEA emphasized educating citizens as much as training specialists.

Growing Pains: The Middle Years

Following a decade of steady growth in appropriations and numbers of programs and projects, with the now flagship Language and Area Centers numbering 106 at 59 different institutions, support from the administration deteriorated. There were calls for the elimination of the program. The rationale offered was that the purposes for which Title VI was enacted had largely been satisfied, and that continuing needs for foreign language and area specialists could be supported through non-federal means. While Title VI was not eliminated, the threat of such an action caused the constituency and other supporters to rally around the program and lobby for its continuation. The efforts of the interest groups were successful, and the Nixon administration's position on Title VI changed. Throughout this period, Congress continued to appropriate funds to support the program. By the mid-1970s, Title VI could be characterized as a modest but stable program.

In 1972, Title VI's scope was expanded beyond its traditional emphasis on specialist training. Funded centers were required to focus on more functional topics and to spend some of their funds on outreach. Title VI also began funding two-year seed money projects that graduate and undergraduate programs could use to internationalize their curricula. The rationale offered by the Office of Education for these new initiatives was that they were following Congressional intent as articulated in the IEA. It was felt that extending the benefits of Title VI to a larger constituency would help insulate the program from future attempts to reduce or eliminate its funding. This bold move also stoked the fires of the two competing camps: those who supported the narrow, specialist-producing role; and those who viewed Title VI as an opportunity to support general enrichment or diffusion of knowledge about international issues. This juxtaposition of narrow versus broad would inform the debate about the appropriate role of Title VI and cause strains among its constituents well into the 1990s.

The original provisions of the NDEA Title VI were folded into the Higher Education Act (HEA) of 1980. The new legislation authorized a new Part B. This new part provided funds on a matching basis for institutions of higher education to develop and enhance their academic programs and provide appropriate services to American firms doing business abroad. This addition reflected Congressional judgment that federal support for international education should address economic productivity as well as foreign policy. Before the end of the 1980s, four additional programs would be authorized under the Title VI umbrella: (1) Section 603—Language Resource Centers; (2) Section 605—Summer Language Institutes; (3) Section 607—Foreign Periodicals Program; and (4) Section 612—Centers for International Business Education Program. In 1992, the reauthorization of the HEA added Section 610—American Overseas Research Centers, and a new Part C, the Institute for International Public Policy.

Title VI: Preparing for the Twenty-First Century

Since its inception, Title VI has formed the keystone of federal support for international education. Though its resources are modest in comparison to most federal programs, it has helped define the development of language and area studies programs in this country. Without the funds provided under Title VI, many of the programs at institutions of higher education focusing on the less commonly taught languages and related area studies would not be sustained. Title VI continues to be the primary vehicle for the production of specialists in foreign language, area, and international studies among federal programs. It also has established an unmatched record of accomplishments in supporting the internationalization of higher education throughout the United States. These programs serve constituents ranging from Ph.D. degree–granting institutions to K–12 schools, as well as the community at large. The programs authorized under Title VI form a pipeline that provides for the training, research, and material needs of institutions as well as students, teachers, and scholars. All of the current programs authorized and funded under Title VI have the common goal of improving and expanding foreign language, area, and international studies in the United States. In addition, an overarching requirement is that these programs share their resources with other institutions and communities through well-planned programs of outreach. This is particularly the case for the network of language, area, and business centers supported under Title VI.

Forty years after the enactment of NDEA Title VI, nine grant programs are currently funded under the authority of Title VI HEA, as amended: National Resource Centers; Foreign Language and Area Fellowships; International Research and Studies; Language Resource Centers; American Overseas Research Centers; Undergraduate International Studies and Foreign Language; Business and International Education; Centers for International Business Education and Research; and Institute for International Public Policy.

Under the Fulbright-Hays Act [Section 102 (b)(6)], four programs are currently administered by the Department: Doctoral Research Abroad; Faculty Research Abroad; Group Projects Abroad; and Seminars Abroad. In the current fiscal year, these programs are supported at a budget level of $60,351,000: $54,581,000 for Title VI and $5,770,000 for Fulbright-Hays. These funds will support approximately 335 institutional projects and programs and 1,144 fellowships. Over the last ten years, using these estimates as the average, Title VI and Fulbright-Hays have supported approximately 3,350 institutional projects and programs and 11,440 fellowships. When tallying the numbers of courses, programs, institutions, and individuals impacted by these 13 programs, Title VI and Fulbright-Hays far outweigh the relatively small federal investment. The evidence clearly shows that the federal interest and support provided by these programs leverages a large amount of non-federal support. For example, a recent survey of Centers for International Business Education revealed that Title VI funds are leveraged with institutional and private sector funds which add an estimated $24.5 million annually, more than three times the federal investment.

The success of Title VI, in large part, can be attributed to the partnership between the Department and its many supporters. We thank all of them for their untiring and dedicated efforts over the years to sustain and grow Title VI to better serve this nation's need for international expertise. While this occasion is primarily designed to celebrate the contributions of Title VI and examine future directions for international studies, I believe it is appropriate that we also honor the many individuals, institutions, and organizations who have contributed to its growth, development, and survival. In the complex and unpredictable post–Cold War world we live in today, Title VI more than ever is critical to addressing the nation's continuing and emerging national needs for international competence. I hope all of you will be a part of the Title VI extended family when we celebrate the fiftieth anniversary of this legislation ten years from now.

REFERENCES

The following sources were consulted in the development of this paper:

Donald N. Bigelow and Lyman H. Letgers, *NDEA Language and Area Centers: A Report on the First Five Years.* Prepared for the U.S. Department of Health, Education, and Welfare, Office of Education. Washington, D.C.: U.S. Government Printing Office, 1964.

John N. Hawkins et al., *International Education in the New Global Era: Proceedings of a National Policy Conference on the Higher Education Act, Title VI, and Fulbright-Hays Programs.* Los Angeles: International Studies and Overseas Programs, UCLA, 1998. The article by Richard D. Scarfo, "The History of Title VI," pp. 23–25, also provided background information for this paper.

Lorraine McDonnell et al., *Federal Support for International Studies: The Role of NDEA Title VI.* Santa Monica, CA: The RAND Corporation, 1981.

U.S. Department of Education, "International Education and Graduate Programs Service: Fiscal Year 1998 Budget Breakout." Washington, D.C., 1998.

Forty Years of the Title VI and Fulbright-Hays International Education Programs

BUILDING THE NATION'S INTERNATIONAL
EXPERTISE FOR A GLOBAL FUTURE

David Wiley

During the past forty years, the contributions of the Title VI programs of the Higher Education Act of 1965 to the vital interests of the United States have been extensive and diverse. The programs serve a broad array of beneficiaries—in the professional foreign policy institutions of government and the private sector, in international business and economic affairs, in the increasingly internationalized institutions of U.S. higher and K–12 education, and in citizen education and exchange programs.

In this paper,[1] I review the history of the establishment of the Title VI and Fulbright-Hays programs in the 1950s and 1960s, the changes in the program over its forty years and the breadth of its current component programs, vignettes of service to government and the private sector especially by the National Resource Centers (NRCs), and the unique characteristics of these programs, particularly the NRCs. I conclude by considering the global and domestic changes that require new directions in Title VI and international education programs in the United States.

New Nations and Nascent International Studies

Throughout these forty years, the creation and gradual evolution of the Title VI Higher Education Act (HEA) and its associated Fulbright-Hays programs has been one of the U.S. government's major endeavors for responding to the growing complexities of global politics and economics in the twentieth century. The very existence of these programs is a clear statement that international programs and international studies are a federal responsibility and that they are vital to serve the national interests of the United States. A brief historical survey provides a view of the national ethos that has enabled these programs to emerge.

The twentieth century has been characterized by a rapidly emerging global economic system and a drive for national self-determination, realities that continually strained the creativity of educators to comprehend these changes and to adjust not only their maps but also their pedagogical goals, teaching materials, and institutions. In 1900, shortly after the Berlin Conference, the world had only 40 nations, and many regions were under colonial rule. By 1920, as the concept of the nation-state spread and the global political framework began to emerge around the League of Nations, 60 nations had emerged. After the surge of decolonization from 1948 to1975, the world had 150 nations. [Today 188 countries are members of the United Nations.]

In the 1940s, the number of U.S. scholars able to comprehend these changes in foreign areas was small, as was the number of university foreign area studies programs. Even at the advent of World War II, few U.S. universities offered Ph.D. degrees in anything other than Western European studies. In fact, at that time, only about 400 Ph.D.s had been completed in the United States concerning foreign area or international affairs, mostly concerning Europe with a few offerings based on a few Asian and Latin American countries. In 1947, excepting Western European studies, there were only fourteen language and area studies programs on all U.S. campuses—six for Latin America, four for East and Southeast Asia, three for East Europe, one for South Asia, and none for Africa or the Middle East.

By 1951, however, that number had grown to twenty-five foreign area programs, including the first African center. In the 1950s, the United States began to assert global leadership, realizing that many of its security and economic interests were now abroad and that it needed to develop new policies and programs in support of these expanded interests. To do so required committing federal funds to promote advanced research and training in foreign languages and international studies. The growth of scholarship about foreign areas in U.S. universities and government support for this body of scholarship have thus developed hand in hand.

The Emergence of the Title VI Program in the 1950s

How did the Title VI effort to build a national core of language and area expertise emerge? In the post–World War II period, quite diverse constituencies in the United States thought it imperative to advocate an increased investment in advanced language, area, and international studies. Throughout the 1940s, academic and governmental bodies had already been developing special initiatives such as the Intensive Language Program (American Council of Learned Societies), the Foreign Language Program (Modern Language Association), and the Army Specialized Training Program. These were early prototypes of language training programs, and aspects of these models would later become incorporated into the National Defense Education Act (NDEA).

Also instrumental in the push to develop U.S. international expertise during this period was a group of liberal influential U.S. senators, representatives, some foreign policy experts, and interested citizens who had actively supported U.S. participation in the League of Nations (1918–40) and the consequent formation of the United Nations in 1945. For example, Senator J. William Fulbright's vision of America's role in the world was built on his own experiences as a Rhodes Scholar at Oxford in 1928 and as president of the University of Arkansas (1939–41). As a recently elected senator, he boldly authored the Fulbright Act in 1946 to institutionalize federal support for research, teaching, and graduate study abroad. He was supported by a bipartisan coalition of senators with a broad international vision, including Hubert Humphrey (Minnesota), Lyndon Johnson (Texas), Estes Kefauver (Tennessee), George Aiken (Vermont), Wayne Morse (Oregon), and John F. Kennedy (Massachusetts).

The appearance in October 1957 of the Soviet satellite *Sputnik* in the night skies over the nation was stunning proof of the USSR's technological leap from its pre-war days, and an unmistakable signal from the Soviets of their seriousness in contending for geopolitical leadership in a world of multiplying nations shedding colonial rule. In this new era of self-determination and independence, the former European colonial powers could no longer guarantee access to the strategic space-age minerals of Africa, Asia, and Latin America. They could no longer exercise any coercion over their former colonies regarding decision-making and voting at the forums of global governance. *Sputnik,* and all it signified, was the catalyst that finally pushed the U.S. government, in 1958, to create the National Defense Education Act (under the then Department of Health, Education and Welfare). NDEA thus heralded a major U.S. commitment to devoting new attention to the world beyond its borders—first to teach more of the uncommonly taught foreign languages, and then to learn in depth about the histories, societies, cultures, and political systems of the key foreign powers as well as of the rapidly multiplying "Third World" nations. The initial phase of this commitment was to encourage study of the less common foreign languages such as Russian, Chinese, Japanese, Arabic, Hindi-Urdu, and Portuguese.

The NDEA established four different programs: (1) the creation of language and area centers, (2) fellowships to students for language study, (3) support for research and studies projects such as language surveys and language teaching development, and (4) language institutes to train language teachers and program administrators. Three years after establishing these programs at American institutions of higher education—the so-called "domestic programs"—the U.S. Congress then passed the Mutual Educational and Cultural Exchange Act of 1961, known as the "Fulbright-Hays Act," to provide for training programs overseas (see below).

Simultaneously, in the late 1950s and early 1960s, the foreign policy experts of the U.S. State Department and the National Security Council, with ancillary support from the Council on Foreign Relations and other non-governmental organizations, advocated increased funding to support foreign language and area knowledge. There was an urgent need to build a more consensual world order based on the concept of détente, "peaceful coexistence," and increasing engagement with the Soviet/Eastern Bloc and the newly independent nations. Under President John F. Kennedy—who considered the United States "the first anti-colonial nation"—the country sought to relate more positively to all of these new geopolitical entities. The United States would have to relinquish its ambivalence about being thrust into a global leadership role, and it would have to demonstrate a greater ability to communicate with these countries. As a world leader, however, the United States was desperately short of the needed expertise in foreign languages and world area knowledge.

As allies in building this new U.S. spirit of internationalism, major foundations such as the Ford Foundation, as well as Rockefeller, Carnegie, and Mellon, joined in by providing additional specialized support. Ford, especially, invested heavily in the "Foreign Area Fellowships Program" for Ph.D. candidates in foreign language and area studies in the social science and humanities disciplines. Ford's investment contributed measurably to building the first cohort of students of non-Western language and area studies in the 1960s, many of whom are now the senior leaders of international centers and programs in the 1990s.

The Fulbright-Hays Act

The passage in 1961 of the Mutual Educational and Cultural Exchange Act ("Fulbright-Hays Act") provided further federal support for strengthening education in the field of modern foreign language and area studies for building the nation's international expertise. As assigned by President Kennedy (Executive Order 11034, June 25, 1962), the domestic needs authorized under Section 102(b)(6) resided in the U.S. Department of Health, Education, and Welfare (DHEW), which at that time had statutory responsibility for educational matters. This focus on the domestic needs was reinforced by linking the programs of Section 102(b)(6) to the objectives of the NDEA Title VI programs. The DHEW, the U.S. Department of State, and the then Bureau of the Budget, along with Senator Fulbright, all concurred that the programs authorized under Section 102(b)(6)—first funded in 1964—were to add an overseas dimension to the domestic NDEA Title VI programs. The four Fulbright-Hays programs, funded under the authorization of the U.S. Department of Education, are (1) Faculty Research Abroad, (2) Seminars Abroad, (3) Group Projects Abroad, and (4) Doctoral Dissertation Research Abroad. All four programs have retained this educationally sound link to the international education programs currently authorized under Title VI of the HEA.

Changes in Title VI with the
End of the Cold War

In 1980, as détente continued, Title VI of NDEA was incorporated into the Higher Education Act of 1965 as Title VI of that act to reflect the lessened focus of Title VI programs to support U.S. government needs and to emphasize a greater focus on their importance as educational programs within higher education. By then, U.S. military and intelligence agencies had already erected large units for analysis and training within their own agencies. Although these agencies sometimes utilized university graduates of the Title VI programs, especially for projects on the Soviet Union and China, their work and training programs were clearly separated from the National Resource Centers and other programs funded under Title VI by the Department of Education.

In the mid-1960s, Congress passed the International Education Act, which, although never funded, had an impact on Title VI in that it helped to redefine and broaden the federal role in higher education. The most important of these ideas, incorporated in subsequent reauthorizations of the HEA, were that national resource centers need not confine themselves to regionally defined international issues, that the international activities of professional schools also receive federal funding along with the social sciences and humanities, and that general undergraduate education also be targeted for international training. Title VI programs are therefore constantly being amended to reflect evolving educational needs and global challenges.

After the end of the Cold War, Congress again reaffirmed and recast the continuing relevance of the Title VI programs. Several administrations, Congresses, and special lobbyists succeeded both in adding new mandates to the foreign area studies programs and in creating new Title VI programs. In its 1998 reauthorization of Title VI, Congress redefined the U.S. interests that the programs were now to address, recognizing the growing effects of globalization, and especially the impact of the new communications technologies, as summarized in (2) of the "Findings" below:

> *FINDINGS*—Congress finds as follows:
>
> (1) The security, stability, and economic vitality of the United States in a complex global era depend upon American experts in and citizens knowledgeable about world regions, foreign languages, and international affairs, as well as upon a strong research base in these areas.
>
> (2) Advances in communications technology and the growth of regional and global problems make knowledge of other countries and the ability to communicate in other languages more essential to the promotion of mutual understanding and cooperation among nations and their peoples.
>
> (3) Dramatic post–Cold War changes in the world's geopolitical and eco-

nomic landscapes are creating needs for American expertise and knowledge about a greater diversity of less commonly taught languages (LCTLs) and nations of the world.[2]

The Ten Title VI and
Four Fulbright-Hays Programs

In the original cohort of Title VI programs formed in 1959, there were nineteen centers of area and international studies (now referred to as the "NRCs"). In 1972, these NRCs had their mandate expanded to include outreach to the media, business, K–12 schools, four-year and community colleges, and the general public, in addition to their traditional teaching and research functions. In the 1980s and 1990s, Title VI underwent reformulation and enlargement, in which a series of special outreach, language, and business programs were established, such as the Business and International Education Program, the Centers for International Business Education (CIBERs), the Language Resource Centers (LRCs), the American Overseas Research Centers, the Institute for International Public Policy, and, most recently, the Technological Innovation and Cooperation for Foreign Information Access Program.

The gradual reformulation of Title VI over the past two decades and in the five-year re-authorization of the Higher Education Act in 1999, and the addition of Fulbright-Hays programs, have thus resulted in fourteen separate programs currently supported by the federal government to address the need for international and foreign language education in the nation. Nine of these are considered "domestic programs," in that their activities take place at U.S. higher education institutions. A tenth, the American Overseas Research Centers, maintains centers abroad. The remaining four are the Fulbright-Hays programs, whose activities are primarily carried out overseas.

In 1999, the U.S. Department of Education made more than 529 international education grants to institutions of higher education and directly supported 1,713 individuals through fellowships and projects in these programs. These 14 programs are summarized in the table below. All of these are administered through the office of the International Education and Graduate Programs Service (IEGPS) of the U.S. Department of Education. The programs are described in greater detail on the World Wide Web home page of IEGPS at <http://ed.gov/offices/OPE/HEP/iegps/index.html>.

Decline in Federal Support
for Expanded Programs

In FY2000, this array of fourteen federal programs was supported with a Congressional appropriation of almost $70 million. Contrary to the perception of some university administrators, the federal budget for all Title VI and associated Fulbright-Hays programs has increased by more than 100% in the 1990s, from

Title VI and Fulbright-Hays Programs in FY1999

Program Type	Program Description
National Resource Centers (NRC)	(FY99: $21,000,100) 109 continuation awards averaging $192,661 at centers for teaching modern foreign languages; instruction on areas, regions, or countries; research and training in international studies or world affairs.
Foreign Language and Area Studies Fellowships (FLAS)	(FY99: $14,900,000) 129 institutional continuation awards averaging $115,504 for approximately 619 new academic year fellowships and 420 new summer fellowships for advanced training of graduate students in foreign language and area or international studies.
Undergraduate International Studies and Foreign Language Program	(FY99: $4,113,450) 59 new and continuation awards averaging $69,720 typically to four-year and community college institutions or consortia to strengthen undergraduate instruction in international studies and foreign languages.
International Research and Studies	(FY99: $3,355,372) 29 new and continuing awards averaging $115,702 for surveys, studies, and instructional materials to improve instruction in foreign languages, area studies, and other international fields.
Language Resource Centers (LRC)	(FY99: $2,884,628) 9 new awards averaging $320,514 for improving the national teaching and learning of foreign languages through teacher training, research, materials development, and dissemination projects.
Business and International Education (BIE)	(FY99: $4,006,369) 53 new and continuation awards averaging $75,592 to institutions of higher education that enter into an agreement with a trade association and/or business for improving the teaching of the business curriculum and to expand the international capacity of the business community.
Centers for International Business Education and Research (CIBER)	(FY99: $7,917,358) 28 new and continuation awards averaging $282,763 to schools of business for curriculum development, research, and training on issues of importance to U.S. trade and competitiveness.
Technological Innovation and Cooperation for Foreign Information Access	(FY99: $1,035,000) 8 new awards to develop innovative techniques using new electronic technologies to access, collect, organize, preserve, and disseminate information on world regions and countries.
Institute for International Public Policy	(FY99: $997,781) A single new award to a consortium to operate an institute designed to increase the representation of minorities in international foreign service, including private international voluntary organizations.

American Overseas Research Centers (AORC)	(FY99: $650,000) 11 new awards averaging $59,091 to consortia to operate overseas research centers that promote postgraduate research, exchanges, area studies, and provide assistance to American scholars.
Fulbright-Hays Doctoral Dissertation Research Abroad	(FY99: $2,094,869) 30 new institutional awards for 95 fellowships to doctoral students for research abroad in the field of modern foreign languages and area studies.
Fulbright-Hays Faculty Research Abroad	(FY99: $891,000) 18 new institutional awards for 19 fellowships for faculty at institutions of higher education to enable them to maintain and improve their language skills and conduct research on topics related to their language and area studies field of specialization.
Fulbright-Hays Group Projects Abroad	(FY99: $2,325,430) 39 new institutional awards involving 464 K–12 teachers, prospective teachers (undergraduate and graduate students), and higher education faculty involved in curriculum development, group research or study projects, or in advanced intensive foreign language programs overseas.
Fulbright-Hays Seminars Abroad—Bilateral Projects	(FY99: $1,112,351) 7 new projects for short-term study abroad for 96 U.S. educators to develop their understanding and knowledge of non-Western societies.

$34 million in 1990 to its present level of almost $70 million. This increase reveals the priority that some members of Congress place on these vital programs.

However, this statistic is misleading in several respects when viewed over the forty-year history of the programs. First, in FY99 the total Title VI budget for the NRCs, FLAS Fellowships, International Research and Studies, and Fulbright-Hays programs—what I would consider the "core academic" programs—was less than half that of 1967 in real terms (adjusted for inflation). This was a consequence of the addition of several new programs with only small increases in the overall budget. As a result, Title VI National Resource Centers (NRCs) in the 1960s had a budget of $282,000 per center per year on average (1999 dollars adjusted for inflation) for their exclusive focus on academic research and training in foreign languages and area studies. In the 1990s, NRCs received an average budget of $193,000 to support faculties that are larger by three- to ten-fold and include the additional outreach programs that were not mandated in the 1960s.

Second, no recent administration has requested a major increase in funding for these programs, in spite of the perception of many that these programs are of vital national interest and therefore a necessary federal commitment. This is because of the pressure in the 1980s and 1990s from both the administration and Congress to avoid budget increases and to decrease federal spending. For instance, under the Clinton administration in FY94–99, when education was being given expanded priority, all other Department of Education programs grew by sizable percentages, whereas the Title VI programs grew by only 3.5%.

As a result, many of these "core" international programs are underfunded and are made tenable only with matching funds from the universities and other recipients who provide 50 percent or more of the federal funding. In the case of the 109 National Resource Centers in African, Asian, Middle Eastern, International, Latin American, Canadian, European, and Eurasian language and area studies, the universities provide the largest share of the total costs of the centers.

The Diversity of International Expertise Contributed by Title VI Centers to Serve the Nation

Too often, the image of these university Title VI NRCs, their faculty, and their work has been of a few professors of literature, linguistics, history, religion, anthropology, and politics studying small groups of people in remote lands at a careful, comfortable pace, all for publishing obscure scholarly works that are more relevant to faculty tenure and promotion than to any real interests of government policy-makers, companies, or the general public. In point of fact, in the 1990s the scale, topical diversity, relevance, and policy engagement of these 109 NRCs are quite astonishing. Today, the area and international studies faculties are far more diverse than the first cohort of nineteen Title VI centers funded in 1959.

In the 1990s, the NRC key faculties contain a wide range of academic fields —including economists, sociologists, foreign policy analysts, agriculturalists, geographers, legal experts, and epidemiologists—and a wide variety of professional faculty. For instance, NRC faculties now contain criminal justice and legal specialists on international crime and terrorism, educationists focused on science and technology training abroad, communication faculty studying foreign broadcasting and Internet diffusion, agricultural economists of food security and micro-enterprise development, fisheries and wildlife specialists attending to world deforestation and fishery depletion, resource scientists studying global environmental issues, and health and medical faculty studying the global spread of malaria, HIV/AIDS, and the new resistant infections.

By including a wide diversity of faculty from the disciplines of natural and physical sciences, humanities, and social sciences, as well as the applied professions (agriculture, business, communication, criminal justice, education, health and medicine, labor and industrial relations, law, etc.), the faculties of these NRCs are large, normally 25 to 60 faculty whose basic professional focus is on a foreign area or region. When professional faculty with a year or more of experience in the foreign area are added to these "key faculty," some of these NRC faculties exceed 100 members.

As a result of this diversity, these NRC faculties are engaged in a broad array of U.S. governmental, non-governmental, business, and educational programs in service of the nation's broad interests. Clearly, in the 1990s, the U.S. Departments of Agriculture, Commerce, and Treasury, the Environmental Protection Agency, and the National Institutes of Health/National Institute of Mental Health, which were conceived originally to serve largely domestic needs, now are deeply immersed in international affairs, policy, negotiations, bi- and multinational exchange, and international decision-making. In addition, the NRCs provide services not only to teachers in K–12 and community college and four-year institutions, but also to the news media, business, ethnic communities, civic organizations, and professional associations working abroad (e.g., in law enforcement, security, public health, and nursing).

Selected cases of such far-reaching service that were elicited from NRC directors include the following:

- When the State Department teaches its officers at the Foreign Service Institute or the Peace Corps teaches its volunteers in Arabic, Hausa, Hindi, Indonesian, Mandarin, Uzbek, and dozens of other LCTLs, they are using methodologies and often specific training materials developed and refined in Title VI language programs and centers. As a service to the nation, many of those much less commonly taught languages, such as Xhosa, Kazakh, and Maya, are not offered in any government institute but only at Title VI centers and their summer intensive language institutes. As a result, many of the NRCs provide translation services in these languages for U.S. agencies, courts, hospitals, and companies.

- When the Centers for Disease Control, the World Health Organization, and the National Institutes of Health meet to discuss the global spread of malaria and AIDS, Title VI faculty from several universities are at the table, at the laboratory bench, and in the field abroad. When the National Science Foundation formed an Advisory Committee for International Programs, Title VI centers provided relevant guidance.

- When the United States was participating in mounting the International War Crimes Tribunal in Bosnia and formulating the new United Nations policy on international drug trafficking, the faculty experts of the Title VI Russian and East European Center at the University of Pittsburgh were engaged.

- When pathbreaking global conferences were organized on issues of women (in Nairobi) and the environment (in Rio de Janeiro), their delegates and many of their materials originated in the Title VI NRC Centers, where there was academic research on issues of gender and minority equity and on the environment long before these topics were popular. Increasingly, these NRCs are engaged in serving the explosion of new minority immigrants in this country—Chinese, Ethiopians, Lebanese, Mexicans, Filipinos, Somalis, Vietnamese, and others—many with strong interests in heritage learning of language and area studies.

- When the United States and Japan discuss economic agendas in their annual parliamentary exchanges and the Carnegie Corporation convenes international experts on cooperation in humanitarian interventions around the world, George Washington University's Title VI International Relations Center is providing expertise.

- In 1998, when the delegates in the Western hemisphere were preparing for the Presidential Summit of the Americas in Santiago, they drew on preparatory materials from "Americas.Net," a project of the Latin American and Caribbean Title VI Center at Florida International University with the universities in Chile, Hewlett-Packard, Microsoft, and BellSouth. A number of the Title VI centers also have mounted definitive international Web sites and e-mail lists on their world area, such as the broad Africa site at the University of Pennsylvania and the Africa study abroad, film and video, and H-Net lists on Africa, and South African higher education sites at Michigan State University.

- When the U.S. Agency for International Development, the World Bank, or Bread for the World discusses the pressing issues of drought early warning, food security, and land tenure in Africa, the African Studies NRCs at Boston University, Florida, Illinois, Michigan State, Ohio State, UCLA, and Wisconsin participate.

- The Title VI Canadian Studies Center at SUNY–Plattsburgh has formed a Canada-U.S. Business Council that enables leaders in business and the U.S. government to receive briefings by leading U.S.-Canada specialists on economic, trade, and political affairs of the United States' largest trading partner.

- When President Clinton visited Africa in 1999, and when U.S. ambassadors regularly prepare to depart for their foreign assignments or when Congressional committees seek testimony on international trade, terrorism, drug controls, and responses to global warming, Title VI NRC faculty provide background papers, briefings, and policy guidance.

- NRC faculty also provide regular assistance to communities, foreign policy associations, fraternal and religious organizations, and members of the general public as they debate key foreign policy issues. For instance, Latin American NRCs have assisted communities in debating immigration and trade policy for Central America and U.S. policy on Cuba and the Panama Canal. Asia specialists in Title VI NRCs have provided analyses of Vietnam policy and China trade and human rights issues in recent years. Africanists in Title VI centers have furnished assessments of the apartheid government in South Africa and of the new movements for democracy across the continent. And Russian and East European NRC faculty have contributed crucial analysis during the transitions at the fall of the Soviet state and the end of the Cold War. NRC Middle Eastern experts counseled on U.S. responses to the political turbulence in Sudan and Algeria. Such use of intelligent academic analysis that is somewhat more distant from the policy decisions of State Department and National Security Council policy-makers helps to ensure that the longer-term interests of the United States and its business and humane interests are being served.

Indeed, wherever there is international diplomacy, public media comment on breaking news, sister city exchanges, trade and business investments, foreign language learning, and educating the next generation about international studies, Title VI faculty expertise is involved—in giving advice on particular issues; in deciding what is important to know; in constructing the courses, colloquia, and conferences for the experts; in writing the textbooks and reference works; in indexing and evaluating the films, videotapes, and texts; and, perhaps most important, in training the next generation of U.S. experts about the global systems, international issues and policy, world regions and countries, and foreign languages.

The Durability and Enduring National Need for Title VI Programs in the Twenty-First Century

In re-examining four decades of the Title VI effort,[3] I see two major complementary forces motivating this relatively small federal program—first, continual innovation for outreach and service to the nation, and second, maintaining the core foundation of training experts in language, area, and international knowledge.

First, in terms of innovation, Title VI and Fulbright-Hays programs have continually evolved and innovated in the past twenty years, responding to the increasing and ever more complex needs for international education by funding an increasing diversity of programs (as in the table above) over and above the original NRC language and area research and training programs.

Second, in spite of real budget reductions, the Title VI NRC programs have used the federal funds to leverage local university and foundation support to build and maintain the core of expertise of new knowledge about international systems, nations, and languages and the training of the next generation of international experts. Only with this continually renewed groundwork can there be high-quality and strategically valuable international knowledge that will benefit diverse U.S. users in government and the private sector.

This uniquely U.S. system does not follow the West and East European patterns of central governmental foreign area institutes. Instead, the Title VI program has established a complex, dispersed, interlinked, and competitively enlarging system of expertise-building that is serving the United States well. Even though Belgium, Britain, France, Germany, Italy, Portugal, and Spain were first to begin carrying out foreign area and language studies of their respective colonies, today it is in the U.S. international studies communities where the largest collections of scholars, experts, libraries, and other resources in the world reside.

In addition, three key elements were central in making possible this unique international studies system. For the sake of U.S. national interests, these elements must continue if these programs are to maintain their value. The first element is a commitment to competition among grantees for Title VI awards as a means of achieving programs that, over the years, are of increasingly higher quality, larger scale, and user relevance, and that maximize the efficient investment of federal and university funds. The Congress and administration did not use the "command and control" model to create and fund all aspects of Title VI programs as the Defense Department did with military industries. Rather, the Department of Education provided incentive funding that rewarded creative university initiatives to respond to the national needs by investing in faculty and administrators, programs, libraries, and foreign language and international studies. The result of this federal leveraging of university funds—in both private and public institutions—was that by the 1980s about 95% of all funding for foreign language and international studies in the NRCs came from the universities themselves. Even in the CIBERs and LRCs, more university funds are being invested than federal funds, even though the match ratio is not as high.

The second key element in the Title VI system has been to achieve quality through merit-based competitions for awards, both institutional and individual. There are no sinecures for the NRCs, and all centers must reapply on the basis of the merit criteria every triennium. At the heart of these merit-based competitions is a peer review process using rankings based on multiple criteria of excellence.

The third key element has been to build these programs for the long term. In contrast to some donors and program funders in foundations and other federal agencies who prize innovation and changing foci more than sustained excellence in priority fields, Title VI programs have emphasized steady and stable growth. While encouraging innovation throughout the system, the U.S. Department of Education has emphasized the long-term building of language capacity, instructional programs, and scholarship for new knowledge. This capacity and programming is built on a continuing accumulation of faculty in diverse disciplines and professional fields with deep experience through immersion in cultures, societies, and nations abroad. As a result, today we have two or three generations of Title VI scholars located in twelve to fifteen centers for each world area (and for international studies) who provide the nation's core expertise and who train the large majority of future internationally expert scholars and professionals.

The Challenges for International Education and the Title VI Programs

Pervasive technological, social, economic, and political change characterize the globe in these post–Cold War years. There are new "consumers" of international knowledge. There are new opportunities to use the electronic technologies that have reached out to homes, schools, businesses, and unions—for building linkages and partnerships with foreign colleagues as well as for better collaboration among the Title VI centers and programs. There is an urgency to revise paradigms so as to adapt to the multipolar world after the Cold War, when older powers wane and new regional powers and global identities ascend. We are beset with new concerns of nuclear proliferation, religious fundamentalisms—both at home and abroad—terrorism, international political and white-collar corruption, organized international crime and the spread of drugs, and the random crime and corruption that they spawn.

The new demands for and transitions toward democratization and human rights require a refined understanding of the politics, societies, and the economies of 170 nations. The turbulence being experienced by many countries for market liberalization linked to the burgeoning pace and scale of international trade and financial flows is transforming corporate ownership, labor relations, and the wealth and power of companies and nations. Pressing environmental issues at the global and local levels demand rethinking the energy and consumption equations in all countries. And in many societies, the interplay of global and local cultures and the emergence of new styles and identities exert demands on the creativity of Title VI centers in designing research and studies to comprehend these changes.

In the face of this scale of global change, every federal agency—not just the Education, State, and Defense Departments—must be concerned with foreign issues and programs. This requires new personnel with global foreign language competence and access to expanding levels of knowledge provided more rapidly than ever before. In addition, across the country, schools and two- and four-year colleges have realized the importance of globalization and of foreign countries; they are therefore demanding new forms of outreach and knowledge from Title VI Centers in order to build their own international capacities.

Finally, there is an explosion of interest in foreign and global issues in professional and science colleges as well as new demands for international components for M.A., M.S., M.B.A., and Ph.D. degrees in fields that have not been concerned with international affairs in the past.

Continuing National Needs and New Directions in Title VI Programs

What impact do these challenges have for Title VI programs? In January 1997, more than 250 scholars, practitioners, policy-makers, and foundation leaders met at the University of California, Los Angeles to discuss the condition and future of foreign area studies and international education in the United States. They reached consensus on a series of twelve continuing and new national needs for international education to respond to the shifts in the political and economic relationships of the United States in the global system. These needs are excerpted from the proceedings of that conference,[4] and summarized below.

- **Addressing the national shortfall in producing language and area specialists**

With a quadrupling of the proportion of Gross Domestic Product accounted for by foreign trade since the 1970s, the United States requires an increasing number of foreign language and area specialists. With the current level of Title VI fellowships and faculty resources inadequate to even meet the universities' replacement needs, there is little capacity to broaden the training and analysis needed for the widening challenges in this era of globalization.

- **Ensuring adequate research and studies on language, area, and international studies issues**

A nation such as the United States, which is so dependent for economic success on information and information technologies, needs to give greater attention to the care and feeding of the research institutions and the scholars who will keep valuable international analysis flowing.

- **Maintaining the breadth of area and international studies training in an era of specialization**

Title VI must guard against simply supporting disciplinary biases that create narrow specialists who must be "retrained" by employers to achieve the needed breadth in order to fulfill crucial roles. Title VI resources cannot cope with all the needs of all U.S. educational institutions; therefore, centers should be encouraged to experiment on the cutting edge of international curriculum, research, and outreach to institutionalize important innovations in instructional methods of internationalizing consciousness, language, experience, and knowledge. Experimenting with distance learning is important, especially in offering the LCTLs.

- **Bridging regional and functional education: linking the international affairs schools, area studies, and other academic units**

There has been too little cooperation among scholars who emphasize the context-based in-depth research of area studies, more applied policy analysis, or foreign policy and international relations programs. In fact, the diversities of these types of scholarship provide fertile opportunities for mutually beneficial collaboration that extends the contributions of the full panoply of Title VI programs.

- **Responding to new foreign language needs**

At least three factors of the post–Cold War period are driving U.S. needs for a growing capacity in learning and using less commonly taught languages. First, widening U.S. economic interests in emerging markets, particularly the "big emerging markets" such as China, Brazil, Mexico, India, Indonesia, Korea, Poland, South Africa, and Turkey, are increasing the need for teaching LCTLs. Second, as the United States assumes the role of broadened leadership in the world political and economic system, the scholarly analytical community needs language capacity for keeping abreast of and providing advanced analysis of a broadened list of countries. Third, the shifting sites of international crisis require national readiness and language capacity to deal with issues such as the Iran/Iraq, Bosnian, and other Middle East tensions; the host of problems in the former Soviet republics; the response to the opening of Vietnam; the religious conflicts of Algeria, Egypt, and Sudan; the shifting politics of Cambodia; the internal convolutions of Peru and Colombia; human rights issues in many lands; and more. For many key languages—in the Middle East, Africa, Europe, East and Southeast Asia, India, Pakistan, and even Latin America—there still is an enormous shortage of up-to-date teaching materials in both print and computer-assisted formats, particularly beyond the introductory level. Even basic reference materials have not been created for a number of the LCTLs offered by some centers. Increased coordination and collaboration among centers are required to develop instructional and assessment materials and to create the technology for language teaching and teacher training. Additional intensive summer language institutes are needed for the LCTLs to meet these increased demands.

- **Bringing standards of functional learning for fluency to language education**

For too long, language education has been a stepchild to the literary and linguistics disciplines, and teaching personnel and program structures have not been oriented sufficiently toward functional literacy and fluency. The universities need a new commitment to language teaching methods that promote proficiency in the most efficient manner. Title VI support is absolutely indispensable in maintaining the instruction that exists in LCTLs. Without this federal support, most of those language capacities in the country, even in the larger research universities, would wither.

- **Encouraging immigrant, gender, and minority diversity in international education programs**

The U.S. population is being transformed by the largest wave of immigration since the turn of the twentieth century. By the middle of the twenty-first century, ethnic or racial minorities will constitute more than half of the population, and they will be increasingly diverse. Foreign area specialists can play an important role in addressing the challenges of this increasingly diverse population. In addition, growing U.S. heritage communities can contribute to both international and multicultural education in a range of areas including research, teacher training, curricular development, public outreach, and language teaching.

- **Planning for cooperation in building the international collections of the nation's libraries**

No U.S. library or library system can cope with the national need for foreign holdings, especially in foreign language materials that are vital for research and teaching about foreign areas. This results from the simultaneous explosion of print and electronic publishing abroad, the surging costs of journals and monographs, unfavorable exchange rates, the high labor costs of cataloging, and the stagnating budgets of university libraries. A critical strategy is to share the effort and expense of acquiring foreign materials, especially those in foreign languages, by coordinating specialized collections at designated institutions that would be available broadly through interlibrary loan. The nation urgently needs a new plan of cooperation among both the university libraries associated with the NRCs, CIBERs, and LRCs (and which engages the Library of Congress, National Agricultural Library, National Medical Library, and Center for Research Libraries), and the many international collections of various federal agencies. Increasingly, the weaknesses of the nation's documentary capacity and the lack of a shared system of collection put at risk U.S. intelligence about foreign nations, economies, and cultures. At the same time, the latest electronic technologies open up new opportunities for collaboration at home and abroad in collection development.

- **Providing experience abroad for faculty and students**
Creating the nation's next generation of foreign language, area, and international studies experts is not possible without immersion and renewing of research experience and language proficiency abroad. A major increase is needed in the capacity of the nation to give its students and faculty the international experiences requisite to language fluency and currency of international knowledge. Fulbright-Hays programs are well positioned to provide such support if adequately funded. Finally, a new interest in study abroad among American undergraduates and their families is challenging universities and national structures to develop more linkages and exchange programs abroad and to encourage intensive language education at home. On campus, much work is needed in these areas: (a) integrating study abroad learning with the domestic curriculum; (b) diversifying the access of students who are ethnic minorities, women, or economically disadvantaged; (c) dealing with the complex issues of curriculum and security abroad; and (d) encouraging new programs in non-Western countries.

- **Strengthening linkages with international education**
  communities abroad
To be effective in building U.S. libraries and foreign area knowledge, Title VI programs need to place more emphasis on linkages abroad, building more collaboratively with scholars and institutions outside the United States. The twenty-first century is an appropriate time to end some of the more unilateral modes of international education and dissemination that were perhaps more relevant to the assumptions of the Cold War and past nationalist periods in Western nations. U.S. libraries, analysts, and scholars need the knowledge, the creativity, and the resources of our international colleagues. Scholars abroad also are struggling to provide education and competence to enable their peoples to cope with globalization and change. Thus we need them at the table with us in developing new knowledge across the globe for a more innovative, intelligent, universal, efficient, just, and sustainable global system.

- **Cooperating nationally in cost-effective outreach**
The outreach mission of Title VI centers has become more important because of the increased need for a globally informed citizenry, not only among undergradu-

ate and graduate students but in civil society at large. As globalization touches every institution of U.S. society, the need and demand for Title VI outreach programs have grown, especially for business, government, K–12 institutions, two- and four-year colleges, professional colleges, and the media. There has been a mixed response of Title VI centers to this challenge. Some centers, finding their Title VI budgets eroded over the years and beset with proliferating demands to serve more diverse needs and clients, prefer to keep their focus on outreach through scholarly publishing and consulting. Much greater use of the Internet and World Wide Web technologies offers more cost-effective provision of reference services as well as encouraging collaboration among the centers. An especially important new agenda for Title VI centers is to better serve the needs of the expanding international linkages and programs of federal and state agencies whose basic mandates have been domestic in the past, but which now face the pressures of globalization.

- **Addressing the national predicament of declining resources for international education in the face of increasing globalization**
There has been repeated concern voiced about the declining funds available for these increasingly important and expanding national needs. Funding for Title VI has not kept pace with inflation. Fulbright Hays funding not only has fallen from levels in the late 1960s as measured in "constant dollars," but has declined in real dollars since the levels of the early 1980s.

Conclusion

The uniquely American Title VI system of foreign area, language, and international education remains exceptional and self-renewing. This is especially important for a nation that seeks to be a global leader in a key period of global readjustment from the polarities of the Cold War. Because of the dramatic and deepening integration of the United States with the global system and other nations and their economies, the U.S. need for enhanced international education is exceptional— for U.S. government agencies, companies, NGOs, educational institutions, and the general citizenry.

As a result of this accelerating pace of globalization, the Title VI centers and their programs are experiencing an exponential increase in demand for language, areal, thematic, global, and outreach services. These requests for new services are arriving at the Title VI centers just when many of their key language and area faculties of the original 1960s cohort of area specialists are nearing retirement, when the long-term erosion of federal support by inflation is becoming increasingly problematic, and when some universities are questioning the wisdom of continuing to fund low-enrollment languages, no matter how nationally strategic they may be.

Yet the new technologies also make possible a broader cooperation and collaboration among Title VI universities and a higher quality of delivery of education and services to their many new clients. The relatively small Title VI centers and programs are strong, although they are suffering the stress of success born of globalization and the increased demand for their services. University budgets alone cannot sustain this national need for international education; therefore, the incentive systems of the federal Title VI programs are absolutely essential. The Title VI programs and centers are a unique national treasure for achieving the long-term interests of the nation and its peoples; but these programs need additional support from the universities, from the foundations, and from the federal coffers. The broad welfare and enduring interests of the peoples of the United States are at stake.

NOTES

1. Christine E. Root provided substantial commentary and editing of this paper.

2. Part A—International and Foreign Language Studies, Sec. 601. Findings and Purposes, in 1998 Amendments to Higher Education Act of 1965, P.L. 105–244, Title VI—International Education Programs. Sec. 601 concerns the Title VI Foreign Language and Area Studies (FLAS) Graduate Fellowships in language, area, and international studies and the National Resource Centers.

3. Major portions of the ideas expressed in this section are drawn from the "Conference Rapporteur's Synthesis," by D. Wiley, chapter IV in *International Education in the New Global Era: Proceedings of a National Policy Conference on the Higher Education Act, Title VI, and Fulbright-Hays Programs,* ed. John N. Hawkins et al. (Los Angeles: International Studies and Overseas Programs, UCLA, 1998), which is available electronically at the Web site <http://www.isop.ucla.edu/pacrim/title6/>.

4. Ibid., pp. 219–224.

Domains and Issues in International Studies[1]

Richard D. Lambert

It is sometimes helpful to take an overall view of our enterprise looking for retro-spective and prospective changes in the form and direction of international edu-cation as it has developed on our campuses. It is probably time for another com-prehensive survey to provide the empirical data on the basis of which such an assessment might rest. In the absence of such a survey, I would like to offer a few impressions of structural issues that face the field. In particular, I will deconstruct the field into some of its constituent domains, discussing some of the enduring problems specific to each domain. At the end, I will briefly discuss the need to rethink the relationship of international studies to the rest of the academic estab-lishment, and to seek ways of making the different domains among us more in-terrelated and mutually supportive. In this paper, I want to focus on two aspects of international studies. First, I will be concerned with the structure of our enter-prise, not so much with the specifics of what we do. Second, I will deal with some durable problems that have faced us over a number of years, many of them taking on a special urgency in the deflationary trend in our external environment, by which I mean the decline in the availability of external funding.

I. Domains within International Studies

The first thing to note is that while we talk of international studies as if it were a single thing, the general rubric includes a number of quite separate enterprises. Some years ago, I was struck by a notion introduced by Robert McCaughey.[2] He argued that international studies was really an "enclosure movement," that is it was formed by taking many disparate academic enterprises that had existed separately and gathering them under a single rubric as if they were both a separate and a homogenous phenomenon. Toward the end of the paper I will discuss the question of separateness. Let us first deal with homogeneity.

There is, of course, a common thread that links all international studies activities: they relate to countries other than our own. However, this shared characteristic of border crossing, while it can serve as a rule-of-thumb definition of international studies, and the associated notion of an internationalization process for campuses, obscures an immense internal diversity within the field. The term international studies denotes a number of quite separate, quite different academic domains which, in practice, tend to behave like separate academic tribes. Each has its own membership, its own folkways, and they rarely come together, let alone intertwine. Intermarriage is almost unheard of. And within some of the tribes there are separate subgroups that act as distinct clans. For instance, within area studies, the distinct area specialist communities tend to behave totally independently of each other. While to the outside world a specialist on China and on Latin America may both be considered fellow area specialists to other academics, to those inside the field, they have very little in common and very rarely act in concert. As I will note toward the end of the paper, one of our greatest challenges for the future is to relate these tribes and clans to each other, to make them mutually supportive and cumulative in their effect.

In the meantime, in discussing the persistent structural issues in international studies, I will take up each of the several domains one at a time. At the end, I will discuss briefly some trends in the field as a whole and some problems that we will have to face collectively. The domains I will discuss briefly may be divided into two sets. First are those that conduct research and teach about international regions or topics. Under this rubric, I will deal with: area studies, transnational studies, and foreign language instruction. Those who belong in my second set of domains tend not to teach about other countries, but conduct their professional activities primarily abroad. The groups I will discuss under this rubric are those concerned with study abroad, foreign students, and international aspects of applied and professional fields.

This division of international studies domains into these two types is, of course, not precise—international business studies falls in both camps—but it does reflect a major contrast in what "international education" is, and how it is administered on our campuses. For instance, the activities of international education administrators, both on their campuses and in their professional organizations, tend to be concerned with the second set of domains—more specifically study abroad and foreign student flows—and have less administrative responsibility for the first of those in the first set of domains—area specialists, transnational scholars, and language teachers. One of the persistent challenges on campuses is to relate the activities in these various tribes to each other, to make them mutually supportive and reinforcing, but unfortunately, on all too many campuses, the international studies administrators can only play a limited role in the first category. And for those who belong to one or another of the international studies domains, crossing the boundaries is difficult, particularly within the larger universities.

II. Internationally Targeted Research and Teaching

A. Area Studies

The first domain is area studies, in which research and teaching are focused on geographically defined nation-states and world regions outside the United States. Area studies as a distinct field emerged out of World War II, and since that time has expanded into a major enterprise, one that in its scale and complexity is unmatched anywhere in the world. The development of area studies had been well documented.[3] Over the years, area studies has been beset by a number of endemic problems, many of which are now appearing in an acute form.

1. FROM EXPANSION TO STEADY STATE OR CONTRACTION

The period of rapid growth of area studies has given it a tradition of expansion. One of the imminent problems facing the field is to move an expansionary orientation to one that is, at best, steady-state, and more likely one of contraction. In the past, this expansion has had two components: a lateral spread through the disciplines and a diffusion down the institutional ladder from research universities to liberal arts colleges to community colleges.

The growth of area studies has been achieved by a lateral diffusion throughout the academic disciplines. Looking back on the current numerous and robust tribes of area specialists it is hard to remember that in the years immediately after World War II area studies comprised a small group of scholars who were mainly historians, philologists, and specialists on literature or art. Middle Eastern studies specialists were mainly Biblical scholars or Islamicists. Indologists were focused on Sanskrit studies, and Sinologists and Japanologists on classical texts and history. The expansion of area studies, accompanied by a shift in its center of gravity, came with the recruitment of substantial numbers of social scientists, particularly anthropologists, political scientists, and to a lesser extent sociologists and economists. One of the persistent problems of area studies, one that is currently bedeviling the field, has been the maintenance of this disciplinary spread. This is a problem of major proportions both at the national level and on individual campuses. The transformation of area studies from a young, expanding enterprise to what the economists call a mature industry changes the institutional context in which area studies operates. In particular, what the economists call obsolete bargains with departmental chairs that resulted in the hiring of area specialists into disciplinary slots are difficult to renegotiate when they come up for renewal. It becomes increasingly difficult to sustain the cross-disciplinary representation within, say East Asian, or African Studies. The recruitment and retention of faculty and students specializing in the quantitative end of the social sciences is becoming particularly difficult.

The second expansionary thrust in area studies has been its diffusion down the institutional ladder. The area studies program model, comprising a loose coalition of faculty members from a wide variety of disciplines who teach a variety of highly specialized courses on a country or region, is most at home on large university campuses. However, many liberal arts colleges have developed core area programs, usually comprising one or two individual specialists in literature, history, political science, anthropology, and perhaps art history or religion. However, given the heavy costs of sustaining a viable minimal area program, with its heavy demands on faculty appointments, expanded library collections, and the introduction of what are often low enrollment language problems, the spread of the area studies program model down the institutional ladder has been difficult to sustain and the prospects for further expansion into the smaller and less selective colleges are dim. It will be especially interesting to note whether a new form of area studies which is appropriate to community colleges with their large and growing portion of the college enrollments, will be invented.

2. DIMINUTION OF EXTERNAL FUNDING

The very substantial growth of language and area studies on our campuses has been made possible by the availability of substantial external funding that has nurtured the various parts of the enterprise. However, this dependence on external funding raises real problems in the deflationary period that clearly lies ahead, a period when funding for international education, in fact for education as a whole, is almost certain to decline. While on most campuses area studies is supported by the institution's own resources, the expansion of the field, and particularly the flagship programs at research universities' campuses, has been nourished by very substantial funding from the major private foundations and by the federal government, particularly first NDEA Title VI and then HEA Title VI. A sharp decline in that funding, which is already underway, is bound to have a major depressing effect on the field. For instance, if Title VI disappears, international studies at a number of major research universities with a half a dozen or so Title VI programs which receive combined federal funding of several million dollars per year, will be devastated. Other universities and colleges will be similarly hit. Since HEA Title VI is due for reauthorization, with some of its strongest Democratic supporters leaving Congress, the ability to maintain this program is in real jeopardy. Funding that currently supplements HEA Title VI with dissertation fellowships is also increasingly tenuous. The loss of federal and foundation support will be particularly devastating if support fellowship money dries up, particularly if support for dissertation-level research disappears. Graduate students training to be area specialists must be able to go to the country of their expertise at dissertation time. If they cannot, the flow of fresh participants into the field will be immensely diminished causing the danger of stagnation.

3. WORLD AREA AND COUNTRY BALANCE

One of the endemic problems of area studies that is partially related to the availability of funding is its dependence on the swings in interest in particular countries or regions among the general public. Of course, international studies as a whole is subject to the fluctuations between public parochialism and cosmopolitanism. In similar fashion, particular countries or world areas are also subject to their own shifts in public attention. For instance, public interest in Southeast Asia was high during the Viet Nam period and has had a modest resurgence more recently with the interest in the economic tigers. Such episodic attention is difficult to sustain. South Asia, particularly India, once received great public and academic interest. It is now barely on the public or academic radar screen. Interest in China and Japan, the Soviet Union, and Latin America remain high. These shifts in public enthusiasm are reflected in the well-being of particular area studies clans on campuses, showing up in such things as enrollment swings, appointments, administrative support, expenditures on library acquisitions, and external funding. One of the major policy issues facing area studies in the future is how to determine and sustain the appropriate balance among area and country competencies among area specialists in the face of these short-term cycles of popular enthusiasm and differential external funding.

4. CHANGING RELATIONS WITH SCHOLARS ABROAD

There is another long-term problem that faces area specialists, one that has a different impact on the various world areas and various disciplines. In the early days of area studies, American area specialists enjoyed an immense advantage over scholars in the countries they studied in the financial and intellectual resources available for their research. Hence, with respect to many countries of the world, their reference group in conducting research on those countries was mainly other American scholars. In many countries, this advantage is no longer quite so clear. The various clans of area specialists have had to adjust to an intellectual environment in which the main body of research and writing lies within those countries themselves. One of the consequences of this development is that their craft is dependent on a continuation of the research-oriented exchange programs that are necessary to support that growing symbiosis and such exchange programs are currently in great jeopardy.

B. Transnational Studies
By transnational studies I refer to those academic pursuits in which a researcher or teacher focuses on an international topic but not on a particular world area or

region. Within this larger tribe I would place such clans as specialists on international relations, comparative studies, security affairs, peace studies, diplomacy, and various thematic topics such as world demography, international trade, world literacy, or the Muslim world.

However, the divide between area studies and transnational studies is not just a geographic one. That area studies and transnational studies represent distinctive intellectual perspectives was vividly brought home to me a few years ago when, as Editor of the Annals of the American Academy of Political and Social Science, I was reviewing for publication twelve articles in a volume dealing with the foreign policy of Scandinavian[4] countries. I noticed that the articles fell neatly into two piles. In one pile all of the explanations for foreign policy were based on analyses of social and political forces within the countries—an area studies perspective. In the other pile, the explanations were framed in terms of the international politico-economic system: battles over international fishery rights, the strategic position of the Norwegian coast in the military defense of Europe, the attractiveness of the European Union, the course of relations with the Soviet Union, and so forth. These authors whose articles fell in the second pile are what I have called the transnational scholars. There is some degree of overlap between transnational and area studies approaches, particularly with reference to the Soviet studies, but by and large they are quite distinct.

1. THE TRANSNATIONAL STUDIES VS. AREA STUDIES OBSOLESCENCE BATTLE

In recent years an interesting scholastic argument has emerged between area studies and transnational studies. Since academic disagreements have a tendency to be translated into obsolescence battles, so has this one. In this battle, area studies is described as the old international studies, and transnational approaches as the wave of the future, one that is superior intellectually to a concentration on a single world area or country.[5] At the very least this debate highlights the rigidities inherited from the decades-old definitions of "areas." The efficiency of the current academic divisions of world areas which follow the old British Foreign Office partitioning of the world is a matter that has received surprisingly little attention. Does including Afghanistan in South Asia make any sense at all? In whose area do the Central Asian states fall? Should North Africa be considered part of the scholarly fiefdom of Middle Eastern studies because of its Islamic orientation, or part of Africa?

However, the argument by transnational scholars is more fundamental than a quarrel about regional boundaries, it is one about legitimacy and obsolescence. These twin arguments about the difference in intellectual perspectives and obsolescence between area studies and international studies was captured[6] recently by Kenneth Prewitt, President of the Social Science Research Council [see Part 2, this volume]. In foreshadowing a new organizational style for the Council, he wrote: "Area studies holds area constant and invites the participation of multiple disciplines, in contrast to traditional comparative studies which held discipline constant and involved multiple areas." I have no comment on the merits of this characterization except to point out that most area specialists work within a single discipline. He goes on to argue that a new global approach both to the subjects being studied and the scholars engaged in that study represents the future of international studies. In the typical combative style of most academic arguments, global studies is the more modern viewpoint that should replace the obsolete older area studies approach. This notion of tribal obsolescence and displacement is even clearer in an earlier *Items* article by Stanley J. Heginbotham, Vice President of SSRC,[7] who argued that area studies was rooted in the cold war and thus was now obsolete. Normally such scholarly storms stay within the academic teacup, but they can and do have immense effect both on the decisions of funders and of academic administrators. The shifts at SSRC and in several of the major private foundations from area studies to transnational studies as the organizing principle for grants and fellowships are cases in point.

2. SOME PERSISTENT ISSUES WITHIN TRANSNATIONAL STUDIES

I shall not dwell at length on the issues that lie within the transnational studies domain of international studies. Let me just mention two or three. First, unlike area studies, the center of gravity for this tribe lies outside the academic community in the foreign relations establishment of the government, the media, and the host of foreign policy non-governmental organizations. Campus-based scholars play a less dominant role in this domain than they do in area studies. Second, there is a constant battle to retain a separate tribal identity from the disciplines as a whole. In particular, political science and economics tend to constantly absorb the work of the transnational specialists' wing into the corpus of the regular discipline. Tribal boundaries are difficult to maintain. And third, this tribe, like area studies, is prone to sub-division into separate clans. For instance, I mentioned earlier such fields as national security studies, the analysis of international organizations, peace studies, and diplomacy. While there is some overlap among the clans, these too tend to be intellectually and organizationally separate.

One of the enduring issues in transnational studies is the construction of a coherent curriculum that embodies the intellectual thrust of the field. In the preparation of an area specialist, requirements for the major can follow a simple pattern: just lengthen the language requirement and increase the number of disciplinary courses on the area that the student is required to take, and include a disciplinary specialization. For transnational scholars, the problem of developing a coherent, bounded, integrated major or concentration for students who are preparing to become experts is a continuing problem. It is illustrated most dramatically in the rapidly growing—on some campuses it is already the largest—undergraduate majors in what is called international studies. Once it moved beyond the intellectual confines of the analysis of interstate relations that used to be characteristic in international relations majors, the disciplinary and topical mix of educational programs that will be required of future transnational studies majors is constantly in search of definition. In particular, how the construction of an international studies major should relate to the first domain, the area studies, and how it should relate to various disciplines is always open to negotiation. And especially troublesome is the relationship between transnational studies and the next international studies domain, foreign language teaching and learning.

C. Foreign Language Education

1. ROLE IN INTERNATIONAL STUDIES

Most foreign language educators do not consider themselves a tribe within international studies. This is so, in spite of the fact that at the undergraduate level, foreign language courses often comprise more that fifty percent of all internationally oriented courses and enrollments on most campuses. Nonetheless, the tribal separation within international studies is nowhere greater than between foreign language educators and international studies more generally. This is true not just from the perspective of foreign language professionals, but the other tribes as well.

The role of foreign language learning in transnational studies is especially uncertain. The mastery and use of a foreign language is presumed to be a defining characteristic of area specialists, although the extent to which this applies in practice varies somewhat by the world area or country being studied.[8] The problem for transnational studies is that, except for English, no one language or combination of languages will prepare a scholar to deal with issues based in many other countries. It used to be that in the traditional study of international relations, the study of French, and perhaps German, would suffice since these were the languages of diplomacy and the scholarly literature dealing with it. As shifting events have changed the focus of world attention, the selection of languages that must be mastered has become increasingly murky. Transnational specialists must be eternally grateful for the hegemony of English throughout the world. I do not want to delve too deeply into the internal issues that have been of long-range concern to foreign language educators. As the former director of the National Foreign Language Center, my comments in this area have been widely disseminated.[9] Let me just mention some of the more durable structural issues, some that have recently emerged, and the steps currently being taken by the field to address them.

2. SOCIETAL CONTEXT AND LIMITED SKILL LEVELS

The basic problem for foreign language instruction in the United States lies in the larger social setting within which foreign language education is situated. The devout monolingualism that characterizes much of American society, nurtured by the ubiquity of English usage throughout the world, limits the effectiveness of the field no matter what its structural arrangements. Deriving in part from the unsupportive social context for foreign language education, there are a number of durable structural issues that face the field. For one thing, the lack of widespread use of foreign languages by Americans limits the ability of foreign language educators to demand that more learners commit enough time to create viable foreign language competencies. The system now educates a large number of students to relatively low skill levels, too low to make foreign language use painless and effective for substantial numbers of Americans. Nonetheless, Americans strongly support the representation of some foreign language instruction in our educational system. The result is that we have a foreign language educational system structured in a fashion that is relatively uncommon. In most other countries, basic foreign language instruction is limited to the secondary schools. In our system, we provide elementary foreign language instruction both in secondary and higher education. Indeed, we have a system made up of two pyramids, one in high school and one in college. Both pyramids have large number of students in the first year and diminishing numbers at subsequent levels, and the two pyramids often have little to do with each other. This arrangement makes it difficult to create continuous and cumulative learning sequences, and to produce very many learners with truly high levels of skill.

This is an issue which the field is beginning to address, both by lengthening the pre-collegiate learning process, and by starting the language instructional sequence in middle and elementary schools. Hopefully, this will create a substantial number of students who have had a long training program in foreign languages, in turn pushing up the level of language instruction, and perhaps the use of foreign language in colleges and universities. The lack of articulation in language instruction between high school and college is being addressed by introducing experimental programs deliberately articulating high school and college language teaching.

3. Language Choice

A persistent structural issue in foreign language instruction is which languages to teach. Currently language choice in the United States is what might be called a constrained laissez-faire, demand-driven system, one in which students make their own choices, constrained by the language competencies of the teaching staff and the enrollment choices. The result has been a continued overwhelming emphasis on Western European languages, but within that category, long-term shifts from Latin and Greek, to German, to French, and now to Spanish. Indeed, Spanish is currently the Pac Man of the foreign language field, gradually swallowing up all other languages. The United States, unlike almost all other countries except Australia where Japanese has been placed at the top of the list, has a deliberate policy of expanding the role of what are called the less commonly taught languages. Instruction in Japanese, and to a lesser extent Chinese and Russian, is more and more available. Yet the problem of how to staff language instruction in the face of unpredictable swings in student preferences, and how to match the language learning experience of our students to the needs of the next, not the last, century remains a problem for our foreign language educational system.

4. Modernizing Instructional Style and Setting Standards

One of the geniuses of the American language educational system is that decision-making concerning the content and style of language instruction is fully dispersed to the level of the individual teachers and school systems. There is no centralized planning mechanism whereby the quality and content can be addressed nationally. This situation has the effect of maximizing local innovation, but it makes it difficult to raise the quality of instruction more generally and more uniformly throughout the system. In recent years, the field has accomplished this through the introduction of a new testing and achievement rating system which emphasizes oral communicative competence rather than grammar and reading skills. That rating system, which emphasizes a preferred pedagogical style, was introduced first as a voluntary, piecemeal movement, and is now more universal and has been reinforced by the more general national effort to adopt outcome standards in a variety of fields.

5. SHRINKING FOREIGN LANGUAGE PROGRAMS

On the whole, these recent developments in foreign language education described above relate to practices within the field, which would produce a more effective teaching of foreign languages. However, recent deflationary trends are having a major effect on the structure of foreign language programs. On more and more campuses there is a radical rethinking underway of the role of higher education in basic language instruction, a series of hard-headed decisions as to how institutions should be staffed to perform that role. Many university administrators and faculty planning groups who, while still believing that every student should have some experience with language learning—hence the language requirement—are now arguing that such experience should occur mainly before students come to college. Consequently, language requirements are shifted to entrance requirements. To the extent that basic language is provided at the college or university level, it is proposed that it be treated as a remedial service, as it is in English, rather than as an activity deserving full college credit. In a similar vein, academic administrators are asking why language teaching must be done by full-time faculty members, or their graduate students. They argue that, for one thing, this system does not deliver the most effective forms of basic language instruction since the interests of the faculty and graduate student teaching assistants are focused on their graduate level research careers, primarily in literature. As an alternative, separate foreign language teaching institutes or centers are being created on a number of campuses. They are staffed with part-time, temporary employees chosen for their excellence in teaching basic foreign language skills. University administrators are also beginning to question the link between the needs of a comprehensive graduate and undergraduate degree program and the provision of language instruction for the general undergraduate student body. Must a major foreign language department have faculty expertise on each literary genre, period, and language? Does it need graduate students in all of these specialties, and should these graduate students be the ones to staff the basic language courses? As a result of this reevaluation, some universities are dropping entire sub-sections of their graduate programs in literature, dispensing with both the faculty and the graduate student body, and creating separate language teaching centers or institutes that are staffed by part-time, short-contract language teachers who do not have full faculty status. This contraction of academic departments, particularly in the humanities, is, of course, not limited to foreign language departments. However, they are more vulnerable because of their link to elementary language instruction. Fortunately, the extreme forms of this contraction in language programs is not yet widespread.

III. International Actors

I turn now to tribes within international education whose function is not the study of other countries and their languages or world affairs, as was the purpose of the first set of tribes. International actors are those for whom the locus of their work is overseas. Included in this category are: (1) study abroad and programs of "faculty enrichment;" (2) foreign student flows; and (3) the overseas activities of the applied and professional schools, and to a lesser degree the scientists. It is interesting to note that one of the reasons why European and American experts on international education tend in conferences to talk past each other, is that for Europeans, the first two of these domains, the flow of students and faculty across national boundaries, are the essence of international education. Americans tend to bring into the discussion many of the other domains, particularly those in our first category, tribes that are conducting research and teaching with respect to other countries.

A. Study Abroad and Faculty Enrichment

1. FACULTY ENRICHMENT—THE NEED FOR ASSESSMENT AND PLANNING

What is usually referred to as "faculty enrichment"—an odd term meaning the dispatch of individual faculty members abroad—is widely practiced as a device for promoting greater internationalization on a campus. In view of this, it is surprising that while there is abundant anecdotal evidence, faculty enrichment has received surprisingly little scrutiny. There is relatively little discussion about whether it is a consumption good for individual faculty members or an investment that brings returns for the institution and its students. Nor is there any research of which I am aware that informs us which faculty to send, where, for how long, to do what; nor do I know of any studies of opportunity costs, that is, whether resources spent on faculty enrichment might be better spent on some other domain of international education. In any event, in view of the general decline in funding for international education at the national and institutional level, this is a domain of international education that may be in considerable jeopardy. Once it is gone, we may come to assess the value of faculty enrichment.

2. EXPANSION AND FILLING IN THE GAPS IN STUDY ABROAD

In contrast to the ad hoc nature of much of faculty enrichment, study abroad is the domain of international education that had received the most substantial and continuous attention from the field. There is, indeed, a very substantial evaluative and planning literature relating to the dispatch of students around the world.[10] Over the past several decades, the structural issues that have received the greatest amount of attention in this domain have to do largely with the expansion and the correction of imbalances in student clienteles. On relatively few campuses, particularly large university campuses, do as many as ten percent of the students study abroad. Much of the effort of international programs offices is directed toward the expansion of the percentage of students who participate. Indeed, in a few institutions the goal is for every student to have the opportunity to study abroad. Further, study abroad programs are becoming increasingly common on community colleges. Accordingly, the overwhelming structural issue for study abroad has been growth.

This concern for growth has been accompanied by attention to imbalances in student participation, for instance, increasing the representation of minorities and students from less affluent families. In addition, there has been a concerted effort to broaden the range of study abroad destinations, developing programs outside of England and Western Europe where most students now go. Special effort has been devoted to the development of programs in Latin America, East Asia, Australia, and to a lesser extent in South and Southeast Asia.

3. CHANGES IN THE TIMING AND FUNCTION OF STUDY ABROAD

In addition to attempts to increase the number of participants in study abroad and to fill in underrepresented student clienteles, a great deal of attention has been given to clarifying and expanding the function of study abroad. Many institutions have paid fresh attention to the academic as contrasted with the experiential content of the study abroad experience. Foreign language study, which comprises the most important official or de facto purpose for study abroad, is being scrutinized more closely. Special efforts are being made to coordinate it with language instruction before departure and after return home. Some institutions have deliberately tried to break out of the confines of the general education/liberal arts focus of study abroad, one which tends to concentrate participants into the sophomore and junior years. They are introducing a larger variety of major-related programs, many of them located in the junior or senior year study programs. It is interesting that very few institutions, to my knowledge, have followed the logic of this trend to promote graduate level and professional school study abroad, which, of course, is more typical of study abroad programs for foreign institutions. The most important example of this shift in the function of study abroad has been the proliferation of internship programs. These work-cum-study programs respond to student demand that experience abroad be viewed as an investment, one that is both educational in the most general sense and one that will embellish their curriculum vitae to help in securing future employment.

4. CHANGING THE ECONOMIC BASE OF STUDY ABROAD

There are several structural problems that have received somewhat less attention but that may have a major impact on the future of study abroad. The first is economic, but not so much the general deflationary trends resulting from decreased external funding that are threatening many of the other domains of international education. On many campuses, study abroad is either a profit center or breaks even financially. In fact, surplus resources drawn from study abroad programs are sometimes used to support other domains of international studies. Such an economic base sometimes derives from the practice of charging normal on-campus tuition for a university or college's study abroad program. If the tuition fee of the overseas institution is considerably lower, the program gains a surplus. Not all programs have this differential and incomes are often balanced out. But the mechanics of such a system guard study abroad programs against some of the deflationary effects of the diminution of external funding for international studies more generally.

There are, however, two major threats to the continuation of this economy in the future. First, students may be encouraged, in part by American national exchange organizations, to take a leave of absence from the home institution, register directly in foreign universities, and then transfer the credit earned abroad back to the home institution. In an era of rapidly expanding tuition at American colleges and universities, this is a very tempting solution for students. Second, the steep increase in tuition in almost all American colleges and universities has been accompanied by a expansion in the tuition discounts given to students in the form of fellowships and subsidized loans. Currently, in most cases these discounts can be spent by the student on foreign study. Were this situation to change, if colleges and universities come to insist that the scholarships and student loans they provide can only be spent at the home institution, the result could have a major impact on study abroad, affecting particularly the participation of students from less affluent families.

B. Foreign Students

Another major domain of international education is the flow of foreign students into our campuses.[11] In spite of many determined efforts by international education administrators to utilize the presence of foreign students as a force for general internationalization of the campus, like other aspects of international studies, the management of foreign student flows is carried out by a separate tribe on the campus, one that has little relationship with the other tribes. Indeed, foreign students themselves have little or anything to do with other aspects of international studies on the campus. There are a number of structural issues that have faced foreign student management in the past and seem likely to become more intense in the future.

1. EXPANDING THE NUMBER OF FOREIGN STUDENTS

The first issue in the management of foreign student flows has to do with the number of such students coming to the campus. Aggregate foreign student enrollments have increased rather steadily over the past decades, with a steeper incline in this decade. This account written several years ago summarizes the trend.

In 1990–91 the Institute of International Education (IIE) census reported 407,529 foreign students registered in American colleges and universities. This represented an increase of 667 percent from the 53,107 students reported in 1960–61. The increase in numbers has been somewhat uneven across the intervening years, in some years slowing to an increase of barely 1 percent. There was an explosive growth of 172 percent between 1960 and 1970, and of 125 percent between 1970 and 1980, but only 25 percent between 1980 and 1990. Current growth is at the rate of 5 percent annually, and the rate of overall increase is currently climbing again.[12]

Several things should be noted in connection with the growth in aggregate numbers. First, its steady growth has been sustained by several radical shifts in the countries providing those students. We have, in fact, been almost magically blessed. Just when one set of countries has diminished as a source of foreign students, another set of countries has come along. The predominance of Latin American and Canadian students in the 1950s was swamped by the influx of OPEC country students in the early 1980s. This flow was replaced in turn by Asian students, most especially from the newly prosperous economic "tigers."

The historical increase in the aggregate flow of foreign students has meant that on many campuses foreign students became an increasingly prominent and in many cases a crucial portion of the student body. Dependence on foreign student flows varies considerably by institutional level. While in smaller institutions, particularly liberal arts colleges and most community colleges, foreign students comprise typically less than ten percent of the student body, in the large research universities, the percentages are much higher. At MIT more than 20 percent of the enrollees are foreign students, and at most of the Ivy League institutions, the student body is composed of approximately 15% foreign students. Thus larger institutions have come to depend on that flow, and many smaller institutions are scrambling to catch up. At the same time, the country of origin and the type of foreign student recruited has changed. Many institutions are only looking for full cost paying students who do not need any of the tuition and living cost discounts that must be provided for many American students. Hence, phalanxes of college and university recruiting teams descend each year on Japan, Hong Kong, Korea, and other parts of Southeast Asia. Estimates place the number of institutional recruiting teams visiting Japan at around 100 each year, and a similar number descend on Hong Kong.

Until recently, the United States had only modest competition in recruiting. American education was extremely attractive abroad, particularly in countries with underdeveloped higher educational systems of their own. The field is no longer quite so clear. The European Erasmus program set up strong currents for movement among the European countries. Over the past decade, the Australians have made an immensely successful effort to recruit students from East and Southeast Asia into what they call "export education," a well-tended supplemental component of their higher educational system. American recruiters are finding Australians to be major competitors particularly in Southeast Asia, a major recruiting ground for American institutions at the present time. The Japanese have launched a major recruiting effort in Asia, although they have a considerable distance to go in making their higher educational system foreign student friendly.

2. THE DEPENDENCE OF GRADUATE-LEVEL SCIENCE AND ENGINEERING ON FOREIGN STUDENTS

The need to maintain and expand the flow of foreign students is especially severe in research universities. The problem for major universities is that the flow of foreign students is concentrated largely at the graduate level. Indeed, as many as a third of the graduate students at most Ivy League institutions are foreign in origin. Moreover, these students are concentrated in graduate programs in science and engineering, so much so that the maintenance of these graduate programs in major universities is heavily dependent on the influx of foreigners to provide a satisfactory level of bright, well educated graduate students.

Once again, we have been lucky. Some hidden hand has expanded the flow of foreign students into our science and engineering departments precisely when the flow of American-born students into graduate programs in theoretical and research fields like physics and chemistry was declining substantially, so much so that the maintenance of graduate faculties has become dependent on the influx of foreign students. This is a major structural problem for universities that is yet to be addressed. The maintenance of a strong flow of highly qualified foreign students in science and engineering is a major challenge, particularly in the face of increasing hostility from the Immigration and Naturalization Service, the rumblings of state legislatures worrying about the support of foreign students by state taxpayers, and the decline of available federal fellowship and research assistance money resulting from the general deflationary trend in education more generally.

C. Business and Applied Disciplines

There are other internationally oriented tribes on our campuses that are not so much concerned with studying other countries, their languages, or international affairs, but are engaged in preparation of students for future careers that will be essentially international in focus. The most prominent among these are the now burgeoning international business programs, many of them supported by federal funds earmarked for international education. In addition, consortia of leading engineering schools have established educational programs preparing students for future connections with Japan.[13] Unlike our first category of international studies, the distinguishing characteristics of the graduates of these programs is not what they know about other countries but what they expect to do there. Nonetheless, they share with traditional international studies programs the intention of educating a variety of internationally oriented specialists.

1. STRUCTURAL PROBLEMS IN INTERNATIONAL BUSINESS AND ENGINEERING PROGRAMS

The structural problems faced by international business and engineering programs are clear. In each case, the professional training program is so extensive that there is little time to fit in the extra courses required to provide the specifically internationally oriented substantive courses. Second, the liberal arts orientation of much of the internationally oriented materials is very much social science and humanities based and shaped to fit within their disciplinary approaches. This limits the relevance of disciplinary international studies courses in the education of professionally oriented students, and there are few faculty members who can face both toward the liberal arts and the professional world.

The limitations of time and mismatch of focus between the needs of the applied disciplines and most of international education is most marked in language training and in study abroad. In a crowded MBA program or an engineering degree there is just not enough open space to provide the immense amount of time it takes to master a foreign language—particularly a language like Japanese—or to allow the student to spend enough time abroad to provide for a significant foreign experience. Moreover, to make the overseas experience directly related to the business and engineering students' future careers demands specially targeted study abroad programs. And more generally, fitting in the supplemental international studies education requires stretching out the degree program, and, not least importantly, raises the price of the degree. The greatest problem of all is to convince employers that the supplemental international training represents substantial value added. Is the supplemental international studies training grafted on to a business or an engineering degree an asset that will lead to better career prospects for graduates? The answer to this question, one that is by no means clear as yet, affects not only the willingness of students to invest in the extra demands on their time and resources in internationally oriented professional education, but in the long run, it also affects the universities' willingness to provide the extra funds to support what can often become quite expensive operations. Some of that cost is now borne by the federal government through HEA Title VI funding for the Centers for International Business Education and Research. As in the case of area studies, it will be interesting to see what will occur if this general support for such programs is discontinued.

2. BLURRING THE BOUNDARIES OF INTERNATIONAL STUDIES

The question of "value added" in international business programs raises a more general issue that returns us to our main discussion of the domains of international studies. One of the major structural problems facing international business programs is that their curricular add-on becomes less relevant when the rest of the training of their profession becomes more cosmopolitan. If all MBA education is oriented toward the international nature of business, what is the purpose of maintaining a special program focused on international business? Cannot, indeed should not, its goals be met by incorporating international materials and perspective in all courses?

This question is even more striking if one considers other parts of the campus, where there are an increasing number of individuals and activities that are substantially international in their orientation. A substantial group of faculty, particularly at land grant universities, devote much of their professional careers to technical assistance abroad. These professionals do not consider themselves part of international studies. The entire world of international science lies outside of what is normally considered international studies, as does international law, public health, and similar activities of other applied and professional disciplines. The way in which they, and their students, relate to their peers in other countries tends to be very different. The support for their activities abroad is very different, as is the mix of international and domestic activities. And even in the social sciences and the humanities disciplines, as they regularly incorporate more and more international information, as the domain of those disciplines becomes truly global, as the fraternity of scholarship becomes more transnational, then the boundary separating international from domestic studies also becomes increasingly blurred. Will the "enclosure" process be diminished, or reversed? What then happens to the special tribes of international studies? In short, one of the most important issues facing international studies results from the growing internationalization of a substantial portion of the academic enterprise.

IV. Conclusion

This brings the discussion full circle, back to McCaughey's "enclosure movement." I have outlined above a number of structural problems facing various domains of international studies on the campus. There are, however, two overall structural challenges facing the enterprise as a whole that are suggested by McCaughey's notion of enclosure. The first is external. The very success of the internationalization process on the campus must lead to a breakdown of the enclosure process. The tribes in international studies that have become a distinct set of people on the campus with a distinct set of functions and a distinct set of intellectual foci will lose their identity. Members of these tribes must then find ways to relate more effectively to larger, more cosmopolitanized disciplinary and professional groups. We in the field must rethink who we are and what are our special characteristics and functions. We must find ways to enhance and become part of the general cosmopolitanizing trends on the campus.

It is clear, however, that some of the functions of the international education tribes require special resources. Provision for sustained and cumulative transnational research and teaching will remain. For instance, the area specialist will still need the extra language, library, and field research opportunities to carry out their craft. Foreign language instruction will still demand specialized staffing, pedagogical technologies, and time commitment. The successful management of study abroad programs will still require special experience and expertise, and the maintenance of a set of far-flung arrangements to make it possible for students to study abroad.

In the new deflationary environment, however, these special requirements of international studies will have to be rethought and reargued. Our case will have to be made not only intellectually and educationally on its own terms, but comparatively, that is, measured against all of the other things that a university might do to cosmopolitanize itself. What are the opportunity costs, as the economists would put it? How we can demonstrate that internationally focused activity serves the institution's central missions, and compared to what?

The second set of structural problems relating to enclosure are issues of internal relations. Perhaps it is time to face the problem that the bulk of this article addresses. How can we blur not only the distinction between international and domestically oriented education, but lessen the tribal divides within international studies itself? For instance, can we transform the obsolescence wars that seem to perpetually pervade the interface between area studies and transnational studies into a discussion of how they can assist each other, recognizing each as representing coherent, but different approaches? Can we bring foreign language learning and use to a more central position in international education, one in which all tribes participate? Can study abroad be tied more directly to the interests and purposes of other components of international education? More generally, can the activities that relate to the study of other countries be related more effectively to those of what I have called the international actors?

To accomplish this blending of tribes will require a more holistic, transtribal view of international education than has typically been the case. There is some evidence that this perspective is already emerging. The recent compilation of a collective research agenda for the internationalization of higher education in the United States adopted such an integrated overview of the field.[14] Much of the recent work in Europe, particularly a set of OECD-sponsored comparative country profiles of international education, takes a similar overarching perspective. It is my hope that the kind of structural and intellectual analysis that I have attempted here will contribute to such a planning process for all of international studies, not just its separate tribes and clans.

NOTES

1. This paper is based on a paper delivered at the 25th anniversary meeting of the Pennsylvania Council of International Education.

2. Robert McCaughey, *International Studies and Academic Enterprise: A Chapter in the Enclosure of American Learning.* New York: Columbia University Press, 1985.

3. See for instance, Richard D. Lambert, *Language and Area Studies Review.* Philadelphia: Social Science Research Council, 1973; and Richard D. Lambert, *Beyond Growth: The Next Step in Language and Area Studies.* Washington, D.C.: Association of American Universities, 1984.

4. Martin O. Heisler, *The Nordic Region: Changing Perspectives in International Relations. Annals of the American Academy of Political and Social Science,* Vol. 512, Nov. 1990.

5. Evidence of this approach may be seen in the recent abolition of their area-focused committees by the Social Science Research Council and the American Council of Learned Societies, and by the shift in the focus of support by a number of the private foundations that have traditionally funded area studies.

6. Kenneth Prewitt, "President Items," in *Items.* Social Science Research Council, March 1996, pp. 15–18.

7. For a spirited rejoinder to this and similar charges, see Gilbert W. Merkx, *LASA FORUM,* vol. XXVI, No. 2, Summer 1995, pp. 5–8.

8. See Richard D. Lambert, *Beyond Growth: The Next Stage in Language and Area Studies.* Washington, D.C.: Association of American Universities, 1984, in Charles Hirschman, et al. (eds.), *Southeast Asia Studies in the Balance: Reflections from America.* Ann Arbor, Mich.: Association for Asian Studies, 1992, pp. 125–34.

9. See Sarah Jane Moore and Christine A. Morfit (eds.), *Language and International Studies: A Richard Lambert Perspective.* Washington, D.C.: National Foreign Language Center, 1993, pp. 3–179.

10. For a recent review of research being conducted on study abroad by various European research organizations, see Alan Smith, Ulrich Teichler, Marie van der Wende, *The International Dimension of Higher Education: Setting the Research Agenda.* Vienna: Internationale Forschungzentrum Kulturwissenschaften, 1994. For the most comprehensive comparative surveys of the structure and impact of study abroad in the United States and the United Kingdom, France, the Federal Republic of Germany, and Sweden, see Carlson, Jerry; Burn, Barbara; Useem, John; and Yachimowicz, David, *Study Abroad: The Experience of American Undergraduates.* Westport: Greenwood Press, 1990; and Opper, Susan; Teichler, Ulrich; and Carlson, Jerry, *Impacts of Study Abroad Programmes on Students and Graduates.* London: Jessica Kingsley Publishers, 1990.

11. For detailed data on foreign students see the annual issues of *Open Doors,* or Richard D. Lambert, "Foreign Student Flows and the Internationalization of Higher Education," in Katharine H. Hanson and Joel W. Myerson, *International Challenges to American Colleges and Universities: Looking Ahead.* Washington, D.C.: American Council on Education, 1995, pp. 18–41.

12. Richard D. Lambert, "Foreign Student Flows and the Internationalization of Higher Education," in Katharine H. Hanson and Joel W. Meyerson, *International Challenges to American Colleges and Universities: Looking Ahead.* Washington, D.C.: American Council on Education, 1995, p. 20.

13. Howard L. Wakeland, "International Education for Engineers," in Richard D. Lambert (ed.), *Foreign Language in the Workplace.* Annals of the American Academy of Political and Social Science, Vol. 511, September 1990, pp. 122–131.

14. Barbara B. Burn and Ralph Smuckler, *A Research Agenda for the Internationalization of Higher Education in the United States.* Association of International Education Administrators, 1995.

2 Current Issues in International Studies and Higher Education

Current debates in international studies have been concerned with the relevance of area studies to academic disciplines, particularly the social sciences, and the need to transcend area studies by examining global phenomena. The study of cultures and societies is a dynamic process. Governments change, boundaries are redrawn, new political actors appear, economic and political problems are resolved, business opportunities emerge, and societies continually borrow and assimilate new cultural ideas. Those who are concerned with area studies typically take these changes into account when doing research on particular countries or regions.

However, competing theories from academic disciplines are affecting the ways in which cultures and societies are now being studied. Today, social scientists, humanists, and others use new theoretical paradigms that replace, reject, or modify previous ones. These new orthodoxies often determine the direction of research, faculty appointments and tenure, funding, and graduate student support.

In the first part of this volume, we documented the history and contributions of Title VI programs. In this part, we have chosen writers who represent various interpretations of the theory and practice of international studies. Robert H. Bates calls for political science students to have not only area and language skills but also training in formal theory, statistics, and mathematics. This "scientific approach" has also dominated thinking in such disciplines as anthropology and sociology. Chalmers Johnson challenges Bates's ideas. He believes that Bates has launched an attack on the "unscientific" nature of area studies in order to advance the "rational choice" agenda. Johnson reaffirms the need for immersion in a particular subject or society, including mastery of language, history, and an understanding of culture. Furthermore, he maintains that, far from being atheoretical, area specialists have produced some of the most notable classics in contemporary social science.

Mark Tessler, with Jodi Nachtwey and Anne Banda, see more positive consequences from the ongoing debate between advocates of area studies and those promoting more scientific approaches. They argue that the alleged division between multidisciplinary area studies and disciplinary social sciences is highly exaggerated and that the substantive knowledge associated with area studies not only can contribute to the development of social science theory but also is essential to it. This represents a meeting point between area studies and theory. Indeed there is a new generation of scholars who are eager to test theoretical approaches in other than Western societies.

Kenneth Prewitt acknowledges that area studies has been "the most successful, large-scale interdisciplinary project ever in the humanities and social sciences." As president of the Social Science Research Council, historically a principal source of research funds for area studies, Prewitt responds nevertheless to changing global realities by presenting a new agenda that would cut across area studies, regions, and disciplines. Peter A. Hall and Sidney Tarrow address the trend toward regional and global analyses as well as the position developed by Bates. They conclude that the greatest danger in studying global trends is that the next generation of internationally oriented social science researchers will give "short shrift to area-based empirical knowledge." Hall and Tarrow thus point out the serious risks presented by these debates for graduate study and for the training of the next generation of researchers.

For some, the priority continues to be acquiring fundamental, in-depth knowledge of particular societies and cultures. For others, broader theoretical considerations are more important. The resolution of this debate will affect the form and substance of international studies taught in universities and colleges and will have ultimate consequences and repercussions for the strategic interests of the United States.

Area Studies and the Discipline

A USEFUL CONTROVERSY?

Robert H. Bates

When arguments become polarized, it often signals that divisions are falsely drawn. Such appears to be the case with this controversy. Why must one choose between area studies and the discipline? There are strong reasons for endorsing both. In this essay, I sketch the current debate and explore the ways in which local knowledge can and is being incorporated into general analytic frameworks. I conclude by stressing the work that lies ahead. In doing so, it should be stressed, I deal only with political science. The dynamics in other disciplines, I have found, differ greatly from those within our own (Bates et al. 1993).

Caricaturing the Present Divide

Within political science, area specialists are multidisciplinary by inclination and training. In addition to knowing the politics of a region or nation, they seek also to master its history, literature, and languages. They not only absorb the work of humanists but also that of other social scientists. Area specialists invoke the standard employed by the ethnographer: serious scholarship, they believe, must be based upon field research. The professional audience of area specialists consists of researchers from many disciplines, who have devoted their scholarly life to work on the region or nation.

Those who consider themselves "social scientists" seek to identify lawful regularities, which, by implication, must not be context bound. Rather than seeking a deeper understanding of a particular area, social scientists strive to develop general theories and to identify, and test, hypotheses derived from them. Social scientists will attack with confidence political data extracted from any region of the world. They will approach electoral data from South Africa in the same manner as that from the United States and eagerly address cross-national data sets, thereby manifesting their rejection of the presumption that political regularities are area-bound. Social scientists do not seek to master the literature on a region but rather to master the literature of a discipline. The professional audience of social scientists consists of other scholars from their discipline who share similar theoretical concerns—and who draw their data from a variety of regions of the world.

Like all caricatures, these depictions distort in order to highlight important elements of reality. The implications of this reality have profoundly unsettled our discipline.

Most immediately, the shift from area studies to "social scientific" approaches has influenced graduate training. Graduate students, whose resources of time and money are necessarily limited, increasingly shift from the study of a region to instruction in theory and methods. When confronted by a choice between a course in African history or one in econometrics, given their constraints, many now choose the latter.

The shift from area specialization to "social science" also alters the balance of power within the academy. Political science departments have long resembled federations, with their faculty in comparative politics dwelling within semi-autonomous, area studies units. Possessing access to resources for seminars, administrative support, fellowships, research and travel independent of the department, the comparative politics faculty has had little reason to defer to the demands of department heads. The move toward a disciplinary-oriented view of comparative politics, and the declining resource base for area studies, has shifted the political center of gravity back to the chairs, who can now apply disciplinary criteria, rather than area knowledge, in evaluating and rewarding professional contributions.

Change in the notions of professional merit also alters the balance of power between generations. Old field hands are giving way to young technicians. It is those in the middle who are the most threatened. Like their elders, they have trained as area specialists; but they are being evaluated by a new set of standards —ones by which they compare unfavorably with younger scholars. The mid-career scholars now scramble to master the new vocabulary and techniques; and departments that once would have readily promoted them too often decide to refrain from doing so, in the expectation of later filling the slots from the best and brightest of the new generation.

The result of these changes is heightened tension within the field, as the controversy resonates with divisions between scholars of different generations, locations within the university, and stages in their careers.

Clearly, the causes of these tensions lie outside the academy: they lie in the rising concerns with government deficits and the end of the cold war. The one has led to reductions in spending for higher education; the other, to a lower priority on area training. For reasons I do not fully understand, rather than cushioning the impact of these changes, foundations have instead exacerbated them by moving in concert with the government. Resources for the study of foreign areas are therefore declining, and we in academics are being required to establish new priorities, as we adjust to tighter constraints.

Reacting to the New Realities

Many departments were once characterized by a core of technocrats, many of whom specialized in the study of American politics, and a congery of others, many of whom studied foreign political systems. Students of American politics viewed themselves as social scientists; but the political system on which they concentrated, they came to realize, was singularly devoid of variation. Even comparisons across states within the greater federation failed to provide insight into differences, say, between presidential and parliamentary systems, much less between polities in market as opposed to centrally planned economies. A vocal minority within American politics had long dismissed students of comparative politics as "mere area specialists"; but the more sophisticated increasingly realized that their hard-won, cumulative, scientific knowledge about politics in the United States was itself area-bound. There therefore arose *among Americanists* a demand for *comparative* political research, and some of the most theoretically ambitious among them sought to escape the confines imposed by the American political system.

On the one hand, this trend creates allies for comparativists who seek to resist retrenchment; their knowledge of political variation has acquired greater significance. On the other, this trend will promote a transformation in the comparative study of politics; it will force those who have a command of local knowledge to enter into dialogue with those who seek to understand how institutional variation affects political outcomes or who see particular political systems as specific realizations of broader political processes.

Pressures from outside the discipline amplify these changes; they emerge from trends that have affected political systems throughout the world. Following the recession of the 1980s, authoritarian governments fell, and the collapse of communism in Eastern Europe further contributed to the spread of democracy. This change underscored the broader relevance of the Americanists' research into elections, legislatures and political parties. The spread of market forces and the liberalization of economic systems highlighted the broader significance of research conducted on the advanced industrial democracies as well. The impact of economic conditions upon voting, the politics of central banking, the effect of openness upon partisan cleavages and political institutions: long studied in the Western democracies, these subjects have recently become important, and researchable, in the formerly socialist systems in the North and in the developing nations of the South. As students of comparative politics have addressed them, they have come increasingly to share intellectual orientations, and a sense of necessary skills and training, with their more "social scientific" colleagues in the discipline.

The attention given to King, Keohane, and Verba's *Designing Social Inquiry* (1994) provides a measure of the impact of these trends. It suggests the urgency with which students of comparative politics feel a need for guidance, as they have sought ways to move from the in-depth study of cases, typical of area studies, to sophisticated research designs, required for scientific inference.

Deeper Fusion

The field is thus undergoing significant changes, and the increased stringency of funding strengthens these trends. Less visible, but highly significant, forces run just below the surface and these too will shape the final outcome. Insofar as they do so, they may well define a new synthesis. I refer to a synthesis not only between area studies and the discipline but also between context-specific knowledge and formal theory, as developed in the study of choice.

Area studies emphasizes the importance of cultural distinctions. Cultures are distinguished by their institutions. Game theoretic techniques, established for the study of economic and political organizations, provide a source of formal tools for investigating such institutions. They show how institutions shape individual choices and collective outcomes, and therefore provide a framework for exploring the origins of political difference.

Cultures are also distinguished by their histories and beliefs. The theory of decisions with imperfect information, newly prominent in political science, can be used to explore the manner in which such differences arise and matter. Individuals with similar expectations, it shows, come to diverge in their beliefs if exposed to different data; persons can be shaped by their histories. Even if exposed to the same data, decision theory suggests, persons will revise their beliefs in different ways, if they bring different likelihood functions to bear upon observations. The theory of decisions thus yields insight into the way in which history and world views shape individual choices and therefore collective outcomes. The theory thus provides a framework for exploring cross-cultural differences.

The relationship between "local knowledge" and rational choice theory can be illustrated by Elizabeth Colson's well-known research into the Plateau Tonga of Zambia (1974). The lives of the Tonga, she reports, resemble the Rousseauian myth, with people residing in peaceful communities, sharing their belongings, and legislating wisely in village assemblies. But, Colson reports, the surface harmony disguises deep fears: of the greed and envy of neighbors, of their wrath, and of their desire and capacity to harm. While the lives of the Plateau Tonga may resemble the accounts of Rousseau, their beliefs, she finds, are better captured in the writings of Hobbes. Colson resolves the paradoxical contrast between beliefs and behavior by arguing that it is the beliefs that support peaceful conduct: people scrupulously choose to act in ways that preserve the peace, she argues, for fear of the violence they would unleash should they impinge upon the interests of others.

Viewed in terms of game theory, Colson's argument represents a claim that behaving courteously constitutes an equilibrium strategy. The strategy is supported in equilibrium by beliefs as to the costs that would be incurred were people to stray from the equilibrium path. It would be easy to use the theory of games to specify the conditions under which the argument follows. More significantly, doing so would suggest additional insights into what must also necessarily be true for the argument to hold. Given that this is so, transforming the narrative into a rational choice account would generate additional testable implications (Ferejohn 1991). Some of these implications might be non-obvious; when this is the case formalization inspires new insights as well. Others might be crashingly obvious. But even jejune propositions, if deduced from a theory, are significant; for when they are tested, it is the theory from which they derive that is put at risk. Embedding narrative accounts in theories thus increases the opportunities for testing; it therefore increases our ability to judge the adequacy of an explanation.

By the same token, theory must be complemented by contextual knowledge. Consider the problem faced by an observer who encounters a person who is inflicting damage upon another. If a family head, he may be refusing a request for bride wealth; if a faction leader, he may be withholding patronage; if a mayor, she may be bringing the forces of the law to bear upon a rival political. Such actions inflict harm. But, in interpreting their political importance, the observer will need to know: Do they represent initial defections? Or do they represent punishments for an earlier defection? Without knowledge of the history, the investigator cannot determine the *significance* of these behaviors. The first history suggests that they should be analyzed as a political rupture; the second, that they should be treated as a punishment phase of a game—a phase that may in fact constitute a prelude to reconciliation. In the absence of local knowledge, the actions remain observationally equivalent; nothing in the theory alone suggests their strategic significance and thus their implications for subsequent interactions. Just as in the parable related by Geertz, a "wink" differs from a "twitch," so too does strategic behavior thus require interpretation. To be analyzed correctly, such behavior needs to be addressed by theory that is informed by empirical observation (1973).

To the degree that rational choice theory comes to occupy a central position within the discipline, then, the conflict between area studies and the "social scientific" core of political science will be misplaced. The approach provides explanations for difference; it requires knowledge of the difference for the construction and testing of its accounts. It provides a framework which transforms ethnography and narratives into theory-driven claims, amenable to refutation, and it requires precisely targeted observations to establish the force of its arguments (Bates et al., 1998).

It is important to realize that the present debate has been energized by adjacent controversies. It echoes recent ideological struggles. The debate over area studies is often exacerbated by debates over the merits of the market, the state, or the impact of the West, with those who endorse area studies viewing those who use rational choice theory as being pro-market, anti-state, and given to applying historically contingent categories in a universalistic manner. And it resonates with earlier battles over the qualitative and quantitative, between numeracy and literacy, and between the humanities and the sciences. In other cultures, well educated people are expected to excel at both; strength in the one need not imply weakness in the other. But the division remains powerful within our own culture, particularly among academics, where it limits and impedes. It reinforces the foundations for the present debate between area studies and the discipline.

Not being hard-wired, the division between "the scientific" and "the humanistic" can be transcended. The issue is not whether to use the left side of the brain rather than the right. It is, rather, how to employ both. The combination of local knowledge and general modes of reasoning, of area studies and formal theory, represents a highly promising margin of our field. The blend will help to account for the power of forces that we know shape human behavior, in ways that we have hitherto been able to describe but not to explain. It is time to insist upon the pursuit of both rather than upon the necessity of choosing sides.

Conclusion

To pursue this agenda, departments will have to accommodate the special needs of graduate training in comparative politics. For not only will our students need to possess area skills, such as languages; they will also need training in the skills long expected of students in the American subfield: formal theory, statistics, and the mathematics to do both. Others will need to train in economics as well. Just when university administrators are seeking to reduce the length of time necessary to secure a degree, this subfield will need to accommodate longer residencies. Administrators and department heads will have to adjust their programs accordingly.

Perhaps as a complement, departments will also have to re-think their approach to evaluating junior personnel. Unless fortunate enough to be a native speaker of a foreign language or to possess an unusually strong mathematical background, most junior faculty will not be able to consolidate both area and analytic skills prior to facing the tenure hurdle, much less to produce research demonstrating a confident command of both. In making promotion decisions, then, rather than focusing purely on product, attention will have to be placed on investment: If initially in command of research methodologies, have the young scholars used their initial years to learn the history of their area or its languages? If emerging from an area-based program, have they taken themselves to the classrooms in the statistics, economics, or mathematics departments? The deliberations regarding tenure in comparative politics may therefore have to differ from those in other portions of the discipline. Questions such as these will have to be addressed and the answers given greater weight than in other subfields.

In earlier decades, the Social Science Research Council gave mid-career grants, enabling professors to return to the classroom. These grants virtually made possible the creation of "hybrid" fields, such as economic history. Historians trained as economists, and economists as historians. Clearly, the creation of such an awards program would represent a timely response to the present crisis.

How will we know when reconciliation has been achieved? One test will be the capacity of someone who has invested heavily in the knowledge of an area to respond to a dean, provost, or departmental chair who inquires: "What has the study of your area contributed to the broader discipline?" Each of us who specializes in the study of an area should be able to respond to this question. We will, I am afraid, increasingly have to do so.

NOTE

This article draws heavily on Robert H. Bates, "Area Studies and Political Science: Rupture and Possible Synthesis," *Africa Today,* vol. 44, no. 2 (1997), special issue on "The Future of Regional Studies." I wish also to thank Timothy Cotton and Peter Hall, and the junior fellows of Harvard Academy, especially Daniel Posner, for their tough criticisms. I have failed to incorporate many of their suggestions, and therefore must assume complete responsibility of the defects that remain.

REFERENCES

Bates, Robert H., Jean O'Barr, and V. S. Mudimbe. 1993. *Africa and the Disciplines.* Chicago: University of Chicago Press.
Bates, Robert H., Avner Greif, Margaret Levi, Jean-Laurent Rosenthal, and Barry Weingast. 1998. *Analytic Narratives.* Princeton, N.J.: Princeton University Press.
Colson, Elizabeth. 1974. *Tradition and Contract.* Chicago: Aldine.
Ferejohn, John. 1991. "Rationality and Interpretation." In *The Economic Approach to Politics,* ed. Kristen Renwick Monroe. New York: Harper Collins.
Geertz, Clifford. 1973. *Interpretation of Cultures.* New York: Basic Books.
King, Gary, Robert Keohane, and Sydney Verba. 1994. *Designing Social Inquiry.* Princeton, N.J.: Princeton University Press.

Preconception vs. Observation,

OR THE CONTRIBUTIONS OF RATIONAL CHOICE THEORY AND AREA STUDIES TO CONTEMPORARY POLITICAL SCIENCE

Chalmers Johnson

A curious and little-noted ideological development accompanied the end of the Cold War. Just as the United States was stridently proclaiming its "victory" over the materialism of the former USSR, its academic political science establishment was endorsing a form of economic determinism that is more rigid and less insightful than the Marxism it had seemingly just discredited. This is so-called rational choice or public choice theory, the attempt to apply the neo-classical (i.e., the University of Chicago Economics Department's) model of a market to politics. This exercise infects political science with the same flaws that an extreme version of laissez-faire ideology has inflicted on economics. As Robert Kuttner (1997, 30) notes, "Nearly half the articles in major political science journals have reflected a broad public choice sensibility." It also leads to jejune turf wars and attempts to excommunicate from university political science departments those now identified as heretics, typified by Robert H. Bates's (1996) "Letter from the President: Area Studies and the Discipline."

Reprinted with permission from *PS: Political Science & Politics*, vol. 30, no. 2 (June). © 1997 by American Political Science Association. Reprinted with permission of the publisher and the author.

It seems obvious why some political science pedants want to emulate economics. They envy the prestige attached to academic economics in contemporary Anglo-American political culture and would like to acquire a little of that aura of authority for themselves. As Jim Richardson (1997, 56) puts it, "In the contemporary West, above all in the 'Anglo-Saxon' societies, accreditation in economics is coming to be analogous to membership in the Communist Party in the former Soviet Union—a sine qua non for a role in policy making or for acceptance as an authoritative commentator—and familiarity with the discourse is analogous to command of the esoterics of Marxist-Leninist ideology."

In the jargon of these self-promoters, the intervening variable is "science." Economics is thought to be scientific because some of the relationships in its models can be expressed as simultaneous equations or other forms of mathematical expression. In emulation of this practice, for the past decade and more the *American Political Science Review* too has littered its pages with equations so complicated as to make the formulae for derivatives used to hedge large investment portfolios look like child's play. As Martin Anderson (1992, 101) puts it, "The main problem is not that much of the writing of academic intellectuals is too mathematical, but that it is insignificant, unimportant, trivial. If the ideas were significant and important ones couched in the language of mathematics, that would be fine, for presumably it could be reworked into English. But if the writing is devoid of any merit, expressing it in plain English would expose the intellectual sham."

In order to advance the rational choice agenda within academic political science, Professor Bates has launched an open attack on what he calls area studies. He proposes that since scholars who have acquired the skills to do empirical research in non-Anglo-American environments do not fit his definition of a "scientist," they should be discriminated against within the discipline. "Area studies has failed to generate scientific knowledge," he writes (Bates 1996, 1). Area specialists have "defected from the social sciences into the camp of the humanists." A certain sign of this "defection" is the area specialists' commitment to the study of "history, languages, and culture." Area specialists lag behind others in terms of "their familiarity with mathematical approaches to the study of politics." Most irritatingly, they often stand in the way of the plans of rational choice vanguards who want to take over departments and establish what they like to call a "paradigm" of standards for the discipline. Such a paradigm is needed in order to protect rational choicers from criticism and allows them to rig the customary systems of peer review in their favor. "They [area specialists] often oppose the appointment of those who have trained in such areas [as algebra, etc.] but who may be deficient in language skills." According to Bates (1996, 1), "wily directors" of area centers can "become independent of departmental chairs." He evidently considers this wily because whenever the marketplace of ideas is actually allowed to function in a university, area specialists attract more customers than the scientists do. Hence Bates intones: "I have long regarded area programs as a problem for political science."

One of the ironies of the we-too-can-be-economists fad in political science is that rational choice theory represents one of the last gasps of "modernism"—i.e., the belief that science and materialism equate with "progress" towards the best of all possible worlds—and fails even to consider the new realms of complexity opened up by the postmodern perspective on race, gender, and culture. "The rational-choice segment of political science," writes David Hollinger (1997, 347–48), "has been as far removed from the identity debates as have been the model-building economists. . . . Critics accuse the rational choicers of failing to illuminate anything of genuine significance to the study of politics, just as model-building economists are sometimes accused . . . of avoiding the complexities of the real world with the determination of Methodists avoiding a local saloon. Rational-choice scholars [have] responded . . . by insisting that they actually offered a general, impeccably scientific approach to all politics that promised to create a universal explanatory theory. Nowhere in the social sciences and the humanities is the Enlightenment flame of epistemic universalism kept with less respect for the concerns of thinkers who believe this flame to be a flash of artificial light."

American academic economics remains the last great modernist project awaiting the attention of post-modernist critics and serious deconstruction. This would involve above all placing works such as Paul Samuelson's *Foundations of Economic Analysis* (1947)—perhaps the last great modernist text still read with the naivete of a turn-of-the-century progressive—in their true political setting and displaying their ideological uses in the Cold War, regardless of the alleged intentions of the author. It is possible that some of contemporary neo-classical economics and its offspring could survive a post-modernist critique of their alleged scientific credentials. But rational choice theory has come nowhere close to providing models of political process that approximate those of Samuelson fifty years ago. Unfortunately, Kuttner's (1997) example of the payoffs from rational choice theory is not a caricature: "Public choice claims that office holders have as their paramount goal re-election, and that groups of voters are essentially 'rent seekers' looking for a free ride at public expense, rather than legitimate members of a political collectivity expressing democratic voice. Ordinary citizens are drowned out by organized interest groups, so the mythic 'people' never get what they want. Thus, since the democratic process is largely a sham, as well as a drag on economic efficiency, it is best to entrust as little to the public realm as possible." This might pass as an official statement of Singaporean ideology or even help explain the current enthusiasm among America neoconservatives for the authoritarian oligarchies of East Asia, but as political science it is dangerous nonsense (Heilbrunn 1996).

Nowhere do the rational choicers look more sophomoric than when contending that rational choice theory contains a unique capacity to transcend culture and reduce all human behavior to a few individual motivational uniformities. Bates (1996, 2) thinks that "cultures are distinguished by their distinctive institutions" and that rational choice theory provides "the tools with which to analyze institutions." He is confident that his set of deductive axioms when allied with game theory "will lead to scientific progress." But he fails even to acknowledge the existence of evidence that rational choice's key assumption, i.e., that all behavior can be reduced to rational individuals' short-term attempts to maximize their utility, is both wrong and culture-bound. This failure is the strongest indicator that rational-choice theory is more an ideological expression of United States' interests in the post–Cold War period than an attempt at social science. Greider (1997, 187) expresses the basis of this ideological interest in these terms: "As the organizational structures of global industrial firms gradually converge, a profound debate is forming between two competing capitalist systems: the American model of independent, profit-maximizing enterprises versus the cooperative and state-administered version in Japan. One promotes Anglo-Saxon legal rules to ensure free-wheeling competition. The other constructs webs of business relationships and social obligations among many firms. One preaches a laissez-faire approach to managing the overall economy. The other plans national strategies for industrial development and actively supervises competitors in the marketplace. One thrives on individualism, the other on loyalty."

In short, the rational choice project not only does not transcend culture and may itself be an expression of contemporary American culture, it also fails even to understand the concept of culture that it repeatedly attacks. Contrary to the view that culture is merely a set of institutional alternatives, I believe the present understanding of culture dates from Thomas S. Kuhn's *The Structure of Scientific Revolutions* (1962). In that pathbreaking work, Kuhn provided a historicist and relativistic explanation of culture (i.e., for a particular society's structure of values and how this interacts with its division of labor) that is more empirical and less easily transcended than Marx's reduction of culture to the interests of a ruling class. Rational choice scholars like to cite Kuhn without ever appreciating that the lasting effect of Kuhn's breakthrough was to take "the glitter off of the more extravagant claims of the scientific method in the humanities and social sciences (Bender 1997, 25)."

This view of culture, which rational choice theory trivializes, makes it the master concept of all social science. It also leads directly to genuine area studies since it requires that for a researcher to break free of his or her own culture, he or she must immerse "oneself in one's subject, learning the language, living with the people, and getting to understand the society so thoroughly as a participant that it problematizes one's own place as an objective observer (Suehiro 1997, 20–27)." This is what social scientists do naturally when studying their own culture, and it is what they *must* do in order to study another culture. There is no alternative or rational-choice shortcut. I will return to this point in my conclusion.

Equally important, rational choice theory also has no way to account for cultural change, and its conclusions are therefore commonly outdated by cultural developments that rational choice theory ignored. As an example, consider the impeccably rational-choice-cum-inane-quantification treatment of Japan's ruling party that the *American Political Science Review* published five months after the party had lost power (Cox and Rosenbluth 1993). Never once did the authors' allegedly powerful theoretical apparatus suggest to them that in the post–Cold War period the Liberal Democratic Party had lost its most important cachet, its anticommunism, and that even though it had long ago rigged the political system so that it could not lose at the polls, it might simply collapse from internal irrelevance and infighting. Something similar was happening in Italy at the same time, but rational choice theory does not promote meaningful comparisons. One of the reasons why Kuhn's model continues to have such currency today is precisely because it contains a genuine theory of cultural change, which Kuhn calls a "scientific revolution."[1]

Rational choice theory on the concept of culture is simply puerile; rather than transcending culture, it appears merely to reflect the particular parochialisms of American culture and what *Daedalus* calls "American academic culture."[2] As even Bates himself inadvertently acknowledges, rational choice theory is inseparable from the overgeneralization of American political culture. "Developed for the study of politics in the United States, these tools [rational choice theory] are increasing being applied elsewhere," writes Bates (1996, 2).

In order to do this, Bates understands that an analyst will have to learn *something* about the foreign country he or she is studying. "These tools," he writes, "cannot be applied in the absence of *verstehen* (1996, 2)." But *verstehen* if it means anything at all requires skills and tools that the rational choice adept specifically rejects. The joke that much American social science on the enrichment of East Asia (e.g., Paul Krugman [1994], who has argued that it is a flash in the pan) comes from people with no more knowledge of the area than they acquired from flying over it during daylight applies specifically to the rational choice theorists. Rational choice scholars explicitly refuse to acquire the tools needed to attain *verstehen* through their own efforts, and are left to rely on graduate students from the country under study.

Bates's gloss on the *verstehen* problem is an old confidence trick. It proposes that the relationship between area specialists and rational choice theorists is that of a hierarchy, with the area specialist in the role of a gold miner digging away at the cliff face of a foreign culture, while the rational choice theorist is the master goldsmith who can turn this raw ore into beautiful things. "I do not regard area studies as an intellectual rival," writes Bates (1996, 2); "rather I regard it as a necessary complement to the social sciences." In Bates's vision of how academic life should be organized, "They [area specialists] would record the data from which political inferences would be drawn by social scientists residing in political science departments."

One problem with this proposed division of labor is that these social scientists do not produce beautiful objects but junk and real area specialists have a much better record of producing theory than their self-proclaimed theoretical rivals. By theory in this context I mean the formulation of apparent relationships or underlying principles of observed phenomena that have to some extent been verified. Theory in this sense stands in contrast to the concept of hypothesis. This kind of theorizing is inherent and routine in area studies but is nonexistent in rational choice analyses.

Contrary to Bates's contention, area specialists within political science and related disciplines have produced some of the most notable classics of contemporary social science. In my view, such a list would include Barrington Moore, Jr. (Russian area specialist), *Social Origins of Dictatorship and Democracy: Lord and Peasant in the Making of the Modern World* (1966); Lucian W. Pye (China area specialist), *Asian Power and Politics: The Cultural Dimensions of Authority* (1985); Robert A. Dahl (U.S. area specialist), *Modern Political Analysis* (1970); Robert Putnam (with Robert Leonardi and Raffaella Y. Nanetti) (Italian area specialists), *Making Democracy Work: Civic Traditions in Modern Italy* (1993); Albert O. Hirschman (Latin American area specialist), *Exit, Voice, and Loyalty* (1970)[3]; G. William Skinner (China area specialist and a very mathematical one at that), *Marketing and Social Structure in Rural China* (1965); Cynthia Enloe (Southeast Asian area specialist), *Ethnic Soldiers: State Security in Divided Societies* (1980); Guillermo O'Donnell (Latin America area specialist), *Modernization and Bureaucratic Authoritarianism* (1973); Juan Linz (Spanish area specialist), *The Breakdown of Democratic Regimes* (1978); Philippe C. Schmitter (Latin American area specialist), ed., *Patterns of Corporatist Policy-making* (1982); and Paul Kennedy (diplomatic historian), *The Rise and Fall of the Great Powers* (1988). As an area specialist of China and Japan, I consider my own books derived from study of the Chinese revolution (*Peasant Nationalism and Communist Power,* 1962) and from study of the postwar Japanese economy (*MITI and the Japanese Miracle,* 1982) as aiming for the same level of theoretical discourse as the books listed above. Equally important, these books intend to communicate knowledge about some important parts of the world to citizens of democratic polities. These books concern real world politics, not the doodles of game theorists still stumped by the prisoner's dilemma.

I have tried to think of one book in which rational choice theory has been applied to a non-English-speaking country with results even approximately close to the claims made for the method. I cannot.

Another irony of the fad for rational choice theory in political science is that it is occurring just as the model science, economics, is starting to back away from its basic theory. Economics today is rethinking whether the "as if" assumptions in its models diverge too far from reality.[4] Economists are undertaking these reforms because the anomalies in the paradigm have become too numerous for comfort and also probably for practical reasons. Massive and sustained downsizing based on pure laissez-faire theory has started to hit the professional classes in the United States, and some members of comfortably tenured academia have begun to realize that this theoretically sanctified practice might ultimately impinge on them. A purely rational choice analysis of American universities today, many of which look as bloated as IBM before the value of its shares collapsed, suggests that they are ripe for a good dose of Maggie Thatcherism. Even Nobel laureate Robert M. Solow (1997, 56–57) has started to acknowledge that "the part of economics that is independent of history and social context is not only small but dull" and that "theory is cheap, and data are expensive."

Just as James Baldwin (1963) once wondered why anyone would want "to integrate into a burning house," young political scientists should be asking themselves the same question. In recent months George Soros, William Greider, and Robert Kuttner have all drawn attention to the economic contradictions of the global economic system and to the need for the United States to confront the weaknesses of its own dogma (Soros 1997). When George Soros argues that financial prices are always "wrong" in that they never reflect economic fundamentals and William Greider points out that overproduction and the abandonment of a powerful rule-setting function by governments portend a new global collapse of demand, neoclassical economics and its offspring rational choice theory are in serious trouble. If prices are wrong, they cannot be a guide to making rational choices; and if the only answer to inadequate demand is state action, then political science's contemporary disparagement of the state (something that assuredly does not occur, for example, in China) is a form of unilateral disarmament.

Kuttner (1997) points to three fundamental flaws in the model of the market derived from neo-classical economic theory, each of which applies with even greater force to rational choice theory as it is applied to politics. The model (a) oversimplifies the dynamics of human motivation to such an extent that it turns the "as if" assumptions underlying the model into science-fiction; (b) it misunderstands that civil society needs political rights in which some things are not for sale; and (c) it misprices many things (e.g., national currencies), which means that pure markets do not yield optimal economic outcomes. This critique returns us to the preoccupations of Adam Smith's *Wealth of Nations*—the things that the state must do in order to allow a market economy to exist and flourish, even from a minimalist perspective (nightwatchman, defense, education of the labor force, etc.). State and market coexist symbiotically; the model of the neoclassical market does not recognize this.

To conclude, neither neoclassical economics nor rational choice theory provides a mechanical alternative to genuine social science analysis, i.e., what political science but no other discipline of the social sciences calls area studies. This means immersion in a subject or a society that the political analyst is studying, including mastery of the relevant languages and history, participant observation, and an empathetic attempt to understand its culture (in the Kuhnian sense). The problem with knowledge gained in this manner is that in its totality it is incommunicable except perhaps in novels or to those who have similarly immersed themselves in the object of study. This is where social science discipline comes in. It provides the concepts and vocabulary with which to communicate knowledge gained through area studies, and the attempt to express area studies knowledge in disciplinary terms unavoidably involves inductive theorizing about the results of research. Graduate study of a discipline such as political science is intended to introduce and explain the ideas, concepts, and terms that must be used to communicate doctoral and professional area studies research to those who have not personally immersed themselves in the research. But knowledge of the political science discipline is in no way a substitute for area studies. It is merely the means of communicating them, without which they emit no more of an intellectual message than the raw materials of cultures themselves.

Herbert A. Simon, political science's first Nobel laureate, is arguably the leading role model for the discipline as it exists today. Another equally distinguished political scientist, Charles E. Lindblom (1997, 228), writes, "About Simon, we might suggest that he made his several great contributions to the study of behavior and society by distancing himself from the dominant interests of political science." Pondering the current fad for rational choice theory, I think that is good advice.

NOTES

1. For an application of Kuhn's concept of culture and cultural change to political systems, see Chalmers Johnson, *Revolutionary Change* (Stanford University Press, 1982, 2nd ed.).

2. See the issue devoted to "American Academic Culture in Transformation: Fifty Years, Four Disciplines," *Daedalus,* Winter 1997.

3. For those who might doubt that Albert Hirschman could be called a Latin American area specialist, see Hirschman, *Journeys Toward Progress: Studies of Economic Policy Making in Latin America* (New York: Anchor Books, 1965); and Hirschman, ed., *Latin American Issues: Essays and Comment* (New York: Twentieth Century Fund, 1961).

4. See, e.g., John Cassidy, "The Decline of Economics," *The New Yorker,* December 2, 1996, pp. 50–60; Partha Dasgupta, *An Inquiry into Well-Being and Destitution* (Oxford: Oxford University Press, 1994); "Rational Economic Man: The Human Factor," *The Economist,* December 24, 1994, pp. 90–92; Robert Kuttner, "Peddling Krugman," *The American Prospect,* Sept–Oct, 1996, pp. 75–85; and Alan Tonelson, "The Perils of Techno-Globalism," *Issues in Science and Technology,* Summer 1995, pp. 1–8.

REFERENCES

Anderson, Martin. 1992. *Imposters in the Temple: American Intellectuals are Destroying our Universities and Cheating our Students of Their Future.* New York: Simon & Schuster.

Bates, Robert H. 1996. "Letter from the President: Area Studies and the Discipline." APSA-CP: *Newsletter of the APSA Organized Section on Comparative Politics.* 7(1): 1–2.

Baldwin, James. 1963. *The Fire Next Time.* New York: Dial Press.

Bender, Thomas. 1997. "Politics, Intellect, and the American University." *Daedalus* (Winter).

Cox, Gary W., and Frances Rosenbluth. 1993. "The Electoral Fortunes of Legislative Factions in Japan." *American Political Science Review* 87(3): 577–89.

Greider, William. 1997. *One World, Ready or Not: The Manic Logic of Global Capitalism.* New York: Simon and Schuster.

Heilbrunn, Jacob. 1996. "Yew Turn: How the Right Embraced 'Asian Values.'" *The New Republic,* 9 December.

Hollinger, David A. 1997. "The Disciplines and the Identity Debates, 1970–1996." *Daedalus* (Winter).

Krugman, Paul. 1994. "The Myth of Asia's Miracle." *Foreign Affairs* 73(6): 62–78.

Kuhn, Thomas S. 1962. *The Structure of Scientific Revolutions.* Chicago: University of Chicago Press.

Kuttner, Robert. 1997. "The Limits of Markets." *The American Prospect* (March–April).

Lindblom, Charles E. 1997. "Political Science in the 1940s and 1950s." *Daedalus* (Winter).

Richardson, James L. 1997. "Economics: Hegemonic Discourse." *Quadrant* [Melbourne] (March).

Solow, Robert M. 1997. "How Did Economics Get That Way and What Way Did It Get?" *Daedalus* (Winter).

Soros, George. 1997. "The Capitalist Threat." *The Atlantic Monthly* (February).

Suehiro, Akira. 1997. "Thinktanks and the Evolution of 'Chiiki Kenkyu,' Japan's Area Studies." *Social Science Japan* (February).

Introduction

THE AREA STUDIES CONTROVERSY

Mark Tessler, Jodi Nachtwey, and Anne Banda

Growing tension between regional specialists and discipline-oriented social scientists has emerged as a major issue in the fields of international, comparative, and area studies. At the heart of the controversy is an important disagreement about social science epistemology, about what constitutes, or should constitute, the paradigm by which scholars construct knowledge about politics, economics, and international relations in major world regions. This controversy is the result not only of shifting intellectual currents within many social science disciplines but also of external factors, such as changing priorities for U.S. government and private foundation funding. With emphasis increasingly placed on scholarship that is global in perspective and informed by social science theory, these developments have threatened regional studies programs or, at the very least placed these programs on the defensive.

The area studies controversy, as it is known, has been particularly intense in political science. Thus, in an article entitled "Political Scientists Clash over Value of Area Studies," *The Chronicle of Higher Education* reported the charge that "a focus on individual regions leads to work that is mushy" (Shea 1997). The most important criticism reviewed in the article is the contention that area specialists are hostile to social science theory, meaning that they have no interest in either

Reprinted with permission from *Area Studies and Social Science: Strategies for Understanding Middle East Politics,* ed. by Mark Tessler with Anne Banda and Jodi Nachtwey. © 1999 Indiana University Press. The first half of the introduction is reproduced here.

the development or application of insights which transcend particular times and places. A related criticism is that their research lacks conceptual sophistication and methodological rigor. Similar complaints have been presented in *PS: Political Science & Politics,* a quarterly publication of the American Political Science Association. In June 1997, for example, the journal featured a section containing three articles on "Controversies in the Discipline: Area Studies and Comparative Politics." Articles in the prominent scholarly journal *Daedalus* have also explored this issue. They note that while the controversy may be most pronounced in political science, it is by no means limited to that discipline (Slow 1997; Bender 1997).

Against the background of these tensions and controversies, the present volume offers a collection of essays and research reports by scholars who are grounded in both area studies and their respective social science disciplines. All are Middle East specialists and nearly all are political scientists, although the disciplines of economics and history are also represented. In most cases, authors either take a self-conscious look at some portion of their past scholarship or present the results of a current research project, making explicit and then evaluating the relationship of this work to both their academic discipline and the field of Middle East studies. The essays were first presented at a conference at the University of Wisconsin–Milwaukee, where they formed the basis for an interdisciplinary discussion of the area studies controversy.

The Middle East is by no means the only world region for which these concerns are relevant. On the contrary, the area studies controversy involves criticisms directed at all area studies research. Thus, while a focus on the Middle East offers an excellent opportunity to examine this controversy, this collection seeks to do more than illuminate the foundations of political research in one particular region. The volume's larger purpose is to explore the relationship between area studies and theoretical social science as paradigms for the study of any major world region. By presenting some of their scholarly work and then discussing the ways in which this research is informed by, and contributes to, both theoretical and area-specific considerations, the contributors to this volume provide a basis for thinking about how and for what purposes scholars seek to produce knowledge about a particular country or region. All of the authors conclude that scholarship is especially productive when informed by disciplinary considerations, and by a concern for theory in particular, while at the same time being fully grounded in the real-world circumstances of the countries or regions under study. The essays also show that research which draws upon and integrates social science and area studies perspectives his yielded valuable results in the study of the Middle East.

Area Studies and Disciplinary Social Science

The tension between area studies and disciplinary social science is not new. Discipline-oriented scholars, who place emphasis on the development of general theoretical insights, have for many years argued that the work of area specialists lacks rigor, and, above all, that it is not scientific in that it favors description over explanation, lacks analytical cumulativeness, and shows no interest in parsimony and generalization. Area studies research, these critics also contend, is overly preoccupied with detail and specificity. Though rich in factual information about particular places or particular times, it offers little to those with broader interests, applied, as well as theoretical.

Analytically oriented social scientists have also received their share of criticism. They have been charged with faddishness and oversimplification, with engaging in sterile debates about conceptual and theoretical frameworks, and with constructing highly abstract models that provide little real insight into the complex behavior patterns or events they purport to explain. Discipline-oriented scholars may not be drowning in minutiae, as critics charge is the case with area specialists, but their work is often perceived to be irrelevant, having little or no connection to real world situations. This is the case in particular for international and cross-cultural research, where, according to area specialists, insights uninformed by a knowledge of the languages, cultures, and histories of particular regions are highly unlikely to be meaningful or even accurate.

Posed in these terms, the intellectual divide between the two scholarly approaches may be overstated. Neither area studies nor disciplinary social science should be viewed in such stereotypical terms. Each is more diverse and tolerant than this portrait might suggest, and many scholars have recognized the value of incorporating insights from both paradigms. Nevertheless, this should not obscure the very real tension that has long existed, as will be readily attested by those who have witnessed the contentious debates surrounding personnel decisions in many university social science departments. The divide has also been reflected in scholarly journals, with disciplinary journals and area journals rarely having the same contributors, or even appealing to the same readers. Even with tolerance and mutual respect, which unfortunately have not always been present, area specialists and discipline-oriented social scientists have, to a very significant degree, inhabited two different scholarly worlds.

Several recent developments have sharpened the divide between these two perspectives, and, as noted, placed area specialists on the defensive. In disciplines like political science and economics, for example, increasing sophistication in quantitative data analysis and the popularity of rational choice theory as an approach to model building have created new orthodoxies and diminished the importance attached to foreign language proficiency and overseas research experience. Rational choice theory, in particular, sees behavior as rooted in the self-interested cost-benefit calculations made by all men and women, and it is accordingly skeptical about the inclusion of cultural factors in explanations of behavior.

At the other end of the spectrum, trends associated with postmodernism in some disciplines, most notably anthropology and sociology, have called into question the possibility of objective scholarship and led some to condemn cross-cultural field work on both intellectual and political grounds. Also known as "reflexivity" or the "reflexive turn," this intellectual orientation asserts that since all knowledge is a product of the interaction between observer and observed, the quest for research findings that are intersubjectively transmissible, the foundation of science and cumulativeness, is inevitably doomed to failure. Objective social science, in other words, is said to be an illusion. Admittedly, some trends associated with postmodernism are much less absolute, calling simply for greater self-awareness regarding the subjective elements of data collection and field work, including those pertaining to the researcher's motivations. Others, however, insist that there is no possibility of empathetic understanding or even accurate observation across lines of culture. The same is said to apply to divisions based on race, gender, and other critical social categories.

A concern with "Orientalism," which is not new, has also had something of a chilling effect on area studies scholarship. The charge here is that many area specialists consider behavior to be determined primarily by cultural influences, and that they accordingly place the people they study outside of science by seeking to explicate the unique culture and history that makes them behave as they do. Among the results of such research have been studies with titles like "The Arab Mind" and "Temperament and Character of the Arabs," which critics of Orientalism condemn as stereotypical, one-dimensional, reductionist, and deterministic (Said 1978, pp. 309–311). In response to such criticism, reflecting a desire to avoid the stereotyping about which critics of Orientalism quite properly complain, a tendency has developed to question the value of any research that gives prominent attention to cultural and historical factors when studying non-Western societies. This tendency, once again, places area studies scholarship on the defensive.

Challenges to area studies have also been based on considerations of relevance. Specifically, area studies is said to be a product of the Cold War, developed with federal funds in the 1950s and 1960s in order to ensure that the United States would possess the knowledge about Third World countries needed to compete effectively with the Soviet Union. This global confrontation was often described at the time as "the struggle for men's minds." While most area specialists did not see their scholarly mission in such terms, support for the study of less commonly taught languages and for overseas research in developing countries was made possible by an American government and several private foundations that saw strategic value in the collection of detailed information about Third World societies. Support for the study of Second World societies and languages, said to be necessary so that the United States would know its enemy, was also provided. The National Defense Education Act, passed by the U.S. Congress in 1958, was particularly important. The graduate fellowships it provided for advanced training in foreign languages and area studies laid a foundation for the entry into American universities of a large new corps of regional specialists.

Today, however, new global realities, coupled as they are with a concern for reducing the federal budget in the United States, have led many to argue that area studies is an anachronism. An influential expression of this view was provided by

Stanley Heginbotham, vice president of the Social Science Research Council (SSRC), who in a 1994 article called for less attention to in-depth studies of regional particularisms and more attention to themes of global relevance (Heginbotham 1994). The SSRC subsequently refocused its program of "area" research grants and announced that it would henceforth encourage "thematic" studies addressed to such global concerns as ethnic conflict and transitions to democracy, preferably to be examined in comparative investigations within or even across world regions.

The Ford Foundation, the Mellon Foundation, and the MacArthur Foundation have all begun to move in this direction as well. The Ford Foundation, for example, which provided major support for the establishment of area studies programs in the 1950s and 1960s, in December 1996 announced a new grants program devoted to the "revitalization" of area studies. Apparently judging the training and research associated with area studies to be in need of reform, the foundation is encouraging area programs to reexamine their goals and is offering assistance to those prepared to move in new directions. Ford also joined with the MacArthur Foundation several years ago to encourage research on global rather than regional problems, and the Mellon Foundation has taken a similar approach in its program on cross-regional issues.

The end of American-Soviet rivalry is only one part of the new reality that critics of area studies cite in order to justify their calls for attention to global rather than regional issues. Other trends, some associated with the end of the Cold War and some reflecting the revolution in communications and information technology, are also transforming the environment within which scholarship takes place. One important consideration is that political and economic liberalization is breaking down national barriers and forcing an increasing number of countries, whether they wish it or not, to deepen their involvement in the world economic and political system. However different might be their cultures and histories, events and developments in countries around the world are increasingly subject to the same global influences.

Similarly, the communications revolution is breaking down isolation and fostering the development and worldwide dissemination of common cultural forms and shared behavioral norms. Francis Fukuyama calls this "The End of History" (Fukuyama 1992). According to this argument, a process of global integration and linguistic and cultural consolidation is taking place. Western culture and the English language will play an increasingly important role in the non-Western world, just as a continuing expansion of the dominant languages and cultures in these regions will further reduce, and perhaps eventually eliminate, the great diversity that has marked Third World societies in the past. According to critics of area studies, these trends are another reason why it is no longer important for Western scholars to acquire detailed information about the history, culture, or languages of most developing countries.

Area specialists have begun to respond to this constellation of charges and challenges. At the center of their response are two interrelated arguments: first, the research agenda of many area specialists has a strong theoretical focus and, accordingly, the alleged division between area studies and disciplinary social science is highly exaggerated; and second, the kind of substantive knowledge associated with area studies not only *can* contribute to the development of social science theory, it is in fact essential.

Many scholars working under the umbrella of area studies are concerned with, and have in fact produced, broadly generalizable theoretical insights. A good example, and one which shows that this is by no means a new phenomenon, is the work on cultural pluralism by Crawford Young, a political scientist and Africanist at the University of Wisconsin–Madison (Young 1976 and 1993). Although trained as an area specialist and using a traditional case study methodology, Young has nonetheless made major theoretical contributions to our understanding of how political identities are formed and subsequently change. The theoretical contributions of numerous other area specialists could be similarly cited, including Barrington Moore, Theda Skocpol, Lucian Pye, Lloyd and Suzanne Rudolph, Leonard Binder, John Waterbury, Albert Hirschman, Guillermo O'Donnell, and Philippe Schmitter, among many others.

Reflecting on this situation, John Creighton Campbell, an Asia specialist at the University of Michigan, asserted that "most of the things that people say about area studies are silly. . . . Most of the stuff that people say area studies should be doing is what area studies is already doing" (Shea 1997, p. 13). The same point was made by Peter A. Hall and Sidney Tarrow, political scientists at Harvard and Cornell, respectively. Writing in 1998, Hall and Tarrow rejected the claim that area specialists focus only on detailed descriptions of individual nations or regions. They noted that many scholars concerned with theory, including Charles Tilly, Benedict Anderson, Donald Horowitz, and Michel Crozier, have drawn upon "deep and context-rich knowledge of a particular society or region to develop propositions of general applicability." Thus, they concluded, the charge that area specialization is incompatible with theoretical inquiry is "little more than a misleading rhetorical exercise" (Hall and Tarrow 1998, p. B5) [p. 99, this volume].

Area specialists frequently argue not only that their work is compatible with a concern for social science theory, but that the quest for theory cannot be pursued meaningfully without attention to the kind of contextual knowledge that area studies research provides. They note, for example, that theory construction often begins with observation, with the delineation of variance that hypotheses are then formulated to explain. Further, the hypotheses themselves will have explanatory power only to the extent that they are neither trivial nor obvious. Finally, hypotheses cannot be tested without the development of measures that are valid within the social and cultural context from which data are drawn. All of this, however, requires an ability to recognize, understand, and evaluate the facts on the ground, which is precisely the kind of knowledge associated with area studies.

An argument along similar lines is advanced in relation to rational choice theory by Robert Bates, a political scientist and African specialist at Harvard.

Bates's own work on African markets, like that of Young on cultural pluralism, illustrates the theoretical contributions that can and often do grow out of area studies research (Bates 1981 and 1989). In addition, however, Bates contends that the kind of knowledge produced by area specialists is essential for the development of social science theory. To illustrate this point, he cites the work of several anthropologists and states that without the kind of cultural knowledge produced by their studies it would be impossible to evaluate the significance of the alternative behaviors among which individuals must choose, and hence to apply rational choice theory (Bates 1997) [p. 51, this volume].

Hall and Tarrow write in the same vein when responding to the charge that globalization has made area studies increasingly irrelevant. Expressing concern about recent trends in political science and economics, they take issue with claims that "rational-choice analysis (which uses econometric models and game theory to study how people make decisions) can explain the behavior of Japanese politicians and bureaucrats without much reference to Japanese culture" (Hall and Tarrow 1998, p. B4). Thus, like Bates, they insist that while rational choice theory may provide a useful conceptual framework for analyzing decision processes, this framework can be applied to particular cases only if information about the meaning and importance attached to alternative courses of action is available.

Some scholars add that this is precisely what discipline-oriented social scientists do when they study their own society and culture, and so it is puzzling that they should have difficulty understanding why it is essential for the development of theory that applies to other parts of the world. According to one account, this in fact makes culture the "master concept of all social science." Meaningful social inquiry, this argument continues, requires that one "immerse oneself in one's subject, learning the language, living with the people, and getting to understand the society so thoroughly as a participant that it problematizes one's own place as an objective observer" (Suehiro 1997, pp. 20–27). This point of view is cited in an article by Chalmers Johnson, a prominent Asianist from the University of California. Johnson goes on to write that "this is what social scientists do naturally when studying their own culture, and it is what they *must* do in order to study another culture. There is no alternative or rational-choice shortcut" (Johnson 1997, p. 172) [p. 61, this volume].

Disagreement about the value of case studies, a mode of inquiry strongly identified with the research of area specialists, reflects a methodological dimension of the area studies debate. Some social scientists have argued that case studies are either inherently atheoretical or, at best, useful only for *generating* testable hypotheses. As early as 1963, Donald Campbell and Julian Stanley characterized the case study as a "one shot" methodology that "is of no scientific value" (Campbell and Stanley 1963). Arend Lijphart's influential article in the *American Political Science Review* several years later expressed similar, if somewhat less categorical, reservations about the theoretical value of case studies (Lijphart 1971). Yet area specialists insist that in-depth case studies are fully compatible with systematic social science inquiry. Clifford Geertz, for example, writing in response to early criticisms, justified case studies as necessary to provide the "thick description" without which the complex interrelationships among social processes and events cannot be meaningfully unraveled (Geertz 1973).

More recently, area specialists, as well as some others, not only have continued to insist that case studies offer an opportunity to test research hypotheses, they have also proposed innovations designed to enhance the value of case studies for broader comparative and theoretical inquiry. Many of these innovations, including contributions by Harry Eckstein, Alexander George, and Robert Yin, are summarized in a useful article by David Collier. Collier reports that in-depth case studies can be extremely useful in hypothesis testing and theory building, and he notes in this connection that some social scientists have "dramatically recanted" their earlier charge that such research is without scientific merit (Collier 1991, p. 23). Collier also reports that case studies have been used effectively in rational choice analysis, as in the work of Christopher Achen and Duncan Snidal, for example (Achen and Snidal 1989).

Beyond these arguments about epistemological and methodological considerations, area specialists often make several additional observations, some calling attention to the strengths of their own approach and others to the deficiencies they find in social inquiry that is excessively abstract and theoretical. With respect to the former, they insist that many of the intellectual considerations which generated support for area programs in the past are as relevant today as ever. These include the importance of interdisciplinary scholarship, since complex real-world problems rarely fall entirely within the purview of a single discipline. They also include a need to transcend ethnocentrism and Western bias, not only to ensure accuracy and relevance but also so that insights derived from the study of one region or culture might contribute to innovative thinking about other regions or cultures. Intellectual considerations of this sort, as well as strategic calculations associated with the Cold War, led the Social Science Research Council and the Ford Foundation to invest heavily in area studies programs in the 1960s (Ward and Wood 1974), and area specialists insist that these concerns are no less important than in the past.

Area specialists also sometimes insist in this connection that the significance of their investment in acquiring research skills be recognized and appreciated. For example, few social science Ph.D. programs require more than four or five courses in formal theory and quantitative methods; this is usually considered adequate to prepare students for "scientific" research. By contrast, twice that number of courses is necessary to establish proficiency in many less commonly taught languages. Area specialists rightly claim that the effort and accomplishment reflected in such preparation is, at the very least, no less praiseworthy than the training in social science research methods that others have acquired, and which they themselves have very often acquired as well.

So far as the work of discipline-oriented scholars is concerned, there are complaints both about a double standard and about relevance. Area specialists note, for example, that many of these scholars produce descriptive and atheoretical studies of American society and politics. They are, in effect, American area specialists. There is nothing wrong with this, of course. On the contrary, this research is often quite valuable. The complaint is that the work of these "Americanists" is valued and considered mainstream by political science, economics, and other social science disciplines, while the same appreciation is not extended to area specialists who do descriptive work or study contemporary issues in other parts of the world, especially the non-Western world.

More serious, perhaps, is a contention that it is actually disciplinary research, rather than scholarship associated with area studies, which most often is of little real-world relevance. This charge has been leveled at both quantitative analysis and rational choice theory. A recent article by Johnson, for example, argues that mathematical formulas are no substitute for significance and then suggests that the latter is frequently lacking in quantitative social science. In this connection, Johnson endorses the view of Martin Anderson, who writes that "the main problem is not that much of the writing of academic intellectuals is too mathematical, but that it is insignificant, unimportant, trivial. If the ideas were significant and important ones couched in the language of mathematics, that would be fine, for presumably it could be reworked into English. But if the writing is devoid of any merit, expressing it in plain English would expose the intellectual sham" (Anderson 1992, p. 101).

With respect to rational choice theory, Johnson states that he cannot think of a single book "in which rational choice theory has been applied to a non-English-speaking country with results even approximately close to the claims made for the method" (Johnson 1997, p. 173). Similar criticism has been advanced by others. For example, as noted, Hall and Tarrow challenge the claim that political behavior in Japan can be fully understood without reference to Japanese culture. David Hollinger offers a more sweeping condemnation, accusing the rational choicers "of failing to illuminate anything of genuine significance . . . of avoiding the complexities of the real world" (Hollinger 1997, pp. 347–348).

REFERENCES

Achen, Christopher, and Duncan Snidal. 1989. "Rational Deterrence Theory and Comparative Case Studies." *World Politics* 41 (2): 143–169.
Anderson, Martin. 1992. *Imposters in the Temple: American Intellectuals Are Destroying Our Universities and Cheating Our Students of Their Future.* New York: Simon & Schuster.
Bates, Robert. 1997. "Area Studies and the Discipline: A Useful Controversy?" *PS: Political Science & Politics* 30 (2): 166–169 [see p. 51, this volume].
———. 1989. *Beyond the Miracle of the Market: The Political Economy of Agrarian Development in Kenya.* Cambridge: Cambridge University Press.
———. 1981. *Markets and States in Tropical Africa: The Political Basis of Agricultural Policies.* Berkeley: University of California Press.
Bender, Thomas. 1997. "Politics, Intellect, and the American University." *Daedalus* (Winter).

Campbell, Donald, and Julian Stanley. 1963. *Experimental and Quasi-Experimental Designs for Research.* Chicago: Rand McNally.

Collier, David. 1991. "New Perspectives on the Comparative Method." In *Comparative Political Dynamics: Global Research Perspectives.* Dankart Rustow and Kenneth Paul Erickson, eds. New York: Harper-Collins.

Fukuyama, Francis. 1992. *The End of History and the Last Man.* New York: Free Press.

Geertz, Clifford. 1973. "Thick Description: Toward an Interpretative Theory of Culture." In *The Interpretation of Cultures.* Clifford Geertz, ed. New York: Basic.

Hall, Peter, and Sidney Tarrow. 1998. "Globalization and Area Studies: When Is Too Broad Too Narrow?" *The Chronicle of Higher Education,* 23 January [see p. 96, this volume].

Heginbotham, Stanley. 1994. "Rethinking International Scholarship." *Items* 48 (2–3): 33–40.

Hollinger, David. 1997. "The Disciplines and the Identity Debates, 1970–1996." *Daedalus* (Winter).

Johnson, Chalmers. 1997. "Preconception vs. Observation, or the Contributions of Rational Choice Theory and Area Studies to Contemporary Political Science." *PS: Political Science & Politics* 30 (2): 170–174 [see p. 58, this volume].

Lijphart, Arend. 1971. "Comparative Politics and Comparative Method." *American Political Science Review* 65 (September).

Said, Edward. 1978. *Orientalism.* New York: Pantheon.

Shea, Christopher. 1997. "Political Scientists Clash over Value of Area Studies." *The Chronicle of Higher Education,* 10 January.

Slow, Robert. 1997. "How Did Economics Get That Way and What Way Did It Get?" *Daedalus* (Winter).

Suehiro, Akira. 1997. "Thinktanks and the Evolution of 'Chiiki Kenkyu,' Japan's Area Studies." *Social Science Japan* (February).

Ward, Robert, and Bryce Wood. 1974. "Foreign Area Studies and the Social Science Research Council." *Items* 48 (4): 53–58.

Young, Crawford. 1993. *The Rising Tide of Cultural Pluralism: The Nation-State at Bay?* Madison: University of Wisconsin Press.

———. 1976. *The Politics of Cultural Pluralism.* Madison: University of Wisconsin Press.

Redefining International Scholarship

Kenneth Prewitt

I.

Many readers of *Items* will know that the American Council of Learned Societies (ACLS) and the Social Science Research Council jointly sponsor a number of regionally defined scholarly committees, familiarly known as "the joint committees." These committees collectively cover a large part of the world's regions: Africa, Asia (five committees), Eastern Europe, the former Soviet Union, Latin America, Near and Middle East, and Western Europe. In some instances dating to the 1950s, these committees have long taken responsibility for advancing scholarship on the world areas, a task which has involved the administration of fellowship programs, language institutes, summer workshops, commissioned studies, research planning conferences, publications, institutional partnerships, and much more. In the earlier years the primary focus was on informing the U.S. about foreign places; in more recent periods, there has also been an emphasis on working with scholars from these regions—approximately 40 percent of the joint committee members today are non-Americans.

The enterprise of academic training and promotion of scholarship organized through area studies (of course not just the joint committees) has been impressively successful in the terms set forth in the 1950s and then elaborated in subse-

Reprinted with permission from *Items,* vol. 50, no. 1 (March) and *Items,* vol. 50, nos. 2/3 (June/September). © 1996 by the Social Science Research Council.

quent decades. This accomplishment is well-known and need not be detailed in this brief note. Suffice it to say that the United States is today vastly more informed about the world beyond its borders than it was a half-century ago—and this is so whether our referent is the foreign policy apparatus, the research universities, commercial enterprise, nongovernmental organizations, or the reading public.

From the narrower perspective of the humanities and the social sciences, area studies has successfully brought together language and literature, history, philosophy, geography, anthropology, sociology, political science, economics, psychology, and other relevant scholarly traditions to provide a comprehensive interpretation of a bounded geographic area. Area studies holds area constant and invites the participation of multiple disciplines, in contrast to traditional comparative studies which held discipline constant and involved multiple areas. Area studies, consequently, has been the most successful, large-scale interdisciplinary project ever in the humanities and the social sciences.

The many accomplishments of area studies notwithstanding, most readers of *Items* will know that area studies as commonly understood is being freshly examined, even questioned, on a number of campuses, among funders, and, not surprisingly, by the ACLS and the SSRC. In this self-examination the academic community is hardly alone. From United Nations agencies to international corporations, from nongovernmental organizations to the state department, the traditional region-by-region organization is found to be poorly aligned with the tasks and opportunities of the contemporary world.

For the ACLS and the SSRC, two central considerations drive the reexamination of area studies. These considerations are the foundation for a new international program the Councils will jointly propose this year. One consideration derives from changes in world conditions and the other from changes in world scholarship.

World Conditions

One of the frequently remarked consequences of the globalization accelerated by new information technologies and post-1989 market forces is that "areas" are more porous, less bounded, less fixed than we previously assumed. Diasporas lead to continuous redefinition of who belongs to what place, and thus confuse the very notion of place as a marker of social identity. Area studies traditionally had a fairly clear grasp of what was meant by "here" and what was meant by "there." But when areas, from remote villages to entire continents, are caught up in processes which link them to events that, though geographically distant, are culturally, economically, politically, strategically, and ecologically quite near, the distinction between "here" and "there" breaks down. To learn more and more about social conditions in a particular area, then, means to learn more and more about how that area is situated in events going on beyond its geographic borders —but not thereby outside its economy or ecology or culture.

And, self-evidently, the obverse holds as well. Globalization does not render the specifics of place inconsequential. Whatever may be meant by the term "globalization," the phenomenon to which it points is clearly constructed from dozens to thousands of separate places, not all marching in some lock-step pattern. Misplaced "global village" metaphors notwithstanding, globalization does not inevitably lead to homogenization. It produces winners and losers, the included and the excluded. And the way in which these winners and losers respond to new opportunities, and fresh defeats, is no less conditioned by their separate histories and unique cultural perspectives today than it was in times past.

In short, the global-local notion is not a methodological metaphor invented by social theorists; it is the lived experience of billions of people. And it is being lived today in ways unanticipated even a decade ago.

This raises not just new scholarly questions but a host of new practical problems. These problems weigh heavily on those who are working toward a world less inequitable, less insecure, less inhumane, less unjust than the one we presently experience. The social sciences came into existence toward the end of the last century in response to what were then viewed as the urgent problems of the day. And for a century the results of quality scholarship have found users among persons working to make the world more equitable and secure and humane and just.

The practical challenges are being thought through anew, as globalization shows evidence of presenting new perversities and plagues, different ways to kill and impoverish, unexpected instabilities and insecurities. That the 21st century will require its own coping mechanisms, policy instrumentalities and social formations appropriate to new problems is not in doubt, though what those will be and how well they will work certainly is.

In this effort to cope and renew and invent, there will be a searching for insights and theories of the sort that only disciplined analysis can generate. Our question must be whether the humanities and the social sciences are preparing themselves to provide those insights and theories.

The Councils believe that a number of discrete and separated "area committees," each focused on a single world region, is not the optimum structure for providing new insights and theories suitable for a world in which the geographic units of analysis are neither static nor straightforward. The Councils believe as well that if scholarship is not rooted in place-specific histories and cultures, it will miss, widely, the nuances that allow us to make sense of such phenomena as international labor flows, conflicting perspectives on human rights, alternative paths to democratization, violent responses to perceived territorial threats, and differing visions of the relationship between humans and nature. As we reflect, then, on a world shaken loose from its familiar moorings, we have no choice but to ask if there might not be better ways to advance international research and to prepare the next generation of scholars.

World Scholarship

When area studies (American style) were being launched a half-century ago, the ACLS and the SSRC took for granted that the disciplines to be involved in area scholarship would be propelled largely by developments in the American academic community. This was not merely myopia or arrogance speaking. It was an assessment of the comparative resources held by the U.S. And this resource advantage—the depth of the humanistic and social science disciplines, the organizational know-how of U.S. academics, the vast postwar expansion of higher education, and generous funding by private foundations and, following Sputnik, by the federal government—did give the American scholar off to Kampala or Santiago or Delhi or Hong Kong a near monopolistic advantage.

Under these circumstances it was understandable that the reference point and audience for the area scholar were those fellow Americans hard at work on a different but equally fascinating feature of Uganda or Chile or India or China. From this, of course, emerged university-based area centers, as young Ph.D. candidates returning from the field gravitated to colleagues, of whatever discipline, with whom insights could profitably be compared. University administrators cooperated, especially when Title VI funds became available. In the maturation of area studies, the joint committees were central actors. They helped to shape the research agenda, allocated training fellowships and travel funds, and worked to establish national organizations and journals dedicated to advancing knowledge on the different world regions.

Though this American-centric version of the story slights the important role of British, Canadian, German, and French scholars, neither these countries nor any other created, or is now likely to, the extensive array of programs and institutions that collectively define area studies in the United States.

This American near-monopoly on studying foreign places gave way first, of course, in Europe, then in Latin America, and gradually across nearly every world region. If not universally so, certainly scholarship of the kind practiced by American area studies is now internationally produced.

This has far-reaching implications. In the first instance, one's colleague in the study of Uganda, Chile, India, or China is as likely to be a scholar from that country—or from Europe or from elsewhere in Africa, Latin America, Asia—as to be an American. Moreover, those colleagues will not view themselves as "area specialists." The Ugandan historian, Chilean sociologist, Indian economist, or Chinese linguist—whether they study their own or some other part of the world—take as their peer community historians, sociologists, economists, or linguists. The international production of knowledge is now largely discipline-based.

This in turn is pulling more non-area American scholars into the international arena. There has always been comparative politics, comparative sociology, comparative literature—drawing from but not limited to area studies. Scholars of international economics and security have at times come out of area studies, but that has been the exception rather than the rule. Historians not of a place but of a phenomenon—of art, of war, of revolution—roam across borders and boundaries. More recently cultural psychology has emerged as a sub-field bridging anthropology and psychology and, in some instances, bringing in the new biocultural specialties.

These exceptions notwithstanding, discipline-based scholarship in the United States has been American-centered. This inward focus—parochialism one might say—is in rapid retreat. Partly this comes from what was earlier mentioned: good colleagues *in the disciplines* are to be found all around the world. To be current in econometric modeling, gerontology, sociolinguistics, or cultural analysis requires more than knowing what one's U.S. colleagues are doing. Moreover, as U.S. universities seek new ways to internationalize, they are involving units from across the campus—from professional schools to physics, from ethnic studies to economics—in cross-national efforts of student recruitment, visiting scholars, exchange programs, and collaborative research.

Probably most significant in the gradual (though certainly not completed) de-parochialization of the disciplines is the array of fresh research questions that draw their theoretical excitement or methodological challenge from the variations presented by examining them in non-American settings. The commonplace observation with which we started, local variations in the context of strong tendencies toward globalization, comes into play at this point. Name your topic— child-parent bonding, identity politics, transitions to market economies, energy consumption—and chances are high that the comparisons that will most matter cross area and cultural boundaries.

Changes in how scholarship is and increasingly will be practiced require changes as well in how international scholarship is advanced, at least for the ACLS and the SSRC.

A New Structure for the Councils

The issue of how best to organize international research and training at the Councils has benefited from the attention of the officers and the boards of both the SSRC and the ACLS, as well as from exchanges with officers of the Ford and Mellon Foundations (without whose core support the international program would shrink to a set of activities hardly justifying the label "program").

And, of course, the community of interested scholars has actively engaged the issues. There have been lively discussions with members of the present joint committees, as well as a flood of memos and letters representing the views of close to 200 scholars. These discussions and commentaries have been substantively rich, thoughtfully constructive (in nearly every case), and, for this reader, instructive. The new structure, to be described in a subsequent issue of *Items,* is being shaped by these exchanges, but is not likely to please everyone or to be viewed as fully responsive to specific (and often contradictory) advice.

As we try to take into account and be responsive to the changes in world conditions and in world scholarship noted in these cursory comments, we will also be mindful of why we have an ACLS and an SSRC and why the two Councils find merit in working together. Scholarly insularity is an ever present tendency within the humanities and social sciences. It occurs when scholars from one discipline don't talk to those from other disciplines, when scholars in one part of the world (or who study one part of the world) don't know what is going on in other parts and don't talk to those who do, when globalists construct research projects that float free of history and place, and when scholars talk only to other

scholars. The Councils have been and will continue to be a counterforce to parochialism and to insularity.

II.

The March 1996 issue of *Items* included a "Presidential Items" comment setting
forth a background logic for the substantial reorganization of the joint ACLS and
SSRC international program. I commented on changed world conditions and resulting transformations in world scholarship, suggesting that these changes called
for new structures through which to pursue international scholarship. More specifically, the comment implied that the familiar "joint committees" would be de-
commissioned; and it concluded with a promise to include in the next issue of
Items a fuller account of what a replacement structure would involve.

This essay describes the prospective network of committees and activities
that will serve as a platform for the jointly administered international research
and training program of the Councils. One feature of that program—dissertation
field research opportunities—is not here described in detail, but will be the subject of a presidential commentary in the next issue of *Items*.

Redefining International Scholarship

Starting shortly after World War II, American higher education expanded its expertise about parts of the world that previously had been remote from mainstream
academic concerns. Nearly half a century later, under the label of "area studies,"
there is now a significant number of scholars trained in a wide range of languages,
histories, and cultures, as well as in the methodologies of their academic disciplines. An infrastructure of academic programs, library and teaching resources,
publications and scholarly associations also has been established. The joint committees of the ACLS and SSRC can take some credit for the fact that the quality of
American teaching and scholarship dealing with parts of the world outside Europe and North America has reached a level of insight, subtlety, creativity, and
self-reflection that would not have been imaginable when area studies programs
were first established. In the process, area studies affirmed the power of new
ideas to change longstanding assumptions and challenge conventional wisdom,
not least about ourselves and the relationships that bind us to the world.

Area studies, of course, proceeds largely in terms of geographic boundaries,
especially those that have prevailed since the Second World War hastened the
end of the colonial empires. Obviously geographic boundaries have always been
somewhat blurred and porous, what with cultural borrowing, trade routes, security alliances, population movements, and world religions. But the last half-century, characterized by a nation-state system and superpower confrontation, has
been an historical period during which it made sense to organize knowledge pro-

duction with distinctions between Asia and Western Europe, or Africa and the Middle East, or Latin America and the Soviet Union much in mind.

Now free from the bi-polar perspective of the Cold War and increasingly aware of the multiple migrations and intersections of people, ideas, institutions, technologies and commodities, scholars are confronting the inadequacy of conventional notions of world "areas" as bounded systems of social relations and cultural categories. Critical problems and critical research issues appear in forms that overwhelm conventional definitions of area and region—from the quality of economic, political, and environmental life around the globe to the conditions for ensuring the security and well-being of all people. These contemporary issues inspire new and urgent questions about history, religion, and artistic expression that highlight the contingent ways in which people have interpreted the conditions of their lives. It follows that we need new intellectual concepts and new ways to organize scholarship.

I. Basic Principles
The Councils have found it conceptually useful to draw a distinction between traditional area studies, on the one hand, and area-based knowledge, on the other. Area studies has taken regions in their totality as its primary unit of analysis. To be an area scholar is to participate in an enterprise that seeks to know all that can reasonably be known about a world region—its languages, history, cultures, politics, religions. Traditional area studies is primarily knowledge about an area.

Area-based knowledge starts with knowledge about an area, but then applies that knowledge to processes, trends, and phenomena that transcend any given area. It is our working premise that areas, from remote villages to entire continents, are caught up in processes that link them to events, that, although geographically distant, are culturally, economically, strategically, or ecologically quite near. To learn more and more about values or social conditions in a particular area, then, means to learn more and more about how that area is situated in events going on beyond its geographic borders—but not thereby outside its culture or economy or ecology.

Self-evidently, the obverse holds. Globalization does not render the specifics of place inconsequential; it reinforces the specificity of place. It is not homogenization. It differentiates, producing winners and losers, the helped and the hurt. And the way in which these winners and losers respond to new opportunities and fresh defeats is no less conditioned by their histories and values than it was in times past.

We use the term "area-based knowledge" to point toward a scholarly enterprise that can interpret and explain the ways in which that which is global and that which is local condition each other. Any number of phenomena—religious fundamentalism, for instance—occur on a global scale and yet vary dramatically from one place to the next. For the Councils, then, one outcome of our new focus on area-based knowledge will be to enhance our capabilities of incorporating area studies into new arrangements, thereby repositioning its contribution to research and training. Because area studies remains disturbingly vulnerable to shifts in funding trends, and to changes in the intellectual climate within the academy, it is worth emphasizing that the repositioning herein recommended is an effort by the Councils to insure a durable place in intellectual life for area studies. Methods of inquiry developed by and for area studies will continue to have a central role in the international program structure of the Councils. We will continue the effort to integrate an area-based epistemology into discipline-based studies, and vice versa. Just as one would not expect the disciplines to advance in the absence of methodologies of quantification, they cannot advance in the absence of methodologies which reveal the varieties of human experience in the larger world.

In addition to bringing the particular to bear on the general and facilitating interregional comparisons, area-based knowledge has a larger epistemological role to play in contemporary scholarship. Here we have in mind the philosophical debate that contrasts "views from nowhere" with "views from somewhere." Whether there are transhistorical principles from which can be derived universal truths is not something to be sorted out here. But we do suggest that this "views from nowhere" argument needs its philosophical opposition. Area-based knowledge, broadly understood, anchors the position that views do come from somewhere; that they are historically and culturally rooted. A commitment to area-based knowledge, then, is centrally important to a key philosophical debate underway in intellectual communities around the world.

A commitment to area-based knowledge is also a commitment to scholarly traditions more prominent in the humanities than in the social sciences. The Councils readily acknowledge that holding their respective constituencies together in a single program has its challenges. If they have been successful during the long involvement with the joint area committees, this has been because the different sets of disciplines have had unique contributions to make. Area-based knowledge necessarily involves understanding the histories, value systems, and languages of specific cultures, just as it involves understanding their politics, social structures, and economies.

II. Continuing Tensions

We begin to see how this basic commitment to area-based knowledge is manifest by considering a few of the familiar tensions that occupy any organization responsible for research planning and training. We believe it will help the reader to see where the Councils are going if we also make clear what our position is with regard to these tensions.

GLOBAL VS. LOCAL

Remapping the boundaries of international studies is intended to reconfigure the forms of social knowledge that emerge from the study of place. The rationale for area knowledge is no longer only the task of helping one society (the United States) to understand the "foreign other." It is now also the more subtle task of sorting through the ways in which the global and the local interpenetrate one another in a changing, heterogeneous world.

This task requires area knowledge, but also comparison across areas. It requires tools and techniques that help the scholar to link local experience to broader contexts and to treat the local experience as the foundation for constructing models, building hypotheses, and testing theory. Area-based knowledge is of course not in opposition to discipline-based knowledge. It is informed by and informs disciplinary work.

We can better identify how the new program intends to position itself intellectually by reflecting more generally on the global vs. local issue. The fact of globalization is virtually uncontested and is empirically confirmed in analyses of capital flows, mass migrations, flexible labor regimes, telecommunications networks, tourism, and cultural transfers. Not always appreciated, however, are the novel ways in which globalization locates people, resources, beliefs, and information along new routes, in the process forging social connections between individuals and institutions which never before had contact or a common agenda. As noted above, area studies as a structure for organizing academic inquiry is challenged by these global processes. Its familiar geographical boundaries have been disrupted, and today appear less stable, more permeable and fluid. Different phenomena of interest to the research community lead to different configurations of areas. In this flux the familiar country and regional labels given to us by the cartographers still matter, seriously so, but it would be limiting indeed if area knowledge were confined within these jurisdictional boundaries.

Transnational labor flows provide a clear example of the tensions posed by global processes for the boundaries of area studies, and illustrate the value of integrating knowledge of place with the tools and insights of the disciplines. Those involved in such flows, and there are millions, are connected with multiple households as well as with multiple communities and countries. They are citizens of no place and yet of multiple places. Transnational labor flows necessarily involve a dense web of people, ideas, and resources passing through existing political and economic structures, although not smoothly or predictably. The genealogy of labor flows cannot be untangled without reference to the specificities of given places and their histories. Yet such questions as why workers cross national boundaries, which workers move, what happens to those who do not move, and how workers experience their transition into new national labor markets are concerns that transcend place. They can be more fully comprehended by subjecting them to the methods of the social sciences, for example through anthropological insights into the changing dynamics of households during the transition from command to market economies, sociological contributions to the understanding of social movements generated by the entry of foreign workers into new labor markets, and economic models about the implications of social policy for labor mobility. Equally important, these mass migrations upset established ways of assigning meaning to social experience. Thus they create problems and opportunities for artistic and religious ways of interpretation and expression as people seek to establish continuity or to articulate new cultural juxtapositions.

It is one of the paradoxes of globalization that as it promotes integration, it frequently leads to the proliferation of difference. As the world is being drawn together through global transportation and information systems, peoples are asserting difference and rejecting sameness on an unprecedented global scale, and with consciousness that these assertions take place on a global stage. Recent waves of racism, nationalism, fundamentalism, and communalism underline again the persistence of the local. It is not surprising, therefore, that studies of race, ethnicity, gender, religion, and nationalism—all carriers of the local and vehicles of the difference—are issues preoccupying many disciplines. These studies document that even the most global of phenomena—the Internet, for example, or international travel—are far from equally available. Area-based knowledge traces the patterns of inclusion and exclusion, and helps us to see more clearly the ways in which global forces distribute rewards and penalties.

Globalization provides powerful support for reconceptualizing the meaning of place in the contemporary world, and for promoting analytic tools that permit us to grasp the interconnection of the specific and the general. The new international program structure reflects our conviction that in the 21st century local cultures cannot be fully studied in isolation from global cultural and technological forces. The argument is simple but consequential. At a moment when disciplinary and area knowledge are often depicted as opposing epistemologies, the Councils insist on the need for the productive interaction of both. The value of this commitment becomes even more evident when we move beyond the boundaries of U.S.-based social science and humanities, and begin to conceptualize international studies as a truly international endeavor.

AMERICAN-CENTRIC VS. INTERNATIONAL SCHOLARSHIP

By the end of the Second World War, American scholars had begun to redefine their concerns as international, and as explicitly political. The new mandate of comparative politics for example, according to a 1944 report, was to serve as a "conscious instrument of social engineering" by "imparting our experience to other nations and integrating scientifically their institutions into a universal pattern of government" (*American Political Science Review* 1944: 540–48). The study of world regions has long since moved beyond the notion that science is the instrument of modernity and an instrument best wielded by scholars based in the United States. Despite these critiques, often led by humanists, we continue to wrestle with the legacy of the postwar construction of area studies as a project to export American experiences abroad, and with the notion that there exists a universal pattern of government (electoral democracy) and a universal pattern of economic organization (markets). Among other things, these notions created powerful rationales justifying federal support for area studies programs.

We do not wish to convey the sense that area studies has been static. Quite the contrary, scholarship on world regions has moved a considerable distance from its postwar origins. Challenges to the postwar conception of area studies have been sharply expressed by scholars in the United States, especially within the humanities. Humanistic scholarship has become fertile ground for critiques of the universalist claims of modernity (and of the social sciences). Our understandings of the ways in which different people respond to the changing contexts of their lives have been made more complex by the encounter with realities too diverse to be managed, integrated, or made American.

Nor do we wish to replace the unsatisfying dichotomy of postwar area studies, that of modernity versus tradition, with an equally unsatisfying, post–Cold War dichotomy about globalization versus "the local." What characterized the former was a concern to replace the fixed structures of tradition with the dynamic, change-promoting structures of modernity. What we expect to characterize the latter is a concern with blurred boundaries, overlapping categories, and the heterogeneity of contemporary experience. In place of the notion that U.S. concerns and research priorities will define the intellectual terrain of area studies, the new program will more fully acknowledge that there are may forms of knowledge that arise out of different intellectual traditions and historical concerns.

The development of major scholarly communities around the world opens up new opportunities for international studies to be international in form as well as content. Though research has always been an international enterprise, American-based scholarship in the social sciences and humanities held an unusually privileged position in the decades immediately following World War II. That era has passed; the United States is a diminishing point of reference for many scholars located elsewhere.

The Councils have been centrally involved in this transformation of scholarship, in their effort—led by the joint committees—to strengthen the social sciences and humanities in dozens of countries around the world and, to the extent practical, to involve leading Latin American, African, Asian, and European scholars in Council-supported activities. At present, for example, approximately 30 percent of the joint committee members are non-American.

The Councils' new program takes the further internationalization of knowledge production as a key task. It will do so in terms of partnerships with non-American institutions, in its establishment of collaborative research networks (see below), and in its choice of problem areas to investigate. Part of this effort necessarily involves helping the U.S.-based social science and humanities disciplines to see themselves in less American-centered terms, an effort helped along by the development of a more internationally organized intellectual community.

AREA STUDIES VS. DISCIPLINE-BASED SCHOLARSHIP

A more thoroughly internationalized program of organizing research is important from another point of view, i.e., that of the U.S. discipline-based scholar. A largely discipline-controlled academy has often treated area studies as peripheral. Space does not permit engaging this issue fully, though perhaps mention should be made that most American discipline-based scholars have been engaged in area studies without recognizing it. It is just that they have taken the features of American politics or society or culture or history as their reference point. Indeed, in the program set forth here the Councils see much merit in treating North America as an "area" equally with other areas in its involvement in the globalization trends referenced above.

The internationalization of knowledge production has far-reaching consequences for the American-centric social science and humanistic disciplines. Because important scholarship is increasingly practiced in many parts of the world, to be current in econometric modeling, gerontology, comparative literature, or cultural analysis requires more than knowing what one's American colleagues are doing. As the discipline-based social scientist or humanist seeks out colleagues abroad, American-centric scholarship begins to fade. Probably more significant in the gradual (though certainly not completed) deparochialization of the disciplines are the theoretical challenges highlighted by the task of explaining local variations in the context of strong tendencies toward globalization. Comparisons that matter very often cross area and cultural boundaries.

The proposed program takes advantage of these tendencies, as well as the present inclination of many American universities to internationalize, to hasten the integration of area-based knowledge into disciplinary work.

BASIC VS. APPLIED

Probably no dichotomy has so haunted attempts to organize intellectual life as that which opposes basic vs. applied research. Although there have been many creative efforts at blending or relabeling to try to escape this dichotomy, in the end there is a difference between scholarship which is curiosity-driven and that which honors the principle of knowledge for its own sake and scholarship in service of broad social goals.

The differences are particularly important to recognize in a program that promises to join the humanities and the social sciences. For while both sets of disciplines incorporate basic and applied principles, the humanities are often regarded by skeptics as aloof from socially relevant issues. On the contrary, the humanities have much to say about the very issues of political and social identity, cultural transformation, changing gender role, and social cohesion which roil so much of the contemporary world. We fully expect the new structure to focus that scholarly energy. Humanistic scholarship is primarily interpretive and valuative, employing methodologies that are pragmatic, strategic, and self-reflective depending on the questions posed. The questions, in turn, depend on context and the new program will be a dynamic context for humanistic inquiry.

To address, then, how the Councils view the new program along the basic-applied continuum requires that we again situate the program in the changed world conditions.

Only seven years have passed since the end of the cold war. In this short time, discussions of globalization, identity politics, democratization, and many other dramatic changes in the organization of social life have become commonplace. Yet we have only begun to explore the true meaning and significance of phenomena that have raced beyond the vocabularies to which we have grown accustomed. That existing categories come across as increasingly obsolete is not surprising, for they were constructed largely by an international scholarly community seeking to interpret a world in which nation-states remained the central actors, linked to one another by security alliances, trading partnerships, the U.N. system, and the Bretton Woods institutions.

That familiar world has slipped away, and the world that is replacing it features stresses and strains that are poorly understood and even more poorly managed. Scholars confront the rapid proliferation of new issues and new relationships, including climate change and environmental degradation, religious upheavals and challenges to modern value systems, population growth and vast flows of refugees, pandemic and emergent diseases, and industrial relocation and emerging markets. These processes have brought new actors to the fore, including global corporations, transnational religious movements, international NGOs, and international media empires. Issues of religious concern, cultural identity, and political community are now played out in new contexts.

Established political and cultural institutions are only partially managing to keep pace with these developments, often yielding place to new sites and forms of intervention. International human rights policy, for example, has been defined and often implemented by non-state actors, a dramatic but hardly isolated example of the role of transnational NGOs. Propelled by video and e-mail technologies, such issues as domestic violence and child labor must be confronted in an immense variety of local contexts around the world in ways that challenge long held assumptions about morality, identity, and autonomy. Similarly, multilateral lending agencies, accustomed to providing assistance exclusively through national governments, are now scrambling to catch up with the micro-credit revolution, a revolution whose origins and early practices emerged in a social space defined by neither the market nor governments but responsive to local forms of social solidarity.

These are illustrative of broad patterns. And if it is a truism to observe that the world is changing, so it is to observe that intellectuals are in the early stages of providing the concepts and constructs that will be drawn upon by those who have to manage or cope with these new conditions. Anyone who participates in meetings on any of the dozens of vexing topics confronting the international policy community—food security, literacy, human rights, refugee flows, fertility rates, emergent viruses, civil violence, climate change, trade imbalances, structural unemployment, historical preservation—will have heard the plea for "better understanding" of the human dimension or the social context or the cultural constraints. The plea, however phrased, is in fact an appeal for the kind of social intelligence that the social sciences and humanities are expected to provide.

We are motivated to respond to this plea, though in ways that we believe make best use of the particular strengths of the two Councils.

Although by no means easily achieved, we hope to promote a scholarship that is critically engaged with the world. An important step in this process is learning to hear how problems are framed outside the academy. Obviously this includes the policymaking community, but it is shortsighted indeed to imagine that policymakers are the only voices that matter. The array of world conditions identified above are being lived out in complex institutional settings, governmental and nongovernmental, market and non-market, in isolated environments and in densely linked networks. We strongly believe that, without having to sacrifice any academic autonomy, many scholars—however they describe their purpose—

will need to come to terms with, and hear from, these multiple settings. In fact, an area-based knowledge system is a vehicle for the expression of voices and perspectives that can easily be ignored in the noise associated with globalization.

Does this mean that the new international program is being converted into a "policy program?" No. The Councils are academic organizations, not think-tanks or contract houses or policy forums. They will remain so. The explanation for this lies beyond any considerations of institutional tradition or historic niche. The fact is that short-term applied research is not likely to reveal the deeper patterns giving rise to the fundamental problems the world community is facing. To the contrary, what basic research is uniquely able to provide is new and deeper understanding of critical phenomena, and indeed of the human condition; societies are inevitably impoverished by the lack of such perspectives, without which, moreover, informed policy debates are impossible. In the familiar phrase, there is nothing so practical as a good theory.

Examples of the power of new ideas to generate change are abundant. It is through the research of social scientists and humanists that we generate new definitions of security—taking into account the identities and vulnerabilities of subnational groups around the world; that we promote insights on structural unemployment—taking into account historical forces seldom captured by the standard policy study; that we produce more nuanced conceptions of democratization—taking into account the multiple ways in which citizenship rights can be extended to new actors or expanded to encompass a broader array of rights for segments of a polity; that we contribute to the eternal human effort to grasp how people understand themselves, their past, and their prospects.

Answers to questions such as these are not likely to be produced on demand. The deeper contours of the human experience are seldom predictable. Unpredictability recommends an important place in the program for undirected research. What we propose, then, is to develop a set of institutional structures through which there can emerge a robust and vital basic research community, one that will be both available and able to help illuminate the core social issues of the moment, whatever those issues might be and without the expectation that such issues are knowable in advance.

The central objective of the new program architecture will be to stimulate basic critical scholarship that brings area-based knowledge to bear on global issues, that fosters integration of that knowledge with theories derived from discipline-based studies, and that is international in its purpose and organization.

III. Architecture of Program: Five Components
The familiar joint committee structure took region as the fixed point, and then varied thematic foci and disciplinary contribution as appropriate. This fixed point was intellectually productive and organizationally convenient. But the logic of the preceding argument makes it clear that the region cannot be the single, fixed referent. Neither, of course, do we intend to propose a program that has a preset topical focus. In our continuing effort to develop and apply area-based knowl-

edge, we will try to create a system in which region and discipline and theme vary according to the research question at hand. The more difficult task is to promote a flow of ideas with sufficient points of convergence around which researchers can assemble as they generate international and interdisciplinary linkages, articulate scholarly research agendas and training needs, and link critical scholarship with issues of societal concern.

The structure we propose represents the most substantial reorganization of the joint international program since the first area committees were established at the two Councils in the late 1950s. Its prospects for success will be enhanced by a process of continuous consultation among the leadership and staffs of the Councils and the scholars, practitioners, and funders whose participation in the program is essential to its success.

An initial step, to which the boards of both Councils are committed, is to decommission joint area committees. This will be accomplished in a manner that does not abandon or neglect ongoing research projects. A number of pre-existing working groups and advisory panels will be kept in place for the duration of specific responsibilities.

Following are the five components of the new program.

• Collaborative Research Networks (CRNs)

The research planning responsibilities of the Councils will be met through collaborative research networks. It is this program element that will advance critical scholarship on topics of pressing theoretical and substantive concern and will reshape the study of such issues by linking scholars separated by boundaries of discipline, region, and methodological tradition. The topics that will give rise to CRNs will depend in part on funding opportunities but also on an assessment of the comparative advantage of the new structure and of the Councils' international contacts. It is not expected that there will be a large number of CRNs; the goal is not topical coverage so much as quality and impact.

It is anticipated that CRNs will vary in how long they will stay in place. Some will last only as long as the specific task that led to their appointment. Other CRNs will become semi-permanent, as they build an ever widening network on, say, religious and ethnic conflict, transitions to democracy, or social development in the context of a global financial system. In other cases, a CRN appointed for one purpose will, in accomplishing that purpose, transform itself into a new CRN. Thus a CRN on agrarian technologies and ecological change might become a new CRN on land use patterns and biodiversity.

The examples could easily be multiplied. The point is that the flexibility of the CRN structure invites it to be a major home to fresh theoretical work, methodological innovation, and innovative arrangements bringing scholars together across regions.

• Human Capital Committee (HCC)

Under the present structure, training activities specific to a given region are attended to by the appropriate joint committees. In shifting from an area-based to an internationally defined structure, training will be designed and governed from a broader perspective. For instance, the new dissertation training program, funded by the Mellon Foundation (see *Items,* vol. 50, no. 4), will focus on exactly the issues set forth in this proposal, and is conceptualized as a single program rather than distributed across the several area communities.

A human capital committee in the new structure will oversee and coordinate the wide range of fellowship and training programs now operating under the auspices of the Councils. It will also work with regional advisory panels and field development working groups to identify areas in which new programs are needed and to ensure that such programs are designed in a manner that takes into account the experiences of similar programs elsewhere. It will also generate an analysis of human capital formation, one focused on training as a component of professional development. More specifically, the HCC will:

(1) consider a given training experience in the context of what precedes it and follows it—the quality and diversity of different recruitment pools to issues of long-term career maintenance;

(2) review the flow of the Councils' projects designed to build local social science and humanities infrastructures in regions where indigenous capacities are underdeveloped or threatened by political, social, and economic turmoil;

(3) consider the need for and coordinate the activities of field development working groups devoted to training specialists on world regions that remain relatively understudied or insufficiently understood despite the postwar achievements of area studies.

Fellowship and training activities have long constituted an integral part of the Councils' programs, accounting for a major portion of annual budgets and staff commitments, especially of the international programs. Indeed, with support from a number of agencies, public and private, domestic and international, the Councils now offer research and training opportunities for graduate students at all stages of progress toward the Ph.D. degree, as well as for postdoctoral scholars in the social sciences and humanities.

We are committed to maintaining and strengthening these programs, which provide opportunities for scholarly innovation at each stage of the professional development of researchers. The new structure envisioned in this proposal will enable us to continue this tradition while taking care to maximize the productivity of human capital investments by integrating them in a comprehensive package of new and existing programs. The comprehensive program of both the HCC and field development working groups (see below) will build on elements in place or being planned. To name the major programs: the International Pre-dissertation Fellowships; Title VIII programs for Eastern Europe and the former Soviet Union; Korea Foundation programs; Bangladesh fellowships; the SSRC/Mellon Minority Opportunity Fellowships; International Dissertation Workshops; the program to train junior Central American scholars in poverty research; seminars for junior economists from post-socialist countries; the new Mellon-funded International Field Research Dissertation Program; the NEH/Ford-funded Advanced Research Grants Program.

• Regional Advisory Panels (RAPs)

The Councils do not believe that area-based knowledge can be developed and enhanced without a way to bring together an interdisciplinary group of scholars—similar to the joint committees—who understand a given region. These regional advisory panels (up to eight are envisioned) will not, as is presently the case with the joint committees, have general authority over research and training. Meeting annually, these panels will bring to bear perspectives of their respective world regions on the research, training, and related components of the new international program. Each RAP will identify how global issues impact and are influenced by the history, culture, politics, and so forth of the region in which it is expert. It will also be their responsibility to strengthen links with regional scholarship. In every instance a RAP will have multinational membership; and we will look for opportunities to build partnerships between RAPs and institutions from a given region.

The projects of the CRNs will frequently crosscut world regions, others will compare two or three regions, and others will be activities best conceptualized as internal to a single region. In each instance, however, the project will contribute to theoretical formulations that are multi-level and multi-regional.

Establishment of regional advisory panels will assure that a research agenda–setting enterprise is informed by perspectives rooted in a serious understanding of what is going on in and between the various parts of the world. Similarly, they will enable the Councils to remain attuned to the broadest possible range of perspectives concerning the issues that international scholarship ought to be addressing, as well as the perspectives through which those questions can most fruitfully be explored. Finally, they will also provide a unique perspective on the human capital–related challenges that confront research communities in different parts of the world, thus ensuring that the Councils are positioned to respond quickly and appropriately to changing needs throughout the world.

• Committee on Engagement

On an *ad hoc* basis the present joint committees took up what we will here refer to as engagement—arguing the importance of area-based knowledge (and all that is required to sustain it) in a variety of fora; talking with and listening to non-academic actors—from governments to NGOs, from multilateral agencies to village organizations—who have a stake in scholarship on the emerging global issues; and making greater use of new information technologies to engage scholars from around the world in the common research enterprise. The Councils believe it is time to more aggressively and self-consciously pursue these goals of engagement.

Comprised of distinguished individuals from a variety of backgrounds, a committee on engagement will articulate and demonstrate the multiple ways in which contemporary societies will benefit from international knowledge grounded in an understanding of local conditions.

Closely associated with this advocacy, but with an important difference, engagement also includes a determined and deliberate effort to insure that the best that international scholarship has to offer finds its way into public and private agencies struggling to manage a world that has slipped free of its familiar moorings. Engagement in this sense involves creating a dialogue between scholars and those who can make effective use of new insights or fresh interpretations.

Finally, a committee on engagement will attempt to grapple with the challenges and opportunities to international scholarship represented by new technological frontiers. The implications of electronic communication vary dramatically for different communities of scholars, both in the United States and internationally. The proliferation of promising projects taking advantage of new technologies—from worldwide web sites, to e-mail discussion groups and on-line data, text, and image archives—constitutes a historic opportunity to connect heretofore diffuse intellectual communities, and to link these communities with practitioners. Progress toward fulfilling this aspiration is uneven. While in some parts of the world and for some scholarly fields new modes of information distribution and retrieval open the door for unprecedented access to scholarship, other regions and fields are hampered by infrastructural or economic barriers. Building on the work in which the ACLS has already pioneered, the Councils have an opportunity to play a leadership role in efforts to extend and deepen the use of new technologies in the production and dissemination of knowledge.

• Field Development Working Groups

The new structure proposed in these pages builds on the strong platform of U.S. area studies developed over the past decades. This platform is not uniformly strong, however, and the new program will remain involved with field development efforts focused in the United States. Drawing on non-core funding, the Councils will appoint field development working groups whose task is continued attention to training on relatively understudied world regions. Encompassing support for language training, field research and/or academic infrastructure, field development working groups may from time to time emerge from and be connected to discussions taking place in the RAPs and HCC. But their primary mission is with the U.S. academic community, and thus will be generated and governed somewhat independently.

IV. Conclusions

Five entities have been separately described but each is interdependent with the others. The human capital committee, for instance, cannot function without access to information about what is happening in regions around the world, and neither can it proceed in the absence of links with the methods and theories being generated by the collaborative research networks. Similarly, the committee on engagement must incorporate perspectives from each of the other four program components to connect them effectively with perspectives from outside the academy.

Linkages across program components are essential if we are to avoid and overcome the ever-present tendency toward scholarly insularity. Such insularity occurs when researchers from one discipline do not talk to those from other disciplines, when scholars in one part of the world (or who study one part of the world) do not know what is going on in other parts and do not talk with those who do, when globalists theorize in ways that float free of history and place, and when scholars only talk to other scholars.

Linkage will be strengthened through two basic principles that will govern administration of the new program: overlapping committee membership and multiple staff responsibilities. It will be common, for example, for a collaborative research network to include members from a number of the regional advisory panels. And the same small staff, of course, will be simultaneously working with all five of the components.

The structure is thought of as an integrated system, but one that is intentionally open-ended and multidirectional. Many things will happen simultaneously. Area-based knowledge will be tested by its deeper engagement with the disciplines. U.S. perspectives will be challenged through sustained interaction with non-U.S. academic communities. Discipline-bound certainties will encounter the local knowledge of area specialists. Academic agendas will be exposed to the concerns of practitioners.

There is a degree of messiness inevitable in an open-ended structure with multiple tasks. We will live with this messiness, adjusting and, perhaps, improving as we go. We are pleased to announce that the Ford Foundation has provided a core grant to the Councils to allow them to undertake the changes outlined above.

Globalization and Area Studies

WHEN IS TOO BROAD TOO NARROW?

Peter A. Hall and Sidney Tarrow

Every era has concepts that capture the public imagination, and "globalization" has recently emerged as one for our time. The term conveys a sense that international forces are driving more and more developments in the world, and thus crystallizes both the hopes of some people that we will finally achieve a global society and the fears of many others that their lives and jobs are threatened by forces beyond their control.

The term is useful in many ways, in many countries. At a recent lecture in Italy, when the leader of the largest federation of Italian unions was peppered with questions from the audience about the Italian government's impending pension reform, he switched the topic instead to the pressures of globalization. As one of our colleagues observed: "He wanted to talk about globalization, because he didn't know what to say about Italy's domestic problems."

For academic policy makers, foundation executives, and researchers, terms such as globalization have a natural allure, offering new mysteries to be unraveled and new ways of packaging or organizing research. In 1993, the Ford Foundation and the MacArthur Foundation inaugurated a joint project on globalization, and the Mellon Foundation initiated a program on cross-regional issues. Globalization has been taken up by many institutions—not least among them the

This article originally appeared in *The Chronicle of Higher Education,* 12 January 1998. Reprinted with permission of the authors.

Social Science Research Council. The council's president, Kenneth Prewitt, has argued that its traditional support for area studies—the field that develops knowledge about specific countries and regions—must be built on general theoretical frameworks that highlight global trends, such as rising levels of ethnic conflict.

It is true that much may be gained from analyzing global trends. The nations of the world have been growing more interdependent, and the interest that globalization inspires offers opportunities to examine that interdependence more closely. However, there are also dangers implicit in this focus on global trends. Paradoxically, even as it draws attention to the importance of developments around the world, such a focus threatens to undermine America's knowledge about other nations, by diminishing attention to the cultural, historical, and political context of trends in particular regions.

The paradox partly stems from the tendency of many people who are concerned about globalization to assume that international forces are responsible for a growing range of domestic problems. The economist Paul Krugman, of the Massachusetts Institute of Technology, observed in an article in the *International Herald Tribune* last year that there is "an odd sort of agreement between the left and the right to pretend that exotic global forces are at work even when the real action is prosaically domestic." Many governments, for example, are inclined to blame rising levels of unemployment on global pressures, even when the difficulties are rooted in structural problems of their domestic economies.

In addition, the allure of globalization has grown just as area-studies programs in many universities have come under pressure from a number of directions. The end of the Cold War precipitated cutbacks in government support for many programs devoted to the study of what was once the Communist bloc and to the parts of the third world that were caught up in it. At the same time, the rise of new academic paradigms that tend to devalue culturally specific knowledge in such disciplines as political science and sociology—once bastions of area studies—has offered tempting ways of theorizing about other nations with little need for scholars to develop specific knowledge of regions and countries. For example, claims that rational-choice analysis (which uses econometric models and game theory to study how people make decisions) can explain the behavior of Japanese politicians and bureaucrats without much reference to Japanese culture have ignited a significant debate in political science.

These developments are widening the gap between the social sciences and the humanities. Robert Bates, president of the comparative-politics section of the American Political Science Association, recently observed in the section's newsletter that many political scientists "see area specialists as having defected from the social sciences into the camp of the humanities" by virtue of "their commitment to the study of history, languages, and culture, as well as their engagement with interpretivist approaches to scholarship."

Even in the humanities, however, some universities are considering closing down Russian-language departments in favor of broader "modern literature" programs. In such instances, a focus on globalization seems to offer a way to limit support for area studies, while preserving the appearance of teaching international studies.

Thus, in one of the great ironies of current American scholarship, programs that support our reservoir of knowledge about other countries are being threatened just as Americans have become intensely aware of how closely their own fate is tied to events abroad. Even the Central Intelligence Agency is complaining that it cannot find recruits with an adequate knowledge of other languages or regions of the world.

No wonder that several journals and newsletters in political science have featured debates in recent months about the future of area studies. In essence, the debates are about whether area studies is useful, and, if so, how studies of specific regions or countries should be pursued.

Unfortunately, too often the debate is marked by pervasive ambiguities about the nature of area studies and the alternative forms that internationally oriented social science might take. The concept of area studies has three quite distinctive connotations among scholars. First, it is sometimes used to refer to a detailed description of a nation or region that does not explicitly seek to generalize beyond the specific case.

Second, the term can refer to studies that build on a relatively deep and context-rich knowledge of a specific society or region to develop propositions of more general applicability. The French sociologist Michel Crozier, for instance, used a detailed examination of the ways in which French organizations work to amend Max Weber's classic theory of how bureaucracies operate.

Third, the term can mean interdisciplinary teaching or research by clusters of scholars grouped together in a program focused on a particular region of the world. In this sense, the term refers to the many centers found on American campuses that focus on the study of Latin America, Africa, Europe, or other parts of the world. The value of area studies to the social sciences depends heavily on which sense of the term one is using.

In our view, even area studies in the first sense has value. Those scholars most committed to the development of "portable truths" must still rely on area-specific information if they are to produce accurate generalizations. The powerful theories of the sociologist Charles Tilly about the development of the state, for instance, draw on the work of many historians, and the sweeping arguments of Donald L. Horowitz, a professor of law at Duke University, about the causes of ethnic conflict build on anthropological work done in many individual cultures.

In political science, sociology, and economics, however, many scholars challenged this type of area studies during the 1950s and 1960s, arguing that research has to be oriented toward generalizations applicable across many societies. As a result, it is area studies in the second sense of the term—meaning work oriented toward producing general propositions—that predominates in most social-science fields today. To scholarship in this vein, we owe some of the most fruitful propositions ever to emerge from the social sciences and much of our understanding of nations other than the United States. In recent decades, for example, such work has significantly enhanced our understanding of the conditions necessary for a successful transition from other forms of government to democracy.

Yet much of the debate about area studies today proceeds as if the research of scholars in area studies still focused only on detailed descriptions of individual nations or regions. In the social sciences, the contention that area studies must use knowledge about particular regions to make more broadly applicable generalizations won out 20 years ago. To invoke it again seems little more than a misleading rhetorical exercise. The research of most area specialists today already aims at cross-national generalizations, on such diverse topics as the conditions that precipitate peasant rebellions and the circumstances that encourage women to join the labor force.

The value of area studies in the third sense of the term—interdisciplinary programs that bring specialists on a particular region of the world together—is a different issue, because it speaks to the fruitfulness of alternative ways of organizing teaching, research, and intellectual exchange. Because discipline-based departments already exist, the issue here is whether it is useful to provide support for area-studies programs as well. As their critics point out, area centers have financial and intellectual costs. Their central purpose is to enhance interdisciplinary exchange among scholars interested in a specific region of the world, and to the degree that they succeed, the intensity of interchange within individual departments may be diminished.

A number of considerations, however, convince us of the continuing value of area centers. First, much of the most influential work in the social sciences long has been generated by scholars informed by precisely the kind of interdisciplinary exchange that area centers facilitate. For example, the sociologist Barrington Moore's great 1966 book, *Social Origins of Dictatorship and Democracy*, was based on work that he did at the Russian Research Center at Harvard University. Similarly, the political scientist Benedict R. Anderson's inspiring 1983 work, *Imagined Communities: Reflections on the Origin and Spread of Nationalism*, was written while he was at Cornell University's Southeast Asia Program.

Second, given the strong hold that disciplines already exercise within institutions, the presence of area centers would seem to be a small, yet much-needed, incursion on their control over the organization of knowledge and teaching. Third, the foreign visitors whom area centers attract not only provide students and faculty members with insights about other parts of the world, but also bring American scholars into direct contact with the diverse research agendas and approaches to research being developed elsewhere in the world. It was partly through such contacts, for example, that new approaches used by Latin American scholars to study development—and the way that third-world countries depend on more-advanced nations—became influential in the United States.

Some scholars suggest that international studies should concentrate more heavily on comparisons, not just among nations, but among regions. Cross-regional studies are clearly valuable, and we have too few of them. However, that is not a coincidence. Apart from large-scale statistical studies—which are appropriate for analyzing only such problems as the determinants of economic growth or the bases for demographic changes—cross-regional comparisons are inordinately expensive and difficult to do with accuracy. Where accurate observations depend on a deep contextual knowledge of the nations at hand, even acquisition of the requisite language skills can be a daunting task. We should encourage the development of cross-regional inquiry, but not press it on everyone interested in international studies.

Moreover, because resources for research are scarce, we need to weigh carefully which regional comparisons would be most fruitful. If key variables in the analysis cannot readily be measured in aggregate terms, or potential causal relationships are not already well known, comparisons of cases found inside one or two nations may yield more-insightful results than comparisons of many nations. The political scientist Harry Eckstein, of the University of California at Irvine, developed a powerful theory about how authority relations in the family influence forms of democracy, based on an intensive study of Norway. Many fruitful theories about the relationship between politics and economic development have been developed through comparisons within one region, such as Africa or Latin America.

Finally, the fate of area studies is especially consequential for graduate training. While it is important that doctoral students whose work focuses on other areas of the world acquire the theoretical and methodological tools central to their disciplines, it is also important that they secure adequate empirical knowledge of the countries about which they write. Pressures to shorten graduate programs and the scarcity of fellowships already threaten the ability of many students to secure the fundamental knowledge of a region on which their future scholarly work will be based. We are at risk of graduating students who know a great deal about the arcane details of their professors' writings but very little about the parts of the world that feature in their own. Area-studies centers have long provided crucial logistical and intellectual support for graduate students seeking to acquire the international knowledge that they need.

The greatest danger in the current debate over area studies is that, in the name of studying global trends or advancing overarching theories about them, the next generation of internationally oriented social-science researchers will give short shrift to area-based empirical knowledge. Driven by shifts in the incentives that foundations offer and discouraged by tight university budgets, graduate students may find themselves echoing the Italian labor leader who tried to dodge domestic issues: They may turn to globalization because they don't know what to say about the internal complexities of the societies they are studying.

3

Accomplishments and Challenges in International Programs

In this section we have brought together articles that reflect important trends and directions on university and college campuses. Those concerned with international teaching, research, and outreach face a number of common challenges and opportunities. These include implementing new techniques in foreign language instruction, developing access to library materials through technology, coping with the high cost of foreign books and periodicals, increasing the international dimension in teaching and research in schools of business, offering outreach to public groups beyond the campuses, and providing opportunities for undergraduates to directly experience other cultures and societies. These topics, as well as papers by two university presidents on how to internationalize their campuses, are explored in depth in this section.

From its inception, Title VI gave primary emphasis to language teaching and learning. Richard D. Brecht and A. Ronald Walton document the key role that the federal government has played through Title VI in supporting the less commonly taught languages. At the same time, they call for improved quality of instruction and a broad range of language programs to meet changing needs.

John D. Metzler acknowledges that Title VI Centers have played an important part in providing different outreach opportunities but sees the need for outreach to be more directly connected to scholarship. He believes that these centers have the obligation and the opportunity to work with a variety of publics to enable them to take full advantage of new international options. Metzler calls for a more robust internationalization of almost every aspect of U.S. domestic life, and also for more creative uses of technology in implementing outreach.

In recent years, the U.S. Congress and the Department of Education have recognized the importance of international content in business school curricula and research. Title VI funding has helped business and professional schools to expand their international missions. Richard W. Moxon, Elizabeth A. C. O'Shea, Mollie

Brown, and Christoffer M. Escher examine trends in global business, survey international business needs, and discuss improvements in business and university programs.

Research universities and smaller colleges may pursue different approaches to increasing the international experiences of their faculties and students. Robert A. Scott, president of Ramapo College of New Jersey, provides a framework for how a small public college of liberal arts, sciences, and professional studies has been able to forge its identity as an institution committed to international as well as multicultural education.

Barbara B. Burn compares study abroad programs in several countries and the language requirements for participation in them. Her results generally show that there is an increase of study abroad programs in these countries but that students tend to go for shorter periods than in the past, and to more programs that do not require foreign language study. An increased interest in overseas study programs by professional schools is encouraging. Finally, Seth Spaulding, James Mauch, and Lin Lin devote considerable attention to the contribution of foreign students on U.S. campuses, and how their presence affects policy issues regarding recruitment, credentials accreditation, educational costs and benefits, academic concerns, and the internationalization and cultural diversity goals of institutions of higher education.

These articles describe what some U.S. colleges and universities have done to provide their students and faculties with international opportunities and experiences and to reduce curricular parochialism. Other schools employ different programs and approaches to achieve these same ends. What is clear in all these essays is the recognition that international dimensions are integral to the educational goals of higher education in the United States.

National Language Needs and Capacities

A RECOMMENDATION FOR ACTION

Richard D. Brecht and A. Ronald Walton

Abstract

The federal government, through Title VI of the Higher Education Act, has played a vital role in supporting language study in the United States, especially the less commonly taught languages (LCTLs).[1] While this legislation has subsidized to a large extent the bulk of the training, particularly in the least-commonly taught of the LCTLs, it also has played a critical role in building and maintaining the expertise base of all the LCTL fields.

In the past decade, the situation in the world and on the nation's campuses has changed considerably, and these changes have significant consequences for this nation's language needs and capacities.

- The new political, economic, and social conditions in this world now require more citizens to be competent in more languages for more applications than ever before;

- For the foreseeable future, financial pressures on institutions of higher education now make language expertise and program maintenance, let alone expansion, extremely difficult.

Reprinted with permission, International Studies and Overseas Programs (ISOP), University of California, Los Angeles, California, from the publication *International Studies Education in the New Global Era: Proceedings of a National Policy Conference on the Higher Education Act,* 1998.

Given this situation, more needs to be done within higher education to expand the availability and improve the quality of instruction in the increased number and broader range of languages demanded by the new circumstances in the world. The national need for linguistically competent citizens, tied as it is to the nation's security, is a federal responsibility, and Title VI is positioned to continue to play a leading role in this regard.

The recommendations of this report focus on building infrastructure, particularly for the languages of greatest need and weakest capacity, in order to support directly institutions wishing to initiate or enhance current offerings in the LCTLs and to maintain an otherwise precarious national expertise base.

Introduction

The National Foreign Language Center (NFLC), a privately funded language policy "think tank" located at the School for Advanced International Studies of Johns Hopkins University, was awarded a grant from the United States Department of Education (Center for International Education) in 1995 to assess the language component of Title VI of the Higher Education Act (HEA). This present report on the state of language needs and capacities in Title VI and in the nation as a whole relies upon the preliminary results of that study as well as on the accumulated experience of the National Council of Organizations of Less Commonly Taught Languages (NCOLCTL) and the NFLC. The latter organization has amassed a significant body of research and policy formulation on our nation's language needs and capacities.

Background

Since World War II, the United States has been almost alone among countries of the world in defining its need for foreign language competence to include the languages of practically every country and even of many ethnic regions within countries. The Soviet Union's surprising capability in nuclear weapons development and launching and the jolt to our national confidence that those technical developments produced provided the impetus for the National Defense Education Act (NDEA), including a specific title (Title VI) addressing a clearly perceived enhanced national need for language competence. Through that legislation Congress acknowledged the global language needs of the country by directing significant funding for languages that were not "generally available in the United States." It also clearly confirmed the important role of universities in building and maintaining the required capacity in language. Since that time Title VI support has continued to assist universities to train and maintain the expertise required by this global language mandate as well as to provide significant amounts of on-site language instruction. In short, Title VI of the NDEA and HEA has been a confirmation of the federal mandate to address national language needs on a global scale as well as to assign a major role to the campuses to help meet those national needs.[2]

Title VI and the National Language Capacity

It is not an exaggeration to say that many, if not most, of the LCTLs in this country would not or could not be taught if it were not for Title VI. This assertion is supported by interviews with language specialists as well as with university administrators around the country. It also follows from a comparison of the enrollment statistics for languages in Title VI and non–Title VI institutions. An analysis of the MLA survey of language enrollments in two- and four-year colleges and universities throughout the country in the fall of 1995 reveals that only sixty-four institutions in the United States have language programs supported by Title VI (leaving aside Canadian and International Studies). Based on the following statistics, one can assert that this small group of institutions constitutes the essence of this nation's capacity to teach the LCTLs at the university level.

- Outside of French, German, Italian, and Spanish, the Title VI–supported programs in these institutions account for 22.5% of undergraduate language enrollments and 59% of graduate enrollments. Clearly, these sixty-four institutions are carrying a hugely disproportionate burden for instruction in the LCTLs, particularly given the fact that they represent 2.66% of the 2,399 colleges and universities in this country offering language instruction in the United States.[3]

- If one focuses on the least-commonly taught languages, i.e. omitting the ten with the most enrollment (Arabic, Chinese, French, German, Hebrew, Italian, Japanese, Portuguese, Russian, and Spanish), the sixty-four Title VI–supported institutions account for 51% of the undergraduate and 81% of the graduate language enrollments!

The contribution of Title VI–supported institutions goes well beyond language instruction. As the graduate student enrollment numbers above make clear, the nation's future experts are receiving their language training overwhelmingly in these institutions. In addition, there are other indicators that Title VI support has been instrumental in building and maintaining the expertise base of language fields, again particularly in the LCTLs:[4]

- From 1988 to 1995, Title VI NRCs have supplied more than a quarter of the Ph.D.s in the LCTLs. (These do not include dissertations in literature or area studies.) In many LCTLs, the percentage of Ph.D.s produced at Title VI–supported institutions is even higher: 40% in Chinese and Japanese, and even higher for many of the least-commonly taught languages. And this percentage has risen significantly over the past decade: 1982–87, 15.2%; 1988–92, 35.6%; and 1993–95, 44.7%.[5]

- A sampling of the research published on second language acquisition in the LCTLs from 1992 to 1995 shows that Title VI National Resource Centers contributed almost half of all published research. (This sample of twenty-five LCTLs includes sociolinguistics, descriptive linguistics, and language policy.) This contribution increases to more than 60% of the research published on the Least Commonly Taught Languages.[6]

These figures point unambiguously to the Title VI legislation and the institutions it supports as the foundation of this nation's capacity in the LCTLs. However effective Title VI may have been in the past in sustaining the LCTLs, there are clear indications that needs are changing and expanding rapidly.

The New Context

In the past few years, the situation in the world and on the nation's campuses has altered considerably, and these changes have significant consequences for this nation's language needs and capacities.

Our Changed World and Consequences for Language Learning

The astonishing developments of the past decade have resulted in new political, economic, and social orders as well as having produced a revolution in communication, all of which has had a significant effect on the language needs of our society:

- **Political.** The new world order presents challenges to governmental and NGO activities in the political arena, as more peoples around the world assert their independent identity and all too frequently come into conflict with newly created indigenous minorities or with neighboring countries engaged with similar territorial and cultural problems. Naturally enough, language plays a major role in this self-identification, when local as well as national ethnic groups insist as never before on communication in their own language. For example, *linguae francae* such as Russian, Serbo-Croatian, and Afrikaans now are replaced by Belarus, Kazakh, Slovenian, and Zulu, to name only a few, just as the notion of "Chinese" has given way to distinctions such as Mandarin, Cantonese, and Taiwanese.

- **Economic.** International trade, specifically exports, which constituted a small fraction of the U.S. economy in the early 1960s, now represents a major driving force.[7] The NAFTA and WTO are now in place, and American participation in other agreements for the Western Hemisphere and the Pacific Rim is being pursued (FTAA and APEC). This new world economic order entails intensely expanded interactions among representatives of diverse cultures on a day-to-day basis on behalf of large corporations and medium and small businesses. This is particularly true as America attempts to export its services to the world (Brecht and Walton 1995). In addition to the increases in numbers, the kinds of cultures with which Americans must interact are shifting radically. The cultural "safe havens" for Americans of Western Europe are being rapidly replaced in economic impact by the truly foreign cultures of Asia, where Americans are much less comfortable linguistically and culturally.

- **Social.** Governments and NGOs around the world are cooperating on social issues as never before. Environmental protection, law enforcement, disease control, humanitarian aid, and a host of other issues are now being addressed globally literally by hundreds of nations.

- **Communications.** Transportation and communications have expanded to the point where the traditional physical restrictions of time and space are less and less a factor in people's ability to interact. The clearest example is perhaps the Internet, through which tens of millions of people communicate, approximately half of whom live outside of the United States. In this context more people from more cultures than ever before in history are interacting directly with one other, and the potential for expansion is virtually without limit.

Such a litany of changed circumstances impinging on intercultural communication and language use easily could be expanded, but this list is offered merely as a broad perspective on the following discussion. The conclusion, though, is inescapable: these changes entail a major expansion in the educational mission of government, private, and academic institutions in the language (and culture) area. To prepare citizens for this new global environment, our education and training institutions must offer more languages (and more difficult languages), for more purposes, to a more diverse clientele than ever before.

A New Campus Environment
Just as one can point to the rising need to expand language and cross-cultural communication education on campus and beyond, so too can the realities of steady or even shrinking resources be assumed as a permanent aspect of most if not all educational institutional planning. The maintenance of expertise and of programs, let alone the expansion envisioned here, will thus require an infusion of new resources or at least a reorganization of existing ones.

The problem of shrinking resources is exacerbated on campus by the almost insignificant enrollments in languages other than Spanish, French, and German, as student demand more and more drives educational investment.[8] In addition, efforts at expanding investment in language face resistance born of the general negative attitude toward language study on the part of many students, faculty, and administrators, which is reflective of the American society as a whole. All too often, there is a general sense that, on the one hand, something is broken in the way languages are taught because few seem to graduate with usable skills; and on the other, there is a suspicion that maintaining a number of language programs has to be wasteful on some level. This general attitude toward language, unfortunately, is based more on intuition than it is on real evidence or even explicit argumentation. It is fed by a number of considerations, including the high cost of such a labor-intensive enterprise as language teaching. Nevertheless, the result of these factors on campuses across the country is a general erosion of support for language, accompanied by pressure for downsizing or elimination of all but the largest-enrolled languages. It is, thus, no coincidence that, as the MLA statistics cited above make clear, many of the least-commonly taught languages are taught only at Title VI–supported institutions.

Finally, costs for attaining functional competence in language have increased significantly with the shift in focus in the national imperative to non-European languages, especially the languages of Asia. Russian takes approximately twice as long to acquire as French; Arabic, Chinese, Japanese, and Korean, as much as three to four times as long. If one adds to this the small class size characteristic of instruction in many of the LCTLs, then it is clear that the cost of producing functional competence in these languages is much higher than for the European cognate languages.

Capacity and Needs

An overall framework against which to assess national needs and capacities can be summarized as follows:

Tactical level	**Demand**	**Supply**
Strategic level	**Needs**	**Capacity**

We define these terms as follows:

- *Demand:* the specific tasks for which language competence is actually being used;

- *Supply:* the availability of language competencies and modes of sourcing and housing;

- *Needs:* the perceived or latent conditions (harmful or beneficial) that can be improved or exploited by language competence;

- *Capacity:* the ability to produce linguistic competence designed to meet demands which are driven by real or potential need.

In terms of this framework, it is logical to assume that Needs provoke real Demand, for which an immediate Supply is generated, which in turn depends upon an institutionalized system characterizable as Capacity. This enriched market-oriented framework is called for by studies such as *Russian in the United States: A Case Study of National Language Needs and Capacities,* which concluded that a simple "supply and demand" view of language has serious flaws when it comes to strategic national needs, and that significantly more attention has to be paid to defining national needs and insuring underlying capacity, particularly in times of uncertain market forces.

The NFLC further has defined our national capacity to provide instruction in a language as a function of the strength of a language "field" in the U.S. (Brecht and Walton 1993). The strength of a field in turn depends on the existence (and quality) of a strong "architecture," which can be understood to consist of base structures, infrastructure, and flagship programs. Very simply, effective instructional programs depend on the existence of a field infrastructure supporting materials development, teacher training, study abroad programming, testing and assessment systems, data collection, and information-sharing networks, among other things. Based on this characterization of strength, languages such as French, German, and Spanish can be seen not only to be popular among students at the secondary and tertiary levels, but to have at their disposal a strong supporting infrastructure. The LCTLs, on the other hand, are generally much weaker in this regard and, accordingly, that much more handicapped in expanding and/or improving instruction across the board.

The National Council of Organizations of Less Commonly Taught Languages (NCOLCTL) comprises sixteen national language teachers' organizations, including African, Arabic, Cantonese, Chinese, Hebrew, Japanese, Korean, Russian, Slavic, South Asian, Southeast Asian, and Turkic.[9] At its inception in 1987, the members of the NCOLCTL stated clearly that their greatest common needs were for teaching materials and teacher training. However, in spite of this general consensus, in the LCTLs the range of variation among languages with regard to infrastructure strength and weakness is significant. For some languages, Russian for example, teaching materials are plentiful and excellent, but standardized testing instruments are not available; for many other of the least-commonly taught languages, the availability of a basic textbook, or even a dictionary or up-to-date grammar, is problematic.

Given the basic fact that our national capacity to mount programs producing proficient users of a language depends on the existence of materials, teacher training programs, study abroad programs, etc., it is imperative to focus on strengthening these infrastructure elements. In so doing, all programs across the nation can be enhanced simultaneously, and students in all institutions can receive the benefit of the improvement.

Needs

In order to determine the strengths and weaknesses of our national language capacity and the real and specific needs of the languages taught in the United States, in particular the LCTLs, the NFLC has worked with NCOLCTL and their individual fieldwide organizations, visited dozens of campuses across the country, conducted fieldwide studies in the principal LCTLs (Brecht, Caemmerer, and Walton 1995; Jorden and Lambert 1991; Moore, Walton, and Lambert 1992) and is at present in the process of surveying all existing fieldwide organizations specifically for this purpose. This experience has produced the following taxonomy of LCTLs and a list of specific needs.

Classification of Languages
The wide variation of strengths and weaknesses among the LCTLs makes some kind of rough taxonomy necessary (Brecht and Walton, 1993). There are at least

three relevant criteria for this classification: enrollments, institutional availability, and strength of field architecture. What follows is an updated classification of the LCTLs, which is based on the Fall 1995 MLA enrollment data as well as on a very tentative assessment of field strength. It should be understood more as illustrative of the differences involved rather than as a rigorous specification of where a language stands in the United States. Indeed, although scholars may argue over where a given language belongs, the relevant issue is still the diversity of the LCTLs.

- **Group One: The Principal LCTLs (Chinese, Japanese, and Russian).** These languages, studied by tens of thousands of students every semester, mirror, although on a much reduced scale, the commonly taught languages in being generally available in schools and universities around the country. Compared to the other LCTLs, they can be seen to have significant strength in their field architecture, although with important weaknesses. The principal problem with these languages, though, is their degree of difficulty, which makes it virtually impossible for students to reach even a minimal functional ability without extensive immersion study in-country. Finally, although the national demand for all three of these languages currently is expanding rapidly, at the school and university levels this growth is reflected in student enrollments only for Chinese and Japanese, while Russian enrollments are declining at an alarming rate (Brecht, Caemmerer, and Walton 1995).

- **Group Two: The Less Commonly Taught LCTLs.** In this category belong the languages that are studied only by several thousand students every semester nationwide: Arabic, Hawaiian, Hebrew, Korean, Portuguese, Swahili, and perhaps a few others. These languages present a very mixed picture with regard to difficulty: Arabic and Korean are Category Four languages, which in the State Department's classification refers to those languages requiring the most time to learn. Other differences among these languages include institutional availability and strength of architecture. They seem to share, however, at least to date, the common fate of not being able to extend their enrollments, as Chinese and Japanese have done in the past decade.

- **Group Three: The Much Less Commonly Taught Languages.** There are approximately twenty non–West European/non–North American languages taught in the United States, each of which has undergraduate and graduate enrollments across the country ranging in the hundreds (again, as per MLA Fall 1995 statistics). Most importantly, for these languages, instruction is consistently available only in a handful of institutions in the United States. These languages include Armenian, Czech, Hindi, Indonesian, Mongolian, Persian, Polish, Serbian/Croatian, Tagalog, Thai, Turkish, Vietnamese, and Yoruba, among others.

- **Group Four: The Least Commonly Taught Languages.** In addition to the languages above, the formal educational system in the United States offers approximately eighty other "least commonly taught" languages, whose total national enrollments range from dozens to the single digits. These languages, even more than the preceding group, occupy a very marginal position in the educational system, being offered often only at one or two institutions across the United States in a given year, often on an "on-demand," individualized learning basis, and supported by very meager learning and teaching resources. Here belong Bengali, Burmese, Cantonese, Hausa, Punjab, Shona, Slovak, Slovenian, Ukrainian, Uzbek, Wolof, and Zulu.

- **Group Five: The Rarely (or Never) Taught Languages.** Finally, there are many other of the world's several thousand languages which can be viewed as important to our national interest and which are rarely or never taught in the United States. For some of these languages, there is linguistic and anthropological expertise available; for many others, sufficient basic expertise is totally lacking. In this class of languages belong all the Chinese languages (except Mandarin and Cantonese), all nonstandard Arabic, the Central Asian languages, most of the languages of Africa, and many others such as Lao, Georgian, Malay, and Sinhala (Dwyer and Wiley 1980).

Specific Needs of the LCTLs
The needs that all these languages share, although in varying degrees, include:

TEACHING MATERIALS

Many, if not most, LCTLs are in desperate need of teaching materials, including basic texts as well as customized learning modules, both in the traditional text format as well as in more technologically enhanced modes. The existence of good materials is particularly important for the LCTL fields, where much of the learning takes place with untrained native-speaking tutors, or often students are completely on their own. Materials are particularly valuable as well for these fields where teacher training programs are rare or nonexistent—as they are for most of the LCTLs.

Even where materials exist, say for Russian, the rapidly changing world of the former Soviet Union makes updating, particularly of cultural materials, a necessity. (For example, with hyperinflation rates in Russia the unit of currency known as the "kopeck" has simply gone out of use, and the value of the ruble makes facility with very large numbers now needed as never before.)

While materials are desperately needed, a process must be found that will guarantee that resources invested in producing them will be effective: that good materials will be developed and that they will be used broadly by teachers around the country. A prerequisite for this is a fieldwide consensus on a standardized learning framework, the specific purpose of which is to guide materials development as well as curricular design and teacher training.[10] Such a framework would represent the collective wisdom of a field and serve as a guide, or a mandate, as programs nationwide seek to meet the needs of their students each in its own unique local context. The consensus a framework such as this represents can ensure that the traditional fatal flaw of idiosyncratic materials development will be avoided, and that potential investors will once again have confidence in the enterprise.

Teacher Training

Professional development is a national priority uniformly across the language teaching profession.[11] This is becoming especially important now that theoretical and applied research in language acquisition is beginning to produce results that are directly beneficial to the learning and teaching experience. If any benefit to the student is to be realized, however, the research results have to be made available and accessible to the classroom teachers in ways that they understand and that they can use. This requires a continuing and expanded investment in faculty development programs, which for the LCTLs are too rarely offered due to cost and the dearth of trainer expertise.

Expertise Base Strengthening

Materials development and teacher training do not exhaust the principal needs of many of the LCTLs. Any production of textbooks and the like have to be preceded by research on the language itself and the development of even the most basic tools, such as dictionaries and grammars. Many languages simply never have had good dictionaries and grammars at their disposal; for other languages, dictionaries and grammars are often completely out of date, having been developed decades ago often by amateur linguists. With the expansion in the number of languages demanded today, this need has become even more acute.

Study Abroad Programs

The new imperative for language includes the "truly foreign languages" (Walton and Jorden 1987) of the Pacific Century; and, as a result, the time needed to attain functional proficiency in these languages has risen significantly. As mentioned above, Russian, Arabic, Chinese, and Korean take two to four times as long to acquire as do Spanish and French! This exponential demand on time and resources is best accommodated by placing students in-country, where the "time-on-task" is essentially a student's entire waking hours. However, the design and management of effective in-country immersion programs are extremely complex and require significant expertise and resources. Fields need assistance, particularly where the resources are limited and the in-country cultures are "truly foreign" for the American student.

Networking Facilities

Finally, all the LCTL fields have teachers and researchers, as well as learners, who are operating alone or in very small numbers and who are geographically widely dispersed. To assist these practitioners and learners, mechanisms are needed to gather and disseminate information and data, as well as to build strong learning and teaching communities. Ties also have to be made and sustained with the *heritage language communities in this country, which constitute perhaps our nation's greatest resource in the LCTLs.*

In concluding this list of the immediate needs of the LCTL fields, one must reiterate that each language has its own specific needs. Accordingly, only field experts can properly assess and target priority needs. For example, while a national decision to fund the development of testing instruments for a given language may constitute a valuable contribution to a field, the actual practitioners might well make the case that for them basic textbooks are a more pressing need.

Strategic Recommendation

More needs to be done to expand the availability and improve the quality of instruction in the broader swath of languages demanded by the new political, economic, and social conditions in the world. Strategies should be targeted that will provide direct and relevant assistance to nascent, established, and threatened language programs on our nation's campuses. Given the range of languages needed and the diversity of needs of the fields involved, we recommend a general strategy to focus on building field architecture, which is particularly important for the languages of greatest need and weakest capacity. This strategy is aimed specifically at enabling language fields to provide direct support to institutions across the country that wish to initiate or enhance current offerings in these languages.

Accordingly, we recommend the establishment of "national language field resource centers" (NLFRCs), whose principal mission is to serve the nation as its principal source of information, communication, and the products and services supporting the teaching and learning of the languages in their world area. Each center, in cooperation with existing professional organizations and enterprises, will assume general responsibility for field development: for assessing the field's needs, for meeting those needs, and particularly for providing direct assistance to institutions to establish new or improve existing language programs. To put it succinctly and concretely, anyone anywhere who is interested in a specific language will know that there is a number to call or a URL to address, where high-quality information and assistance is available on demand.

In order to address this fieldwide mission, these NLFRCs should meet the following qualifications:

1. Each center should be language field–oriented. It should serve a specific language or group of languages. Therefore, the center has to have at its disposal nationally recognized experts in these languages and particularly in the acquisition of these specific languages.

2. Each center should be fieldwide. It should draw expertise from across the field, wherever it resides: in this country or abroad, in colleges and universities or in associations or research institutes; in the academic, private, govern-

ment, heritage, and overseas sectors. The center should have a working relationship with the leading field associations and institutes. Finally, the center should be linked by the Internet to institutions and individual scholars and teachers around the country.

3. The center should have the capability to collect relevant data, materials, and services wherever they exist and disseminate them on demand to institutions and individuals. This presumes a Web-based site responsible for the collection and dissemination of expertise and resources.

4. The center's focus should be on applied as well as basic research, so that it can bring the results of the latest research to bear directly on the design and management of products and services needed for language teaching and learning.

Each NLFRC's responsibilities would include:

1. Model curriculum and program design;

2. Materials design and production, including technologically enhanced (interactive, multimedia, Web-deliverable) materials and learning environments;

3. Intensive summer language-training institutes for students as well as teachers;

4. Teacher training;

5. Fieldwide networking and information sharing;

6. Data collection and dissemination;

7. In-country immersion language program support;

8. Facilitation of fieldwide consensus on standards and learning framework to guide materials development, teacher training, and curricular design; and

9. Networking among the academic, heritage, government, private, and overseas sectors.

These centers should not concentrate and control all the field's resources; the notion of "letting a thousand blossoms bloom" makes more sense in the development of language instruction in a variety of institutions across the country. However, these blossoms are not blooming; most of the nation's programs in the LCTLs need more expertise and resources. In order to meet these needs most effectively, the fields need a mechanism, owned by its established experts, which carefully husbands its scarce resources and accepts responsibility to provide the safety net under its instructional programs nationwide.

Conclusion

Title VI of the NDEA and now of the HEA has been the principal motivator and the major contributor—along with a relatively small set of universities—in maintaining LCTL programs on our nation's campuses. Without Title VI, many of the LCTL programs would simply disappear.

The language needs of this country, however, are greater than ever before in its history, even if the demand in many sectors is latent, i.e. not reflective of the true national need. Since these needs are national, they should continue to be, at least in part, the proper responsibility of the federal government.

With this expanded need, campus programs require more and better materials, teacher training, and many other supporting structures and services. This assistance can be provided by the language field, if the field itself has sufficient infrastructure. While the federal support provided by Title VI has been critically important, not enough has been done in the past to build the LCTL fields, which are generally not strong enough to provide direct assistance to campuses in meeting their expanded language needs.

A way must be found to continue to sustain the LCTLs while expanding their number on campus and improving the quality of instruction. This must be done within highly restricted budget constraints. Accordingly, a recommendation aimed directly at strengthening infrastructure by establishing National Language Field Resource Centers is the most cost-effective, efficient, and quality-assured strategy to accomplish this end. This is particularly important for the languages with the fewest resources and for those whose difficulty makes the cost of instruction two or three times that of the more accessible languages.

The proposed centers form a safety net responsible for ensuring that the national interests are served across the board in a particular language or group of languages. They should exist to serve programs, teachers, and learners directly, effectively, and with maximum cost-efficiency. Such a network of centers would guarantee a baseline level of expertise and resources to sustain threatened programs and to assist in program proliferation, as the national need is more and more matched by real demand for language competence and student enrollment in our schools and in higher education begins to reflect real demand. In sum, a mechanism is proposed whose function is to build and support the infrastructure of a given language field, which in turn sustains and enhances all the nation's institutions, rich and poor, in offering the broad range of languages the United States needs.

NOTES

1. The term "less commonly taught language" (LCTL) in this country traditionally has referred to all languages except French, German, & Spanish. While the enrollment patterns of students at the secondary and tertiary levels is changing dramatically, there is reason to continue the designation with some additional distinctions to be discussed below.

2. In recognition of this global language need, in the postwar period various federal agencies established language training facilities, including the Defense Language Institute, the Foreign Service Institute, as well as the language training facilities at CIA and

NSA. These facilities are charged with meeting the immediate language needs of the federal government as they arise.

3. The impact of these numbers is only slightly mitigated by the fact that these sixty-four institutions are among our nation's largest.

4. French, German, and Spanish, in the main, have been supported by school systems and higher educational institutions in this country, although the role of Title VI even with these languages has not been insignificant.

5. Data on dissertations on foreign languages was gathered through a search of the Dissertations Online database for the following: all dissertations in foreign languages (but not literature or area studies); all dissertations in the LCTLs; all language dissertations at Title VI centers; and all LCTL dissertations at Title VI centers. The search was limited to the period 1982–1995. Italian, German, Spanish, and French were excluded from the initial search. Subsequently, Western European LCTLs were removed from the data as well in order to determine their contribution to the overall number of doctoral degrees earned in the LCTLs.

6. A search for publications on research in SLA and related topics (including sociolinguistics, descriptive linguistics, and language policy) was performed on the Language Learning and Behavior Abstracts (LLBA) bibliographic database. Twenty-five LCTLs, representing all categories of LCTLs, were sampled. The abstracts sampled included abstracts of journal articles, review articles, books, textbooks, chapters in books, and dissertations. Book reviews were excluded from the sample. The LLBA on-line bibliographic database was chosen because it provides as part of each citation the home institution of the first-listed author of the publication.

7. "From 1985 to 1994, exports rose from 7.2 percent to 10.2 percent of the nation's gross domestic product . . ." Such numbers provoke judgements like ". . . trade specialists say, foreign growth is the best hope to animate the United States economy."

8. The enrollment data for two- and four-year institutions are now available from the Modern Language Association for Fall 1995.

9. This is the first organization in this country dedicated to the improvement of our national capacity specifically in the LCTLs. It has received almost a decade of support from the Ford Foundation.

10. The National Council of Organizations of Less Commonly Taught Languages, funded by the Ford Foundation and headquartered at the National Foreign Language Center, held a conference on January 26–27, 1996, in Washington, D.C. to present and discuss the Language Learning Frameworks (LLFs) for the LCTLs that have been developed by the Council's member organizations over the last three years.

11. AATF and AATG, for example, have been involved in this endeavor for a number of years.

REFERENCES

Brecht, R. D. 1995. *NFLC Policy Issues.* Washington, DC: National Foreign Language Center.
Brecht, R. D., J. Caemmerer, and A. R. Walton. 1995. *Russian in the United States: A Case Study of America's Language Needs and Capacities.* Washington, DC: National Foreign Language Center.
Brecht, R. D., and A. R. Walton. 1993. *National Strategic Planning in the Less Commonly Taught Languages.* Washington, DC: National Foreign Language Center.
Dwyer, D., and D. Wiley. 1980. *African Language Instruction in the United States: Directions and Priorities for the 1990s.* East Lansing: African Studies Center, Michigan State University.

Jorden, E. H., and R. D. Lambert. 1991. *Japanese Language Instruction in the United States: Resources, Practice, and Investment Strategy.* Washington, DC: National Foreign Language Center.

Moore, S. J., A. R. Walton, and R. D. Lambert. 1992. *Introducing Chinese into High Schools: The Dodge Initiative.* Washington, DC: National Foreign Language Center.

Walton, A. R., and E. H. Jorden. 1987. "Truly Foreign Languages: Instructional Challenges." *Annals of the American Academy of Political and Social Sciences* 490: 110–24.

International Outreach for the New Millennium

John D. Metzler

Abstract

As we approach the twenty-first century, the United States must prepare for an in-creasingly inter-connected global society. The U.S. academy, particularly through the Title VI Centers and their outreach programs, has a unique opportunity and obligation to work with a variety of American publics in enhancing the capability to negotiate and take full advantage of new international opportunities. Outreach programming from Title VI Centers and programs plays an important role in pre-paring the populace for these opportunities. It can provide assistance to U.S. for-eign policy professionals and the Congress, as well as state and local govern-ments; it can lead to innovations in foreign language and international studies curricula in both K–12 and post-secondary institutions; it can assist U.S. compa-nies to take advantage of international trade and support local, state, and national agencies in developing initiatives abroad; and it can assist the media in becoming more comprehensive and accurate in their international coverage. A more robust commitment to and focus on outreach functions is needed if the national needs are to be met in the face of relentless internationalization of almost every aspect of U.S. domestic life. The small amounts of outreach funding available and the

Reprinted with permission, International Studies and Overseas Programs (ISOP), University of California, Los Angeles, California, from the publication *International Studies Education in the New Global Era: Proceedings of a National Policy Conference on the Higher Education Act,* 1998. This is a slightly revised version.

many other activities "mandated" for the Title VI National Resource, Foreign Language Resource, and International Business Centers, however, results in a sometimes ambivalent university commitment to expenditure for outreach personnel and programming. Moreover, in spite of rhetorical commitment to service, outreach or service is often peripheral to the culture of many universities and is perceived as not being important to scholarship. This paper will address the great national need for foreign language and international studies outreach for a variety of U.S. populations, institutions, and agencies. We also (i) explore ways in which outreach can be promoted as an integral part of scholarship and the core agenda of the university, (ii) critique established and current outreach initiatives, and (iii) survey new ways of doing outreach through collaborative endeavors and the creative use of technology.

Background

The Mission
There is a wide consensus within the internationalist community that as we approach the twenty-first century our planet is becoming increasingly inter-connected. This process of "globalization" presents on the one hand tremendous opportunities for economic growth, increased political freedom, and social development; however, on the other hand, globalization also presents the possibility of dangerously increased economic disparity, political destabilization and social disintegration. Internationalist scholars from across the disciplines can play an important role in generating and disseminating knowledge which is essential to realizing the potential of globalization while concurrently minimizing its risks. In this regard the U.S. academy, particularly through the Title VI Centers and programs, has a unique opportunity and obligation to work with a variety of American publics in enhancing their capability to negotiate and take full advantage of new international opportunities, while minimizing the risks to international peace and security.

Outreach programming from Title VI Centers and programs can and should play a central role in realizing this agenda by disseminating appropriate knowledge and enhancing the analytic capabilities of individual citizens, business personnel, educators at all levels, the media, and policy makers at the local, state, and federal levels. However, in order to realize these achievable goals a more robust commitment to and focus on the outreach functions of the Title VI National Resource, International Business, and Foreign Language Resource Centers is imperative.

The objective of this paper is to explore ways in which we can more clearly define the outreach agenda in the age of globalization and to develop guidelines and strategies that will facilitate the realization of these important goals.

There is undoubtedly a consensus among the individuals, universities and organizations working in the international arena that National Resource Centers should engage extra-university communities by addressing issues related to globalization. However, there is little consensus as to how central this outreach mandate should be to the larger agenda of international education in the academy generally and of Title VI Centers specifically. If outreach is to fulfill its potential, university-based international units will have to actively engage this debate. To be effective in this endeavor it is essential that we first:

- understand and address the problematic of outreach and its current peripheralization within the academy;

- critically assess the normative outreach endeavors of Title VI National Resource Centers (NRCs), Centers for International Business Education and Research (CIBERs) and National Foreign Language Resource Centers (NFLRCs), celebrating outreach achievements while challenging our shortcomings.

Peripheralization of Outreach within the Academy

One of the central problems of outreach work in Title VI Centers has been that although outreach has been mandated since the early 1970s it has traditionally been perceived as peripheral to the main objectives, goals, and tasks of the Centers. This is not surprising given the institutional context of the larger academy in which Title VI Centers operate.

OUTREACH AS PERIPHERAL TO KNOWLEDGE GENERATION

The academy—even those which pride themselves as "land-grant" institutions—have had an ambivalent and often ambiguous relationship with the concept and practice of outreach. From the perspective of the academy the primary tasks of the academy are:

- The production of knowledge which is achieved through scholarship/research;

- The training of the next generation of scholars/researchers (producing the producers of knowledge) which is achieved through quality graduate education programs;

- The dissemination of knowledge through the traditional medium of undergraduate instruction.

Dissemination of knowledge beyond the traditional modalities of undergraduate and graduate education has seldom been given much support within the academy, beyond the sometime established practices of:

- University-based extension services to rural and agricultural communities;

- Post-graduate professional association with academy alumni—e.g., relationships with K–12 educators, medical personnel, business persons, engineers, etc.;

- Recent computer (Web-based) distance education with focus on degree programs.

But even in these situations the relationship between the academy and "clients" has been an uneasy and often uncomfortable one. The "clientele" relationship (often one-way dissemination of knowledge) is not conducive to trust and collaboration, nor has this relationship been seen as being an integral part of scholarship, the production of knowledge, and the primary function of the university. Moreover, and relatedly, the academy has often treated academics who are involved in outreach activities as being "second-class," as not being committed to real scholarship.

Parenthetically, Title VI programs that are thematically based or hosted by professional units, for example, CIBERs, may find it easier to do outreach, given the disciplinary tradition of working with "clients" external to the university. On the other hand, area studies centers housed in the more normative and traditional social science and humanities administrative units have a more restricted tradition of working with communities outside of the academy and, consequently, may perceive outreach to be of limited value.[1]

OUTREACH AND THE UNIVERSITY REWARD STRUCTURE

Given these realities, it is not surprising that the academy's reward structure has traditionally devalued outreach in terms of its reward and tenure structure. Even at land-grant universities which claim a tripartite reward structure—research, teaching, and outreach—outreach is seldom (outside of extension appointments) given weight in terms of tenure, promotion, and salary considerations. Consequently, outside of the units with traditions of outreach (agriculture, medicine, education), scholars who see the value of outreach as a legitimate and important part of the academy often minimize their own outreach activities.

Title VI international centers are for the most part administered and supported by a core faculty who come from this disciplinary tradition, i.e. the social sciences and humanities. Consequently not many Title VI directors, and fewer of the centers' core faculty, perceive great value in doing outreach. This frame of mind and consequent practice (or lack thereof) is sanctioned by the larger university culture and structure, including deans or directors of international programs, as well as central university officials, who in most cases provide no leadership in the area of outreach.

Moreover, it is clear that many Title VI directors perceive that the International Education and Graduate Programs Service (IEGPS) of the U.S. Department of Education assigns low priority to outreach—both in terms of the competition point system and the manner in which outreach is assessed and monitored. Consequently, although we do not have definitive data, the evidence indicates that most Title VI Centers do not have a full-time person appointed to outreach. Quite often the outreach functions are part of the numerous responsibilities of an assistant or associate director, or they are handled by a part-time person, not infrequently by a graduate assistant.

Until Title VI Centers are pressured from their university administration and IEGPS/USED, and until there is a change in the manner in which it is perceived, outreach will remain peripheral and, as a result, will likely be poorly done and have little lasting impact, locally, regionally, or nationally.

Addressing the Outreach Problematic

I would argue that for the outreach endeavor to be taken seriously in the academy our initial task will have to involve a two-pronged agenda to demonstrate the following:

OUTREACH IS COMPATIBLE WITH AND STRENGTHENS SCHOLARSHIP

We need to convince the academy that outreach can and should be perceived as central to the scholarly enterprise, and not simply a peripheral activity which can be done in a haphazard manner by graduate students or "para-"professional, "want-to-be" scholars. That is, outreach should be viewed as:

> . . . a form of scholarship that cuts across teaching, research and service. It [at its optimum] involves generating, transmitting, applying and preserving knowledge for the direct benefit of external [to the university] audiences in ways that are consistent with the mission [of the academy].[2]

Moreover, as Ernest Lynton has observed:

> For pragmatic . . . as well as substantive reasons, we believe that it is necessary to reexamine prevalent conceptions of what it means to be a scholar. Balance of esteem among research, teaching, and outreach requires the recognition that teaching and outreach not only are essential activities, but that they constitute as much an intellectual challenge as research, and are equally integral parts of the professional work of a scholar. . . . Scholarly research occurs when the facts and figures are transformed into new knowledge. Similarly, just as research is more than the gathering of information, so are teaching and outreach more than the transmission of facts. *All three activities advance knowledge by the process which transforms information into understanding. Knowledge is based on but transcends information, and the transformation of information into new knowledge is the essence of scholarship* [emphasis added].[3]

OUTREACH IS CENTRAL TO THE FUTURE OF THE ACADEMY

A fairly high percentage of Title VI Centers are housed in public institutions, most of which are AAU research universities, and some of which are land-grant institutions. These institutions are publicly funded and, according to their own mission statements, must serve the citizens and institutions (public and private) which fund them. Obligations to the citizens have traditionally been fulfilled, it is argued by the academy, by providing on-campus training in the form of undergraduate and graduate education. With the notable exceptions of outreach done by some professional programs such as agricultural and education extension work, public universities have done little outreach or service to non-campus communities. Indeed, there is ample current evidence that the public perceives institutions of higher learning to be increasingly insulated from the realities of the "real world."[4]

I suggest that outreach can play a central role in reestablishing trust and connection between the academy and the public. This pragmatic argument goes beyond recognizing the important public relations value in establishing meaningful programmatic relationships with the public through meaningful and well constructed and administered outreach programs. A number of leading experts in higher education have cogently argued that as we "bridge to the 21st century," the scholarly endeavor requires reform, which in part can come only from redefining the role of the academy and scholarship in larger society. As the late Ernest Boyer asserted:

> We proceed with the conviction that if the nation's higher learning institutions are to meet today's urgent academic and social mandates, their missions [and practices] must be carefully redefined and the meaning of scholarship creatively reconsidered. Redefining [scholarship] means bringing to scholarship a broader meaning, one in which legitimacy is given to the full scope of academic work.[5]

International outreach, obviously, can play only a modest, but potentially important, role in this endeavor. As with other university outreach endeavors, successful international outreach will depend on increasing support from the academy and the U.S. Department of Education. Realistically, increased support for international outreach will only happen if outreach, broadly defined, is perceived to be essential to the reformulation of scholarship and the revitalization of the academy.

History and Current Status of Title VI Outreach

Area and international thematic studies centers, CIBERs, and NFLRCs traditionally have focused their outreach in one of four areas:

- K–12 educators and students

- Educators in institutions of higher education

- Business community, usually small- and medium-scale businesses

- Community-based organizations—service clubs, religious organizations, etc.

Outreach to K–12 Educators and Students
I was unable to carry out a systematic survey of outreach activities by NFLRCs and NRCs, but based on my ten-year experience of working in the outreach field, I would suggest that most of the Title VI Centers (i.e. area and NFLRCs) which have active outreach programs place emphasis on outreach to K–12 educators

and students. This tradition of emphasizing K–12 education in outreach endeavors is based on several factors:

- The IEGPS of the U.S. Department of Education has for many years given priority to outreach endeavors to K–12 educators and students. Title VI Centers have responded to this priority by emphasizing K–12 in their outreach endeavors (however limited their overall outreach program may be).

- Many Title VI administrators and faculty share with the IEGPS the belief that K–12 outreach projects are the most effective in terms of return for effort. Given the limited priority given to outreach by many centers, well conceived and executed programs for K–12 educators are perceived to be the most efficient use of scarce outreach resources. However, effective K–12 programs necessitate considerable resources particularly in terms of time commitment by outreach personnel, a factor which is often ignored by resource-poor outreach programs.

- There is a widely shared conviction among Title VI Centers that outreach resources should be allocated to activities which have the greatest potential for promoting international competency and understanding. This conviction converges with an equally widely shared perception of the ameliorative potential of education. Consequently, there is an acceptance of the argument that K–12 outreach, with the possibility of shaping the minds and attitudes of America's youth, should be given high priority.

- Given the previous points, Title VI Centers often appoint to the outreach positions persons who have a background in K–12 education. Outreach coordinators with K–12 experience are likely to continue to emphasize outreach to schools, and teachers and may feel uncomfortable in undertaking initiatives outside this arena.

- Even in cases where outreach coordinators have no direct K–12 experience, they report that they and the faculty recruited to assist in special programming (workshops, institutes) indicate a higher comfort level in working with educators than with other extra-university populations. Even when the "snobbery factor" is taken into consideration there is strong anecdotal evidence that university faculty are more responsive to and more effective in working with educators than with other groups.

TYPES OF K–12 OUTREACH

Outreach programs have been involved in numerous types of outreach endeavors to the K–12 community.

- *Teacher In-Service Workshops.* One of the most popular and effective modes of outreach to K–12 educators (if planned and executed in a professional manner) has been in-service programming. Such programming usually allows for an in-depth exploration of issues to a group of teachers. When in-service workshops are sponsored by individual school buildings or school districts it provides an opportunity to impact teaching throughout the building or district. This is much more effective than providing one-on-one consultation to individual teachers. Teacher in-service workshops also provide an ideal locale for collaborative efforts between regional centers. (Collaboration is addressed in greater detail below.) Numerous Title VI Centers have also sponsored special summer programming for teachers. Examples of effective and rewarding summer programming are National Endowment for the Humanities Summer Institutes (or Seminars) for Teachers which focus on African, Asian, or Latin American studies, and the Fulbright-Hays Group Projects Abroad, which heavily subsidize four-week international study-travel programs for educators, and collaborative summer institutes for foreign language teachers, such as the Taos Institute for Language Teachers.

· *Resources to Teachers.* Many outreach programs continue to provide consultation to individual teachers, even though these services are not emphasized. In addition many Centers have outreach resource collections which are specifically oriented to K–12 educators. Such collections contain reference books, model curricula, introductory level texts, trade books, textbooks, music, slide collections, computer simulations, videos, etc. In some institutions which host more than one Title VI Center, resource collections have a common location.

· *Outreach through State and National Teacher Organizations.* A number of outreach programs have developed positive working relationships with state and national level disciplinary associations. Area and thematic centers have often concentrated on state level Councils for the Social Studies, state level Geographic Alliances, and working with the educational programs of state level Councils for the Humanities. Additional efforts should be undertaken to effectively take advantage of the opportunities offered by national level organizations through their conferences and publications.[6] The NFLRCs have been quite successful in working with state and national level foreign language associations in influencing important changes in foreign language curriculum and pedagogy. These endeavors stress inter-center collaboration and have national as well as local impact, and are important and should be encouraged.

· *Curricula and Textbooks.* In addition to resource collections a number of outreach programs have targeted their resources to the development and marketing of curricular modules in the social studies and humanities for different grade levels. Other centers have been involved in collaborative endeavors in the critical review of global studies textbooks.[7] Other programs have undertaken the task of publishing texts for K–12 educators.[8] Several outreach programs have produced short videos for teachers and students.[9] These endeavors are very commendable, but also very time-consuming, and beyond the scope of what many outreach programs are able to undertake.

· *Student-Oriented Activities.* Although many outreach programs will facilitate classroom presentations, most programs minimize these activities on the conviction that classroom presentations are very time-consuming and have minimal value in reaching teachers. However, there is a large body of anecdotal evidence that classroom presentations, particularly by international students, can have a tremendous impact on students.[10] Other programs have worked with extra-university groups in working with K–12 students in activities such as Model United Nations, Model Organization of American States, and Model Organization of African Unity. Centers that have worked with students in these fora have found these activities to be very rewarding. Moreover, there is considerable anecdotal evidence that a number of the students exposed to these programs have gone on to major in international studies in their undergraduate careers.

· *Foreign Language Instruction.* Some Title VI Centers have emphasized outreach to language teachers. This, of course, is particularly, but not exclusively, true of the NFLRCs. These initiatives have generally emphasized one of three curricular objectives. The NFLRCs have focused primarily in promoting curricular and pedagogy reform in the teaching of the more commonly taught foreign languages at the K–12 level: French, German, and Spanish. A number of Latin American and African programs have worked with teachers of Spanish and French to encourage the infusion of African and Latin American cultural studies into the teaching of French and Spanish respectively. Other Centers have worked with teachers of less commonly taught languages such as Arabic, Chinese, Japanese, and Swahili, among other languages which are taught in American high schools. Some of these centers have also sponsored Group Projects Abroad for foreign language teachers.

Outreach to Higher Education

In their reports to the IEGPS, most Title VI Centers indicate outreach activities which focus on faculty at institutions of higher learning. However, many of these activities are not exclusively outreach activities (e.g. special on-campus seminars, conferences, and events to which faculty from other institutions are invited). That is, many of these reported activities are not perceived by the centers as fulfilling outreach functions but are primarily valued for their contribution to other areas of scholarship.

There are however a number of Title VI Centers that are involved in outreach programming specifically oriented to faculty at institutions of higher learning. Many of these endeavors have been cross-regional and cross-thematic, resulting from collaboration of several area studies centers, international studies programs, CIBERs, and NFLRCs at the same or neighboring institutions. A number of such endeavors have focused on working with consortia of either liberal arts colleges or community colleges. Examples of collaborative endeavors will be noted below.

Specialized outreach to faculty at higher education institutions has focused on five activities/objectives:

- *Curriculum Development for Infusion of International Modules.* Many community colleges and small liberal arts colleges cannot offer regionally specific or even internationally focused courses in the humanities (literature, music, art, religious studies, etc.) or social sciences (history, anthropology, economics, geography, sociology, political science). Therefore outreach programs for college faculty often focus on developing the knowledge base and skills necessary to infuse international (including regional-specific) modules into existing undergraduate courses. A number of Title VI Centers co-sponsor curriculum development workshops and institutes for faculty. These institutes are often co-sponsored by one or more regional studies programs, CIBERs, and NFLRCs.[11]

  A number of CIBERs have initiated collaborative programs internationalizing business curricula for faculty at community and four-year colleges. It would be beneficial to explore ways in which Title VI NRCs can collaborate with individual or consortia of institutions that have been awarded Title VI Internationalizing Undergraduate Awards in order to develop programs to meet their international education objectives.

- *Internationalizing Campus and Student Life.* A number of Title VI programs collaborate with external consortia to assist in internationalizing campuses through the promotion of a variety of activities: visiting scholar programs; international/global festivals; international music and film series; and programs which facilitate international students from Title VI institutions to visit campuses which have little international presence.

- *Outreach to Local Communities.* Many small colleges, particularly community colleges, have a rich tradition of outreach to the local community. A number of Title VI outreach initiatives in higher education have focused on assisting smaller colleges to "internationalize" their community outreach activities. Such activities include facilitating community colleges' efforts to assist local businesses to take advantage of international business opportunities.

- *Scholarly Opportunities.* The most frequent outreach activities to scholars at smaller institutions are programs which allow faculty to take advantage of the superior resources at Title VI institutions to enhance their own scholarship. Programs for these colleagues include visiting fellow programs which allow individual scholars to carry their own scholarship to more formal seminars which provide specialized training.[12]

- *Teacher Education.* Given the emphasis the IEGPS and Title VI Centers have placed on outreach to K–12 schools and educators, it is surprising and disturbing that there have been limited attempts and fewer successes in internationalizing teacher education programs. In fact, even though there is a growing appreciation of the importance of educating a globally competent generation of Americans, the greater streamlining of teacher education programs has on occasion resulted in the removal of global education electives from the teacher education curriculum. It is vitally important that the IEGPS/USED and Title VI Centers explore ways in which they can actively engage teacher educators in the project of internationalizing K–12 education through incorporating global education in the teacher education curriculum.

Outreach to Community Groups
Most Title VI Centers have experience in working with various community groups in promoting international competency and understanding. For the most part these endeavors have not been systematic or part of an established effort (such as programs for K–12 educators). Rather, most area and international thematic centers have worked with local religious groups and civic organizations (Rotary, Lions, Kiwanis, etc.) in response to specific requests for information related to special international projects being undertaken by those organizations. For example, a church or civic organization may be involved in raising funds in support of an international project and may ask a Title VI Center to assist in providing background information on the region (or crisis) and perhaps to give advice on logistical issues.

Title VI Centers should assess the opportunities for outreach to community groups. Should these opportunities be given higher priority? Or is the effort too time-consuming for often limited results, which takes away from targeted outreach efforts at the regional and national levels?

Outreach to Businesses
Prior to the creation of CIBER programs most Title VI Centers did very little systematic outreach to the local, state, or national business community. This is due partially to the difficulty that centers staffed primarily with humanities and social science scholars have in accessing the business community. Moreover, there has often been a mutual discomfort, if not suspicion between the two communities which limited the contact between regional and thematic centers and the business community.

CIBER centers have not only filled this void but they have also drawn area Title VI Centers into outreach to the business community. CIBER seminars for the business community often feature area scholars who make presentations related to society, culture, and politics in the region(s) of focus in the seminar. For example, the CIBER at Michigan State University has involved faculty from the Canadian, Latin American/Caribbean, and Asian Centers in offering seminars on trading opportunities in Canada, Mexico, and Japan, Michigan's three largest international trading partners. The MSU-CIBER has also developed the nationally recognized International Business Academy. This innovative program brings together representatives from five to six mid-size Michigan businesses for monthly day-long sessions over a 15-week semester.

Outreach to the Press and Media

There is a strong consensus among Title VI Centers that the entertainment and news media share responsibility for both the lack of international competency among the American public and for the inchoate opinions and often egregious stereotypes held by many Americans.

Many of the Title VI Centers respond to requests from the news media on issues related to their regions of expertise. Unfortunately, communication between the international scholarly community and the popular news media is nearly non-existent. Ironically the advances in electronics which make possible instant TV access to the "remotest" parts of the world have enhanced the media's possibility of "parachute journalism,"[13] thereby reducing their need to consult international scholars.

An area of potential collaboration between Title VI Centers is the compilation of a comprehensive database of scholars with thematic, disciplinary and regional/country-specific expertise. An easily accessible database could be used by the news media (among other groups) to quickly identify scholars who could provide necessary background to the important international stories.[14] In addition, centers could encourage their faculty with relevant expertise to write unsolicited op-ed pieces on little-understood world events for submission to local and national media.[15]

The effects of the "Tarzan syndrome" in creating and reinforcing images held by Americans of Africans, Asians, and Latinos have been well documented. Consequently, more than a few of the Title VI regional centers have been involved in generating and disseminating reviews of films and videos related to their region.[16] These reviews, inter alia, provide educators at all levels with information which will enhance their ability to identify and select films and videos which are appropriate to the intended theme and audience.

Collaboration

Although there are numerous examples of exceptional outreach projects developed by individual Centers working on their own, many programs work collaboratively with other centers, pooling resources in an attempt to provide more effective service. Moreover, it is worth noting that IEGPS/USED has in recent years looked favorably on collaborative outreach endeavors.

Outreach collaboration has taken several forms:

- Joint programming between Title VI (or other non-federally funded) international centers (area studies, thematic, CIBERs, NFLRCs) at the same institution.[17]

- Cooperative programming between analogous centers. Many of the national and regional level seminars and workshops sponsored by Area Studies Centers, CIBERs, NFLRCs, and Undergraduate Centers are collaborative endeavors.

- Collaborative endeavors between Title VI Centers from different universities. While not common, there are examples of joint outreach efforts between Title VI Centers (across regions) at different institutions.[18]

IEGPS/USED, in its proposal guidelines for all international programs, emphasizes the importance of collaboration in outreach endeavors. There are numerous cogent arguments for such collaboration that deserve our attention:

- *Resources/Finance.* Outreach programs are competing with other legitimate activities of the Centers for scarce resources. Moreover, as indicated above, outreach has seldom been given pride of place in the Centers' goals and programs, with the consequence that their programs have had to operate on very limited resources. Collaborative programs between Centers at the same institution, regionally, or nationally, will enhance the capacity of outreach programs to develop and execute effective programming.

- *Regional and National Significance.* Even the most well-resourced, innovative, and effective outreach programs are severely limited by capacity to have a larger regional or national impact, be it on education (K–12 or higher education), the press, business, or public policy. However, well-conceived collaboration between centers has the potential of influence at the regional and national level. [The issue of national level outreach is discussed in greater detail below.]

- *Positive Response to the Challenge of "Globalism."* The issue of "globalism" (also referred to as "globalization") has impacted debates within the Title VI community.[19] The worst-case scenario would indicate a reduction of support for area studies with a corresponding increased emphasis on centers that focus on cross-regional international themes. Collaborative outreach activities co-sponsored by regional and thematic centers have the potential of providing perspective to this debate. Regionally focused or cross-regional seminars are not likely to persuade "globally oriented" clients of the importance of regional perspectives to global problems. However, collaborative outreach programs between thematic and regional centers have the potential to provide fora in which global issues can be explored comparatively in the framework of regional similarities, specificity, and exceptionalism. Such venues are not only vital to the agenda of regional centers but can also provide rigor and authenticity to the study of global themes.

Technology

Electronic and computer technology has the vast potential to radically change the structure of international outreach. The Internet and the World Wide Web provide the opportunity for Centers to share information and resources and provide consultation to "clients" locally, regionally, nationally and internationally. There are a number of examples of electronic international outreach which are instructive.

- *Outreach Web Sites.* By 1999, every Title VI NRC hosts its own Web site. Outreach programs should be central to this endeavor, providing information on outreach services, but also using the site as a means of offering outreach resources and materials (e.g. model curricula, teaching materials which can be down-loaded, etc.). A number of Title VI outreach programs have already developed exceptional Web sites that provide comprehensive services to educators, students, business persons, and the general public.[20] Web sites provide the potential for making local center resources available through digitization to a national and international audience.

- *List Serves.* A number of outreach programs are experimenting with discussion-oriented list serves for educators and other clients. Most outreach list serves are fairly restrictive in scope, bringing together a small group of educators. However, H-Net, the most comprehensive online resource for scholars, teachers and students in the humanities and social sciences, sponsors numerous international multi-disciplinary/regionally specific moderated list serves each with a corresponding Web site. H-Net is encouraging outreach programs from across the regions to develop their own moderated list serves that will be oriented to educators.[21]

Technology will provide the opportunity for modestly resourced outreach programs to provide state-of-the-art services to local, regional, national and international communities. The linking capabilities of the Internet will also encourage collaboration since each Center will not have to develop comprehensive databases but will be able to provide linkages to other institutions and programs which have specialized expertise or electronic holdings.

The Challenge of Multi-Area/Level Outreach: Local, Regional, National, and International

In response to comments from outside reviewers on the reasonableness of expecting Title VI Centers to engage in comprehensive outreach programming to local, regional, and national audiences, the "Federal Regulations for Higher Education Programs in Modern Foreign Language Training and Area Studies" (September, 1996) recorded that:

> The Secretary believes the proposed scope of outreach functions and their point allocations are sufficient to enable all applicant institutions to *demonstrate impact at the national and regional levels* (emphasis added). The Secretary also believes that it is appropriate to expect national Centers to engage in all three areas (education, business, media).[22]

The intent is clear that national centers are expected to engage in local/state, regional, and national level outreach. However, effective as opposed to token, multi-level outreach will necessitate, inter alia, an increased emphasis on and greater resources allocated to outreach on the part of centers. Increased emphasis on outreach, without a corresponding increase in resources, is likely to result in the proliferation of token programs that will have only minimal outreach impact.

Developing meaningful regional and national level outreach projects, given the realities of minimal resources, can be accomplished through the creative initiatives which take advantage of:

- *Use of External Funding Sources.* Outreach programs can take advantage of federal funding programs to develop regional and national level endeavors. For example, a number of Centers have received programmatic monies from Fund for the Improvement of Post-Secondary Education (FIPSE), Fulbright-Hays Group Projects Abroad, National Endowment for the Humanities (summer institutes and seminars for teachers or college faculty) and in collaboration with other institutions, Title VI Undergraduate International Studies and Foreign Language Programs.

  If outreach programming is to meet the challenges of the new century, we will need to look beyond traditional government-funded agencies of programmatic support. Outreach programs should actively engage the foundations (Ford, Kellogg, Mott, Rockefeller, Spencer, Pew, etc.) to support innovative programming.

- *Inter- and Intra-Institutional/Center Collaboration.* In order to develop effective programs that have regional and national impact, NRCs, CIBERs, NFLRCs, and Undergraduate Centers have increasingly emphasized collaborative outreach programming, seeking partners within their own institutions, with corresponding Centers at other institutions, and across thematic and regional areas.[23]

- *Collaborative Programming with Outreach Clients.* In addition to collaborating with other Centers, effective outreach can be done through developing collaborative (as opposed to "one-way") projects with potential outreach clients. For example, a number of Centers have co-sponsored Title VI Undergraduate International Studies and Foreign Language Programs to create programs which have integrated the resources of the Centers with a consortium of under-resourced institutions.[24]

  It should be noted that while such programs are carried out at the state or regional levels, they provide model projects and relationships which can and do have national significance.

- *Work with National Level Disciplinary and Cross-Disciplinary Organizations.* A number of Title VI Centers have worked closely with national level organizations such as the Global Forum and The National Association for the Social Studies in promoting an international agenda. Personnel from some centers have been involved in working with their national level disciplinary associations to facilitate national guidelines and recommendations for infusing international and regional studies into disciplinary curricula.[25]

· *Use of Technology/Internet.* Of limited expense, and in terms of breadth of dissemination, potentially the most effective method of outreach to local, regional, national and international clients is the use of the Internet. As indicated above, the effective use of the Internet will both necessitate and facilitate multiple levels of collaboration and "linkage" between the unique resources and offerings of cooperating Centers.

A word of caution may be advisable as Centers debate the question of prioritizing outreach efforts in terms of local, regional and national initiatives. Some outreach programming, such as services provided through a Web site, will service clients at all three levels. However, there are some types of programming that can only be done effectively at the local and/or state level, and these should not be automatically discounted in an effort to have regional or national impact in our outreach programming. For example:

· Given that education policy in the U.S. is a local district and to a lesser extent state function, outreach to K–12 educators is probably most effective when oriented to the district and state level. This of course does not negate the importance of developing instructional materials, audiovisuals, etc. that can be disseminated nationally. Nor is it an argument against sponsoring regional or national level institutes for K–12 teachers. But it should be recognized that while such programming is national in terms of its recruitment, it is local in terms of the impact. That is, teachers participating in national or regional level institutes will have minimal impact on national or even state educational policy, but they are likely to impact the internationalizing of teaching (be it foreign languages, language arts, or the social studies) within their own schools and districts.[26]

· Outreach directly to business communities is often most effective when done on a direct, "face-to-face" basis.[27] This is probably a truism, regardless of the potential clients, be they community groups, religious organizations, the media, etc.

Outreach programs which have the greatest impact at the national level may well be programs that are locally or regionally focused, but which serve as models for adoption nationally.

Additional Issues

This paper cannot address, even in minimal detail, all of the issues related to the development and administration of effective international outreach endeavors at Title VI Centers. In this final section I would like to briefly address a few issues for consideration:

· *Financing Outreach.* A strong argument can be made that given the importance of outreach, IEGPS, centers, and universities should allocate more funds to outreach endeavors. However, given the budgetary realties and the legitimate needs of other center activities, it is not realistic to expect higher levels of funding. Consequently, outreach programs, if they are to have impact, will have to actively seek alternative sources of funding. There are two methods of raising additional funds for outreach, which while promising are also problematic:

- *External Grants.* A number of outreach programs have received external funding for outreach programming. Grants can facilitate wonderful outreach initiatives,[28] and should be cautiously pursued. However, grant monies in outreach are usually for special programs and are not aimed at increasing the institutional capacity to do sustained outreach. Consequently, once the project is completed, there is usually no internal capacity to sustain the project. Moreover, grant seeking, writing, and subsequent administration demands a huge time commitment on the part of outreach professionals. Without adequate university/center commitment to outreach in terms of personnel, it is impossible to obtain and administer outreach grants.

- *Fee for Service.* In order to fund outreach activities, centers are increasingly offering outreach services on a fee-for-service basis. This system works very well in situations in which the "client" is anxious for the service and has the ability to pay for the service. CIBERs, for example, have been able to develop extensive and comprehensive programs for target members of the business community on a fee-for-service basis. Educators, on the other hand, at both the K–12 and undergraduate level, are frequently receptive to outreach initiatives, but are often unable to pay for the services rendered. Consequently, centers who have traditionally reached out to the educational community are faced with a dilemma of providing services to only those school districts or colleges which are able to pay for services, and discontinuing services to less-resourced institutions.

- *Outreach to Local, State, and National Government Agencies.* A number of CIBER centers, at times in association with area studies centers, have developed innovative linkages with state level international business offices, providing consultation on international trade.[29] Area studies centers, however, have been less successful in engaging state and local agencies which have international responsibilities. In this age of "globalization" it is imperative that governmental agencies, which have responsibility for establishing and administering international policy, have access to the tremendous expertise that resides within the associated faculty of Title VI Centers. Serious exploration of ways in which we constructively engage these agencies should be a priority of Title VI Centers.

- *Niche or "Targeted" Outreach.* The current reality in most Title VI Centers proscribes multi-level and multiple outreach endeavors. Some Centers have attempted to engage in numerous outreach endeavors even though they do not have adequate human or financial resources to adequately support them. Consequently, the majority of the attempted programs do not succeed, leaving a negative "aftertaste," both to the client and to the center staff, with the unintentional consequence of reinforcing negative attitudes towards outreach.

A more positive strategy for a center where outreach is under-staffed and under-funded would be to develop an outreach niche for the Center and target resources to this activity. Such a strategy is likely to result in positive outreach experiences that can be used as capital to slowly invest in an expanding outreach program.

· *Outreach to "Non-Traditional" Clients.* With the exception of CIBERs, which have a natural client in the business community, and NFLRCs, which have a target outreach clientele among foreign language teachers, Title VI Centers have not attempted to service communities with which they may have a thematic or regional connection. Area studies centers, the largest set of Title VI institutions, for example, have not attempted to cultivate relationships within the U.S. ethnic or "heritage" communities whose ancestors (distant and immediate) migrated from the regions they study.

I would suggest that while our mandate stipulates that we provide outreach programming to all U.S. communities, regardless of ethnic or regional heritage, it would be mutually beneficial to explore fuller linkages with these communities.[30] In addition to providing scholarly affirmation for the richness of their history and sociocultural heritage, such linkages have the potential of developing important grassroots (at local and national level) support for National Resource Centers.

Another important population which has not been traditionally serviced by the outreach endeavors of Title VI Centers are Americans who live in rural areas. Computer technology as it becomes more readily available in rural areas will provide a medium through which centers can provide service to these communities. However, technology alone is not sufficient. Centers, particularly those at land-grant universities, should explore opportunities to collaborate with existing university-based structures of outreach such as 4-H Clubs, and university-based state extension services.[31]

· *Outreach through Continuing Education Programming.* Most universities which host Title VI Centers have continuing education programs which provide off-campus credit courses for "non-traditional" students. International centers should explore the possibility of offering international and foreign language courses to this growing community of adult students.[32]

Conclusion

Within the greater Title VI community there is a clear and strong consensus that the U.S. is not adequately prepared to meet the economic (competitiveness and sustainable development), political (security, democratization, and peacekeeping), social (meeting and maintaining an adequate standard of living), and cultural (sociocultural fissures, "universalization of knowledge") challenges of globalization. This consensus further recognizes that the academy has a central role to play and a social responsibility to address this need.

Traditionally the academy has confronted societal crises and needs through the production and dissemination of knowledge necessary to ameliorate problems. Internationalists within U.S. academies feel confident that provided adequate resources we can bring to bear our considerable intellectual resources to address the challenges of globalization through research (producing new knowledge), graduate education (training new internationally competent researchers), and undergraduate education (training globally competent citizens). However, to adequately prepare U.S. citizens, businesses, educators, and institutions of the state (local, state, national level) and civil society to face the challenges and take advantage of the opportunities of globalization, it will be imperative for internationalists within the academy to reach out beyond the traditional confines of scholarship.

As argued above, the challenges of globalization provide the academy with an obligation and an opportunity to re-connect with the public through the effective provision of outreach services which will assist individual Americans, as well as institutions in the private, civil, and public sectors, to develop the level of global competency necessary to realize international security and prosperity.

NOTES

1. March 10, 2000. This is not an indictment of the marvelous community services provided by humanities and social science units through university-based museums, music programs, and distinguished lecture series, etc.

2. *University Outreach at Michigan State University: Extending Knowledge to Serve Society.* (A Report by the Provost's Committee on University Outreach, October, 1993, p. 1.)

3. Ernest Lynton, "Scholarship Recognized." (Unpublished manuscript submitted to the Carnegie Foundation for the Advancement of Teaching, 1992.)

4. There are numerous examples of this alienation between public-funded academies and the public. One of the most troubling examples is the apparent strong public support for attempts in the Minnesota State Legislature to reform the tenure system and structure at Minnesota's public universities.

5. Ernest Boyer, *Scholarship Reconsidered: Priorities of the Professoriate.* (Princeton: Princeton University Press for the Carnegie Foundation for the Advancement of Teaching, 1990, p. 13.)

6. A number of regional outreach councils, for example, have edited special regionally/globally focused editions of *Social Studies,* the monthly journal of the National Council for the Social Studies.

7. The Middle East Studies Association Outreach Council has completed a comprehensive review of social studies textbooks; the South Asian Studies Association and the Outreach Council of the African Studies Association are undertaking a similar review.

8. The South East Asian Studies Center at Columbia University, for example, has coordinated the publication of a number of resource books for teachers.

9. For example, the outreach program of the African Studies Program at Boston University has produced an excellent video which introduces Africa and challenges commonly held stereotypes.

10. Consequently, a number of programs are involved in collaborative efforts which facilitate presentations by international students in K–12 classrooms. For example, the African, Asian, and Latin American centers at Michigan State University assist a locally based group, Community Volunteers in International Programs, to recruit and train international students for classroom presentations. Similarly, at Indiana University, eight area studies centers collaboratively support the Global Speakers Service, which arranges for international students and scholars to speak at schools and civic organizations.

11. At Michigan State University, three Title VI Centers (African Studies Center, Center for Latin American and Caribbean Studies, and the Center for the Advanced Study of International Development) have collaborated in several outreach programs to four- and two-year colleges. The most extensive of these is the Michigan International Development Education Outreach Network (MIDEON) which administers a variety of outreach programs to faculty from 21 participating liberal arts and community colleges.

12. A number of regional and international Title VI Centers have had programs which facilitate visiting faculty research. An example of this type of specialized training is the CICALS Program (Consortium for Inter-Institutional Collaboration in African and Latin American Studies), a collaborative outreach endeavor by the Michigan State University College of Arts and Letters, African Studies Center, Center for Latin American and Caribbean Studies, and three college consortia (Great Lakes Colleges Association, Association of Mid-Western Colleges, and 19 Historically Black Colleges and Universities). CICALS programming has brought consortia faculty to MSU each summer for a four-week intensive language program in either Portuguese or one of three African languages (Amharic, Swahili, Shona). The following summer these scholars participate in a four-to-six-week research project in one of the language areas—Brazil, Ethiopia, Kenya, or Zimbabwe.

13. This term refers to the tendency of the U.S. press to (a) cover only crises in developing areas, and (b) with little background, "parachute" into the troubled areas to bring an instant interpretation of the crisis to the American public.

14. This could be an activity promoted by the outreach councils of the area studies associations.

15. For example, during the recent crisis in the Great Lakes region of East Africa, a number of Africanist experts on this region submitted detailed but accessible analyses of the crisis.

16. The Middle East Studies Association has sponsored a project which has systematically reviewed many of the feature and documentary films which focus on this region. Similarly, the *Africa Media Program,* housed in the MSU African Studies Center, is undertaking the systematic review of many of the feature and documentary films on Africa which are available in the United States. These reviews will soon be accessible on the AMP Web site.

17. For example, the international programs at the University of Illinois publish a joint newsletter to teachers. At Michigan State University, the African Studies Center, the Center for Latin American and Caribbean Studies, and the Center for Advanced Study of International Development have collaborated in outreach programming to both K–12 and higher education. In addition they have cooperated with the MSU CIBER in outreach endeavors to both businesses and college faculty. There are many other examples of this type of systematic cooperation between Title VI Centers at the same institution.

18. For example, in Michigan there has been programmatic cooperation between Title VI Centers at MSU (Africa and Latin America) and the University of Michigan (Middle East and Asia-S.E. and Japan). Moreover, the outreach coordinators of these institutions work together in lobbying the Michigan State Department of Education on issues relating to international/global education.

19. See Stanley Heginbotham, "Rethinking International Scholarship: The Challenge of Transition from the Cold War Era," *Items* [Social Science Research Council] 48, nos. 2–3 (1994), and Kenneth Prewitt's address to the Title VI directors in Sante Fe (November 1996).

20. For example MSU's CIBER program has developed a very comprehensive Web site on international business which is widely used by businesses nationally and internationally. The African Studies Program at the University of Pennsylvania has the most comprehensive outreach site currently available; it is accessed by thousands of clients each week.

21. H-AfrTeach, cosponsored by the Africa outreach programs of Boston University and Michigan State University, has been on-line since 1998. H-Asia/Teachers, and H-Latin America/Teachers should be operational by 2000. These list serves will provide educators with the opportunity to seek advice and to share curricular/teaching ideas and the associated Web sites will provide educators with a comprehensive menu of regional-specific resources.

22. *Federal Register* (vol. 61, no. 186, Tuesday, September 24, 1996, p. 50193).

23. An example of outreach collaboration across thematic areas is the joint programming in developing "business" language skills in which some CIBERs and NFLRCs are involved. For example, MSU's CIBER and NFLRC are involved in developing German "business" language skills among U.S. business persons and business majors.

24. For example, MIDEON (see footnote 11), a consortium of MSU (CASID, ASC, CLACs) and 20 Michigan community and four-year colleges, received a Title VI Undergraduate grant, 1993–1996.

25. For example, see Sven Groennings and David Wiley (eds.), *Group Portrait: Internationalizing the Disciplines.* (New York: The American Forum for Global Education, 1990).

26. Again, this is not an argument against working at the state and national levels, say through disciplinary organizations, such as the national (or state level) Council for Social Studies, to promote internationalizing of the curricula. Such outreach endeavors can be effective, but research on teaching strongly suggests that successful changes in teaching are most easily achieved through direct contact with teachers (long-term in service and institutes).

27. An example of this is the nationally recognized International Business Academy sponsored by MSU-CIBER. This innovative program brings together representatives from five to six mid-size Michigan businesses for monthly day-long sessions over a semester. This program, while certainly a national model, is effective only at the state or local level.

28. Examples of externally funded outreach endeavors are listed earlier in the text.

29. For example, the MSU-CIBER, with assistance from the MSU Center for Latin American and Caribbean Studies, has worked closely with the International Trade Office of the Michigan Department of Commerce in promoting trade relations with Mexico.

30. This suggestion in no way negates our obligation to do outreach to the wider American community. Indeed, for almost all regions represented by Title VI NRCs, the "majority" culture desperately needs a clearer understanding and appreciation of Africa, Asia, Latin America, etc.

31. David Hansen, Associate Dean of Agriculture, The Ohio State University, for example, is very keen on exploring ways in which Title VI Centers can provide services to rural communities through collaboration with university-based outreach structures, such as extension services.

32. For example, Robert Lapiner, Dean of Continuing Education at UCLA, orally indicated that UCLA offers a wide variety of international and language courses to nontraditional students through their continuing education program. He indicated that in developing these courses he has worked closely with the faculty of the international centers at UCLA.

Changing U.S. Business Needs for International Expertise

*Richard W. Moxon, Elizabeth A. C. O'Shea,
Mollie Brown, and Christoffer M. Escher*

Abstract

This paper presents the results of a survey of over one hundred U.S. corporations
and twenty business schools. The goal was to discover whether the needs of businesses are changing as a result of trends in the global business environment. The
study finds that (1) international business is expected to grow rapidly over the
next decade; (2) the emerging markets of Asia, Latin America, and the former
Soviet Union are becoming more important for U.S. companies; (3) small companies and service industry firms increasingly require international expertise;
(4) companies see the need for improvements in their level of expertise; and (5)
they also seek improvements in university programs. Similar to previous studies,
the survey finds that (1) there is only a limited need for U.S. nationals to fill
positions in overseas offices; and (2) little value is given to people with language
and cross-cultural skills unless they also have business skills, overseas experience, and interpersonal skills. The survey raises questions as to whether universities and Title VI are overemphasizing certain aspects of international education
and underemphasizing others.

Reprinted with permission, International Studies and Overseas Programs (ISOP), University
of California, Los Angeles, California, from the publication *International Studies Education in the
New Global Era: Proceedings of a National Policy Conference on the Higher Education Act,* 1998.

Introduction

The purpose of this study is to investigate the needs of U.S. firms for international expertise. The global environment has been transformed over the last decade by geopolitical and technological changes. This paper used a survey that intended to examine how these changes have affected the international staffing and educational needs of business and to project future needs.

The paper begins by reviewing major changes in global business and their potential implications for the demand for different international skills. Then the results of a survey of over one hundred businesses and twenty business schools are presented. Finally, the paper looks at the implications of the survey for university programs and for Title VI program priorities.

Trends in Global Business

Global Integration

Economies have become far more integrated during the last decade, and this trend promises to continue. Global competition is pervasive, affecting industries and firms that never before were concerned with international markets or competition. Global and regional trade pacts have linked economies and made it more feasible for companies to approach international business with a set of globally similar products and approaches. At the same time, U.S. style business education has spread around the world, with the result that U.S. companies can hire foreign managers who have the equivalent of U.S. business degrees.

These trends suggest on the one hand a growing need for international expertise as global markets expand. They also suggest the need for people who can work across borders to transfer best practices among different national affiliates. Multinational teams will become more common, and more people will travel internationally. Many managers must be ready to work internationally. On the other hand, there may be less need for expatriates to be sent abroad on long-term assignments.

Electronic Communications Revolution

Low cost electronic communications by phone, fax, and electronic mail are making global messaging pervasive. In the past, phone and fax costs limited personal communication to important matters. Now more and more people are able to communicate daily about relatively less important issues. And while most international communications used to be by international specialists—managers in the international departments of businesses, for example—today many others are involved.

This trend may accelerate the dominance of English in international business. Certainly a relatively smaller proportion of the U.S. nationals engaged in international business communications will be expected to have foreign language proficiency.

Emerging Markets

The most important international business developments of the last decade are the integration of the formerly socialist economies into the global economy, and the liberalization of trade and investment in the developing world. These "emerging markets" have augmented the global economic arena, and can be expected to continue to lead growth in international business. Since these countries tend to have business systems and cultures that are relatively unfamiliar to U.S. nationals, the demand for specialized international expertise may be expected to grow. On the other hand, their adoption of more market-oriented policies reduces the "exotic" nature of these economies, suggesting that country-specific expertise may be less necessary for success.

New Global Players

Globalization and the liberalization of trade and investment in emerging markets have drawn more companies and new industries into international business. Many service industries that had been minor participants in global business, especially telecommunications, energy, and other infrastructure industries, are now aggressively expanding. And many more small firms are finding that they are able to participate in the global economy. These trends suggest a growing demand for international expertise, but also that new kinds of international know-how may be needed.

Questions

Based on these perceptions regarding the changing needs for international expertise, a survey was designed to examine the following questions:

- Is there a growing need for international expertise by U.S. companies?

The authors wish to thank the CIBERS at the following universities for their cooperation in conducting this survey:

Brigham Young University/University of Utah
Columbia University
Florida International University
Georgia Institute of Technology
Indiana University
Michigan State University
Ohio State University
Purdue University
Rutgers, State University of New Jersey
San Diego State University

Texas A&M University
University of California, Los Angeles
University of Colorado at Denver
University of Connecticut
University of Hawaii at Manoa
University of Illinois at Urbana-Champaign
University of Memphis
University of Michigan
University of Pittsburgh
University of Southern California
University of Texas at Austin

Figure 1. Number of International Business
Survey Respondents by State (109)

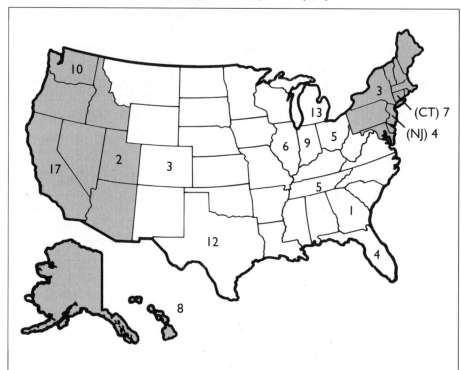

- What is the nature of international expertise required by U.S. companies?
- What is the relative importance of different types of expertise?
- Are companies able to find the kinds of expertise they need, and how are U.S. universities doing in supplying the needed expertise?

Survey Design and Participants

Survey Administration
The design and administration of the survey was coordinated by the Center for International Business Education and Research (CIBER) at the University of Washington. A total of twenty-one other CIBERs participated in the project. Each participating CIBER administered the survey questionnaire to businesses in its region and to faculty and staff at its university.

A total of 129 business questionnaires were completed. Of these, 109 were completed by managers responsible for some aspect of the international business

Table 1. Number of International Business Respondents

Company Size	Service Companies	Manufacturing Companies	Total
Small	20	16	36
Medium	15	13	28
Large	21	24	45
Total	56	53	109

for the companies. In many cases, the questionnaire was completed by the head of international sales or business. Another 20 questionnaires were completed by a member of the company's human resources department. It is important to note that in this paper only the responses of the international business managers are reported. It was found that many questionnaires from the human resource managers were incomplete, perhaps reflecting their relative unfamiliarity with the company's international business. This may be an important finding in itself, exhibiting some disconnection between international operations and hiring needs.

A total of 46 business school questionnaires were completed, 31 of which were from faculty, and 15 from career services professionals. We had intended to compare the career services responses with their corporate human resource counterparts. However, because we could not use the responses from the human resource professionals, the responses from business school career officials were inapplicable. Thus, only the business school faculty responses are reported in this paper.

Business Respondents

The map in Figure 1 shows the geographic distribution of international business respondents, and Table 1 shows the distribution by company size and industry sector. The intent of the survey was to achieve a balance of responses geographically and by size and sector. The concern was not to achieve a statistically representative sample of all U.S. companies, or even all companies engaged in international business. It seemed important to examine whether there were significant differences among sectors and sizes of firms, and for that purpose a balanced sample was preferred.

The purpose of the survey was to assess the perceptions of U.S. managers of firms with experience in the international market, rather than to get a representative sample of all U.S. companies. Figure 2 shows that international sales in the surveyed companies represented an average of over 36 percent of total sales. While there was great variety in the importance of international business, all companies had some international operations, and for many, international sales represented over half their total sales. Table 2 shows that companies of all sizes and in all sectors had a high average level of international sales. The sample of companies included companies that were mainly exporters, as well as companies whose international sales came mostly from overseas plants or offices.

Figure 2. International Sales: Percent of Total Sales

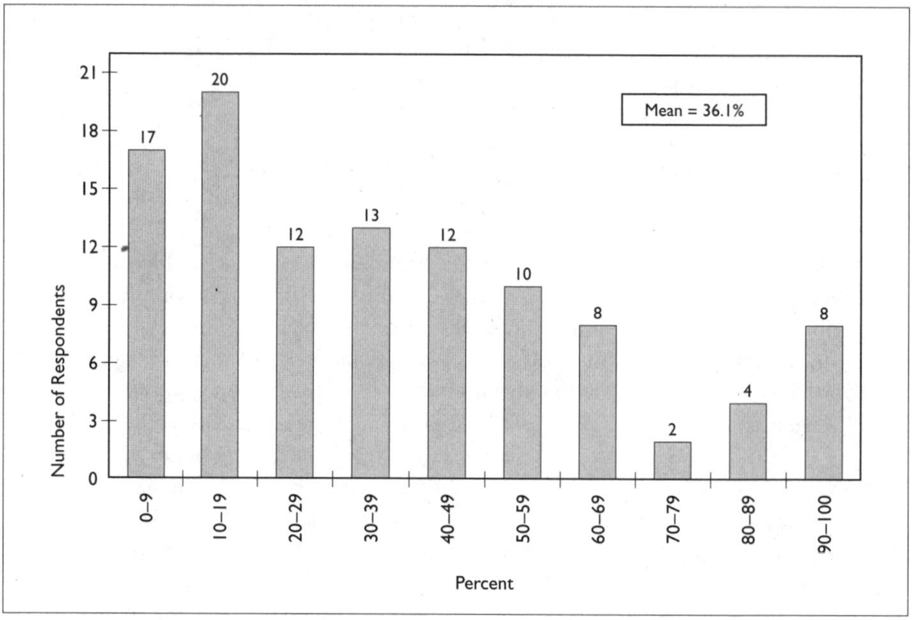

The business respondents had a relatively high level of international experience, as shown in Table 3. The average rating of 2.6 is on a scale in which 3.0 represents extensive international travel, living, or work. On the other hand, the self-reported foreign language proficiency of the business respondents was not very high, as shown in Table 4. The average rating of 2.0 represents only modest ability in one or more foreign languages.

Survey Results

What did the business respondents say about their future needs for international expertise? The survey asked them about the overall expected growth of international sales and staffing, about the relative importance of different regions and countries, about the relative value of different kinds of expertise in their international operations, and about the need for improvement of international expertise in their companies.

Growth of International Business

The majority of companies reported that international business is expected to grow strongly over the next decade and to assume a much greater importance within their firms. Figure 3 shows the breakdown of responses. Recognizing that

Table 2. International Sales: Percent of Total Sales

Company Size	Service Companies	Manufacturing Companies	Total
Small	52.9	34.1	44.6
Medium	21.9	34.0	28.0
Large	26.8	40.5	34.0
Total	35.3	36.9	36.1

Table 3. International Experience of Respondents (averages)

Company Size	Service Companies	Manufacturing Companies	Total
Small	2.7	2.7	2.7
Medium	2.2	2.6	2.4
Large	2.7	2.5	2.6
Total	2.5	2.6	2.6

Scale: 1 = none/very little; 2 = some; 3 = extensive.

Table 4. Foreign Language Skills of Respondents (averages)

Company Size	Service Companies	Manufacturing Companies	Total
Small	2.3	1.5	1.9
Medium	1.7	2.1	1.9
Large	1.9	2.6	2.3
Total	2.0	2.1	2.0

Scale: 1 = little or none; 2 = some; 3 = considerable; 4 = great.

Figure 3. Future Importance of International Business

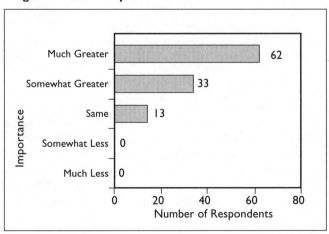

Table 5. Expected Change in Number of Managers Abroad (averages)

Company Size	Service Companies	Manufacturing Companies	Total
Small	7.1	6.9	7.0
Medium	6.8	7.2	7.0
Large	7.7	7.4	7.5
Total	7.2	7.2	7.2

Scale: 1 = great decrease; 3 = some decrease; 5 = no change; 7 = some increase; 9 = great increase.

Table 6. Expected Change in Number of Domestic Managers in International Business (averages)

Company Size	Service Companies	Manufacturing Companies	Total
Small	6.7	6.7	6.7
Medium	7.0	6.0	6.5
Large	6.8	6.3	6.5
Total	6.8	6.3	6.6

Scale: 1 = great decrease; 3 = some decrease; 5 = no change; 7 = some increase; 9 = great increase.

these companies are already relatively international, this result indicates that international sales may represent well over half of total sales for many more survey companies in the future. This has obvious implications for the need for international expertise.

The expected international sales growth is reflected in the future managerial staffing needs of the survey companies. As shown in Tables 5 and 6, companies expect an increase in the number of managers in foreign offices and in the domestic side of their international business. The expected increases do not differ greatly among firms of different sizes or business sectors.

Growth of Emerging Markets
Companies were asked about the current importance and projected importance of different world regions to their business. The results are shown in Figure 4. As expected, the most important current markets are those of Western Europe, Japan, and North America (Mexico and Canada). Companies expect all markets to increase in importance over the next decade, but some much more than others. The greatest increases are expected for the emerging markets of East and Central Europe, the Former Soviet Union, China, India, East and Southeast Asia, Brazil, and

Figure 4. Current and Future Importance of Selected Countries and Regions

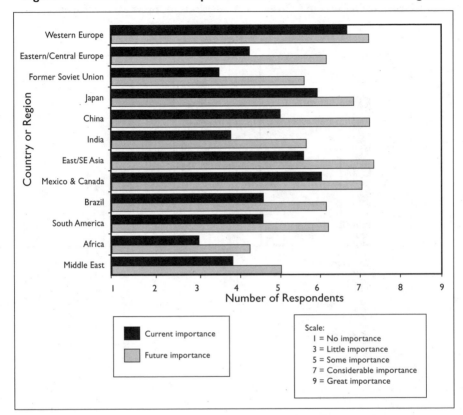

the rest of South America. All areas except Africa are expected to reach a level of "some importance" over the next decade. This indicates that international business managers are taking the emerging market phenomenon seriously and see great potential in these countries.

Staffing of International Positions

How will U.S. companies staff their overseas and U.S. offices? To what extent will companies rely on foreign nationals versus U.S. nationals to manage their international business? Figure 5 confirms the often reported trend towards "localization" of the key management positions in foreign offices. But the survey also reveals that most companies will continue to send some U.S. expatriates to foreign offices and that some firms will rely mostly on U.S. expatriates for key positions.

Figure 5. Future Staffing of Key Management Positions in Foreign Offices

Figure 6. Future Staffing of Domestic Positions in International Business

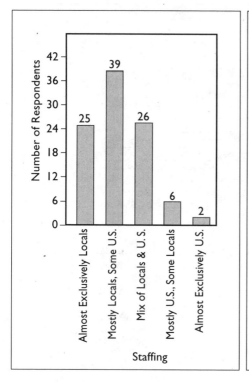

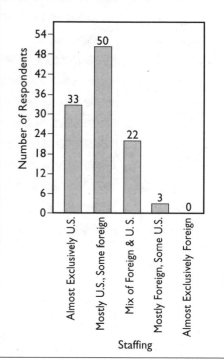

Most firms expect to rely on U.S. nationals for the staffing of most domestic positions in international business, but they also expect a considerable mixing of foreign nationals. The multicultural home office is becoming a reality for many companies, as shown in Figure 6.

Importance of International Expertise
The heart of the survey focused on the perceptions of international business managers regarding what kinds of expertise are needed in the management of international operations. For this part of the survey, the perceptions of international business faculty are also reported for comparison. The results are reported in Figures 7 and 8, which focus first on the managers in overseas offices and then on managers in the domestic side of international operations. In both graphs, the first five items along the left side represent "international" skills, while the last three represent "general" skills which are not specifically international.

Figure 7. Importance of Skills for U.S. Managers Abroad

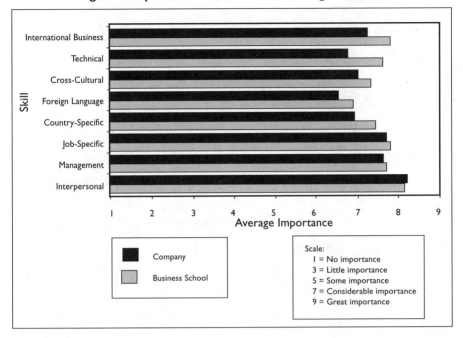

Looking first at Figure 7, there is general agreement between managers and faculty about the relative importance of different skills for managers in overseas offices. The faculty rate the "international" skills slightly higher in importance, which is understandable since the respondents are teaching international courses. The second observation is that the "general" skills—job-specific, general management, and interpersonal—are rated higher than "international" skills. But all skills are seen as important; all are ranked well above "some importance." Foreign language proficiency received the lowest average rating, but it was still seen as between "some" and "considerable" importance.

Figure 8 shows many of the same conclusions for the domestic side of international operations. Again, the faculty and managers are in agreement and the "general" skills are rated as most important. Foreign language and country-specific skills are rated as less important for international managers in the U.S. offices, but both are still seen as having at least "some" importance.

There was broad agreement in the perceived importance of different types of expertise among managers in companies of different sizes and in different sectors. For this reason these results are not reported in detail in this paper. One exception was the perceived importance of foreign language in the domestic po-

Figure 8. Importance of Skills for Domestic Positions in International Business

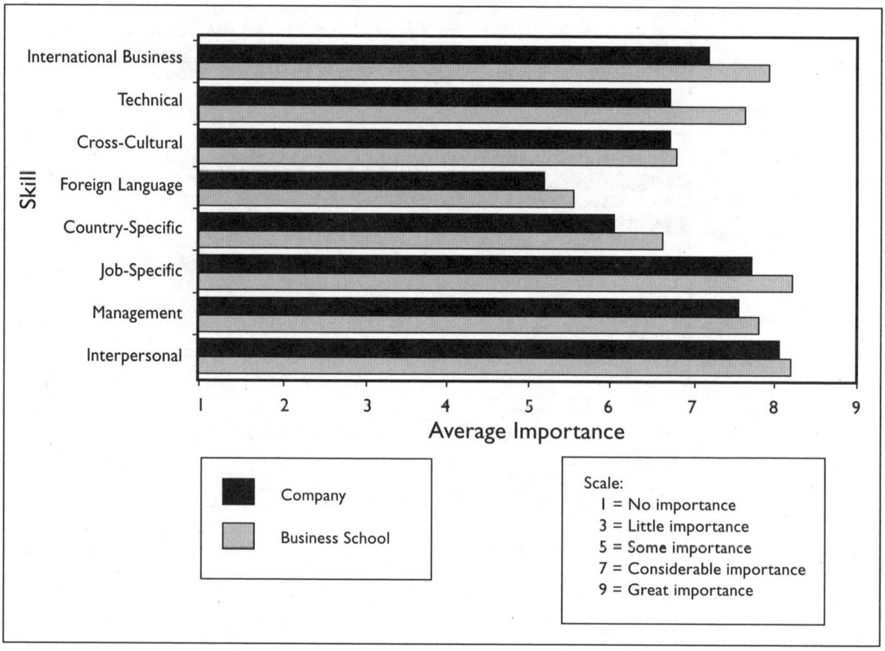

Table 7. Importance of Foreign Language Skills for Domestic Positions in International Business

Company Size	Service Companies	Manufacturing Companies	Total
Small	5.5	5.7	5.6
Medium	5.3	5.5	5.4
Large	5.1	4.5	4.8
Total	5.3	5.1	5.2

Scale: 1 = none; 3 = little; 5 = some; 7 = considerable; 9 = great.

sitions in international business, as shown in Table 7. Small companies rate foreign language proficiency as more important. This is understandable given that such managers tend to be in direct contact with foreign customers and distributors, whereas in large companies the domestic managers often interact with a company-owned sales office abroad with English-speaking managers.

Figure 9. Improvement Needed in Companies' International Expertise

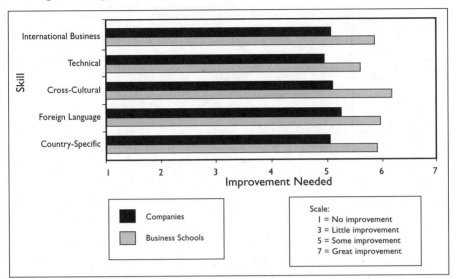

Needed Improvements in Business and University Programs

The survey revealed few dramatic results regarding the needed improvement in the international expertise of companies and the international programs of universities. Figure 9 shows that business managers see the need for "some improvement" in international expertise across the board, with no distinct pattern of where the weaknesses are greatest. The faculty are somewhat more critical, seeing greater need for improvements in U.S. companies.

Similarly, as shown in Figure 10, business managers report "some difficulty" in finding U.S. nationals with various kinds of international expertise, with no clear pattern of where the weaknesses are most salient. Finally, Figure 11 shows that both managers and faculty agree that "some improvement" is needed in university programs, with the faculty again slightly more critical.

Other Comments from Business Respondents

The survey asked business respondents for open-ended comments on the topics included in the survey. While the number of such comments was limited, three types of comments were most common, and add to the analysis reported in the tables above:

- **Real international business experience is most valuable.** Businesses express some skepticism about the value of coursework without firsthand overseas experience. They see foreign study and internships as some of the most

Figure 10. Difficulty in Finding U.S. Nationals with International Experience

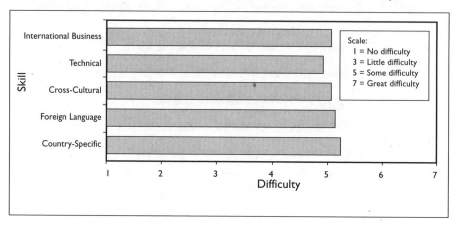

valuable ways that universities can help students acquire international expertise.

- **More graduates need to be globally aware.** Managers often said that all graduates and employees need a global mindset, and that they found that U.S. graduates tended to be less globally minded than foreign nationals. One manager expressed this as "local nationals will run our overseas offices, but everyone at home needs global sensitivity."

- **Student projects with companies are valuable.** Managers report good experiences in working with U.S. business students on projects related to international business. These projects often involve student groups working with small companies to research foreign markets. Managers seem to value this form of university-business interaction.

Conclusions and Implications

Survey Conclusions
Summarizing the findings reported above, the most important conclusions of this survey are:

- International business is expected to increase in importance, and with it the need for managerial staff with international expertise.

- The emerging markets of Asia, Latin America, Eastern Europe, and the Former Soviet Union are expected to increase dramatically in importance. This implies the need for greater expertise in these regions, their cultures, and languages.

Figure 11. Improvement Needed by U.S. Universities in Providing International Expertise

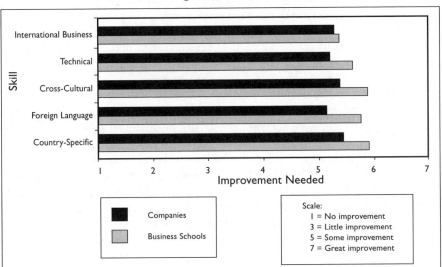

- Many small companies and companies in the services sector are increasingly active in international markets and require international expertise.

- Companies need more managers with global awareness and cultural sensitivity, even if they will not be sent abroad.

- There is limited demand or perceived value for U.S. nationals with language and country-specific expertise unless these are combined with job-specific, management, and interpersonal skills.

Comparison to Previous Surveys

This survey is the latest of several studies in recent years that have looked at the global education needs of U.S. business. While each study has had a slightly different focus, the conclusions of the study presented here are similar to those of previous studies.

Kobrin (1984) surveyed international managers of large U.S. firms to find out what kind of international expertise was perceived as important to success in international business. As in our survey, he found that mangers valued many kinds of expertise, but that people skills were most important. Country knowledge was rated relatively low in importance, but general adaptability and sensitivity to national differences was seen as important. However, managers felt that this general international adaptability was based more on personality than on education. International expertise was perceived as useless without being combined with other management expertise. Like our survey, Kobrin found that foreign language proficiency was seen as an important plus, but not the key success determinant.[1]

Bikson and Law (1994) looked at a small sample of large multinational companies, mostly U.S. based, to analyze the factors contributing to high work performance in a globally oriented firm. Like our study and Kobrin's, they found that the general skills—cognitive and social—as well as personal traits, were rated as most important. Cross-cultural experience and language received the lowest ratings. Cross-cultural competence was seen as important, but colleges could best contribute to this by providing overseas experiences. Interestingly, companies reported that careers were seen as "potentially international." In other words, many of the people being hired out of college would end up working internationally, but it was difficult to predict who they would be when first hired.

CAFLIS (1989) surveyed 99 U.S. companies, mostly large manufacturers, regarding their need for global competence. Global competence was seen as becoming more important. Like other studies, general international understanding and cultural skills were seen as more important than foreign language ability. Language and cultural understanding were not seen per se as criteria for promotion.

Caveats on Survey Results

While the findings of this survey agree in most respects with previous studies, it should be noted that all surveys must be interpreted with caution. The results here are reported as averages, but companies do not generally hire average people. For example, the fact that on average foreign language proficiency is not rated as highly as other attributes does not mean that for some positions it is not extremely important, and may be an absolute requirement. And while it is clear that language and other international expertise is not valued highly unless managers also have other functional/technical expertise, these international capabilities can set a person apart from others whose capabilities are similar in other respects.

Implications for Title VI

Keeping in mind the caveats above, the results of this survey raise some issues related to the relative emphasis that university programs and Title VI funding give to creating different types of international expertise. These are posed here as a set of questions.

Are we overemphasizing

- the creation of international specialists (e.g., area specialists, international business majors)?

- the needs of large companies?

- the traditional markets of Western Europe, Japan, and North America?

- language training and country-specific knowledge?

Are we underemphasizing

- the creation of basic global understanding and awareness for all students?

- the needs of small companies?

- the emerging markets of the world, especially Asia, Latin America, Eastern and Central Europe, and the former Soviet Union?

- overseas experience through foreign study programs and internships?

- the linkage of international expertise to professional skills, and vice versa?

- midcareer training for managers who did not realize when they were students that they would be involved in international business?

These questions are worth debating as we adapt our programs to the needs of U.S. business for the global environment of the twenty-first century.

NOTE

1. Kobrin found that managers proficient in a foreign language rated language proficiency more highly. In the present survey, however, we found no important difference in the rating of foreign language importance based on the respondent's own proficiency.

REFERENCES

Bikson, T. K., and S. A. Law. 1994. *Global Preparedness and Human Resources: College and Corporate Perspectives*. Santa Monica, CA: RAND.
CAFLIS (Coalition for the Advancement of Foreign Languages and International Studies). 1989. *Spanning the Gap: Toward a Better Business and Education Partnership for International Competence*. Washington, DC: CAFLIS.
Kobrin, Stephen J. 1984. *International Expertise in American Business: How to Learn to Play with the Kids on the Street*. New York, NY: Institute of International Education.

Companies

The authors wish to acknowledge the following companies who completed surveys for this paper.

Small Companies (under 500 employees)

Service

ALK Associates
Altoon & Porter Architects
American Collegiate Marketing
Architects Hawaii, Ltd.
Braxton Associates
Cogna International Investment
  Advisors, Ltd.
Desktop Solutions, Inc.
ERS International
Information Management Consultants,
  Inc.
Intercontinental Asset Management
  Group, Inc.
International Legal Group, P.C.
KFC Airport, Inc.
Kroll Associates
Mechanical Dynamics, Inc.
RDA Group of Companies
Tele-Communications International, Inc.
Transacta Realty, Inc.
Walter Group
Wide Fountains International
Wimberly Allison Tong & Goo

Manufacturing

Ansonia Copper & Brass
Bauer Howden
Bry-Air, Inc.
Centigram
Cortelco
Decatur Electronics, Inc.
Dynamo, Ltd.
Flame Technologies
K&W Products
K. Swiss
Maxon Corporation
McGillis Products
Mensor Corporation
Shepherd Color Company
Thomas L. Green & Co.
Varlen Instruments, Inc.

Medium Companies (500–4,999 employees)

Service

Access Graphics
BHP Hawaii
Ducks Unlimited, Inc.
Earth Tech
Experian Corporation
First American National Bank
Imperial Bank
Latham & Watkins
MBI, Inc.
Personnall Decisions International
Spencer Stuart
Wang's International, Inc.

Manufacturing

Acer Latin America
Anchor Industries, Inc.
C&M Corp.
Caterpillar Large Engine Center
Easton, Inc.
Holophane Corporation
Instrumentation Laboratory
Kinetic Concepts, Inc.
Maxell Corporation of America
Mettler-Toledo, Inc.
Robinson Nugent, Inc.
Servco Pacific, Inc.
Varco Pruden Building
Varlen Corp.

Large Companies (over 5,000 employees)

Service	Manufacturing
Airborne Express	3M
Ameritech	Beckman Instruments, Inc.
Andersen Consulting	Boeing Company
Arthur Andersen	Caterpillar
Bank of Hawaii	Cummins Engine Co., Inc.
Carnival Cruise Line	Dana Corp.
Cigna	Dell Computer Corp.
Deloitte & Touche Consulting	Delphi Automotive Systems
Domino's Pizza International, Inc.	Dow Chemical
Eddie Bauer	General Electric Co.
Federal Express	Great Lakes Chemical Corp.
First Chicago NBD	Inland Paperboard and Packaging
Microsoft	Lithonia Lighting
NationsBank	McDonnell Douglas
Novell Inc.	Mettler-Toledo, Inc.
Parsons Infrastructure & Technology Group	PACCAR, Inc.
Price Costco Corp.	Potlatch Corp.
Price Waterhouse	Raytheon Aircraft Company
Seafirst Bank	Schering-Plough Corp.
Steiner Corporation	Sikorsky Aircraft
Towers Perrin	Silicon Graphics
	Thomas & Betts
	Warner-Lambert Company
	Weyerhaeuser
	Whirlpool Corp.

Campus Developments in Response to the Challenges of Internationalization

THE CASE OF RAMAPO COLLEGE OF NEW JERSEY (U.S.A.)

Robert A. Scott

Introduction

We know the imperatives for global education, and they are not new. They just keep growing in number. Economic competitiveness is an imperative; environmental interdependence is an imperative; the increasing ethnic and religious diversity of our towns and schools is an imperative; the fact that many of our citizens work for global or foreign-owned firms is an imperative; the fact that even small businesses must deal with issues of international trade, currency, and products is an imperative; the fact that our college graduates likely will be supervised by or will supervise persons of different racial, ethnic, and nationality groups is an imperative; and yes, national security and peaceful, respectful relations between nations is an imperative. Therefore, our education should prepare students to think and pursue truth on their own and in groups in an increasingly interdependent and multicultural world.

Reprinted with permission from *Higher Education Management,* vol. 6, no. 1. © 1994 by the Organisation for Economic Co-Operation and Development (OECD).

How do we respond to these imperatives? Do we emphasize process or content, skills or concepts, current courses or new and specialized curricula? How should we use interactive computing and telecommunications to connect schools, colleges, and businesses in this country, and make connections with educational partners in other regions of the world? How do we ensure that an emphasis on global literacy does not fan the flames of romance about a foreign culture, but ignore the diversity in our own communities? How do we provide the necessary preparation for current and future teachers and professors? How do we encourage teacher involvement in study and travel in non-Western as well as in Western areas of the world? Of what use is foreign language study in high school or college if students do not have the opportunity to use the language? Which languages should we choose to teach—those important to our state's economic development and international trade strategy, or those chosen because of area populations? In which case will students have the greater opportunity to use their second language proficiency?

How can we be sure that we don't confuse global literacy and the kind of value-void acceptance of ideology described by Diane Ravitch? Or, as she put it elsewhere, how can we be sure we won't sacrifice multiculturalism for a new form of particularism? How can we balance the gods of global literacy and the need for basic skills, two essential ingredients of education which sometimes are thought to be in opposition: with international studies for the suburban elite and basic skills for the urban poor? Can't both needs be tied to the goals of raising student aspirations, reducing attrition, improving attainment, and preparing students for an increasingly interdependent and multicultural world?

During the last several years, it often seemed as if every college and university in the United States, and nearly every higher education association, had become a champion for international education. In 1987, 165 education organizations, many of which had never before found common cause, joined together to create CAFLIS, the Coalition for the Advancement of Foreign Languages and International Studies. The mission of CAFLIS was "to create an action plan aimed at improving the ability of Americans to operate in the international arena and to understand its importance to America's future."[1] To advance this action plan, CAFLIS issued recommendations to the federal government, educational institutions, state and local policy makers, and business-educational collaborators. The most prominent of its recommendations was the creation of a national endowment, similar to the National Science Foundation, to serve as an instrument "for distilling and expressing important national interests" in the area of foreign languages and international studies.[2] In a very real sense, CAFLIS reflected the interests of every collegiate institution.

This seems only natural. Institutions support international education. Three-fourths (77 percent) of all four-year colleges and almost one-half (46 percent) of two-year colleges offer "at least one internationally oriented course in general education requirements."[3] Nearly two-thirds of all four-year colleges have at least one study abroad program of their own.[4] And more than 400,000 students from other countries study in the United States each year at campuses from coast to coast.

However, despite these signs of concern and progress, the results are unimpressive. The great majority of four-year institutions (84 percent) and two-year institutions (97 percent) have no foreign language requirement for entrance.[5] Less than 10 percent of high school students enroll in four years of a foreign language.[6] And relatively few institutions require all students to study a foreign language before graduation.[7] In fact, the United States continues to be one of the few nations in the world where a student can graduate from college without ever studying a second language.[8]

Equally distressing is the fact that "less than 2 percent (about 50,000; 70,000 in 1991–92) of the 12.2 million US college and university students study abroad for credit."[9] The European Economic Community has created a program (ERASMUS, European Action Scheme for Mobility of University Students) which will *add* three times that number to the ranks of European students studying in another country every year. Its goal is 10 percent of European university students per year.

Why haven't we made more progress? The calls to action are numerous and clear. The National Governors' Association said, "All college and university graduates *must* be knowledgeable about the broader world and conversant in another language."[10] The American Council on Education has called for all colleges and universities to "set goals for foreign language competence by the year 2000."[11]

The answers are not simple, of course. Foreign language instruction, study abroad programs, and courses with international content must all compete for priority and resources with courses and programs of more immediate interest to both faculty and students. Change takes will and time and, sometimes, money. Nevertheless, a number of colleges and universities have made significant progress in making the campus more global. In my view, the common ingredients at each are the commitment of the board of trustees and the president, and a clear set of objectives.

The objectives for global education at these colleges and universities seem clear and are well-expressed by the Atlantic Council:

- to provide students with a sense of time and place;

- to challenge students to appreciate the complexity of issues and interests that bear on the relations among nations, regions, and power groups;

- to prepare students to take account of the new and changing phenomena that affect international relations;

- to encourage critical thinking and inquiry about contending concepts and theories of international relations;

- to "de-parochialize" students' perspectives on international affairs;

- to heighten understanding that international relations are not static but subject to constant change.[12]

The imperatives are compelling. The objectives are clear. How do we turn imperatives and objectives into priorities? What are the principles for guiding campus decisions? What is a useful framework for organizing activities and evaluating progress? What are the points of leverage for action? What initiatives should we advocate?

Principles for Internationalizing the Institution

The principles to be used for internationalizing any particular campus will depend upon the goals and objectives established. Will the areas of emphasis be general education, selected majors, area studies, or foreign language proficiency and culture, which are often optional choices for students? Or will the goal be to make global education pervasive throughout the curriculum and extracurriculum in order to affect all students? Is the goal based on an institutional desire to keep up with fundamental industrial, technological and social trends in the United States, or on a need for competitive advantage, or distinctiveness, compared to other institutions?

At Ramapo College, a public undergraduate college of liberal arts, science, and professional studies, and 4,700 students, we developed a strategy that gives emphasis to the international and multicultural dimensions of nearly all fields of study for reasons of institutional mission, strategy, and distinctiveness.

International and multicultural education was chosen as the strategic direction for Ramapo in 1985 not only because the new president believed strongly that every college graduate should be "globally" literate and the recipient of an education based on the liberal arts, but also because Ramapo College has a distinct set of strengths and opportunities. These distinctive features include faculty expertise, student backgrounds, and neighboring international firms, the presence of which suggested that this should be the direction to take in strengthening institutional distinctiveness, attractiveness, enrollment, and resources.

In developing a strategy, it is necessary not only to assess assets and opportunities, but also to develop a set of principles for decision-making. At Ramapo we decided on the following principles to guide us in developing our identity as the "college of choice for a global education."

1. We decided that our strategy should include both international *and* multicultural themes. After all, the United States is part of the world, and we have a great diversity of ethnic, racial, and national groups in our midst. It is just as important for our students to understand the cultural diversity of American society as it is for them to appreciate diversity in the world. Many people seem to think that "international" refers to those "over there," while "multicultural" refers to populations in our own towns, cities, or neighborhoods. We use "global" to cover both terms—international and multicultural or intercultural. Our goal is to provide an excellent preparation for graduates as

citizens and professionals in an increasingly interdependent and intercultural world.

2. We also decided that our theme of international and intercultural education should be pervasive throughout the curriculum, in remedial and developmental courses, general education and area studies, and liberal arts majors, as well as professional studies such as accounting. (After all, if accounting is the systematic assignment of value to assets, and if values and assets differ around the world, then our business students should study comparative accounting as well as international marketing. They do.) We decided on an integrative approach that would make it possible for all programs to be included and would not limit our efforts to particular majors.

3. The Ramapo strategy includes the extracurriculum as well as the curriculum, courses in subject matter as well as in skill areas. Our efforts touch all areas of campus life, including housing, urban internships, field study, cooperative education, and study abroad as well as student and faculty exchanges, visiting international and minority scholars, the use of computing and telecommunications, etc.

4. Our strategic mission embraces research and training as well as undergraduate teaching. There is an important role for our faculty to play through its scholarly and artistic activities and its work with graduate students through joint programs with the New Jersey Institute of Technology, New York University, Rutgers, and the University of Medicine and Dentistry in addition to the state's Minority Academic Careers program.

5. Our initiatives are being developed through campus expertise as well as through partnerships with others, including universities, community colleges, schools, communities, cultural organizations, and corporations whose expertise lies in different areas. In this manner, the sum of what we do can be greater than the total of the individual parts.

It should be obvious that faculty renewal and development is essential to these objectives, and underlies these principles.

Points of Leverage for Action

The points of leverage to raise institutional priority for global education in the curriculum and extracurriculum are the same for every campus, although those employed will vary by circumstance. The key actors in employing these points of leverage will vary as well. They may be the trustees, the president, the academic vice-president, a dean, a department chair, a faculty member, all of the above, or some combination. The first step is for the international education advocate to persuade one or more of these key actors that the imperatives for global education should affect institutional objectives. Once this occurs, the global education prophets can use the points of leverage found in every institution to ensure that international education's priority is sustained or even increased.

The eleven major points of leverage are known to all: the mission statement; the strategic plan; annual academic program and administrative unit reviews; annual goals and objectives for senior officers, including deans; annual budget requests and allocations; staffing decisions; funds for faculty and curriculum development; annual awards, rewards and other forms of recognition for meritorious service, including honorary degrees; the Trustees' agenda; five- and ten-year regional accrediting self-studies; and fund-raising in both public and private sectors. Basically, the advocate of higher priority for global education wants to ensure that it is a central part of the discussion when any of these points of leverage are employed. I think the reason is obvious. They provide the opportunity to ensure that priority follows imperative.

The *campus mission statement* is the institutional expression of educational goals and outcomes; it expresses campus vision, purpose and values. Therefore, it is referenced during discussions of priorities. For international education to be mentioned in the mission statement is the first step toward higher priority. And, as we all know from campus exercises in writing mission statements, these opportunities are available.

Strategic plans include sections on institutional strengths, weaknesses, challenges, opportunities, and both on-campus and off-campus forces for change. The "imperatives" cited earlier make it highly likely that international and multicultural education can gain prominent mention in the strategic plan's environmental scan.

Annual *academic program and administrative unit reviews* should always refer to the mission statement and strategic plan, thus providing an opportunity to assess the degree to which academic programs and administrative units support international and multicultural education and set goals and objectives related to global awareness.

Other points of leverage are used in the same way—with reference to the mission statement and strategic plan—to enhance the priority for global education. The technique works, whether the leverage is the annual goals and objectives of senior officers and deans; annual budget requests and allocations; staffing decisions; the use of funds for faculty and curriculum development; annual awards for promotion, tenure, salary, excellence in teaching or scholarship, or recognition for distinguished achievement in a profession; Trustees' agendas; self-studies for accreditation (especially given the concern of accrediting associations for issues of equity, diversity, multicultural education, and outcomes assessment); or the fundraiser's cue statement, which itself is drawn from the mission and strategic plan. These two documents, often ignored by faculty, are most susceptible to the persuasiveness of the "imperatives," and drive institutional priorities.

This review of the points of leverage is not intended to make it sound easy; it is not. And of course there are other priorities which claim attention in the mission statement and can use the points of leverage to gain priority. But this systematic approach enhances the possibilities for change, and for global education to receive priority.

These eleven major points of decision, and others we could enumerate, offer prime opportunities to express and support campus priorities. These are the points of leverage for institutional change. On each occasion, we should express our commitment to educational objectives that acknowledge the world our graduates will face and the state and national imperatives for global understanding.

So much for a general approach to strategy development. What about a particular campus?

As stated earlier, interest in the international, or global, aspects of education is not new. There have been strong advocates for global education for many years. What is new is the broadening of the term "global" to include multicultural as well as international education, and the convergence of interests as expressed by educators, business and political leaders, and students. The goal is not "international education" alone, but education for an increasingly interdependent and multicultural world, the world our graduates will face, with employees, supervisors, and neighbors from different racial, ethnic, and national backgrounds.

Roadblocks and Strategies

But aren't there roadblocks to such developments? Aren't there structural impediments to change? Doesn't faculty inertia inhibit change? Isn't money the lubricant of change, and isn't it in short supply, even for a noble cause such as international and multicultural education? Aren't there philosophical barriers to overcome?

The answer to each question can be "yes," of course. But for reasons of institutional quality and competitiveness, as well as for reasons of educational philosophy—and for all the other reasons cited earlier—colleges and universities must incorporate the international and multicultural dimensions of various fields of study into the curriculum as a matter of priority.

The fact is that all of our graduates must be educated in content, i.e., knowledge gained through intensive study of both their own culture and a culture other than their own; skills gained through requirements in language, quantitative reasoning, communications, and computing; and abilities, including leadership and interpersonal relationships gained through both the curriculum and extracurriculum, for a new world society to be a reality. This formation is not only self-evident, but also verified by employers throughout the country. We have students tell us they receive offers of employment because of the experience in other cultures they gained through Ramapo programs. Employers say the same.

This formulation of knowledge, skills, and abilities in relation to the increasing interdependence of peoples is important to consider not only as a philosophical rationale for our approach to undergraduate education. It also is important as a set of criteria for evaluating the activities we sponsor to encourage intercultural education.

Imagine, though, the activities created or endorsed on many campuses in the name of international and multicultural education. Think of how columnists, politicians, and many college students and faculty view these themes because of how our college leaders portray them.

In the eyes of many, international education and multicultural education "glorify" the lives and heritage of others while containing actual or veiled criticisms of our nation's past. To many, international education is needed for reasons of economic competition, and multicultural education is needed for reasons of guilt, with those to be studied portrayed as victims. In both cases, the student is posed as voyeur, looking in without understanding the "other" in relation to himself, or herself in relation to the other. How else can we explain the fact that on many campuses, international programming is principally related to business and economics, with student exchanges in mostly English-speaking countries, and on many others, "multicultural" programming is devoted to the subject as victim or to separating students by background? Look at the course titles in the humanities at many colleges for examples. What do these approaches have to do with the "increasing interdependence" of peoples cited in the rationale for a more global education?

The goal of an education for this emerging world should be to understand ourselves, i.e., our knowledge, values, and beliefs, in relation to others, and others in relation to ourselves. Our students must not only master content and skills, but also develop attitudes of respect and concern for others. How can we accomplish this if we deny the heritage of where we live, and compete for "victim" status?

At a recent meeting of university leaders from Asian and Pacific Rim countries, this point was made in a different way. The executive director of an association of southeast Asian universities asserted that Americans are interested in international education for reasons of economic competition, and that Asians are interested in international education for reasons of mutual respect and cooperation. While the assertion may be overstated, there is some truth to it. Most U.S. educators seem to advocate international education for career and other self-serving reasons. And they endorse multicultural education as a palliative, not because it has something important to say.

The goal of education must be to enhance the abilities of students to learn and pursue truth on their own and in groups. The reason for emphasizing global or "intercultural" education is to help ensure that students have the ability to understand themselves in relation to those who are from different backgrounds, and of understanding others in relation to themselves. To accomplish this, we need to study differences by making comparisons in many dimensions. To ignore beliefs and values, customs and institutions, both over time and from place to place,[13] and only to dwell on the unfortunate and painful though true past of a people, is to make it seem as if human nature is the same everywhere, that only the form of "colonial" rule is different. This is short-sighted. We must move beyond "correcting" history to comprehending it.

According to the anthropologist Clifford Geertz, "the image of a constant human nature independent of time, place, and circumstance, of studies and professions, transient fashions and temporary opinions, may be an illusion, that what (humans are) may be so entangled with where (they are), who (they are), and what (they believe), that (their nature) is inseparable from them. It is precisely the consideration of such a possibility that led to the rise of the concept of culture and the decline of the (Enlightenment's) view of (human nature). . . . (humanity) unmodified by the customs of particular places do not in fact exist, (and have) never existed," says Geertz.[14] "This makes the drawing of a line between what is natural, universal, and constant . . . and what is conventional, local, and variable extraordinary difficult" to discern.[15] The conclusion is that humanity is as various in its essence as it is in its expression. And that goes for "us" as well as for "them."

What Geertz does not make explicit, but which he seems to include in his thinking, is that while "essence" and "expression" vary widely across cultures, there are many commonalities as well—identification with a group, grounding in a place, acculturation of values and beliefs, the need for respect, safety, and hope.

The historians Will and Ariel Durant certainly underscored those basic truths in their discussion of race in history. In their brilliant critique of "race theory," they trace the impact of invasions, intermarriage, and imitation on the development of various civilizations; the extraordinary accomplishments of those cultures; and the influence of geographical opportunity and economic and political developments—rather than race—on those civilizations.

"It is not the race that makes civilization, it is the civilization that makes the people: circumstances geographical, economic, and political create a culture, and the culture creates a human type," or tradition. "In the long run such differences of tradition or type yield to the influence of the environment."[16]

Unfortunately, the courses and activities called international education and multicultural education at many colleges seem to deny these conclusions. Instead of aiming to understand the essence as well as the expression of another people, commonalities as well as differences, even of those in our own communities, educators tend to deal in broad generalities. They offer a survey on trade or on exploitation, but not an introduction to what it means to be another—any "other."

I believe the goal of intercultural education should be for students to attain proficiency or competence, however defined locally, in a culture other than one's own. That is, through learning, experiencing, and communicating, students should attain the knowledge, skills, and attitudes necessary to discern the essence of another culture as well as to recognize its expression; and to compare both in deep ways to one's own. To do so, one must attain at least the same level of understanding of one's own culture, in order to be able to discern its essence as well as its expression, its commonalities and differences when compared to others.

But what do many colleges do? They provide a superficial survey of Western history and lump all of African-American heritage into a "Black Studies" course or the 28 days in February. They do the same with Latino heritage and Asian heritage, when they do anything at all. In so doing, they deny our students the opportunity to know the rich diversity of cultures within the African, Latin, and Asian experiences. These educators meld dozens of different "essences" into three forms of "expression," and fail to demand that students put themselves in the position of "other."

There are serious educational consequences that result from these approaches. After all, our own understanding of what we mean by international and multicultural education affects our thinking about campus mission and policies on the curriculum, degree requirements, student and faculty recruitment and retention, affirmative action, and orientation upon arrival at and departure from the college, among other activities.

Complex Issues Made Manageable

It is for these reasons that I say colleges and universities which espouse international and multicultural education often ignore complex issues, including the fact that African-Americans, Asian-Americans, and Latinos are not monolithic groups, as college programming often suggests; that relations between and among these groups, and between and among them and international students and faculty, are often complicated by prejudices brought to this country; and that there are important lessons to be learned by studying ethnic or inter-group relations in other countries.

Too many students think of Africa as a nation instead of as a home of nations. Few students know of the African diaspora and the existence of African heritage in scores of countries. With so little understanding, how can they make sense of the term "African-American"?

The same can be said for Asian and Latino heritage. Our students know so little, and often we are to blame. In our courses and in our celebrations, we must peel back the layers of meaning to reveal the richness of diversity.

We are also often to blame for our students' ignorance because we organize our curricula and activities as if the international is bilateral: the United States and the Far East; the United States and Africa; the United States and Latin America, etc. We seem to forget—except in a few classes—that other nations have relations between and among themselves independent of the United States; that the geographic orientation of countries is not the same around the world (*to wit,* the Far East is not the far east from everyone's perspective); and that inter-group relations forged elsewhere, especially when based on limited awareness and the antagonism over scarce resources, may cause difficulties even in a third country.

The lessons to be learned by studying inter-group relations in other countries seem to be lost on our institutions. Clearly the relations between and among ethnic, national and racial groups in our country can be illuminated by studying inter-group relations in Europe, Asia, Africa, and South America as well as in North America. But why is one the subject of international education, while the other is considered multicultural education? We and our students are of the same world, and need to understand ourselves and others as part of it.

The international and the multicultural are threads in the same cloth. After all, what is multicultural to us is international to others. That is why we must understand ourselves in order to understand others.

One of the advantages and attractions of this approach is that it can be inclusive of all faculty; it is not the exclusive domain of just a few in a precious center of study. But even with these attractions, the change to increased international and multicultural programming requires a strategic plan and process. As with any plan, this strategy requires goals and objectives which attract the professional interests of faculty; an understanding of both mission and markets; a set of principles for the development of new courses and programs; and a planning process which attracts the involvement and commitment of faculty and staff, includes assignments for responsibility and a schedule for deadlines, and a system of evaluation. With expertise identified and commitments understood, funds can be sought with greater assurance. At Ramapo, we can attest to the possibilities.

We established *six* broad objectives for our efforts, all designed to overcome barriers. These initiatives included: *a)* professional development for faculty and staff, with funds for travel, books and materials, consultants, visiting scholars, and faculty and staff exchanges as high priorities; *b)* curriculum development, including released time for revising current courses and developing new courses, scholarship and creative endeavors; *c)* skill development, including languages, computing, international telecommunications capability, tele-conferencing, audio-conferencing, and televised programming; *d)* experiential learning, including theme dorms, study abroad, student and faculty exchanges, urban internships and professional practice through international cooperative education placements; *e)* programmatic partnerships with schools, colleges, community organizations and corporations; and *f)* the recruitment and retention of students, with particular emphasis on international and minority students.

Criteria for Assessing the Impact of Programs

No matter how limited or pervasive the programming is to be, assessment should be designed into it from the beginning. We need to know the impact of the plan on faculty, the curriculum and extracurriculum, and students. Assessment must be routine.

At the more *general level,* we need to assess: *a)* the continuing commitment of the board of trustees and the president to achieving the objectives, especially to the review of how these objectives are related to the mission statement, program reviews, staffing decisions, and budget requests; *b)* the role of faculty as the major determinants of the substance and quality of the programs; *c)* the recruitment and retention of faculty essential to the programs; *d)* the centrality of international and multicultural education to skill, liberal, and professional studies; and *e)* the curricular and extracurricular opportunities for students to develop attitudes, skills, and knowledge that prepare them for citizenship and careers.

At a more *specific level,* we need to assess actual progress toward specific goals and objectives. At Ramapo, this means an assessment of: *a)* the number of faculty and staff who participate in professional development related to the mission for global education; *b)* the consequences of that experience; *c)* the number and distribution of courses revised or added and related to global education; *d)* enrollment in courses related to these goals and objectives; *e)* the development and use of audio and video telecommunications; *f)* the number and quality of study abroad, international cooperative education, student and faculty exchanges, visiting scholars, and urban internship programs; *g)* the number of students participating in these programs; *h)* the number, quality, and results of partnerships with schools, business and community groups; *i)* the number and distribution of minority and international faculty by program; and *j)* the number and success of international and minority students recruited and retained.

I think a useful framework for planning and evaluation is a "grid," a matrix with nine cells. The columns are labeled "campus," "curriculum," and "community." The rows, labeled on the left, are "learning," "experiencing," and "communicating." As the reader can visualize, this grid has great potential for planning and evaluation.

By "learning," I include the various sources for students to enhance their knowledge, skills, and attitudes. On campus, this includes the extracurriculum as well as the curriculum. Under curriculum, we include the international as well as the multicultural, the study of a culture other than one's own as well as one's own, to learn by examining commonalities as well as differences.

By "experiencing," I include the involvement of international students and scholars on campus as well as international cooperative education, study abroad, and field work in ethnic communities. Under "communicating," I include telecommunications as well as foreign language instruction and computing.

Brief Summary of Progress to Date

The six broad areas of initiative at Ramapo have specific goals and a formal system of assessment. For example, in the area of faculty development, we set goals for a professional development program for all faculty members. The program helped create a common ground for intellectual discourse on global (i.e., international and multicultural) education, and to enhance faculty expertise. We specifically allocated funds—and sought new funds—for this purpose. Additional initiatives toward this goal included faculty seminars on particular areas of the world, such as Latin America, East Asia, and Africa; a research institute; major conferences; new faculty hired in foreign language and area studies; visiting scholars; and other professional development opportunities, including released time and travel funds for scholarship.

Nearly three-quarters of the full-time faculty participated in the professional development seminars. In addition, about 5 percent of full-time faculty each year are visiting scholars from other countries, including Fulbright Scholars, an annual scholar supported by the Italian government, Princeton-in-Asia Fellows, and participants in our faculty and foreign scholar exchange programs in Argentina, Volgograd, Puerto Rico, France, Japan, Italy, China, Taiwan, England, Jamaica, and elsewhere. These scholars are from all fields—sciences, humanities, and social sciences. We also have been approved to participate in the Diplomat-in-Residence Program of the US State Department. By refurbishing an old house on campus, we have created a center for visiting American and international scholars to live and to host seminars in a conducive, "special" setting.

The second major initiative concerned curriculum development. The goal of this initiative was "to infuse international and multicultural dimensions comprehensively throughout the curriculum." Approximately seventy new courses or major revisions of existing courses were produced by faculty participants in the Professional Development Seminar. The new or revised courses are found in the Freshman Seminar Program, developmental reading, general education, honors seminars, new minors and majors, as well as in new language offerings in Italian, Japanese, and Chinese to accompany traditional offerings, which included Russian. In addition, a semester-long lecture series, a weekly television program, and plans for new summer institutes resulted from the curriculum development initiatives.

We still have a long way to go, but foreign language courses have almost quintupled and foreign language enrollments have more than tripled in just a few years. The increase in foreign scholars and international students has helped inspire these increases, both by their presence on campus as well as by their participation in courses as teachers and students. But the general level of expectations and increased opportunities for study abroad also helped increase the number of students studying foreign languages. In support of these language courses, library and media acquisitions were made, and a new language lab facility was constructed.

The major headway in foreign language instruction has been made in Italian. While some on campus urged us to expand Russian or start Chinese, I thought we should start with Italian for students of traditional college age and Japanese for adult American employees of Japanese-owned firms. After all, more than one-third of New Jersey residents are of Italian descent, and Ramapo students fit that same profile. In addition, many thousands of New Jersey residents work as managers for the scores of large Japanese corporations located within a twenty-mile radius of the college. Both languages contribute significantly to our language enrollments. Italian programs include a film and culture series, intensive weekend immersion courses, and study abroad. Japanese programs include international cooperative education, study abroad, and The Japanese Culture Society (a community group serving as a "bridge" between American and Japanese families by offering educational, cultural and social programs).

The third goal concerned communications, including specific skills and capabilities in languages, computing, and telecommunications that would enhance the learning and career opportunities of Ramapo students. The centerpiece of this initiative is the International Telecommunications Center, with world-wide satellite capabilities for television reception, audio- and video-conferencing, and broadcast quality television production facilities.

These facilities are used by faculty and students in business, the humanities, social sciences and sciences for course enhancement, and by students in business and communications as subjects of study. Audio-conferencing also holds great promise for use in assessing student progress while they are engaged in study or internships in other countries, and for faculty planning study abroad programs. Other facilities include the foreign language laboratory and the "ICONS" (International Communications and Negotiations Simulation) Project Room. During this past year, Ramapo faculty held more than 60 audio and video tele-conferences and assisted several major corporations in tele-conference productions. In addition, Ramapo now serves the area community college and sixteen school districts by means of fibre optic cable-supported tele-courses, and provides Japanese language tutoring to high school students in 19 states as the second national site for The Satellite Educational Resources Consortium (SERC) Japanese program located in Nebraska.

The audio and video conferences provide a means of bringing the world to the classroom, and the classroom to the world. Among other activities, Ramapo students in class held tele-conferences with a university class in Italy discussing the European perspective on American foreign policy during the Gulf War; a group in Cuba discussing freedom of the press; and a local village leader and ecologist in Brazil discussing the ecology of a rain forest. A course matches the reading requirements for a course at Volgograd Pedagogical University with one at Ramapo College, with a tele-conference every three to four weeks to allow students to discuss the readings and their observations on the future, including career prospects. This project is certainly enhanced by the fact that the professors and several students have visited the others' institution.

The fourth goal was to expand an already comprehensive program of experiential learning opportunities for all students. These out-of-classroom experiences, guided by both College offices and student clubs, provide a bridge to the world beyond the campus and include a greatly expanded set of study abroad, exchange, and routine tele-conference opportunities in England, France, Italy, Israel, Japan, the CIS, Jamaica, Costa Rica, Puerto Rico, Spain, Belgium and Australia. Faculty study tours and visiting scholars add China and Kenya to our world coverage. All of these activities are seen as "building blocks" rather than as capstone experiences.

Each year now five to ten of our faculty and more than 100 students travel abroad for study. We try to design these exchanges so that they result in substantial campus-wide benefits as well as personal enrichment for the individuals involved. We hope that each arrangement continues to expand the opportunities available to faculty and students over time. My goal for international experiences is 100 percent of students and faculty by the year 2000, using telecommunications as well as in-country exchanges and international cooperative education.

One of the most exciting features of the programs created under our goal for experiential learning is the international cooperative education program. This program permits Ramapo students to work abroad in a salaried position while earning academic credit for a project directed by a Ramapo faculty member and a supervisor in the host country. To date, scores of students, including minority, adult, and disabled students, have participated in international cooperative education placements in six countries, including Russia, Japan, and Norway. As an added attraction, students from these countries can participate in cooperative education in the United States while living and studying at Ramapo. The basic premise of the program, of course, is that if students can find a placement at IBM in Paramus, why not at IBM in Paris? Student expenses are offset by corporate grants and employment.

Experiential education includes extracurricular activities as well as academic study. The Model United Nations debate club competes successfully with Harvard, Georgetown and Army each year; a theme dorm devoted to international concerns adds to the richness of campus life; and students participate in urban area internships and mentoring programs.

The fifth goal concerns the enhancement and extension of Ramapo's outreach activities in international and multicultural programs to area high schools, corporations, other colleges and universities, county colleges, and the general community in northern New Jersey. Ramapo has assumed a leading role in the region by organizing several important and successful programs with local high schools, including the Foreign Policy Consortia of schools, colleges and corporations, and the STAIRS (Students Annual International Relations Seminar) program. Approximately 200 students from 20 high schools participate in STAIRS each year.

We have intensive pre-college partnership programs with urban schools as part of our multicultural concerns. We have shared Fulbright scholars with area schools and colleges; we have had a joint Fulbright-Hays Group Projects Abroad Grant for travel to Japan with Kean College; we co-sponsor an archaeological dig in Israel with four other colleges; and now lead a state-sponsored project in collaboration with the Council of New Jersey Consortia for International and Global Education. The Council includes four consortia consisting of 24 colleges and universities, 10 community colleges, and three school districts, as well as numerous professional education associations, state agencies, and community organizations.

We work with Italian as well as Japanese community groups on programs for education and culture, as well as mutual understanding, and with corporate groups in a variety of ways. The International Business major and the International Telecommunications Center have professional advisory boards. In addition, we offer courses and programs on business, language, and culture to American and foreign employees of international and multinational firms. We are partners with Rutgers, the Port Authority of New York and New Jersey, and the Department of Commerce in the New Jersey Center for International Business Education. Through all these activities, we have greatly expanded not only our educational activities but also our fund-raising potential and results.

The sixth goal concerns the recruitment and retention of students who reflect the multicultural nature of American society as well as students from other countries. During the past few years, Ramapo has experienced a 250 percent increase in enrollment of foreign students and a 60 percent increase in minority students. International students now represent about 5 percent of full-time students. Retention for these students has reached 80 percent. The same process worked with both groups: set goals, define actions, raise funds for scholarships, monitor progress and refine goals and actions. Ramapo students now come from 15 states and 50 countries.

The recruitment of faculty and staff has also been affected by our concern for international and multicultural education. In addition to the visiting scholars, 40 percent of new faculty appointments in the past six years have been to minority scholars.

The recruitment of both students and faculty has been assisted by our partnership programs with urban schools such as West Side High School in Newark and our transfer articulation agreements with community colleges which enroll substantial numbers of international and minority students.

For each of these major goals, there are objectives, assignments of responsibility, time tables, and annual, sometimes quarterly, assessments. We have a system of academic program reviews, administrative unit reviews, an internal audit system for operational as well as fiscal matters, and annual performance reviews. We monitor progress toward our goals, with particular concern for student skills, knowledge, awareness, attitudes, and aspirations. We have a special office to assist faculty and staff in seeking corporate, foundation, and government support for our initiatives.

One of the interesting phenomena in the implementation of strategy and the assessment of results is that the more we do, the more we learn. At Ramapo, we continue to extend the frontiers of what we thought possible. Hence, we need to consider new forms and subjects of assessment.

Reflections on the Ramapo Experience

Ramapo's initiatives in global education, both international and multicultural, were greatly assisted by a special three-year grant of $3.4 million from the State of New Jersey's Governor's "Challenge for Excellence" Grant Program. We completed this funding in 1989, and, with the assistance of The American Forum for Global Education, reviewed progress in the attainment of goals. The original proposal was structured around a strategic vision that would be followed with or without the extra state assistance and with a four-year financial plan that would show how the initiatives would be continued after the conclusion of the three-year grant period. It was our assumption that the strategic vision was of sufficient merit to attract private funding as well as other sources of public support. Indeed, we have received generous private and federal as well as other state grants to support the initiatives. These grants include support from Becton Dickinson, IBM, Matsushita, Sanyo, Sharp, Sony, and Title VI of the US Department of Education.

The Challenge Grant award was divided into two nearly equal parts, with one-half financing the renovation and equipping of a facility to become our International Telecommunications Center, and one-half for various forms of faculty, staff, and curriculum development, programs for student recruitment and retention, and related outreach efforts. New faculty were added in foreign languages and additional staff were added to the cooperative education program to start the new international cooperative education initiative. At the conclusion of the three-year grant period, the state provided $750,000 as a permanent addition to the base budget to support high priority initiatives. Private grants enabled us to add the equipment which was deleted from the recommended base budget addition.

There were many unexpected but beneficial consequences of the Challenge Grant support and the initiatives related to it. Furthermore, we underestimated the positive results of the grant. The governor wanted his Challenge Grant program to result in greater distinctiveness and prestige for the State's colleges, and we benefited far more than we ever thought we would. Some objectives which we thought were tremendously far-sighted and ambitious at the time we developed the proposal have proven to be only somewhat far-sighted, and not quite as ambitious as we probably could have made them. In the area of telecommunications, however, we are far ahead of all but the largest research universities in terms of equipment and capability. In other areas, I wish we had been more ambitious, especially in adding staff for foreign language and humanities programs. However, we asked the state for as much as we thought we could, and were the only grant recipient to receive all that we requested.

Some have described aspects of our Challenge Grant initiatives as "sowing a thousand seeds" and awaiting the results. While we certainly had a more goal-oriented approach than this suggests, there is some truth to the notion of allowing many flowers to bloom before deciding which to cull and which to cultivate. As a result, many individual faculty members established linkages with institutions in other countries, even when it did not seem at all certain that those linkages would build on campus strengths or add to all-college opportunities for faculty and students. The successor organization, the Center for Intercultural Education, has developed clear guidelines and priorities for the continuation and establishment of linkages. Nevertheless, we supported some travel and summer study in countries where it was not clear that sustained programmatic initiatives would result. We took risks, and that was appropriate. We need to encourage faculty to explore possibilities.

The initiatives for international and multicultural education were based on the principles of pervasive programming and institutionalized activities that would become part of the fabric of the institution. We were more interested in making all programs infused by global awareness than in the creation of separate and precious programs. It was interesting, therefore, to realize the importance of having some programs specifically identified as international or multicultural, and as resulting from Challenge Grant support. The two examples to be cited are the program in International Business and the International Co-op program. Without these programs, it would be possible for an outsider to review an index of programs and wonder about the impact of the grant. Visible symbols are important to reflect progress, even if they underrepresent the degree of progress made.

Through these initiatives, Ramapo has been strengthened, student and faculty aspirations have been raised, retention has been improved, and our education has been enhanced to prepare students more fully to live and work in an increasingly interdependent and multicultural world.

In addition, Ramapo has gained new status in government, business and education circles. When the new Governor wanted to meet senior executives of Japanese firms, he asked us. When the Department of Commerce Division of International Trade wanted advice on international business education, the staff asked Ramapo. Our faculty, staff, and students have received recognition world-wide for their accomplishments.

It is appropriate to wonder whether alternative formats would have been more successful, and a more effective foundation for future development. The pervasive approach which we undertook is not suitable for every institution. However, I believe that our initiatives support the notion that one can affect and improve the education of all students by selective initiatives in programs such as the freshman seminar, general education, and enhanced majors such as that in American Studies—which views the history of America from the perspective of a visiting scholar from another country—and the increased emphasis on the history and culture of other peoples throughout traditional majors where appropriate.

The developments traced here are ongoing, but received major funding support between 1985 and 1990. In calendar year 1990—the last half of Fiscal Year 1990 and the first half of Fiscal Year 1991—New Jersey's colleges and universities lost more than 25 percent of their state support. As a consequence, we had to make some rapid and difficult decisions about the allocation of campus funds. We emphasized audio more than video tele-conferences; we reduced staffing and reassigned responsibilities; we eliminated some activities; and temporarily, we reduced support for faculty and staff development and library and media purchases. Therefore, in addition to making changes by refining earlier initiatives, we actually had to curtail developments. For example, for the foreseeable future, we will limit international co-op assignments to those we have already arranged, and won't add new sites. We also will arrange to place students from other institutions for a fee and impose increased charges for co-op and study abroad assignments. We also have increased our financial aid budgets, in part to assist student international experiences. We have been able to manage these changes, I believe, because we have an institutional priority, we have a faculty-staff-administration-trustee commitment to a clear set of goals, and our approach is pervasive. Our international and multicultural initiatives are not lodged in one vulnerable office; they are everywhere.

In a curious way, our experience of the past two years may actually help make our initiatives a better model for others. We have learned what we can do with money and without money. We know the ease and low cost of audio conferences as a supplement to the classroom; we know the advantage of international cooperative education as an alternative to study abroad; we know the benefits of partnerships to ensure that the "whole is greater than the sum of its parts"; we know that foundation and corporate grants are available for curriculum change and that new federal initiatives are open. We know that major help is available from the American Council on Education and other associations. We know that the biggest challenge is to make choices among numerous opportunities.

Conclusion

In conclusion, I wish to emphasize three points drawn from these thoughts. First, we as educators must ensure that our students understand the depths of diversity. They must know about commonalities as well as differences, strengths as well as weaknesses, values as well as practices.

Now, I understand there are limits to what we can teach and what we can require. That is why I emphasize that our mission is to enhance the ability of students to learn on their own, and in groups, and why I stress the attainment of mastery in a culture other than one's own. The goal is to understand the "other," any "other" or "stranger," not attempt to offer courses in the extensive array of cultures represented throughout our country. Each college should decide on the limited number of particular cultures it will include, given its location and the demographics of its students.

Second, we educators must ensure that our students understand and appreciate that they are the "other" to many in this world. They must know that we need to know ourselves—the history, literature, and heroes of the peoples who built our civilization, our institutions and our values—if we are to understand our commonalities and differences when compared to others. Without this knowledge of others and ourselves, we are left with ignorance, fertile ground for suspicion and fear.

Third, we educators must ensure that our students develop a level of competence in a culture other than their own. Only by knowing our own culture, and by having some degree of mastery of another culture, can one begin to put himself or herself in the boots or shoes or sandals of another. A superficial survey course cannot accomplish this. Not even proficiency in a foreign language studied in the best labs with the best teachers can assure this. And not all students can afford to study for a year in another country, or take the "Grand Tour" upon graduation.

But all colleges can use three strategies to help students gain this knowledge. The first is through the curriculum, courses as well as requirements. The second is through experiences, such as one-month, summer-long, and semester-long periods of study and work in another cultural setting. Cooperative education placements in this and other countries are important parts of this strategy at Ramapo.

Finally, telecommunications, especially audio-conferencing, can be an inexpensive way to make it possible for students of all backgrounds to discuss similarities and differences with students, village officials, and educators in other settings. "Macro" topics such as democracy quickly are joined by immediate concerns about family and careers when students meet electronically, just as they do when they meet in person. When scheduled several times throughout a semester, these discussions can successfully help students begin to see themselves in another. A start has been made.

Taken together, courses, lectures, field experiences, and electronic meetings can help us and our students see that international and multicultural education are part of the same fabric, complementary measures to prepare graduates for an increasingly interdependent and intercultural world—here and there.

NOTES

1. Robert M. Rosenzweig, "The CAFLIS Action Plan," *Educational Record,* Spring, 1990, p. 13.

2. *Ibid.*

3. Richard D. Lambert, *International Studies and the Undergraduate.* American Council on Education, Washington, D.C., 1989, p. 109.

4. *Ibid.,* p. 11.

5. Lambert, p. 62.

6. *America in Transition, The International Frontier.* Report of the Task Force on International Education, p. 4. Copyright 1989 by the National Governors' Association, 44 North Capital Street, Washington, D.C. 20001-1572.

7. *Ibid.*

8. "What We Can't Say Can Hurt Us: A Call for Foreign Language Competence by the Year 2000." American Council on Education, Washington, D.C., 1989, p. 10.

9. *Exchange 2000: International Leadership for the Next Century, A Report to the Nation on the Role of International Exchange Programs in Meeting United States and Global Needs at the Turn of the Century.* The Liaison Group for International Education Exchange, Washington D.C., 1990, p. 6.

10. *America in Transition,* p. vii.

11. "What We Can't Say Can Hurt Us," p. 3.

12. *Post World War II International Relations as a Component of General Education in American Colleges and Universities.* The Atlantic Council of the United States, Washington, D.C., 1989, p. 7.

13. Clifford Geertz, "The Impact of the Concept of Culture in the Concept of Man," in *The Interpretation of Cultures.* New York: Basic Books, 1973, p. 35.

14. *Ibid.*

15. *Ibid.,* p. 36.

16. Will and Ariel Durant, "Race and History," in *The Lessons of History.* New York: Simon and Schuster, 1968.

Study Abroad and Foreign Language Programs

Barbara B. Burn

The apparent increase in foreign language requirements at high school and college levels is resulting in more college students knowing what it is to study a foreign language and the anecdotal evidence suggests that they are liking the sense of achievement it can give. Will this increase in foreign language enrollments by college students heighten their interest in study abroad? Alternatively, will fewer college students study languages, at home or abroad, because they "got it out of the way" in high school? These questions demand solid research, not just the anecdotal attention which they often receive.

A serious look at the role of study abroad in the foreign language programs of American colleges and universities must take into account that relatively few American undergraduates study abroad. According to the Institute of International Education's (IIE) most recent report, *Open Doors,* American students studying abroad (in 1993–94) were 76,302. This represents a minuscule proportion of all students in US higher education. However, if one looks more closely at IIE's data gathering and other relevant circumstances, IIE's figures may significantly underestimate the number of American students who study abroad. There is a potential that many US students who study abroad are not included in the figures. There are those whose colleges and universities may not know that they are

Reprinted by permission from *International Education Forum,* vol. 16 (Spring). © 1996 by the Association of International Education Administrators and Washington State University Press.

abroad, universities which do not report to IIE, and universities which do not grant credit for coursework taken abroad. Other students included in IIE's survey are the US students enrolled in foreign medical schools and the college-age children of Americans abroad in the military, business and non-governmental and other organizations, who pursue at least part of their higher education in their host country. In short, the impact of study abroad on US colleges and universities and especially on their foreign language programs may be far more significant than IIE's low figures suggest.

It is useful to consider the formula used by the European Community to calculate participation and goals for EC students' participation in the intra-EC student exchange known as ERASMUS (Expanded Regional Action Scheme for the Mobility of University Students), now one part of the new SOCRATES program which has succeeded ERASMUS. The ERASMUS goal—that ten percent of all students in higher education spend at least one term/semester in a higher education institution in another EC country—was interpreted to refer not to the total student population but only one-fourth of it, on the grounds that the average degree period in EC (now EU for European Union) higher education systems is four years, and that the number of study abroad students should be compared to a one-year student cohort, not total enrollments. Using this formula, US study abroad students constitute some 3% of all undergraduates rather than the tiny percentage often cited of under 0.5%, a more significant if still small proportion.

The preparation of this paper involved the following undertakings:

1. A comparison of US study abroad programs in several foreign language countries offered during the academic year in 1986–87 and 1994–95, to see if trends in time periods, admission requirements, and the priority given the use of the host country language in the program increased or decreased over this period;

2. An Internet survey of study abroad offices at US colleges and universities to inquire about their experience with foreign language study and trends in study abroad programs;

3. A questionnaire mailed to several dozen higher education institutions in continental Europe to ask if they are offering more courses using English as the language of instruction today compared to five or so years ago, and if the number of US students enrolled at these institutions has increased over the same period, and;

4. Discussion with the board of directors of the Association of International Education Administrators (AIEA) comparing their recent experience versus five years ago in motivating students to study foreign languages.

Findings from the above date collection and assessment efforts are presented below.

US Study Abroad Programs: Role of Foreign Language

Information on US study abroad programs used in comparing 1986–87 and 1995–96 offerings was obtained from the Institute of International Education publication, *Academic Year Abroad,* for the years involved. Annually, IIE requests US colleges and universities to send it information on their study abroad programs: location, time period, admission requirements including knowledge/previous study of the host country language in such nonspecific terms as: working knowledge, good command, mastery, fluency, solid background in, some knowledge of the language preferred, and thorough knowledge. A number of institutions give their language requirement in terms of numbers of semesters, quarters, or years of prior language study, but do not specify if the study should be intensive or non-intensive.

Some colleges and universities do not specify any language requirement although they may well have one. It seems that many institutions are deliberately imprecise about the level of language to allow flexibility in recruiting and filling programs.

Nor is information on the use of the host country language clear. For 1995–96, a common phrase on how courses are taught is: "in English format" or "in French, German, etc. format." What this means in terms of language of instruction can be difficult to determine.

The tables presented below give an overview of study abroad programs in terms of time period, language requirement for admission, and language instruction in the programs together with total number of programs (SAPs).

TABLE 1
Programs in JAPAN

Time Period	1986–87	1994–95
Academic Year	21	41
Semester	15	40
2 years	1	—
6 years	1	—
TOTAL	38	81

Language Requirement for Admission		
3 years	—	1
2 years	1	15
1 year	4	20
5 semesters	—	1
3 semesters	—	2
not specified	22	—

Instruction in Language		
In English	16	
In English & Japanese	18	

	1986–87	1994–95
In Japanese	1	
Courses for foreigners	5	

(Nearly all programs teach in English and Japanese, and offer beginning and intermediate Japanese.)

As can be seen from Table 1, the main changes since 1986–87 are:

- total programs more than doubled;

- semester programs increased much more than academic year programs;

- more programs require less than 2 years of Japanese language study for admission. Fewer require 2 or more years.

While IIE's *Academic Year Abroad* gives a useful overview of the increase of study abroad programs in Japan in the last decade, a recent study, *Rethinking the US-Japan Educational Exchange: The Collegiate Level,* provides a comprehensive review and analysis of US study abroad in Japan. According to this study, even though enrollments in Japanese at US colleges and universities grew at the rate of 95 percent in the period 1987–91, a much higher rate than for other foreign languages, the enrollment of US students in post-secondary institutions/programs in Japan dropped by nearly 9% between 1991–92 and 1993–94. After having increased from 1,532 in 1989–90 to 2,120 in 1991–92, in 1993–94 the total was only 1,834.

The growth in US study abroad in the period 1989–92 can in all likelihood be attributed in large part to the dramatic increase in Japanese language enrollments in the US in the late 1980s, an increase paralleled by the increase in study abroad programs in Japan. The subsequent drop in American students studying in higher education institutions in Japan can probably be linked to the very high cost of living in Japan compared to the US, more than the equivalent of $20,000 for an academic year.

Recent changes and new developments in Japan promise to increase the number of US students who study there. The enormous imbalance between the Japanese students attending post-secondary education institutions in the US, over 45,000 in 1994–95, has aroused concern on the part of the governments in both countries. This is prompting efforts to increase scholarship support for American students studying at Japanese universities under reciprocal exchange agreements, and encourage the national universities in Japan to develop academic programs that can attract more US students. The programs will combine the teaching of Japanese with coursework in English. This approach characterizes most of the existing US study abroad programs in Japan. Thus, it appears that trends toward reshaping Japanese programs will better reflect the interests and needs of US students in Japan. After lagging behind burgeoning enrollments of Japanese in US colleges and universities, US student enrollment in Japan may continue to rise.

TABLE 2
Programs in GERMANY

Time Period	1986–87	1994–95
Academic Year	33	32
Semester	47	80
Other:		
1 qtr, 4 wks, 8 wks, 2 trimesters	6	—
TOTAL	86	113
Language Requirements for Admission		
3 years	2	1
2½ years	2	11
2 years	30	37
1 year	12	1
12 credit hours	—	1
Other, e.g. advanced proficiency, intermediate, good/thorough knowledge, previous study, Middlebury summer program		

The main points relevant to study abroad and the role of foreign language study are the following:

- While the number of US study abroad programs in Germany increased from 86 to 113 during the period involved, part of the increase resulted from a dozen of the additional programs situated in what was formerly East Germany, some of which date from before reunification.

- The number of academic year programs (they typically involve and require more knowledge and study of the German language) decreased from 33 to 32, from close to 1/3 to under 1/4 of the total.

- German language study increased in the number and proportion of all study abroad programs requiring two or more years of German language study for admission: from 35 or over 1/3 of all programs in 1986–87 to nearly 50 programs or close to 1/2 in 1994–95.

The increase in study abroad programs in Germany in the last decade is all the more noteworthy because the growth rate in German language enrollments in US higher education was only ten percent or less from 1986–1990, much lower than for Japanese, Spanish and Russian. However, a survey of study abroad and foreign language study (by the author in the mid-1980s) showed that of more than 60 US study abroad programs then offered in the Federal Republic of Germany, some 2/3 required at least two years of college level German or equivalent for admission, and expected students to do some or all of their coursework in the regular offerings of the host institution. Apparently as numbers of US programs in Germany have increased, expectations of German proficiency for students have diminished. This shift is common to programs and institutions that increase their enrollments and move from selective to less selective admissions, as with most higher education systems in the world's industrialized nations.

TABLE 3
Programs in FRANCE

Time Period	1986–87	1994–95
Academic Year	43	49
Semester	89	152
1–2 quarters	11	4
2 wks (Art Program in English)	1	—
TOTAL	144	205
Language Requirement for Admission		
3 years	3	9
5 semesters	5	5–6
2 years college	43	63
Intermediate proficiency	9	11
5 quarters/15–20 qtr hrs	4	3
Solid background, mastery, good command, working knowledge, fluency, French preferred/helpful, etc.		
Not specified	30	50

The above table shows developments similar to those for US study in Germany programs, namely a major increase in the number of programs, but many more in the semester than academic year, and with a decline in the proportion of programs requiring at least two years of college level study of French or equivalent for admission, from 62 percent to 45 percent.

Study abroad advocates especially regret the trend towards study abroad for one semester only rather than for a full academic year. Language acquisition is far less when study abroad is only a semester rather than a full academic year or more. This development is a result of diminished financial aid available to American students whether they study in the US or abroad and the increasing tuition costs on home campuses. It may also be a result of the concern of some American colleges and universities, mainly in the private sector, to keep students at the home campus in order to capture income from their tuition and room and board.

Survey of US Study Abroad Offices

Last September US professionals in study abroad advising and program administration were surveyed regarding their experience on whether study abroad trends in the last five to eight years have encouraged or discouraged foreign language study by US students. The survey was sent through what is known as SECUSSA-L, a network with around 700 subscribers who discuss issues relating to study abroad through electronic mail. Subscribers are mainly drawn from SECUSSA, the study abroad section of NAFSA: Association of International Educators.

The rationale for the survey indicated the author's concern that the number of students motivated to study foreign languages in preparation for study abroad may be declining because more US college students are studying abroad in places other than Continental Europe, such as in Africa and Australia. Another concern was stated indicating that the increase in study abroad by students majoring in professional fields, such as business and engineering, may similarly reduce foreign language study because these students often do not or cannot include language courses in their academic programs.

The more than two dozen study abroad professionals who responded to the questionnaire, while representing only a small fraction of US colleges and universities involved in study abroad or even of SECUSSA-L subscribers, constituted an impressive cross-section. They included large and small institutions, more in the private than public sector, and widely dispersed geographically, except that none were from the northwest. The respondents were not fully representative for the reason that persons subscribing to SECUSSA-L are by definition computer literate. Responses to the main issues raised in the survey are summarized below:

- In the last 5–8 years, did your students' participation in language immersion programs abroad increase (80%) or decrease (20%)? Level of decrease: 20–0%.

- Did student participation in programs located in foreign language countries and requiring some language study while abroad but otherwise taught in English increase (50%) or decrease (20%)? The other respondents reported no change. One respondent reported that its study abroad programs in foreign language countries require students to study the host country's language.

- Over half of respondents reported an increase, often of 30–40%, of students enrolling in study abroad programs in foreign language countries that did not require study of that country's language.

- Nearly half of respondents reported a substantial increase in students' participation in study abroad programs in English-speaking countries: from 10 to 40%.

In response to a question regarding the factors that best accounted for the changes mentioned above, almost no respondents attributed changes to changed foreign language requirements in local schools or in their own institutions. About one-third agreed that study abroad programs which require foreign language study while abroad or in countries whose language is not taught at their institution have increased in the last 5–8 years. Respondents were almost unanimous in underscoring the increased interest in study abroad of students in majors that make including foreign language study difficult (largely prescribed and sequential course requirements, as in business, engineering, the sciences, etc.). The reaction to the suggestion that students perceive foreign language study as unnecessary because English is spoken everywhere was indignant rejection.

Survey respondents pointed to the decline in foreign language majors as a possible reason for an increase in student participation in study abroad programs having no foreign language requirements and/or an increase in their participation in study abroad in English language countries. Another suggestion was a decrease in the number of entering freshmen with a strong background in French, and, to a lesser extent, in German. One respondent commented that the national trend to centralize international programs in a single office directly increased study abroad at his institution. As a consequence of centralized study abroad advising students now experience positive encouragement.

While many respondents offered thoughtful comments, the two quoted below illustrate well the dimensions of the challenge of encouraging more and longer foreign language study in the US.

> In a way that is inconceivable to me, the thought process among a number of non-study abroad people and faculty in general does not include previous study of a foreign language even when the students are being sent to study in a country which is not English-speaking! When the courses are being taught in English, somehow it is felt that the foreign language will be learned through osmosis and exposure to the foreign culture!

> As international educators, we can encourage students to start early with language preparation so that they can choose a study abroad immersion program and we can also encourage our universities to offer strong language programs. Since there are more languages than any university could possibly offer, it is also important that we offer study abroad programs where students can begin language study on-site.

The SECUSSA-L survey of study abroad professionals in the US, while not claiming to be broadly representative in the responses it elicited from a broad cross-section of these professionals, indicates the following:

1) While more college and university students are pursuing study abroad in English language countries and in programs not requiring foreign language study, study abroad in foreign language immersion programs and in programs requiring study of the host country language has increased.

2) The study abroad interest of students in professional and other fields whose majors find it difficult to fit foreign language study into their academic programs is markedly increasing. This should be a positive development in strengthening the career preparation of the increasing number of Americans whose professional careers will be more and more international.

A Look at the European Community

For the third information-gathering effort to identify how trends in US study abroad may have impacted foreign language study in American higher education, a questionnaire was faxed to approximately thirty higher education institutions in continental European countries, including universities, business schools, and technical schools. In addition, a letter was sent to several persons who, because of their professional involvement and commitment to international education and exchange, would probably have informed comments on the interrelationship between US study abroad trends and foreign language study in the US.

The focus was whether and to what extent higher education institutions on the Continent offer more courses in English today than a few years ago. One assumption made was that to accommodate UK students wanting to study on the continent under ERASMUS but often lacking foreign language skills to do so or to attract more US students—also all too monolingual—institutions were offering more courses in English. Another possible reason was that few students from many countries are apt to pursue studies in "small language countries" such as Scandinavian countries, Belgium and the Netherlands which require them to become proficient in a language that few people speak.

Hardly a dozen institutions responded to my questionnaire. Almost without exception they were from the "small language countries." The paucity of responses was, however, more than offset by the insights and detail given.

On the assumption that more US students would enroll in programs offered in English to respond to the demand for them from British students, insight into increased enrollments of British students in English language courses was required. In the last five or so years the increase has been very limited (as have been total enrollments), other than at the Catholic University of Louvain where students from the UK have doubled. However, overall the number of courses taught in English in spring 1995 compared to five years earlier had definitely increased. The figures reported ranged from "hardly any," "few," and "none," to 20, over 20 and 50.

Only 6 of 30 universities enrolled more students from the US in 1994–95 than five years previously, and few enrolled more than ten. The enrollment of US students increased, but only at a few universities, most notably the University of Amsterdam and the Catholic University of Louvain.

Comments from some of the respondents were informative:

From a university in Denmark: "Very few foreign students consider knowledge of a minority language such as Danish as a qualification towards their future career and, therefore, do not want to spend time learning it. Therefore, an increasing number of courses and even full degree programmes are being taught in English at Danish universities."

Schools of business seemed to offer more courses in English and to attract more UK and US students to them than do many universities. The former made clear, however, that their teaching courses in English is as much for their own students as for those from English-speaking countries. This might be somewhat comparable to the US program, "Teaching Across the Curriculum," which encourages students and faculty who are not in foreign language learning/teaching to pursue foreign language experience, not just in foreign language departments and courses, but in other departments that agree to offer some of their regular courses in one or more foreign languages.

The response from a university in the Netherlands, active in international education, underscores a point relevant to US international education. This Netherlands university is offering courses in English not so much to recruit UK or US students but to provide courses useful to students for whom English may be their second language, such as their own students. Below is an excerpt from this university's response:

> Five years ago few courses were taught in the English language, mainly in European Studies. Now over 50 courses are taught in English, spread over a great variety of departments.
>
> You have to keep in mind that we are a "small language country" and that we have not created those courses for US students only but for students who, in general, have English as their first or second language.
>
> We do see a growing interest in studying at our university among US students due to the offer of courses taught in English language, but this coincides with interest in learning our language as well.

Although responses from continental European universities were limited, the return rate may have emphasized the survey's lack of relevance to them. To date, few higher education institutions in the European Community are offering their regular courses in English, either to accommodate ERASMUS students from the UK or to recruit students from the US; countries such as Denmark and the Netherlands are the main exceptions. Indeed, they probably have an advantage over the European countries whose languages are more widely spoken in recognizing that students must be multilingual.

Some Informal but Relevant Comments from AIEA Executive Committee Members

The Executive Committee of the Association of International Education Administrators has approximately twelve members: the president, vice-president, immediate past president, secretary, and treasurer with others elected at-large for three-year terms. They typically represent higher education institutions active internationally with central offices that coordinate a range of international involvements. Those present at the October 1995 meeting represented all major geographic regions in the United States (plus one in Germany), large and small institutions, public and private, historically black, land-grant, and liberal arts. Mostly senior administrators and managers, they have strong experience with technical assistance, international factory development, curriculum development and with study abroad as part of their international mandate.

A pause in business discussions afforded a rare opportunity for an impromptu exchange on the issues raised in this paper, to tap into the knowledge and views of this unusually experienced small group.

Suggestions that shifts in US study abroad towards shorter periods and away from foreign language requirements or immersions are probably not unrelated to falling enrollments in foreign languages met with considerable understanding but also counterevidence and arguments. Well informed on developments in higher education and study abroad programs, the AIEA Executive Members gave the following examples:

- Professional school programs provided an increasing rather than decreasing impetus for foreign language learning. The University of Texas at Austin now has or is developing MBA joint degrees in Germany, France, and Mexico using these countries' languages.

- Examples were offered of programs abroad both requiring and not requiring knowledge of the host country language. The former were viewed as the majority.

- A US university which has previously required study abroad students to study the host country's language while abroad may diminish this requirement in order to send more business students on study abroad.

- The assertion that it is better to send a sizable number of students abroad with limited foreign language skills than only a few with strong foreign language proficiency received the group's warm endorsement.

- The tongue-in-cheek observation that a study abroad program claiming in recruiting that its students survive with no skills in the host country language downplays the reality, namely, that living with families and interacting in the local culture hooks the US students on studying the language.

Overall, the comments of AIEA's Executive Committee fit well with the responses to the SECUSSA-L survey. More US students are studying abroad if for shorter periods. More students in professional fields are studying abroad and more wish to do so. More American students are commited to learning foreign languages, to better prepare themselves to function in a global society and community.

Need for More Research

While this paper has explored one aspect of study abroad by US students and its possible impact on foreign language study in the US, the findings point up how little is known about study abroad and its contribution to foreign language and other international learning. As noted by Ulrich Teichler of the University of Kassel, "Most of the research available on academic mobility and international education seems to be occasional, coincidental, sporadic, or episodic." An exception was the Study Abroad Evaluation Project, a major research undertaking on the structures and impacts of study abroad programs offered by higher education institutions in France, the Federal Republic of Germany, Sweden, the United Kingdom, and the United States.

The recent publication of the Association of International Education Administrators, *A Research Agenda for the Internationalization of Higher Education in the United States, Report and Recommendations of an AIEA Working Group,* argues that serious public policy questions are being raised about the value and importance of federal and other public support to international education. The Working Group's report states that "a diversified set of research activities is urgently needed to inform the debate" on these policy questions, and that among one focus of the research should be the outcomes and contributions of study abroad and international exchanges. As individuals and organizations pursue this research, we may be better able to answer some of the questions raised in this paper.

The Internationalization of Higher Education

POLICY AND PROGRAM ISSUES

Seth Spaulding, James Mauch, and Lin Lin

We are now living in an era of rapidly developing globalization. No nation can live independently of the others. There is a clear interdependence of people, of media, of national security and economic interests among nations. Accordingly, universities and colleges are confronted with the need to internationalize for the purpose of producing globally competent citizens. These citizens must be empowered by experience, be committed to lifelong learning, and be aware of cultural diversity. They must recognize global interdependence, be capable of working in various environments, and accept responsibility for world citizenship.

Over the years, there has been considerable interest in the internationalization of higher education and, in fact, there has been significant international activity on campuses in most countries. Many scholars would claim that universities and colleges, by their very nature, are universal and that a discipline or profession must be open to ideas, issues, and research from throughout the world if it is to be modern, scientific, and of long-term significance to national development.

As nations and citizens increasingly recognize the interdependence of na-

This is a revised version of the article by James Mauch and Seth Spaulding, "The Internationalization of Higher Education: Who Should be Taught What and How," which appeared in *Journal of General Education,* vol. 41, pp. 111–129. © 1992 by The Pennsylvania State University. Reproduced by permission of the publisher.

tions, the flow of students and faculty members among universities of different countries, and the internationalization of the curriculum are becoming significant issues. These issues, in turn, are becoming international in themselves, with universities in various countries competing for outstanding foreign scholars and students, and attempting to internationalize their curriculum for the purpose of improving their ability to prepare modern, scientific, and competitive citizens, faculty, researchers, and students.

The "internationalization of higher education" means encouraging student and faculty exchange programs; bringing international concerns and issues to teaching, research and service activities of an institution; holding educational conferences; internationalization of professional writings; and providing educational and cultural aid to other nations. It also means constant efforts to reduce curricular parochialism and to open institutions of higher education to new ideas and international views. In a word, it encompasses various forms of intellectual, cultural and educational exchanges between two or more nations in the world (Adams & Garraty 1960; Deutsch 1970; Jenkins 1983; Gutek 1993).

This paper will focus on policy and program issues in international higher education. It will review the issues and problems currently faced by educational policy makers and higher education institutions in areas of international education, and suggest research agendas, including the possibility of developing research on campuses in various countries and regions beyond the statistical information currently available on international students and student exchanges.

A word on terminology: "international students" are often called "foreign students." In Great Britain and Australia, they are commonly called "overseas students." In this paper, the terms "international students" and "foreign students" will be used interchangeably. "International education," in turn, may be used somewhat differently by each of several professional groups. Those interested primarily in international student exchange think of international education as the exchange of students. NAFSA, originally founded in 1948 as the National Association of Foreign Student Advisors, in 1964 changed its name to the National Association for Foreign Student Affairs. It has now (as of 1990) become NAFSA: Association of International Educators, though it remains primarily concerned with student exchange and to some degree with the teaching of English as a foreign language. It publishes occasional directories of people and institutions involved in international educational exchange (NAFSA 1995) and various studies of education systems in other countries, often in cooperation with AACRAO, the association representing collegiate registrars (discussed below). Other professional associations, including the Comparative and International Education Society and those involved in area studies associations and in many area study centers on campuses, tend to use the term "international education" to mean broader concerns of global, multi- and inter-cultural education involving the internationalization of the curriculum and the encouragement of international research by both faculty and students. This range of interests is both a strength and a weakness in the area. It is clearly positive that a number of different kinds of specialists are interested in the broad field of international education. However, when policy issues are discussed, each of several professional and academic interest groups may take divergent positions without consulting one another.

Policy Issues

The issues vary somewhat from country to country and institution to institution. Clearly, there is much greater variety in institutional policies among colleges and universities in a highly decentralized system as that in the United States than there is in countries with a more centralized higher education system, e.g. France (Clark 1983). But no matter what the country, the broad issues generally have to do with the kinds of encouragement the government and the individual universities should offer domestic faculty and students to become involved in international activities (teaching, research and service); the extent to which international students should be recruited and supported; the extent to which international students can be integrated into the life of the university so that both domestic and international students benefit equally from the experience; and the extent to which foreign study and exchanges for domestic students should be organized and supported.

International student issues are often at the core of policy issues. Essentially, these involve decisions as to the numbers of international students appropriate, the costs and benefits involved in their education, the services they need, and the academic concerns and opportunities raised by their presence on campus. Each of these issues is related to broader policy concerns of governments and academics. Some of these relate to foreign policy, foreign aid or immigration issues; others relate to the educational goals of institutions of higher education and how best to meet them.

These issues, in turn, must be examined in the context of the changing higher education environment in individual countries and regions. Issues such as autonomy and accountability; of privatization of higher education; of universities and national development; of changing roles of universities; of evolving notions of research and development; and of changing political contexts all will affect the way internationalization of higher education will be viewed in the future (Morsy and Altbach 1993). We shall not attempt to deal with all of these issues in this paper, but those interested in future research might pursue these relationships.

The Major Participants in International Education

The internationalization of higher education often means different things to different participants in higher education. Participants include policy-makers and administrators in government and in higher education institutions; they include the faculty and students (both domestic and foreign) in institutions of higher education; they include business and industry, the parents, and the public. Other

participants include sponsoring and funding agencies, both in sending and receiving countries, and such international agencies as the United Nations Development Program (UNDP) and the various specialized agencies of the United Nations (UN).

Some of these participants conceptualize international education as exchange
programs, whereby local students are sent abroad for study in summer programs
or longer programs in cooperation with higher education institutions abroad. Others see international education primarily as the education of foreign students.
Still others see international education as a concern for introducing more global
concepts or issues into the curriculum of higher education; these see the curriculum issue as providing opportunities for the best and fullest application and utili-
zation of knowledge without artificial national, racial, ethnic, or religious boundaries. Many institutions see international education, in part, as overseas projects,
often assisting developing countries in the context of economic and social programs under bilateral or multilateral technical cooperation agencies; some encourage collaborative research with overseas faculty and institutions (Bailey, Buchanan, and Holleman 1990; National Task Force 1990; Tonkin 1984).

Interests in international education are often ideological. This is especially
true of government support for internationalizing higher education. Recent policies of the U.S. and the UK governments, for instance, towards higher education
are a part of a conservative ideology that, on the whole, has negatively affected
higher education budgets and has thus encouraged a harder look by university
administrators at costs, such as fees charged foreign students. At the same time,
governments which see internationalization of higher education as consistent
with an inter-related world economy often place high priority on subsidizing international elements of higher education. Such may, in part, be the current motivation in Japan and Australia, both of which are stepping up activities to attract
foreign students and to encourage the international involvement of their institutions in technical cooperation projects, especially in the Asian region.

Foreign Student Issues in
National Policy Context

Some policy issues concerning foreign students on any university campus are
reasonably straightforward. How many foreign students does the university want,
in what academic areas and at what levels and why? How will they be recruited
and screened so that they most likely will be able to handle the work? How much
will foreign students pay and for what? Other issues suggest a somewhat more
complex matrix of concerns. If the university sees a value in having foreign students, how can legislatures and politicians be convinced of their value when some
may feel that foreign students compete with local students? To what extent will
foreign students be used as teaching and research assistants and in what areas?
When they are so used, what are the problems and the training needs to assure
that they perform well? How much will the needs of the foreign students and their

countries be taken into account when structuring the course of study for each student? How will foreign students be used to enrich the campus and the community while they are on campus? How will counseling and other services be provided to foreign students? How much should the university assist foreign students in returning home and getting placed in employment? How much should the host university cooperate with foreign students' home country institutions in arranging teaching and research opportunities there? How international and multinational does an institution wish to be in its faculty, students, curriculum and research?

A number of these questions can be answered only in the context of governmental policy; some governments (national, provincial or local) establish quotas for foreign students; others establish fee schedules or even visa charges designed to recover supposed educational costs. Some countries (for example, France, Germany, Russia, and most eastern European countries) charge little or nothing to either domestic or foreign students; others have generous scholarship aid in the assumption that foreign student programs are sensible elements of foreign policy. In decentralized systems of higher education, as in the United States, each individual institution, within policies formulated by state governments, sets its own policies concerning foreign students. These policies, however, are affected by immigration rules concerning international students and by various legislative and policy trends having little to do with institutional funding.

Policies vis-a-vis foreign students are often reactive rather than pro-active. During periods of economic stagnation and of conservative political domination, many host countries change their attitude toward foreign students, tightening visa requirements, charging higher tuition and other fees, and generally becoming less welcoming. Many institutions of higher education, at the same time, need foreign students during such periods in order to fill the spaces available in some academic areas, and often to fill teaching and research assistantships at the doctoral level. Few host countries have established a clear-cut, long-term policy toward foreign students which is based on reasoned judgement concerning academic and foreign policy goals (Lin 1998; Spaulding 1980).

This is not to say that there have not been numerous commissions, studies, recommendations, and occasional laws dealing with international education (as with the unfunded International Education Act of 1966 in the U.S.). Few have had, however, any long-term impact. One such commission in Canada has suggested that all universities enroll a minimum number of foreign students; Canada's Bovey Commission recommended, in 1985, that the proportion of foreign students not fall below five percent of enrollment.

The United States has been the leading recipient of foreign students over the years since World War II, although France, the United Kingdom, and other European countries have been major players in terms of attracting foreign students, especially from former colonies. According to Zikopoulos (Institute of International Education 1993), during the 1950s and the 1960s, the United States became the recipient of nearly one-third (34.75%) of all foreign students in the world, and was followed by France (10.77%), the Federal Republic of Germany

Table 1. Development of International Student Enrollment in Higher Education in the United States

	1954–1955	1969–1970	1975–1976	1984–1985	1997–1998
International Student Enrollment	34,232	135,000	179,340	342,113	481,280

Sources: Broaded 1993; Dalili 1982; Evangelauf 1985; Institute of International Education 1994, 1995, 1998

(7.29%), and the United Kingdom (5.6%). In the late 1990s, the United States remained the number one host country while the order of the next three, the UK, France and Germany, has varied from time to time (UNESCO 1992, 1993, 1994, 1995, 1996, 1997, and 1998).

The growth of the international student population in the U.S. during the past 40 or so years has also been dramatic (see Table 1). Many international students come from developing countries to universities in industrialized nations. Of about a million such students world-wide in the mid-eighties, about two-thirds went to the U.S., France, Germany, England, and the U.S.S.R. By 1984, China was eleventh among countries providing students to the U.S.; but in 1989, the Chinese student population had surpassed those from Taiwan and Japan, two leading international-student providers to the U.S., and had become the largest international student group in the country. In 1994, there were 44,380 Chinese students in various American colleges and universities, constituting about 10% of the total number of international students in the United States. By 1997, however, Japan passed China as the largest contributor of international students sojourning in the U.S., although China continued to enroll the most students in major research universities. Community college enrollments jumped by nearly 20% from 1993 to 1997, while research institutions have had an international student increase of only about 2.1% during those five years (Broaded 1993; Editing Committee of Chinese Students and Scholars Overseas Series 1992; Huang 1995; Institute of International Education 1996, 1997, and 1998).

Zikopoulos (Institute of International Education 1993) specified that the number of American institutions that enrolled international students increased from 1,712 in 1960 to 2,417 in 1992. By 1996, in turn, IIE reported that some 2,579 institutions enrolled international students in 1995–1996. Exchanges among European countries, however, have been hampered by lack of equivalencies in degrees, programs and structures of universities from country to country, though there are efforts to create mechanisms for increased exchanges. Some of these are discussed in later sections of this paper.

In the U.S., the general international student enrollment is not only increasing in absolute numbers but is also a growing percentage of total students during the past several decades. In 1954–55, for example, there were 34,000 international students, constituting 1.4% of the U.S. enrollment (Institute of International Education 1990). Forty-four years later, that number had increased more than tenfold to about 481,280 students from overseas, and the percentage rose to 3.4% of the total enrollment in higher education (Institute of International Education 1998).

A number of factors have contributed to the rapid increase of the international student population after World War II. In the United States, the federal government passed several major pieces of legislation that concern the provision of assistance to students and governments of the Third World countries. These have included the Fulbright Act of 1946, the Marshall Plan of 1948, the Smith-Mundt Act of 1948, the Foreign Assistance Act of 1961, the Mutual Educational and Cultural Exchange Act of 1961, and the International Education Act of 1966 (although the latter was never funded). These major pieces of legislation were designed to assist the educational and cultural development of emerging countries and provided the initial momentum for international student exchange (Lin 1998; Spaulding & Lin 1997).

By the early 1990s, most international students tended to be in business and management (19.5%), engineering (19%), math and computer science (9.4%), and physical and life sciences (8.5%), although there are substantial numbers in other areas also (Institute of International Education 1990). In 1997–1998, the trend basically remained: business and management (20.9%), engineering (14.4%), math and computer science (8.5%), and physical and life sciences (7.7%). Foreign students are of critical importance to some advanced fields, particularly the physical and natural sciences, business administration, engineering, and computer sciences. As the number of U.S. citizens earning science and engineering doctorates has been declining, their places have been taken by foreign students. Foreign students with temporary visas earned 30% of all physical science Ph.D.s and 45% of the engineering doctorates in 1988. In some large research universities, foreign students actually outnumber domestic students in doctoral programs such as business and engineering. If the trend continues, it may be that the majority of faculty members in these areas will be foreign nationals or immigrants since future faculty members are prepared in doctoral programs. For example, in 1985, two-thirds of all post-doctorate engineering positions went to non-U.S. citizens (Pool 1990).

Why do so many foreign students choose U.S. institutions instead of other alternatives? Kaplan (1983), an American scholar, explained:

> The developing nations have sent us their youths because they saw the way we lived and they aspired to share in the wonders of the world the United States had created for its people. In order to improve the standard of living of their people, the nations of the Third World sought greater efficiency in the operations of the structures of government and industry. They recognized the need for people with special training to achieve greater efficiency. They could see that the United States had efficiency— it had a telephone system that worked, a postal system that served the people, a bureaucracy that seemed to respond to the wishes of the people.

To sum up, there are several inter-related reasons, no one of which is a sufficient reason in itself:

First, U.S. institutions and society are relatively free and open to ideas. This is a relatively multi-cultural society, with less conformity demanded than elsewhere. Religious and political dogmas tend to be suspect, more open to question, debate, and investigation. This is attractive to many overseas students.

Second, the time to complete a course of study is seen as reasonable. In Japan and some European countries, earning a Ph.D. can take nearly a decade, and often requires foreign students to learn the national language, which is seen as less easy to learn or less universal than English. Also, U.S. institutions offer professional masters degrees that enable students to complete graduate work in less time than a doctorate requires. Many countries, heavily dependent on trained personnel, cannot wait a decade for students to return.

Third, accredited institutions of higher education tend to be seen as serious about their role. When, in the U.S., an institution is accredited to educate students in, for example, medicine, the health professions, nursing, library science, education or other professions, there are public assessments of the programs and institutions, and other published data as well which indicate the nature and quality of the institution.

Fourth, officials responsible for sending students to the United States to study perceive that these are more likely to complete their work than students who stay home.

Fifth, the English language is an important consideration. To be a student in another country requires long, hard study, and a high level of language competency and dedication. The student not only has to listen to lectures, but write papers, with proper grammar and vocabulary appropriate to the country and the discipline. All examinations are written in the foreign language. A decision to study in a foreign country and language entails an enormous investment. The student who invests that much time and energy in learning a language, as well as a body of literature, may choose English because it has become the language of international trade, communication, and scholarship, and it opens many opportunities (Mauch 1984).

Quantifying the Benefits

The reasons why there are rarely coherent, long-term national policies in the foreign student arena are various. For one, it is difficult to quantify the benefits from hosting foreign students. Most academics feel that the quality of education is improved when there are students and faculty from different cultures on campus. The internationalization of higher education provides, as many people would claim, an opportunity to make higher education truly universal, with young people learning during their periods of formation that we are indeed one world, with issues and problems which are universal and which require world cooperation to resolve. Noronha (1992) pointed out that international education has brought "a global perspective and a sense of prestige to many campuses." But these very positive benefits are difficult to evaluate in quantitative terms.

Many foreign policy specialists and even politicians feel that there is a long-term value in having students trained in their universities return to home countries to become leaders in politics, business, the military, and in other areas. International students often represent the intellectual and social elite of their home countries. Lee, Abd-Ella and Burke (1981) observed that many leaders of government, industry, technology, education, and science were drawn from among international students. Lin (1998) noted, for example, that in China, the late former Premier during Mao's era, Zhou Enlai, and the successor of Mao as the most powerful figure in the Chinese government, Deng Xiaoping, were once poor international students in France during the 1920s, having to work part-time to keep their studies going. Later they became the top leaders of one of the most populous and influential countries in the world.

Essentially, educational exchange can further a country's long-term political and economic goals. Kneedler (1991), for example, pointed out that the policy of encouraging international students to study in the U.S. has contributed to the country's continuing political and economic influence on other parts of the world. The Institute of International Education (1994), the largest and most active non-profit organization in the field of international education exchange, also maintains that foreign students who were educated in the United States, especially those in the areas of business and engineering, may later work in positions that would help facilitate international trade between the United States and the sending country. This is an area often dubbed "public diplomacy," essentially referring to activities involving citizens of nations rather than the traditional diplomacy involving only governments and their foreign ministries. But how do you quantify this benefit? How much is this worth to host governments in terms of financing the costs associated with international students on campus?

Australia is among the countries that have been reassessing the amount they are willing to subsidize of the cost of educating foreign students. The Goldring Committee in 1984 provided comprehensive information concerning the overseas student population in Australia, and thereafter the government announced policies to gradually increase their overseas student charge. For a time after the introduction of this new policy, enrollments of international students dramatically declined, although informal education (short-term training, etc.) increased. By the early 1990s, however, the Australian government initiated new initiatives to increase economic and cultural linkages with Asia and many new programs to subsidize foreign students were put in place. From January 1997 to January 1998, Australia increased its international student enrollment by 14% compared to the U.S. increase of 5.1%. Australian increase of students that year from some Asian countries is even more dramatic. Japanese enrollment increased 14.9 percent vs. 1.7% in the U.S.; Chinese enrollment increased 29.4% vs. 10.5% in the U.S.; 21.1% increase of Taiwanese students vs. 1.2% in the U.S. (Institute of International Education 1998). It appears that the Australians now see foreign student exchange as important in foreign policy and they are putting into place a broad range of policies to encourage international students, especially in the Asian region.

Such cost/benefit questions are especially significant in times of financial austerity. When universities are cutting back rather than expanding, the prudent administrator looks for ways to save funds where it will least affect the health of the institution. Budget restraints have been deep at many universities in countries that host the majority of foreign students. Even the prestigious universities such as Oxford are finding that they do not have the funds for filling faculty vacancies and for other core institutional costs. Is it any wonder that questions are being raised as to the costs of international students on campus?

What Are the Real Costs?

At certain periods in some countries, the debate in policy circles concerning financing of higher education has somewhat eclipsed the more substantive concerns about internationalizing higher education. Higher education is seen by many as something needed by domestic students and supported by their parents, and foreign students are expected more and more to pay what is considered the full cost of their education. Study abroad programs, similarly, are generally expected to pay their own way. This raises the question of the real cost of foreign students on campus. Marginal cost (actual money spent for each additional student) may be far less than the average per-student cost, especially in academic areas where there are empty spaces. In addition, up to a certain point, institutional expansion may provide economies of scale, with average per-student cost declining.

A number of macro-studies suggest that international students are a new resource, contributing financially to the country both in tuition fees and in living costs. Evangelauf (1985) indicated that a survey showed that two-thirds of the international students paid their expenses primarily from their own money or with help from their families. Zikopoulos (Institute of International Education 1988) also reported that the great majority of foreign students (77.2%) financed their studies primarily with funds originated from outside the United States; only a relatively small portion of the students (21.9%) received primary support from U.S. sources. Some ten years later (1997–1998 academic year), 76% of international students received their funding from outside the United States (Institute of International Education 1998). The IIE in 1988 estimated that each year, more than $2.5 billion was devoted to the education of students from other countries in the United States. Hayes and Lin (1994) estimated that international students annually contributed $6.8 billion to the U.S. economy in tuition and fees; and an additional $3.5 billion was spent by these students for living expenses and other purchases in U.S. towns and colleges. In 1997–1998, the IIE (1998) reported a combination of foreign expenditures of $7.5 billion on tuition and cost of living by international students. Todd Davis, director of research at the Institute of International Education, considers international students as important assets to higher institutions and to the states where they are situated. He indicated that "foreign students bring dollars to the campuses; foreign scholars bring connections and expertise"; and should they decline in number, this would affect American higher institutions economically and academically (Desruisseaux 1995). Policy-makers now appear to be moderating the tendency in the early '80s to raise foreign student tuition to astronomical highs and many are attempting to attract more international students in the future.

The concern for costs has created a patchwork of policies in many countries. In Canada, foreign students pay anywhere from 50–300% over what domestic students pay. In England, the fees for international students rose dramatically in the early '80s to the point where enrollment dropped off equally dramatically. From 1979/80 to 1983/84, foreign student enrollment dropped by almost 40%. In the U.S., public universities often charge international students high out-of-state tuition while many private institutions do not.

High fee structures not only limit the number of students coming from abroad, but they also limit those who do come to children from wealthier families (most international students being self-supporting or supported by their families). Some countries and institutions that have relatively high fee structures can grant scholarships to poorer international students; others, such as France, charge little to any international student who succeeds in gaining admission.

A number of private institutions in the U.S. that have excess capacity have, in recent years, stepped up recruitment of international students in order to maintain enrollment levels at a minimum necessary to maintain full academic programs. Some of these institutions have established offices to recruit and serve international students and some have even set up special academic programs that they feel are relevant to the needs of international students. Some colleges may be using deceptive advertising in their efforts to fill vacancies with international students. The extent to which this is a problem is unclear, but the issue is one that is important to reputable organizations concerned with the education of foreign student issues in the United States (Council of Graduate Schools 1991).

Collaborative Institutional Arrangements

Many major research universities have programs that encourage the international exchange of students and scholars. For example, at the University of Pittsburgh, there is a University Center for International Studies under which reside various area studies centers, e.g. Asian, Latin American, and Russian and East European, within which faculties and programs collaborate. Some professional schools on campus have international program offices as well (education, business and engineering are examples). These offices and centers have established scores of relationships with universities and scholars abroad and have taken leadership in internationalizing the curriculum on campus. Many smaller, primarily undergraduate colleges, have established international offices, often to recruit foreign students, but occasionally to establish joint programs with institutions abroad. Community colleges, e.g. Lansing Community College and Valencia Community College, often have student and faculty exchange programs, often the result of institutional arrangements. Such programs not only encourage exchange of scholars, but also encourage collaborative relationships with universities in other nations (Bailey, Buchanan, and Holleman 1990).

Such cooperative research and academic exchange programs often arrange for American students to study abroad. This raises few problems from a substantive point of view unless students wish to transfer course work home. Western European governments and universities, for instance, have for years been aware of the desirability of increasing student exchange among universities in the region, but problems of differences in curriculum and degree requirements have severely limited such exchange to very small numbers of students (Sayegh 1990). The situation may be changing with the European Community acceptance of the European Regional Action Scheme for the Mobility of University Students (ERASMUS) to encourage student flows (Sayegh 1990).

On the faculty research side, international collaboration has not always meant truly joint research enterprises. More and more, however, truly joint research efforts are the rule, and research networks in several fields have produced remarkable results over time. The International Education Achievement Association, which has produced the many achievement and educational indicators studies, is an example.

Comparability of Degrees

The United Nations Educational, Scientific and Cultural Organization (UNESCO) and others have done numerous studies concerning the equivalency of degrees (including its pioneering *World Guide to Higher Education* in 1982), but commonly understood standards of transferability of credit among and between countries are far from being achieved. With a number of universities adopting a cumulative course credit system, such as that in place in the United States, comparability may be more achievable in the future (Spaulding and Lin 1997).

European nations have been concerned with the mobility and recognition of university degrees for some time (CEPES 1985; Mohr and Liebig 1988). In the European Community specifically, with the gradual collapse of national boundaries in the 1990s, there is a particularly keen interest in finding ways to make it easier for students and faculty to cross boundaries. In order to do this, the Community has ERASMUS, which is moving ahead rapidly to provide the infrastructure and to encourage institutional changes necessary to foster such mobility. One of the first steps was simply to get a listing of the institutions and the programs in the Community, and a remarkable publication which does just that—and which includes information on how ERASMUS operates—was issued (ERASMUS 1988). Clearly, the European higher education panorama will be changing dramatically over the next few years, and this will affect the international education programs of countries outside the region which have exchange arrangements with countries of the Community (Council of Europe 1990).

Perhaps the best efforts to date to come up with information on comparability of U.S. and foreign degrees are the various publications (sometimes joint) of the American Association of College Registrars and Admissions Officers (AACRAO) and NAFSA: Association of International Educators. The National Council on the Evaluation of Foreign Student Credentials of AACRAO includes NAFSA and other higher education organizations. Many workshops on individual countries and closely related countries have been held, each issuing a report, and nearly 100 country or regional guides have been issued to date. These describe the educational systems in countries examined, and attempt to establish U.S. equivalents of degrees offered at both school and higher education levels. These recommendations are advisory and are accepted as institutions and their faculties see fit.

With complex countries such as India, the problem of establishing comparability is immense. For example, in a joint report (AACRAO/NAFSA 1986), "Projects for International Education Research" workshop held in 1985, India is listed as having over 125 universities and university-level institutions recognized by the Association of Indian Universities and over 5000 recognized colleges, all with over three million students. The report attempts to describe degrees in differing academic areas, suggesting, in general, that master's degrees in India are the equivalent to an undergraduate degree in the United States and that bachelor's degrees are only worth credit toward advanced undergraduate placement in the U.S. Such broad generalizations often lead to a lack of recognition of outstanding bachelor's and master's programs in some institutions that may be equal to or even surpass U.S. standards for the same degrees. Considerable emphasis is placed on the number of years that a country includes in basic education and the number of years required for various degrees, with little attempt to differentiate content at the various levels. Thus, a three-year bachelor's degree in India will never be recognized by AACRAO/NAFSA as the equivalent of a U.S. bachelor's, even though a U.S. four-year program might not have the depth of some Indian programs.

Host Institution Contacts
with Home Countries

Some institutions that are serious about the quality of international students, especially at the graduate level, have tried home-country recruitment and interview visits. The faculty members involved in such efforts not only are able to better judge the quality of applicants through such visits, but also often develop a better understanding of the context from which the foreign students come. This helps the faculty members to appropriately enrich the academic program to suit foreign students, and often develops into inter-institutional relationships that go far beyond student exchange.

Occasionally, this kind of relationship will develop into various kinds of degree programs delivered in non-traditional ways. Many institutions have developed distance education programs or even campuses abroad in cooperation with local institutions. Even more common are various kinds of collaborative activities between American colleges and universities and foreign institutions.

At the University of Pittsburgh, for example, there is an ongoing doctoral degree program in higher education management begun in 1997 in cooperation with Rangsit University in Thailand. It was designed to provide practicing higher education administrators in Thailand a full doctoral program without their having to spend the usual three or more years in Pittsburgh away from their higher education posts in Thailand. A group of 11 Thai higher education administrators participated in the initial program. They first studied at the University of Pittsburgh for eight months from September 1997–April 1998, then returned to their home universities to continue their jobs, returning to the University of Pittsburgh for another four months from September to December 1999. American professors in higher education administration from the University of Pittsburgh travel to Thailand to teach during the periods when the administrators are there. The courses offered in Thailand are arranged during summer periods and are very intensive (each lasting about 3.5 to 4 weeks). This program is under a fixed-fee contract with Rangsit University and per-student charges are considerably lower than those of a resident international student who is full-time on the Pittsburgh campus. Moreover, students can continue working while they are studying, with no more than eight months away from their home campuses at any one time.

Such programs encourage students from other countries to remain home after they receive their degrees. Studies of the migration of high level talent generally show that there are numerous factors operating in the "brain-drain" phenomenon. If the institutions from both countries are in good contact, and if students are counseled concerning opportunities at home, then fewer international students will be likely to migrate (Spaulding and Flack 1976; Altbach and Wang 1989).

Migration-of-talent issues, of course, are complex. In countries where there is an over-production of university graduates there may be an advantage to the country of some out-migration. Egypt is a case in point. Excess high-level manpower exported by Egypt produces considerable foreign exchange (large sums are returned by Egyptians working abroad) and diminishes the political pressure for jobs that might occur if out-migration were not available as a safety valve. For years, American, Australian, and Canadian universities have filled academic openings with foreign, or foreign-trained scholars. This international movement of scholars has brought a wealth of knowledge, practice, and policies to home institutions of higher education (Altbach, Kelly, and Lulat 1985; Lin 1998).

Curriculum and Related Policy Issues

Programs, curriculum, and infrastructures to encourage internationalization of campuses are undergoing scrutiny and debate. Often the benefits of such programs are not well thought out. Area studies programs that exist on major university campuses in some form are often dominated by the humanities and the social sciences, with little participation by the professional schools. The international interests of professional schools are often concentrated on participation by the faculty in a variety of consulting and technical assistance projects which may little impact on the curriculum, if at all. The inter-connection between student exchange policies and the internationalization of the curriculum is often not examined.

Historically, in the U.S., for example, even though many colleges and universities opened wide their doors and enthusiastically encouraged international students to come, not all educational institutions were prepared to satisfy the programmatic goals of international students. Many of them were indifferent to the presence and special needs of these students, and provided little support to assist them in understanding how their training in the United States could be transferred and applied to their home countries. Stephen C. Dunnet of NAFSA, for example, indicated in 1981 that not only were U.S. institutions of higher education indifferent to the adjustment problems of foreign students, they also gave little attention to such problems as the relevancy of American educational programs for the developing world. Inter-disciplinary work, in turn, essential to understanding international social, economic and cultural issues, is hampered by the disciplinary structure of university campuses.

Spaulding and Colucci in 1982 pointed out that at that time few colleges and universities had attempted to adjust curriculum to the needs of international students, many of whom were from developing countries whose manpower and technological problems differed substantially from those of the United States. Even earlier, Moghrabi's study (1972) reported that many international students were not motivated by the curriculum, and a large number of the students interviewed expressed a lack of interest and ability in continuing with their present programs.

There is not much evidence to suggest that the situation has changed dramatically over the years. A recent study conducted by Lin (1998) found that Chinese students at the University of Pittsburgh encountered problems concerning curriculum and program relevance. These problems were especially demonstrated in the non-transferability of certain knowledge that Chinese students acquired in China and the indifference of the university to their special problems and needs.

Essentially, curriculum and related issues on campus are neglected areas of policy study (National Task Force 1990). The new international imperatives suggest the need for internationalizing the curriculum. But to what extent should this internationalization be haphazard as opposed to focussed and purposeful? For instance, in the disciplines and professions, has there been a careful consideration of what domestic students need to know about the world in order to be well prepared? Has there been careful study in the programs that attract foreign students concerning the adaptations that may need to be made?

This is not to say that there has been a lack of task forces, recommendations, and, indeed, funding sources to encourage internationalizing the curriculum in higher education. Area and language centers have been funded by the federal government since the 1960s, first under the National Defense Education Act and later under related legislation. Milestone studies such as the Council on Learning's Education and the World View Project produced several works, including one by Humphrey Tonkin and Jane Edwards (1981) on *The World in the Curriculum.* Richard Lambert's (1980) *New Directions in International Education,* a special issue of the Annals of the American Academy of Political and Social Science, is an example of the interest of those in the disciplines in internationalizing the curriculum. Goodwin and Nacht (1983, 1988), Craufurd and Nacht (1988), and Lulat, Altbach, and Kelly (1986) are other studies of needs in the area. Robert Leestma (1978), then vice president for International Programs of the American Association of State Colleges and Universities (AASCU), wrote on global education issues in *American Education.* AASCU also issued a manual by Harari (1981) on *Internationalizing the Curriculum and the Campus: Guidelines for AASCU Institutions.* Individual universities regularly appoint task forces on foreign student and curriculum issues (for example, International Student Task Force 1983). Some studies on foreign student participation and exchange programs suggest ways in which international students and curriculum interests inter-relate (Goodman 1983).

In the mid-'90s, the Association Liaison Office for University Cooperation in Development (ALO), headquartered at the National Center for Higher Education in Washington with support of the United States Agency for International Development (USAID) and various national higher education organizations, organized a series of policy roundtables exploring the role of higher education in global development. The series examined emerging cross-sectoral issues and the changing circumstances of development cooperation, especially involving higher education. The focus was on new aspects of development problems, innovative and cost-efficient responses, and partnerships for global development.

The goals of the Policy Roundtable Series were: (1) To bring higher education expertise to bear on the identification of key and emerging development problems, strategic approaches for their amelioration, and effective models of partnership for development; (2) To predict and describe the future of development cooperation to advance human, economic, and democratic development; (3) To promote the constructive engagement of informed thinkers from the higher education community and USAID on topics of common concern.

Topics of the roundtable series included: (1) "Assessing Results of Higher Education Development Cooperation"; (2) "The Look of Development Cooperation Ten Years Out: What New Roles for the State, Higher Education, Business and Industry, and the Community?"; (3) "Higher Education, States, the Private Sector, and the Community: New Partnerships for Economic and Human Capacity Development" (case studies presented by higher education/state/business and industry teams); (4) "The Greying of Development Expertise: What's Needed and How Will the Next Generation Get Trained?"; (5) "Increasing the Relevance of Higher Education to Development: What U.S. and Mexican Public/Private

Partnerships Can Do?"; (6) "Coordination and Collaboration in Public Education and Outreach on International Development."

Reports on all of the above policy roundtables are available at <http://www. aascu.org/ALO/pubs.htm>. The one on the greying of development expertise implies that many higher education programs designed to prepare international specialists in various professions have been de-emphasized in the university budget cuts of the eighties and nineties (Association Liaison Office 1996). This roundtable and others undertaken by the ALO have taken the position that internationalizing the higher education curriculum and other international activities are essential if higher education is to play an important role in world development. ALO also sponsors a variety of projects designed to further involve higher education in international university linkages and development activities.

Clearly, institutional policy issues on the internationalization of higher education are many and these, in turn, are further complicated by changing policy climates at the national and international levels. We have only touched on the many issues in this paper, but perhaps this introduction may suggest that more visibility is needed for such issues at all levels: institutional, provincial, national, and international.

Multilateral Policy Studies

In addition to national policy studies, there are numerous international policy studies involving multilateral organizations and regional groupings of countries. Many of these concentrate on issues that can be resolved through collaborative efforts. The United Nations and the specialized agencies within the UN system, such as UNESCO and the World Bank, for example, have worked actively to provide financing for various educational programs and projects in developing countries, most of which have included various kinds of exchange activities. All of this has contributed to the international networking of academics and institutions interested in the development of education worldwide.

Many of these multilateral efforts could be improved with increased participation of national authorities and higher education institutions. UNESCO, for instance, could improve the already impressive coverage of its *Study Abroad* manual (UNESCO 1997) by working with national authorities to collect information in a more comprehensive and complete fashion from institutions that do not respond to their questionnaires. UNESCO's *Study Abroad* was first published in 1948 and has been published regularly since that time, becoming a key reference for individuals and governments who wish to find higher education institutions worldwide that welcome foreign students. The data are compiled from questionnaires sent to governments and institutions and only those that respond by stated deadlines are included. The 1998–1999 edition was compiled by UNESCO's International Bureau of Education in Geneva, Switzerland.

This effort is complemented by Peterson's *Study Abroad* manual, issued annually to help U.S. students find opportunities for overseas study. This manual also lists overseas programs of American universities as well as universities abroad that accept American students for short- or long-term study programs. Peterson's also, of course, publishes a comprehensive set of manuals on American university programs. These manuals are often consulted by international students when exploring study in the U.S.

Organizations such as the AACRAO and NAFSA: Association of International Educators in the United States could initiate contacts with professional governmental authorities abroad, e.g. the Organization for Economic Co-operation and Development (OECD), UNESCO, the European Community (EC), and the Organization of American States (OAS), so as to come up with degree equivalency recommendations useful to all countries. It appears that AACRAO does not cooperate at the moment with the EC's ERASMUS program that is establishing equivalencies among European universities; AACRAO's policy apparently has been largely to ignore other international or regional efforts to establish mutually agreed-upon standards.

The Trans Regional Academic Mobility and Credential Evaluation Information Network (TRACE), organized by several groups and coordinated by the International Association of Universities (September 1989) in Paris, is an example of regional cooperation. Data being collected in the computerized network include: (1) data on systems, structure, and organization of higher education in each country; (2) data on institutions of higher education, including addresses, offices, divisions and subdivisions, admission criteria, programs of study, degrees awarded, and statistics on teachers and students; and (3) data on higher education qualifications and an overview of higher education degrees and diplomas in each country.

More case study and descriptive information is needed on how universities and governments organize and manage services and programs for internationalizing higher education. Many universities have extensive experience with foreign students and issues of internationalization (Blum 1991). Others who wish to move more vigorously into these areas may wish information and technical assistance from the more experienced institutions. Information should be collected and synthesized in a format that can be easily used by policy-makers and administrators in governments and higher education institutions.

Studies on the effects of the presence of foreign students and scholars on domestic issues of cultural diversity would be important. Such studies might enable the academic community to learn about the diversity of ethnic, linguistic, religious, cultural, and political backgrounds. It is often the foreign scholar who sees things differently, who brings diverse experiences, who asks the unusual but penetrating questions. In fact, the curriculum of universities too often omits the great contributions of many other cultures and peoples.

Studies on issues relating to the relevance of university curricula to international students are needed. International students often seek, or are required to seek, academic programs that are relevant to their needs and the needs of their countries. This, in turn, helps to internationalize the host institution. As papers and ideas are shared in classes and seminars, students learn from one another, and the curriculum is enriched. When students do academic work related to their own national needs, they not only enlighten other students, but they also preserve their cultural identity. Clearly, some critically needed skills and knowledge are basic and involve universally relevant subject matter, but if students are continually pressed to study curricula that are related to the host country, both students and hosts lose. The Council of Graduate Schools (1990) makes some very helpful suggestions on this issue.

Tracer studies, to see what has happened to students trained abroad, are badly needed. Such studies can provide information helpful in assessing the impact of such programs; they can also help governments and universities improve their programs and policies based on data rather than on assumptions as to the impact of such study. Again, considerable anecdotal material exists, but there are no systematic efforts to collect this material in a format that would be useful to administrators. UNESCO and the University of Pittsburgh hosted, in 1991, an International Forum of Experts on Research on Higher Education, which recommended greater emphasis on such research (Spaulding et al. 1991).

Such information, indeed, might encourage national governments to give higher priority to international issues in higher education, including but not limited to educational and cultural exchange, as significant elements of foreign policy. Universities and other higher education institutions would be encouraged if they had more consistent governmental support for international participation in higher education policy, management, curriculum, and exchange (National Task Force 1990).

Universities accepting foreign students can also develop policies for a more open international scholarly environment—more open to foreign ideas so as to encourage foreign students and faculty to break down institutional parochialism, to challenge orthodox thinking, and to bring another worldview to the classroom and faculty. This will certainly give a universality to academic institutions. After all, that is at the heart of the real purpose of a university, implied in its name, a place of learning where the universe of ideas, values, skills, and knowledge can freely compete for attention, criticism and support (Tonkin 1984).

Thus it falls not only on academics, but to all who identify with the community of scholars to break down ethnic and parochial superstitions. The sharing of knowledge and understanding is essential to a world growing ever smaller, closer, and more integrated. Knowledge should not be confused with wisdom. Knowledge will not necessarily make humans wise or good, but as scholars share in the discovery and dissemination of knowledge among peoples and cultures, there may be a better chance of developing wisdom and understanding.

The Challenges of the Next Century

Perhaps all can agree with the simple but profound preamble to the UNESCO Constitution: "Since wars begin in the minds of men, it is in the minds of men that the defences of peace must be constructed" (Spaulding and Lin 1997). In the long run, internationalization of higher education will be cost effective today if it contributes, however modestly, to constructing the defenses of peace in the minds of the young who will lead the world tomorrow.

In October 1998, nearly 5,000 participants converged on Paris to attend UNESCO's World Conference on Higher Education. This was one of the largest conferences ever held by this organization. The U.S. government sent an official delegation of 12 members, supplemented by dozens of others who attended at UNESCO's invitation. The Honorable David A. Longanecker, Assistant Secretary for Postsecondary Education, U.S. Department of Education, in his plenary presentation, indicated that ". . . we want to demonstrate our commitment to UNESCO, to internationalizing American higher education, and to working more closely with you, the world leaders in higher education." The conference also adopted a Declaration which the American delegation signed, along with scores of other country delegations, declaring—among over a dozen other articles—that the "international dimension of higher education is an inherent part of its quality. Networking, which has emerged as a major means of action, should be based on sharing, solidarity and equality among partners." It further specified that "regional and international normative instruments for the recognition of studies and diplomas should be ratified and implemented, including certification of skills, competencies and abilities of graduates . . ." (Americans for the Universality of UNESCO 1999).

Challenges remain but the momentum is building. The new century may be a golden one for the internationalization of higher education.

REFERENCES

AACRAO/NAFSA [The American Association of Collegiate Registrars and Admissions Officers; National Association for Foreign Student Affairs; from 1990, NAFSA: Association of International Educators]. 1986. *The Admission and Placement of Students from South Asia: Bangladesh, India, Pakistan, Sri Lanka.* Washington, DC: AACRAO and NAFSA.
Adams, W., & Garraty, J. A. 1960. *Is the World Our Campus?* Michigan: Michigan State University Press.
Altbach, P. G., & J. Wang. 1989. *Foreign Students and International Study: Bibliography and Analysis 1984–1988.* Lanham, MD: NAFSA and University Press of America.
Altbach, P. G., D. H. Kelly, & Y. G.-M. Lulat. 1985. *Research on Foreign Students and International Study: An Overview and Bibliography.* New York: Praeger.
Americans for the Universality of UNESCO. 1999. *Newsletter* (May—special feature on the World Conference on Higher Education). 28 Beaverbrook Road, Ashville, NC 28814.
Association Liaison Office for University Cooperation in Development. 1996. "The greying of development expertise: What's needed and how will the next generation get trained" (June 11). Washington, DC: National Center for Higher Education, Policy Roundtable Series, Higher Education and Global Development.

Bailey, L., Buchanan, N. E., & Holleman, M. 1990. "The LRC's role in helping faculty internationalize the community college curriculum." *New Directions for Community Colleges,* no. 71. San Francisco: Jossey-Bass.

Blum, D. E. 1991. "Reaching out to world develops strong reputation among foreign students." *The Chronicle of Higher Education* (November 27), p. A43.

Broaded, C. M. 1993. "China's response to the brain drain." *Comparative Education Review* 37(3):277–303.

CEPES, European Centre for Higher Education in Europe. (1985). "International mobility and recognition of studies, diplomas and degrees." *Higher Education in Europe* X(4):67–107.

Clark, B. R. 1983. *The Higher Education System: The Academic Organization in Cross-National Perspective.* Berkeley, CA: University of California Press.

Council of Europe Documentation Centre for Education in Europe. 1990. *Newsletter* (April). Strasbourg: Author.

Council of Graduate Schools. 1991. *International Graduate Students.* Washington, DC: Author.

Craufurd, D. G., & Nacht, M. 1988. *Abroad and Beyond: Patterns in American Overseas Education.* Cambridge: Cambridge University Press.

Dalili, F. 1982. *The University's Role in Foreign Student Adjustment.* Akron, OH: Educational Administration, University of Akron.

Desruisseaux, P. 1995. "Number of Foreign Scholars in the U.S. Continues to Drop." *The Chronicle of Higher Education,* pp. A42–44.

Deutsch, S. E. 1970. *International Education and Exchange: A Sociological Analysis.* Cleveland, OH: The Press of Case Western Reserve University.

Dunnet, S. C., ed. 1981. *Needs of Foreign Students from Developing Nations at U.S. Colleges and Universities,* p. xi. Washington, DC: National Association for Foreign Student Affairs.

Editing Committee of Chinese Students and Scholars Overseas Series. 1992. *History of Chinese Studying Abroad.* Beijing, China: China Friendship Publishing Co.

ERASMUS. 1988. *Higher Education in the European Community.* Luxembourg: Commission for the European Community, Office of Official Publications.

Evangelauf, J. 1985. "Number of Foreign Students in U.S. Rises Less than 1 Percent." *The Chronicle of Higher Education,* pp. 31–34.

Goodman, N. G. 1983. "The International Institutionalization of Education." A paper presented to the Comparative and International Education Society Annual Conference, Atlanta, GA.

Goodwin, C. D., & Nacht, M. 1988. *Abroad and Beyond: Patterns in American Overseas Education.* Cambridge: Cambridge University Press.

Goodwin, C. D., & Nacht, M. 1983. *Absence of Decision: Foreign Students in American Colleges and Universities.* New York: Institute of International Education.

Gutek, G. L. 1993. *American Education in a Global Society.* New York: Longman.

Harari, M. 1981. *Internationalizing the Curriculum and the Campus: Guidelines for AASCU Institutions.* Washington, DC: American Association of State Colleges and Universities.

Hayes, R., & Lin, H. R. 1994. "Coming to America: Developing Social Support Systems for International Students." *Journal of Multicultural Counseling and Development* 22:7–16.

http://www.aascu.org/ALO/pubs.htm. Web page of the Association Liaison Office for University Cooperation in Development. Washington, DC: National Center for Higher Education.

Huang, X. X., ed. 1995. *Problems of Chinese Students Studying Abroad.* Hunan, China: Hunan Education Publisher.

Institute of International Education (1988 through 1998 editions). *Open Doors: Report of International Exchange.* New York: Author.

International Association of Universities. 1989. *Activities Report* (September). Paris: IAU.

International Student Task Force. 1983. *International Students at the University of Pittsburgh.* Pittsburgh, PA: University of Pittsburgh.

Jenkins, H. M., ed. 1983. *Educating Students from Other Nations.* San Francisco: Jossey-Bass.

Kaplan, R. B. 1983. "Meeting the Educational Needs of Other Nations," in H. M. Jenkins, ed., *Educating Students from Other Nations,* pp. 253–276. San Francisco: Jossey-Bass.

Kneedler, R. 1991. "American Colleges Should Become More Accessible to Foreign Students." *The Chronicle of Higher Education,* p. B2.

Lambert, R., ed. 1980. *New Directions in International Education.* New York: The American Academy of Political and Social Science.

Lee, M. Y., Abd-Ella, M., & Burke, L. 1981. *Needs of Foreign Students from Developing Nations at U.S. Colleges and Universities.* Washington, DC: National Association for Foreign Student Affairs.

Leestma, R. 1978. "Global Education." *American Education* 14(6):6–13.

Lin, L. 1998. *Chinese Graduate Students' Perception of their Adjustment Experiences at the University of Pittsburgh.* Doctoral dissertation, University of Pittsburgh.

Lulat, Y. G-M., Altbach, P. G., & Kelly, D. H. 1986. *Governmental and Institutional Policies on Foreign Students: Analysis, Evaluation and Bibliography.* Buffalo, NY: Comparative Education Center, Faculty of Educational Studies, State University of New York at Buffalo.

Mauch, J. E. 1984. "Foreign Students: Catalyst for Reducing Parochialism." *International Dimensions of Higher Education.* Pittsburgh, PA: Institute for Higher Education, University of Pittsburgh.

Morsy, Z., & P. G. Altbach. 1993. *Higher Education in International Perspective.* Paris: UNESCO.

McCoy, M. A. 1996. *A Study of the Self-perceived Problems among Asian Students at the University of Memphis.* Doctoral dissertation, University of Memphis.

Moghrabi, K. 1972. "Educating Foreigners in the United States." *Improving College and University Teaching* 20:329–334.

Mohr, B., & Liebig, I., eds. 1988. *Higher Education in the European Community: A Directory of Courses and Institutions in 12 Countries* (5th ed.). Phoenix: Oryx Press.

NAFSA: Association of International Educators. 1995. *Institutions and Individuals in International Educational Exchange: 1995–1996 Directory.* Washington, DC: Author.

National Task Force on Undergraduate Education Abroad. 1990. *A National Mandate for Education Abroad: Getting on with the Task.* New York: Institute for International Education.

Noronha, J. 1992. "International and Multicultural Education: Unrelated Adversaries or Successful Partners." *New Directions for Teaching and Learning* 52:53–59.

Peterson's Guides. Annual. *Study Abroad.* Princeton, NJ: Peterson's.

Pool, R. 1990. "Who will do science in the 1990s?" *Science* 248:433–435.

Sayegh, R. 1990. *International Yearbook of Education,* XLI. Paris: UNESCO.

Spaulding, S., & Colucci, J. 1982. "International Education: United States Perspective." *European Journal of Education* 17(2):205–216.

Spaulding, S. 1980. "Research on Students from Abroad: The Neglected Implications." In G. Coelho and P. Ahmed., eds., *Uprooting and Development: Dilemmas of Coping with Modernization.* New York: Plenum.

Spaulding, S., and Lin, L. 1997. *A Historical Dictionary of the United Nations Educational, Scientific and Cultural Organization (UNESCO).* Lanham, MD: The Scarecrow Press, Inc.

Spaulding, S., & Flack, M. 1976. *The World's Students in the United States: A Review and Evaluation of Research on Foreign Students.* New York: Praeger.

Spaulding, S., Mauch, J., Nyrenida, S., Potter, E., Sabloff, P., & Weidman, J. 1991. *Re-*

search on Higher Education in Developing Countries: Suggested Agendas and Research Strategies. Paris: UNESCO.

Tonkin, H. 1984. "Trends and Issues in the Curriculum." *International Dimensions of Higher Education.* Pittsburgh, PA: Institute for Higher Education, University of Pittsburgh.

Tonkin, H., & Edwards, J. 1981. *The World in the Curriculum: Curricular Strategies for the 21st Century.* New Rochelle, NY: Change Magazine Press.

UNESCO. 1991–1998. *Statistical Yearbook* (issued annually). Paris: UNESCO.

UNESCO. 1997. *Study Abroad: 1998–1999,* vol. 30. Paris: UNESCO.

UNESCO. 1982. *World Guide to Higher Education: A Comparative Survey of Systems, Degrees and Qualifications.* Paris and New York: Bowker, UNIPUB and UNESCO.

Part 4

International Education and Global Studies in Elementary and Secondary Schools

The ways in which international studies is presented in elementary and secondary schools are important for at least two reasons. First, for many American students, K–12 schools may provide the only formal opportunity to learn about the world and how it works. Elementary and secondary schools can make current information about other nations and people interesting and understandable. For the 65 percent of those who complete high school who do enroll in higher education, such precollegiate instruction can also lay the foundation for further study about the world.

Colleges and universities can have an impact on international studies in schools, sometimes in unanticipated ways. For example, a decision at a higher education level to abandon foreign language requirements, for either admission or graduation, may have a deleterious impact on foreign language enrollments at the lower school level. On the other hand, decisions that broaden academic requirements for those preparing to teach may lead to better-prepared teachers of international studies. And international outreach activities offered by colleges and universities are valuable in providing K–12 students and teachers with information and perspectives that would otherwise be unavailable to them.

While there are obvious benefits to be gained when colleges, universities, and schools collaborate to strengthen international studies at the K–12 level, there are also formidable obstacles. Precollegiate education has a different mission, different priorities, and a different culture than do higher institutions. For example, the "foreign language problem" in the minds of many public school educators is not how to teach more foreign languages better. Rather, it is how to teach English as a foreign language to children of foreign birth enrolled in American classrooms.

Another factor that is poorly understood and appreciated by college faculty and administrators is the socialization role performed by elementary and secondary schools. A major task of

American schools is to accept children of diverse linguistic, cultural, and ethnic backgrounds and transform them into loyal, productive American citizens. Therefore, much more attention is devoted to teaching an understanding of American society and culture than to an understanding of other countries. Indeed, the purpose of teaching the geography, history, and political systems of other lands is often to illuminate certain features of U.S. history or foreign policy. In contrast, colleges and universities assume that the socialization task is completed by high school graduation, and that it is therefore not their responsibility.

Public and professional views about what elementary and secondary schools should teach with regard to international studies have varied greatly over the past century. Prior to World War II, the high school world history course was mainly a study of ancient, medieval, and modern Europe, designed to reveal the origins of American institutions and processes. Asia, Africa, Latin America, and other regions of the world were given little attention except to highlight the expansion of European imperialism. World geography taught about the earth's physical features and the distribution of natural and other resources important to Americans.

World War II and the Cold War that followed forced American educators to reconsider their priorities. Clearly, the United States was destined to play a role as a world power. What kind of citizen training was required if the United States was to play this role successfully? Opinions varied. Some Americans, impressed by the breakup of European empires, the emergence of many new nations in the developing world, and the competition with the USSR for friendly allies, believed that it was important for American students to learn about modern Asia, Africa, and Latin America. One result was the appearance of new courses on "Non-Western Studies" or "Area Studies," modeled in part after area studies programs appearing in colleges and universities. Concern about the spread of communism, either as a result of Soviet military aggression or by internal subversion, led to a proliferation of courses on communism and totalitarianism. The best of these introduced students to new regions of the world and alternative forms of political and economic thought.

During the height of these debates, in 1956, the North Central Association of Schools and Colleges established the Foreign Relations Project, whose purpose was to infuse foreign policy topics into the traditional social studies curriculum and foster discussions of current international events. This innovative project produced booklets that formally introduced specific regions of the world to secondary school students. Each booklet was designed to provide background information on important problems confronting that region or nation, to reveal U.S. foreign policy issues concerning these problems, and to encourage students to reflect on what American foreign policy should be toward that region. This continued until 1968 and was a sound approach for its time. It introduced students to other parts of the world while making clear that knowledge of these areas was fundamental for participation as a good American citizen.

Global Perspectives in Education

The demise of the Foreign Relations Project occurred just as a new effort to encourage international studies in K–12 schools was taking place. In 1968, the Foreign Policy Association published the results of a study entitled *An Examination of Objectives, Needs and Priorities in International Education in U.S. Secondary and Elementary Schools.* The study, funded by the U.S. Office of Education, represented a major shift in focus from studying the world as separate countries, cultures, or geographic regions, to one in which the world as a system or as a number of interrelated systems became the object of attention. Interest in "global education," "global studies," and "global perspectives in education" grew steadily throughout the 1970s and 1980s.

Today, the dominant approach to international studies in K–12 schools is one called "global perspectives in education." Its dominance in the literature, if not always in the classroom, is due to three converging factors: It appeals to educators, who hope that international topics will permeate the curriculum and not be merely restricted to single courses; it is congruent with the views of the nation's opinion leaders, who understand America's role in the world and want citizens to support policies favoring international commerce and collective approaches to national security; and it receives support from advocates of various social causes such as environmental protection and human rights, who believe their interests are transnational in scope and not confined to single nations. "Global perspectives in education" is currently more a movement than a curriculum. It is a point of view about the content of courses primarily in the social studies and, to a lesser degree, in other parts of the curriculum.

In one sense, it is a new kind of citizenship education. Whereas the previous approach to citizenship education was directed toward the socialization of youth to become knowledgeable, aware, and active American citizens, global education asks additionally that students become knowledgeable, aware, and active as inhabitants on "Planet Earth." Global education enhances the traditional goals of American citizen training by asserting that good citizenship includes a global perspective.

The three articles in this section all treat some aspect of global perspectives in education. The first article, by Robert G. Hanvey, is based on a study he first published twenty-five years ago, but these ideas are still used as benchmarks for global education, both in the United States and abroad. Their appeal lies in Hanvey's effort to provide an operational definition for the term "global perspective." What would we expect to find in a person who has acquired a global perspective? Hanvey suggests five attributes that distinguish such a person.

The article by H. Thomas Collins, Frederick R. Czarra, and Andrew F. Smith offers specific advice regarding the knowledge, skills, and participation objectives that should guide school curriculum development in international studies. The objectives are structured around three broad themes: global challenges, issues, and problems; global cultures and world areas; and global connections.

Much writing about global education has been in the form of theory, admonitions, and advice. The article by Merry M. Merryfield, a leading scholar on teacher education relating to global perspectives, shows the gap between what global studies advocates believe should be taught and what is actually being taught in the classroom. She also offers ideas about why this gap exists and what might be done to reduce it.

An Attainable Global Perspective

Robert G. Hanvey

The need for education that promotes a global perspective is increasingly apparent. What is less clear is just what constitutes such a perspective, particularly one which young people might actually be able to attain in the course of their formal and informal education. In what follows, I will describe certain modes of thought, sensitivities, intellectual skills, and explanatory capacities which might in some measure contribute to the formation of a global perspective.

What is a global perspective? As conceived here a global perspective is not a quantum, something you either have or don't have. It is a blend of many things and any given individual may be rich in certain elements and relatively lacking in others. The educational goal broadly seen may be to socialize significant collectivities of people so that the important elements of a global perspective are represented in the group. Viewed in this way, a global perspective may be a variable trait possessed in some form and degree by a population, with the precise character of that perspective determined by the specialized capacities, predispositions, and attitudes of the group's members. The implications of this notion, of course, are that diversified talents and inclinations can be encouraged and that standardized educational effects are not required. Every individual does not have to be brought to the same level of intellectual and moral development in order for a population to be moving in the direction of a more global perspective.

Reprinted with permission from a theme issue on "global education" of *Theory Into Practice*, vol. 21, no. 3. © 1982 by the College of Education, The Ohio State University.

With these thoughts in mind we can identify five dimensions of a global perspective. These are:

1. Perspective Consciousness

2. "State of the Planet" Awareness

3. Cross-Cultural Awareness

4. Knowledge of Global Dynamics

5. Awareness of Human Choices

Perspective Consciousness

The recognition or awareness on the part of the individual that he or she has a view of the world that is not universally shared, that this view of the world has been and continues to be shaped by influences that often escape conscious detection, and that others have views of the world that are profoundly different from one's own.

Few of us in our lives can actually transcend the viewpoint presented by the common carriers of information and almost none of us can transcend the cognitive mapping presented by the culture in which we grew up. But with effort we can at least develop a dim sense that we have a perspective, that it can be shaped by subtle influences, and that others have different perspectives. This recognition of the existence, the malleability, and the diversity of perspective we might call perspective consciousness. Such an acknowledgement is an important step in the development of a perspective that can legitimately be called global.

One must make a distinction between opinion and perspective. Opinion is the surface layer, the conscious outcropping of perspective. But there are deep and hidden layers of perspective that may be more important in orienting behavior. For example, in the deep layers of Western civilization has been the assumption that human dominance over nature is both attainable and desirable. This, until recently, has not been a matter of opinion but assumed as a given.

One of the interesting things that reform and protest movements do is to carry out mining operations in the deep layers. They dredge to the surface aspects of perspective that have never before seen the light of day. Once made visible, these may become the foci of debate, matters of opinion. The environmental movement surfaced the assumption of man's right to dominion over nature and thus posed some philosophical choices that had previously escaped notice. The feminist movement raised the consciousness of women and men with respect to "women's place." They labeled the most commonplace behaviors and attitudes "chauvinist," and thus revealed the deeper layers of perspective in action.

I have suggested that with effort we can develop in the young at least a dim sense, a groping recognition of the fact that they have a perspective. And this is very different from knowing that they have opinions. At the present time the schools and the media socialize all of us to be traders in opinion. We learn this through discussion and debate, through the contentious format of forums and organizational meetings, through talk shows and newspaper columnists. We learn, especially, that the individual is expected to have opinions and to be willing to assert them. And we learn tacit rules about "tolerating" differences in opinions so asserted.

We can also learn, if we approach the task with a sure sense of purpose, how to probe the deep layers of perspective. A variety of specialists and social commentators regularly operate in these realms and there are well-developed methods and techniques. Some of these methods can be learned and practiced. For example, some (but not all) values clarification exercises can heighten awareness of otherwise unrevealed aspects of perspective. At the very least it should be possible to teach almost any young person to recognize a probe of the deep layers when he sees it. Such probes come in many forms, from the ironic humor of a "Doonesbury" cartoon strip to the pop sociology of a book like *Future Shock*.

"State of the Planet" Awareness

Awareness of prevailing world conditions and developments, including emergent conditions and trends, e.g. population growth, migrations, economic conditions, resources and physical environment, political developments, science and technology, law, health, inter-nation and intra-nation conflicts, etc.

For most people in the world, direct experience beyond the local community is infrequent—or nonexistent. It is not uncommon to meet residents of Chicago's neighborhoods who have never traveled the few miles to the central business district, or sophisticated New York taxicab drivers who have never been farther south than Philadelphia. If this is true for a geographically mobile society like the United States, it is even more a fact for other parts of the world. Tourism, urban migrations, commerce, and business travel notwithstanding, most people live out their lives in rather circumscribed local surroundings.

Communications Media and Planet Awareness

Direct experience is not the way that contemporary peoples learn about their world. Nonliterate village or suburban housewife, it doesn't matter that one stays close to home. Information travels rapidly and far through the mass media. News of a border crisis in the Middle East reaches within hours the shopkeeper in Nairobi, the steel worker in Sweden, the Peruvian villager. There is now a demonstrated technical capacity for simultaneous transmission of messages to almost the entire human species. The character of the messages is something else again. Here we must ask, do the messages received on those millions of transistor radios and television sets contribute meaningfully to a valid picture of world conditions? That question matters because it is difficult to imagine a global perspective that does not include a reasonably dependable sense of what shape the world is in.

Generally speaking, the media in almost every country will transmit news from around the world. Unfortunately, the fundamental quality of news is its focus on the extraordinary event. An outbreak of influenza is news; endemic malaria is not. A rapid decline in values on the world's stock exchanges is news; the long-standing poverty of hundreds of millions is not. So, there are significant limits and distortions in the view of the world conveyed by news media. Nonetheless, the prospect is not entirely bleak. For one thing, the characteristic interests of the news media can be exploited; events can be staged in such a way as to call attention to world conditions not ordinarily judged newsworthy. A world conference can be convened on food or population or pollution problems. The conference itself is news. More importantly, the condition that gives rise to the conference takes on a new level of visibility—worldwide. And the news media are the instruments of this increased awareness.

Limits to Understanding
There are other sources of distortion. Political ideology chokes off the flow of some information, the defense and security syndrome of nations blocks still other information, and the selective disinterest of audiences constricts yet other channels. As an instance of the first, Americans until recently have had little access to information about Cuba under Castro. As an example of the second, the testing of nuclear weapons by the French and the Indians in recent years produced few hard details about site, yield, fallout, etc. (Governments have ways to obtain the information; publics do not.) As for patterns of audience interest and disinterest, consider how little attention is paid to the affairs of small nations, or to conditions in the rural areas of the world; and with no complaint from the audience.

Finally, there is the matter of the technical nature of world data. There are now unprecedented resources for generating information about the state of the planet, and for sharing and processing the information in order to obtain a sense of the important patterns. But the procedures are highly technical and the results expressed in technical terms. A certain level of education is required to see the full significance of the data.

Overcoming the Limitations
This is an instance where the energies of the schools, properly directed, might resolve the question in favor of the general populace. If from the earliest grades on students examined and puzzled over cases where seemingly innocent behaviors—the diet rich in animal protein, the lavish use of fertilizer on the suburban lawn and golf course—were shown to have effects that were both unintended and global in scope, then there could be a receptivity for that kind of technical information necessary to understand many global issues. Situations such as the depletion of ozone in the atmosphere from aerosol sprays would not seem forbidding;

it would be another instance of a model already documented. Students would have a framework within which to handle it. As for the technical aspects of something like the ozone situation, these do not seem beyond the reach of science and social studies departments that focus cooperatively on the technical dimensions of significant planetary conditions. It may be true that school programs are not typically organized for such a task, but it is not outside the boundaries of our predilections or our capacities.

Cross-Cultural Awareness

Awareness of the diversity of ideas and practices to be found in human societies around the world, of how such ideas and practices compare, and including some limited recognition of how the ideas and ways of one's own society might be viewed from other vantage points.

This may be one of the more difficult dimensions to attain. It is one thing to have some knowledge of world conditions. The air is saturated with that kind of information. It is another thing to comprehend and accept the consequences of the basic human capacity for creating unique cultures—with the resultant profound differences in outlook and practice manifested among societies. These differences are widely known at the level of myth, prejudice, and tourist impression. But they are not deeply and truly known, in spite of the well-worn exhortation to "understand others." Such a fundamental acceptance seems to be resisted by powerful forces in the human psychosocial system.

Several million years of evolution seem to have produced in us a creature that does not easily recognize the members of its own species. That is stated in rather exaggerated form but it refers to the fact that human groups commonly have difficulty in accepting the humanness of other human groups.

The practice of naming one's own group "the people" and by implication relegating all others to not-quite-human status has been documented in nonliterate groups all over the world. But it is simply one manifestation of a species trait that shows itself in modern populations as well. It is there in the hostile faces of the white parents demonstrating against school busing. You will find it lurking in the background as Russians and Chinese meet at the negotiating table to work out what is ostensibly a boundary dispute. And it flares into the open during tribal disputes in Kenya.

There was a time when the solidarity of small groups of humans was the basis for the survival of the species. But in the context of mass populations and weapons of mass destructiveness, group solidarity and the associated tendency to deny the full humanness of other peoples pose serious threats to the species. When we speak of "humans" it is important that we include not only ourselves and our immediate group but all four and one half billion of those other bipeds, however strange their ways.

This is the primary reason for cross-cultural awareness. If we are to admit the humanness of those others, then the strangeness of their ways must become less strange; must, in fact, become believable. Ideally, that means getting inside the heads of those strangers and looking out at the world through their eyes. Then the strange becomes familiar and totally believable. This is a most difficult trick to pull off, but there may be methods that will increase the probability of success. Further, there are lesser degrees of cross-cultural awareness than getting inside the head; these more modest degrees of awareness are not to be scorned.

Knowledge of Global Dynamics

Some modest comprehension of key traits and mechanisms of the world system, with emphasis on theories and concepts that may increase intelligent consciousness of global change.

How does the world work? Is it a vast, whirring machine spinning ponderously around a small yellow sun? Is there a lever we can push to avert famine in South Asia, or one that will cure world inflation, or one to slow the growth of world population? Is it our ignorance of which lever to move that results in tragedy and crisis? Is it our ignorance of how the gears intermesh that causes breakdowns in the stability of the system?

Or is the machine useful as a metaphor? Is it perhaps better to think of the world as an organism, evolving steadily in response to the programming in its germ plasm? Are wars and famines merely minor episodes in the biological history of a planet serenely following a script already written?

The latter view is not a comfortable one for people in industrial societies, raised to believe that almost anything can be engineered, including the destiny of the world. But the machine image doesn't quite work, either, although we continue (as I have done) to speak of "mechanisms." The idea of a machine suggests an assembly of parts that interconnect in a very positive fashion, so positive that when you manipulate one part you get immediate, predictable, and quantifiable response in other parts. That does not seem to describe the world as we know it.

But both machines and organisms are systems of interconnected elements and it is the idea of *system* that now prevails. How does the world work? As a system. What does that mean? It means we must put aside simple notions of cause and effect. Things interact, in complex and surprising ways. "Effects" loop back and become "causes" which have "effects" which loop back. . . . It means that simple events ramify—unbelievably.

But let's begin to talk in more concrete terms. What exactly might the schools teach about global dynamics? The answer proposed here is very selective, with the criterion of selection being, does the particular learning contribute to an understanding of global change; because the control of change is the central problem of our era. There are changes we desire and seem unable to attain. There are changes we wish to constrain and, as yet, cannot. There is also another kind of change: in spite of our difficulties we are growing in our capacities to detect and manipulate change. A global perspective that fails to comprehend both the problems of change and promise of improved control will not be worthy of the name.

Three categories of learning about change suggest themselves:

1. Basic principles of change in social systems

   • the ramifications of new elements in social systems

   • unanticipated consequences

   • overt and covert functions of elements

   • feedback, positive and negative

2. Growth as a form of change

   • desired growth in the form of economic development

   • undesired growth in the form of exponential increase in population, resource depletion, etc.

3. Global planning

   • national interests and global planning

   • attempts to model the world system as related to national policy formulation

Awareness of Human Choices

Some awareness of the problems of choice confronting individuals, nations, and the human species as consciousness and knowledge of the global system expands.

Throughout I have talked of changes in awareness. Awareness of our own cultural perspective, awareness of how other peoples view the world, awareness of global dynamics and patterns of change. In this final section I wish to emphasize that such heightened awareness, desirable as it is, brings with it problems of choice. As an instance, in a "pre-awareness" stage the undoubted benefits of pesticides in agriculture, forestry, and the control of diseases such as malaria provide clear justification for prolific application.

But then information about the dangers of pesticides begins to accumulate. DDT is found in the tissues of organisms far removed from the points of application. Some species are threatened with extinction. Risks not only to present human populations but to future generations are identified. In some countries the use of certain pesticides is halted altogether. A change of awareness has occurred and new behaviors have resulted—in some parts of the world.

Where is the problem of choice? It lies in the fact that pesticides like DDT are still in use. Widely. Hundreds of millions of people depend on DDT to control malaria and agricultural pests. Ask someone in the developed countries if DDT is still in use and he will likely say no, answering in terms of his own country's practices. But pose the question on a world basis and the answer is yes. Viewed as a collectivity, the human species continues to use DDT.

This continued use constitutes a de facto human choice. In a conflict between the rights of living populations to control obvious and immediate threats to health and the rights of other living and future populations to freedom from subtle and long-term threats to health and subsistence, the former wins out. The immediate and the obvious triumph over the long-term and subtle. But although the choice seems to have been made, the *problem* of choice remains. There is a new cognition in the world. We now know that there are long-term and subtle risks. Once we did not. We now admit that other people and future generations have rights. Once we did not. This new knowledge has not had the power to halt the use of DDT where life and health are under severe threat, but it has had the effect of blocking its use in many other parts of the world. To put it simply, there are now two possible behaviors with respect to DDT:

- if it will solve a problem, use it

- *even* if it will solve a problem, don't use it

The second of these behaviors originates in the new cognition, the new awareness of risks and rights.

The DDT situation is simply an instance, a small manifestation of the major cognitive revolution that is now under way. But it is a representative one. Many practices once essentially automatic, whose benefits were assumed, are now questioned. They are questioned because we know new things. We know how to measure minute quantities. We know that factors interconnect in complex ways. We know there are limits to the resources and carrying capacity of the planet. In the context of the new cognition, action does not proceed automatically. Calculations of advantage and disadvantage become explicit and detailed. Choosing a course of behavior becomes a more reasoned process. That shift—from the automatic to the calculated—is a very important expression of the cognitive revolution we are now experiencing.

That cognitive revolution involves a shift from a pre-global to a global cognition. In the pre-global stage, rational consideration of goals, methods, and consequences tends to be limited to the near—the near in time and social identity. The preoccupation with the short-term and the neglect of the long-term has been particularly characteristic of Western industrial societies.

Pre-global cognition is characterized not only by a constricted view of the future but by a relatively simple theory of linkages between events, a linear theory in which some things are causes and other things are effects. This theory leads in its most exaggerated and magical form to the conclusion that conditions are the result of single causes, sometimes personified. In primitive societies this is the basis of witchcraft and ghost beliefs. In a sophisticated society like our own we have the recent example of two presidents who employed the CIA to locate the sinister foreign influence that must surely have been the root cause of the antiwar movement.

The emergent global cognition contrasts sharply with the pre-global. Long-term consequences begin to be considered. Linkages between events are seen in the more complex light of systems theory. Social goals and values are made explicit and vulnerable to challenge. And nations begin to note that their interests and activities are not separable from the interests and activities of others. Further, systematic attention is given to problems that transcend the national, regional, or coalitional; human problems. A global cognition has certainly not been achieved. Pre-global forms of knowing continue to orient much of human behavior. But the transition is under way, driven by the convergent energies of a variety of social movements.

In summary, we are in a period of transition, moving from a pre-global to a global cognition. Global cognition is characterized by new knowledge of system interactions, by new knowledge in planning human action. As such, knowledge and its rational use expands, human choices expand. An awareness of this expanded range of choice constitutes an important dimension of a global perspective.

I have discussed five dimensions of a global perspective. Are there more? I am tempted to be waggish and say no, this is it, the final crystalline truth. But of course there are more, as many more as anyone cares to invent. Such dimensions are inventions, constructs of the mind. This particular set is just one assemblage, a collage of ideas selected and shaped by one individual's proclivities and prejudices. This is not to say there are not real changes under way in human consciousness. I am convinced there are and that they are in the direction of something that can be called a global perspective. But any particular description of that phenomenon is properly suspect. Even this one which is, by coincidence, my favorite.

Guidelines for Global and International Studies Education

CHALLENGES, CULTURES, AND CONNECTIONS

H. Thomas Collins, Frederick R. Czarra, and Andrew F. Smith

Since the end of the Cold War, new forces—cultural, political, economic, and environmental—have swept the world. Americans are re-examining the role of their country in the face of these modern global complexities. Some question the ability of many of our basic institutions, from the government to the military to financial institutions, to cope with these new realities. No institution needs to respond more than our educational system.

Due to high public interest, the United States has an "open moment" to affect crucial change in our nation's schools. With federal support, academic standards have been established in many disciplines, including the social studies areas of history, geography, civics, and economics. Simultaneously, many states are incorporating national education standards into their own curriculum frameworks. These efforts to develop academic standards are laudable, and do contain interna-

Reprinted with permission from *Social Education,* vol. 62, no. 5 (September). © 1998 by the National Council for the Social Studies.

tional components. However, many important issues related to global understanding are either missing or dealt with inadequately.

Our students must be prepared to function in an increasingly interdependent and conflict-prone world. Moreover, schools bear the major responsibility for assuring that the American electorate is both well informed and willing to act responsibly on matters of international significance. Ignoring the global dimensions of education would be a grave mistake.

Educators concerned with the global dimensions of the social studies curriculum need to address many questions. Among them:

- What should our students be expected to know and understand about the world?

- What skills and attitudes do they need to confront problems that are global in scope?

- How well are the global dimensions of learning being addressed by the new academic standards?

- How best can the insights of scholars and practitioners of international relations be incorporated into these standards?

- How can schools increase the global dimensions of education when confronted with many other needs and problems?

In 1968, the U.S. Office of Education funded the development of a list of objectives for international education by the Foreign Policy Association. Since then, individuals and groups—united under the rubrics of world cultures and international studies—have been working to increase the global dimensions of education. Out of their efforts have come many excellent ideas, materials, and programs.

To help those responsible for curriculum development, we have developed guidelines that attempt to summarize what concerned scholars and educators recommend as the international dimension of education for students in kindergarten through grade 12. These guidelines are not "standards" as the term is currently being used; however, we believe they can help to validate local curriculum decisions and ensure that the international dimension receives attention.

We have limited our focus to three broad themes:

I. Global Challenges, Issues, and Problems

II. Global Cultures and World Areas

III. Global Connections: the United States and the World.

Within each theme, we provide: (1) a rationale for study; (2) knowledge objectives as a basis for understanding; (3) a list of skills relevant to evaluating issues; and (4) participation objectives to help students address challenges.

The Guidelines

I. Global Challenges, Issues, and Problems

A RATIONALE FOR STUDY

To identify major global challenges, we examined 75 documents on global and international studies education. These documents spanned the last five decades, and included several reports or surveys written by citizens of other countries. Unfortunately, few authors prioritized their recommendations, meaning that our compilation of global issues reflects only the frequency with which a topic received mention. In some cases, it was necessary to interpret an author's exact meaning. Some rearrangement of topics was also necessary to hold the categories to a reasonable number. However, the ten resulting categories include virtually every issue named by those whose work provides the basis for this compilation.

At the core of all contemporary international and global studies are two concepts: change and interdependence. Engineers quip, "If we can make it work, it's probably already out of date!" A similar rule seems to apply to the major, and largely unresolved, global problems that dominate both scholarly journals and the popular media today. Just as someone claims to "have a handle" on any problem, a new manifestation of it occurs. Proposed solutions are suddenly perceived as inadequate or—as is often the case—found to contribute to a greater problem that was formerly unknown or unacknowledged.

The metaphor of a spider's web applies remarkably well to today's global problems and challenges. Touch that web anywhere, however lightly, and it vibrates everywhere. Similarly, if one "touches" any global problem, one instantly realizes its interdependence with another. As University of Chicago psychologist Mihaly Csikszentmihalyi stated, "It is imperative to begin thinking about a truly integrative, global education that takes seriously the actual interconnections of causes and effects."

Further, it is not overstating the case to say that change and interdependence are so central to all of the social and physical sciences that they deserve continuous attention throughout any program to educate globally literate students. Virtually without exception, those whose thinking we examined named unprecedented change in all aspects of life as something schools should address. The concept of interdependence—often subsumed under "systems perspective" or "systems thinking"—also received nearly unanimous mention.

We identified ten categories of global challenges, issues, and problems as the basis for improved teaching and learning about the international dimension in K–12 schools. These categories are neither exhaustive nor mutually exclusive; in fact, there is significant overlap among some of them. The categories are:

1. Conflict and Its Control: Violence/Terrorism/War:
Low-Intensity to International

This broad heading includes several subclusters. The first is sub-national conflicts, including revolutions, civil strife, assassinations, and rebel or guerrilla activities (often self-identified as "freedom fighters") within a country. Genocide and ethnic cleansing as well as tribalism and secessionist movements may be included in this group.

A second cluster centers on the proliferation of weapons—conventional, chemical, biological, and nuclear—and the arms race, which encompasses sales, sanctions, controls, and trafficking. A third cluster concerns terrorism—state-sponsored terrorism, sanctuaries, social revolutionaries, national separatists, religious fundamentalists—and cross-border conflicts based on irredentism or revanchism.

A fourth cluster involves matters of national security, including the use of force by nations either unilaterally or in combination with other nations. However, we note that arms control, conflict resolution on an international scale, and the formal peacekeeping activities of the United Nations received far less emphasis than conflict itself in the sources consulted.

Schools need to address this crucial area. Given the frequency and intensity of conflict-related issues dominating today's world events, to neglect the study of the methods available to prevent or mediate conflict is a serious omission.

2. Economic Systems: International Trade/Aid/Investment

This category also includes a number of subclusters. The more recent the source consulted, the greater is the emphasis placed on economic problems and issues. The first cluster includes understanding comparative economic systems, e.g., state socialism and other centrally planned economies typified by the former Soviet system and differing from our own. Also mentioned are the transitional and mixed economies typical of many developing nations today. Finally, virtually every source indicates that a working knowledge of our own free-market, or free-enterprise, model is a prerequisite for understanding economic systems different from our own.

The second cluster relates to international trade, encompassing patterns, balance of trade and payments, free trade and zones, trade negotiations—protectionism, quotas, sanctions, and embargoes—as well as tariff and nontariff barriers. Currency exchange (rates, fluctuations) also received mention.

A third cluster focuses on foreign aid, such as purposes, forms, amounts, and conditions as well as the role of donors and multilateral aid programs. Some of the sources placed major emphasis on the need for better understanding of foreign aid. Recent public opinion polls indicate widespread public ignorance regarding all aspects of foreign aid and extraordinary misconceptions concerning the percentage of the national budget devoted to our foreign aid programs. Direct foreign investment, including stress on the role of multinational corporations (MNCs), transnational enterprises (TNEs), and regional trading blocs (EU, NAFTA, GATT, etc.), were also cited as important topics.

Finally, a cluster of economic concerns focused on the specific needs of the developing world, such as debt crisis and relief, preferential trade policies, and protecting infant industries. An understanding of the increasing economic disparities (the rich-poor gap) within and among many world nations also received mention.

3. Global Belief Systems: Ideologies/Religions/Philosophies

Publications from the Cold War period stressed the need for the study of comparative ideologies, that is, Soviet-style communism and its various off-shoots, particularly Chinese communism. Many of the sources consulted emphasize the need for students to study major world religions as a means of better understanding other cultures as well as improving students' understanding of followers of those religions residing in this country. Several sources recommend the study of other nations' or cultures' philosophies. However, in most cases it is unclear exactly what this means. It appears that these references are primarily directed at either political philosophies or ideologies, for example, socialism, communism, and fascism, or thought systems identified with a particular religion, for example, Confucianism, Hinduism, or Daoism. This apparently is seen as a means to better understand and to develop empathy for other cultures.

4. Human Rights and Social Justice/Human Needs and Quality of Life

The category of human rights and social justice includes a broad array of human concerns and topics related to the quality of life worldwide. The more recent the source consulted, the greater the emphasis placed on global human rights. The first cluster focuses on problems associated with human rights and social justice including gender and equity issues, the rights of children (child labor, street children, various abuses), equal access to justice, and rights violations and abuses based on ethnic, racial, sexual, or political identities.

A second cluster—probably the one that has generated the most intense media attention and public concern—focuses on problems concerning food and hunger (chronic malnutrition, famine). Included here are global food security, unequal access to food, food aid, the green revolution, and diseases related to inadequate diet. A third cluster focuses on broad concerns of health, education, and welfare, for example, infectious diseases (particularly HIV and AIDS), inadequate sanitation, drug use (trade, prevention, prosecution), inadequate shelter or housing, illiteracy, low standards of living, and the lack of a social safety net.

5. Planet Management: Resources/Energy/Environment

Virtually every source consulted places major emphasis upon resource depletion—including energy—and environmental degradation or pollution as crucial areas for student study. The resource cluster includes renewable and nonrenewable resources, resource dependence, stockpiling critical resources, recycling, and the role of commodity power in international commerce. The more recent sources emphasize water—its management, reuse, pollution, scarcity, and cost. A few sources cited space as an often overlooked resource.

Topics relating to energy sources—particularly petroleum and nuclear energy—appear on almost every list for study. Production and consumption patterns, proven reserves, costs, the security or dependability of sources, and future oil shocks (OPEC) make up one group of concerns. A second group focuses on alternative energy sources (solar power or hydropower), the problems and potentials of nuclear energy, and the need for conservation.

Studying the condition and care of the environment includes topics such as air, land, water, and seabed pollution; global warming and cooling; ozone depletion; toxic and nuclear wastes (disposal and international trade in); and acid rain. A second set of issues focuses on degradation of the land through erosion, deforestation, drought, or desertification, and reductions in generic, biotic, and species varieties. Some sources also mention carrying capacity and environmental instability as concepts students should understand.

Perhaps no other topic mentioned reflects as high a degree of concern—in a few cases bordering on alarmist—as does the condition of the environment and its care. Schools planning studies of environmentally related topics would be wise to take extra precautions to assure that students are presented with the most balanced and scholarly data currently available.

6. Political Systems: International Structures/Institutions/ Actors/Procedures

Many of the sources examined stressed the need for the study of political systems and ideologies (as with economic systems above) that differ from our own. Under the institutions cluster, the United Nations and its agencies dominate most lists, but the increasing role of regional organizations (NATO, SEATO, OAS, OAU, etc.) also is recommended for study. A second cluster of concerns focuses on the role of alliances, treaties, and negotiations (regarding arms, refugees, trade, and human rights violations). More recent sources mentioned political disintegration, irredentism, secessionism, devolution of nations, separatism, and the opposing trends of regional integration and increased democratization and autonomy. Nongovernmental organizations (NGOs), and their increasing role and presence in international affairs, are also recommended for study. Finally, a cluster focuses on international law and the role of the World Court. Formal study of U.S. foreign policy is also recommended by some authors.

7. Population: Demographic Growth/Patterns/ Movements/Trends

No single problem or concern is listed more frequently than population, particularly its control. Some authors feel that unless present growth rates are checked, particularly in parts of Africa, Asia, and Latin America, solutions to most other global problems will continue to elude us. Basic information on population growth (birthrates, death rates, fertility rates, replacement rates, migration, immigration, and emigration), and its changes, patterns, and trends make up one cluster.

Another cluster focuses on issues that can be controversial, such as family planning and contraception practices, including state-sanctioned abortion or sterilization. It would appear wise that public schools dealing with these topics exercise extreme caution. A third cluster includes a variety of population-related issues, for example, guest workers, illegal aliens, aging, drift to the cities, political asylum, dependency ratios (percentage of a population under 15 or over 65 years old), and the rapidly increasing numbers of refugees and displaced persons worldwide.

8. Race and Ethnicity: Human Commonality and Diversity

Most of the sources consulted feel this topic should be studied by all students, but few provide details. In most cases, "reducing prejudice," "avoiding stereotypes," or "eliminating discrimination" are listed as the goal for such studies. Others stressed "celebrating diversity" or "enhancing students' self-image/concept" as the primary goal. Some scholars and others who included this topic on their lists stress specifics such as race and immigration quotas or preferences, exclusion laws based on race, problems of indigenous ethnic groups, ethnic/cultural roots, color consciousness, and, in more recent sources, ethnic or racially based genocide as well as the ongoing debate concerning Euro-centrism vs. multi-culturalism. In any case, serious consideration of this topic would appear mandatory given our pluralistic society and world.

9. Technocratic Revolution: Science/Technology/Communications

With the exception of communications—often coupled with transportation—this category of issues receives little attention in the earlier sources examined. However, virtually all of the more recent sources emphasize the role that science, technology, and communications play in the lives of all humans. Several individuals note correctly that the study of science and technology provides an ideal vehicle for social studies, math, and science teachers to develop cross-disciplinary lessons and units. Having students discuss both the pluses and minuses of the impact of science and technology on people's lives worldwide is suggested. The communication cluster includes innovations, networking, freedom of use, the information revolution (access to, balanced flow, and censorship) and increasing speed coupled with decreasing costs.

10. Sustainable Development: Political/Economic/Social

Included under this heading is what might be called the "neo" cluster: neocolonialism, neomercantilism and neoimperialism, all manifestations of broader dependency theory issues that include increasing foreign debt and economic imperialism. A second cluster of concerns centers on drift to the cities and explosive urban growth (megacities), often accompanied by increasing social and economic problems and growing city-countryside disparities that cause political instability, often leading to violence. A third cluster includes the role of commodity power and the attempts to form cartels among those developing nations that possess raw materials needed by the more industrialized nations. Also included is the nonaligned movement that, at times, influences voting at the United Nations. A final cluster centers on the internal regional disparities existing in many developing nations, the mistreatment of indigenous peoples in some, and autonomy movements in others.

KNOWLEDGE OBJECTIVES

1. Students will know and understand that global issues and challenges exist and affect their lives. Awareness is a necessary prerequisite to understanding. If we expect today's students—tomorrow's leaders and voters—to make intelligent decisions in the marketplace and at the ballot box, they must have a degree of literacy regarding the global problems, issues, concerns, and trends that increasingly impact their lives. Global literacy does not require in-depth expertise. Rather, it entails reasonable familiarity with a number of global issues that dominate the news, coupled with a working knowledge of the basic terminology and fundamental concepts of these issues. It means knowing enough about some global issues to intelligently analyze others.

2. Students will study at least one global issue in-depth and over time. When studying any complex issue, "a little knowledge is a dangerous thing." Students may be left with the false impression that they have somehow become experts without expending the time and labor that genuine expertise necessitates. Schools may inadvertently contribute to this condition when they insist on coverage rather than depth. To be effective, the serious study of any global issue requires time and depth.

3. Students will understand that global issues and challenges are interrelated, complex, and changing, and that most issues have a global dimension. Students should be encouraged to find the relationships between different domains of knowledge in order to gain a realistic perspective about any global issue. They should become familiar with some of the mechanisms available for managing global problems and to what degree those mechanisms have functioned successfully in the past.

4. Students will be aware that their information and knowledge on most global issues are incomplete and that they need to continue seeking information about how global and international issues are formed and influenced. Global education is a lifelong process. New global issues will emerge in the future, and new insights into current global challenges will be generated. Opinions and attitudes about international topics are influenced by different channels: parents, peer groups, the media, and private and public interest groups. Students need the skills and abilities to examine and evaluate new information, including understanding the biases of the source.

SKILLS OBJECTIVES

1. Students will learn the techniques of studying about global issues, problems, and challenges. The study of any global problem or issue requires time and depth. Having students learn how to learn about global problems and issues may be as important as learning about any single issue.

2. Students will develop informational literacy about global issues and challenges. In our overrich data environment, our chief concern should be to help students, in Charles McClelland's words, "develop criteria for discriminating, evaluating, selecting, and responding to useful and relevant data in the communication flow of reports about conditions and developments in the international environment." In other words, we must help them to become effective at processing data.

3. Students will develop the ability to suspend judgment when confronted with new data or opinions that do not coincide with their present understandings or feelings. When information or beliefs about global issues conflict with students' present perceptions, students must be able to demonstrate thoughtfulness and patience if genuine understanding is to result. Global problems and issues are complex and constantly changing, often reflecting strongly held divergent views. Students must learn to respect such views while maintaining their own right to respectfully disagree.

PARTICIPATION OBJECTIVES

1. Students will approach global issues, problems, and challenges neither with undue optimism nor unwarranted pessimism. The study of any global issue or challenge can become stressful, particularly for younger students. Depending on the topic, such study can leave them fearful or guilt-ridden. Neither fear nor guilt are good motivators, and neither will lead to civic action. Thus, classroom teachers must select issues that are within both the research capabilities and the maturity level of their students. Leaving students frustrated by the enormity of a global problem or feeling guilty because of their inability to "solve" it serves no purpose.

2. Students will develop a sense of efficacy and civic responsibility by identifying specific ways that they can make some contribution to the resolution of a global issue or challenge. School systems have the obligation to foster effective civic action. Despite the complexity of global issues and challenges, students can contribute toward resolving or ameliorating their effects.

II. Global Cultures and World Areas

A RATIONALE FOR STUDY

Interconnected with the theme of global issues, problems, and challenges is the theme of cultures and world areas. Since the 1950s, area or culture studies have been a part of many pre-collegiate curriculums, and in many states, culture studies have been mandated. Yet despite almost 40 years of culture studies and programs, curriculums featuring holidays and food festivals, which contribute little to intercultural understanding, still seem to be the extent of the offerings in many schools.

Education about culture in the 1990s has presented myriad challenges to public school teachers and administrators across the United States. These challenges, for the most part, have arisen from minority groups who cry out for either inclusion or exclusion from what is taught. Many minority groups want their history and culture integrated into the main curriculum, while others desire a separate course exclusively for students of that particular minority. Although these conflicts consume the energies of schools and school systems, larger questions must be addressed by schools and systems that want to teach about the variety of cultures that make up our national and world population: What is culture? What forms does it take? What is important for students to learn about culture and specific cultures? Placing the concept of culture into a larger context may help to define what students should know about local and global cultures.

Most parents expect schools to teach about American civic culture, principally knowledge of democratic values: our Constitution, the Bill of Rights, the Declaration of Independence. Democratic values are a common ground for all Americans. Beyond this, defining American culture, as with any, is difficult because our own culture is so deeply embedded in us that it is difficult for us to see. In addition, the United States is a diverse nation, reflecting the values of different groups. Each day we see many conflicts in schools and communities based on these differences.

Culture should be an important area of study in our schools. Each of us has roots in one or more cultures, and each day we experience a wide variety of behaviors that reflect the values and beliefs of other cultures. However, most students' knowledge of other cultures is superficial or limited to exotic coverage or monolithic examinations. Yet cross-cultural learning is essential for understanding both our own culture and that of others. By studying other cultures, we learn what it is to be human. When studying other cultures, we should look for similarities to our own culture as well as for the differences that make a culture unique. The study of culture is necessary in order to know that other people may view things in ways that are profoundly different from the ways we view them.

KNOWLEDGE OBJECTIVES

1. Students will know and understand at least one other culture in addition to their own. Students should study at least one culture in-depth and from many different points of view.[1]

2. Students will have a general knowledge about the major geographic and cultural areas of the world and the issues and challenges that unite and divide them. Students should study the major geographical and cultural regions of the world as well as some of the major issues and challenges that both unite and divide these world cultural regions.

3. Students will know and understand that members of different cultures view the world in different ways. Differences exist within a culture as well as among cultures. Within cultures, diversity may be affected by factors such as race, class, or religion. Cross-cultural educators state that studying other cultures will help students to understand the values and actions of other people as well as their own.[2]

4. Students will know and understand that cultures change. All cultures have histories, present perspectives, and future orientations. Students should know that cultures are always undergoing change and will continue to change, especially in the 21st century. Many cultures in the world are being changed by technology, migration, and urbanization.

5. Students will know and understand that there are universals connecting all cultures. Universals are the ideas that unite us as humans. Material and nonmaterial cultural elements are things and ideas such as food, housing, the arts, play, language and nonverbal communication, social organization, and the like. Ernest Boyer, an educator of renown, listed the universals of culture we all share: the life cycle, symbols of expression, aesthetics, recalling the past and looking at the future, membership in groups and institutions, living on and being committed to planet Earth, producing and consuming, and searching for a larger purpose.

6. Students will know and understand that humans may identify with more than one culture and thus have multiple loyalties. Every human has values and beliefs. Differences should be respected. Family life, education, and friends and fellow workers shape our worldview and give each of us different sets of values and beliefs.

7. Students will know and understand that culture and communication are closely connected. Languages form bonds that make each culture unique. To fully learn about another culture requires learning its communication system through a study of verbal and nonverbal language.

8. Students will know and understand that cultures cross national boundaries. The modern world, through immigration, migration, communication, technology, and transportation, has broken down traditional cultural boundaries. Many cultures are no longer defined by common geographic areas. For example, there are refugees forced out of their homelands and cultural groups such as the Kurds that have no national homeland.

9. Students will know and understand that cultures are affected by geography and history. Studying the location of cultures and their past history is important to learning about another culture.

SKILLS OBJECTIVES

1. Students will analyze and evaluate major events and trends in a culture. When studying a culture, students should look for events and trends that indicate changes in that culture and be able to analyze how these changes may have an impact on students' lives.

2. Students will examine cultures in the world and recognize some interconnections with their life in the United States. Students should look for events and ideas in other cultures that have an impact on the United States and on its citizens.

3. Students will compare and contrast diverse cultural points of view and try to understand them. Respect for others is at the heart of cross-cultural understanding. Students should learn to listen to various cultural perspectives in order to understand others. However, understanding does not mean agreeing with another point of view.[3]

4. Students will examine the common and diverse traits of other cultures. An open discussion of differences and similarities in other cultures leads to understanding the values and motives of others and is the first step toward the skill of working with others who have different points of view.

5. Students will be able to state a concern, position, or a value from another culture without distorting it, in a way that would satisfy a member of that culture. Understanding other points of view and being able to explain them clearly is a valuable communication skill for all citizens. Understanding other points of view does not necessarily mean that students agree with these opinions. Students should also develop the ability to critique views they disagree with.

PARTICIPATION OBJECTIVES

1. Students will appreciate the study of other cultures. When we study other cultures, similarities and differences emerge clearly in our minds. We are able to put our own cultural values into perspective and thus understand ourselves better.

2. Students will appropriately tolerate cultural diversity. Students should learn to listen to and tolerate the values and opinions of others.

3. Students will seek to communicate with people from other cultures. Students should be given an opportunity to explore their own interests or have their interests stimulated about other peoples and cultures. Students have multiple opportunities to learn about other cultures in both their communities and the larger world. The modern world makes cross-cultural understanding a necessity because of common connections across cultures all over the world.[4]

4. Students will demonstrate an appreciation of universal human rights. Basic human rights should be honored. Students should understand that there are times when the values of individual cultures will conflict with universal human rights. Students should discuss these conflicts and be prepared to defend human rights.

5. Students will meet and learn from people from other cultures. In the modern world, students have multiple opportunities to meet people of diverse cultures. Schools should provide opportunities for students to learn from one another as well as from international visitors and exchange students.

III. Global Connections: The United States and the World

A RATIONALE FOR STUDY

Students need broad-based knowledge of global issues and area and culture studies, but they also need to understand their own connections with these issues and cultures. Helping students understand these connections is a major purpose of international and global studies education. Americans are tied to global issues and different cultures in multiple ways, and students must understand the United States' contemporary and historical connections with global issues and regions. This includes studying traditional topics such as U.S. foreign policy and U.S. participation in international organizations, as well as understanding long-term U.S. political and strategic interests.

Citizens have a responsibility through speaking, voting, lobbying, and other forms of participation to affect international issues and U.S. foreign policies. To an extent, citizenship in a global age is part of the usual citizenship programs, and U.S. foreign policy should be part of the American history standards. Likewise, citizens need to be aware of the channels that influence their opinions on global and international issues, such as the press, media, governmental institutions, and private organizations.

A major problem confronting educators interested in teaching students about global and international topics has been one of relevance. Many Americans believe that global issues are not connected to their daily lives. Others are deeply concerned with the effects of global economic competition. Global problems may appear to be too far away to affect them but, for better and worse, we are increasingly linked to global issues and with peoples and cultures throughout the world. This web of interconnections, which has both positive and negative implications, can be found in local communities, religious groups, social and community organizations, and economic linkages.

KNOWLEDGE OBJECTIVES

1. *Students will identify and describe how they are connected with the world historically, politically, economically, technologically, socially, linguistically, and ecologically.* Every American is connected directly with the world in a variety of ways, for example, the mail; the Internet; ham radios; the telephone; travel; international organizations or religious groups; economic links, such as purchasing products connected with other countries; and the press and mass media. More than 70 "Your Community and the World" studies have been developed that examine the current global linkages of cities, regions, and states.[5]

2. *Students will know and understand that global interconnections are not necessarily benign; they have both positive and negative consequences in the United States and elsewhere.* Global interconnections enhance our lives, and they also may create serious problems. For instance, importing foreign automobiles may add to the diversity and quality of our lives and provide jobs for Americans engaged in their importation and sale, but for workers in U.S. steel mills or automobile factories, these global imports have been devastating. Students need to understand the trade-offs among short-term and long-term consequences of interconnections.

3. *Students will know and understand the United States' role in international policies and international relations, particularly since World War II.* The United States is the sole remaining global superpower. What we do or do not do affects the lives of people around the world. Students need to understand the strengths and limitations of our influence on other nations. Understanding today's foreign policies requires some knowledge and understanding of past foreign policies and issues.

SKILLS OBJECTIVES

1. *Students will recognize, analyze, and evaluate major events and trends in American and world history and examine how these events and trends connect to their local communities and the United States today.* Our lives today are defined by actions others have taken in the past. Understanding past trends and movements is important in understanding today's world. Usually, United States and world history are taught as discrete courses, but the walls between these subjects are artificial. United States history should be taught in a global perspective and world history should include connections with the United States. Both United States and world history should make connections between past trends and the individual today.

2. Students will recognize, analyze, and evaluate interconnections of local and regional issues with global challenges and issues. Global issues do not arise from some far-away place to affect our local communities. Rather, local communities across the world create global challenges and issues. Students should be able to recognize, analyze, and evaluate how local communities contribute to or help resolve global issues.

3. Students will recognize, analyze, and evaluate the interconnections between their lives and global issues. Students should be able to make the link between their daily actions and how those actions—or inaction—influence global phenomena.

4. Students will generate alternative projections for the future and weigh potential future scenarios. The future depends upon actions individuals take. Often, the effects of these actions will be delayed for years. Students need to know and understand that their own actions—or lack of action—can make a difference to the future.

PARTICIPATION OBJECTIVES

1. Students will value participation in the democratic process. Through participation, citizens affect government policies. For example, citizens participate by speaking, voting, lobbying, and contributing to campaigns or causes. Each of these forms of participation affects international issues. While in school, students need to practice these activities where appropriate.

2. Students will tolerate ambiguity. Most global issues will not be resolved soon. Having some tolerance for the ambiguities of this complex world is helpful. This does not mean that students should be tolerant of all behavior or situations; nor does it mean that right and wrong solutions cannot be hidden by ambiguity.

3. Students will read newspapers, magazines, and books; listen to radio and television programs that relate to intercultural and international topics; and actively respond to news articles, books, and programs. Local communities change, as will the United States' role in the world. Students will need to continue to learn about international and intercultural topics. Because citizens learn the majority of their information about the world from the press and mass media, students need to better understand the strengths and weaknesses of these sources of information. Students should be encouraged to actively respond to these "one-way" communication systems by discussing programs with peers, family, and others, and by writing letters to the editorial staffs of newspapers and media stations.

Some Final Thoughts

Global education should provide students with the information and intellectual tools—coupled with the willingness to use them—that enable them to function as competent American citizens in a complex and rapidly changing international environment. The study of global education is not an excuse to neglect the rules of sound scholarship. At times, emotions, personal opinions, and unproven assertions may dominate the discussion of volatile global issues. This is wrong. Students must learn that their feelings and opinions may be understandable, but do not substitute for reasoned judgments based on reputable authorities. However, these difficulties should never provide justification for avoiding the study of topics that may generate emotion and, at times, divisive controversy. Here is where the teacher has the opportunity to model a reasoned, evenhanded approach to potentially volatile topics.

Students also must learn that the published materials on global education vary greatly in their accuracy and reliability. As the late Jean Mayer, a world authority on nutrition and related matters, cautioned one of the authors in working on President Carter's Commission on World Hunger: "Probably one-third of the published materials on food and hunger are accurate, reflect the best current scholarship and should be believed. Another third are either badly dated or only partially correct and always should be used with caution. The other third are badly biased, inaccurate, and grossly misrepresent the problem. Avoid them at all costs!" Educators would do well to keep Mayer's advice in mind when dealing with most global problems.

We must equip students with the knowledge, intellectual skills, and attitudes they need to cope effectively with the global realities they must face as adults. Unfortunately, in many schools, global topics are studied seldom, if at all. Time is spent instead "giving students the background" needed to engage these issues "later on." Unfortunately, "later on" never arrives. Thus, students are forced to form opinions and, ultimately, make decisions about important global concerns in an intellectual vacuum. These concerns are too important to allow our citizens to continue to remain intellectually unprepared.

Individuals working to establish standards that reflect what all students should "know and be able to do" would do well to pay attention to the kinds of student outcomes suggested by those experienced in the international dimensions of education. Further, they should make certain that whatever students "know and are able to do" includes in-depth study of the real problems and challenges facing the human race. John Dewey stated that "School is not preparation for life, it is life." What better way to make school "life" for the next generation.

NOTES

1. Robert Hanvey, in *An Attainable Global Perspective* (New York: The American Forum for Global Education, 1976), describes four levels of cross-cultural awareness: (1) awareness of superficial or visible cultural traits: stereotypes; (2) awareness of significant and subtle cultural traits that contrast markedly with one's own: you are frustrated and confused; (3) awareness of significant and subtle cultural traits that contrast markedly with one's own: you think about it and start to ask questions and understand; and (4) awareness of how another culture feels from the standpoint of the insider: cultural immersion [see p. 217, this volume].

2. Robert Kohls's descriptors of culture are an entry point for students to learn about

the world and other cultures. Under the headings "Some Cultures" and "Most Cultures," he lists points of view or values in relation to the various ways people view the world. For example, in the United States, we generally feel that we have personal control over our environment; however, in much of the world people feel that fate determines what they are to do. Conflict can arise when different cultures with different points of view meet to solve common problems. An awareness of such differences is key to cross-cultural understanding. For a listing of what some cultures believe in and what most cultures believe in, see Kohls and Knight, *Developing Intercultural Awareness* (Yarmouth, Maine: Intercultural Press, 1994), 42.

3. Craig Stori, in *The Art of Crossing Cultures* (Yarmouth, Maine: Intercultural Press, 1990), expresses the cross-cultural process as follows: "We expect others to be like us, but they aren't. Then a cultural incident occurs causing a reaction, such as anger or fear, and we withdraw. We become aware of our reaction, we reflect on its cause, and our reaction subsides. We observe the situation which results in developing culturally appropriate expectations."

4. There are four major traits to be developed and 18 others that support them. They are suggested by J. Daniel Hess in *The Whole World Guide to Culture Learning* (Yarmouth, Maine: Intercultural Press, 1994), 12ff. The four major traits are: (1) a high regard for culture, (2) an eagerness to learn, (3) a desire to make connections, and (4) a readiness to give as well as to receive.

5. Many communities and states have developed "Your Community (or State) and the World" programs. For a list of these programs, contact Dr. Chadwick Alger at the Mershon Center, The Ohio State University, 1501 Neil Avenue, Columbus, OH 43201-2602. Or, contact your state department of education.

BIBLIOGRAPHY

Global Challenges, Issues, and Problems

Brown, Lester, et al. *State of the World, 1995.* New York: W. W. Norton and Company, 1995.

Foreign Policy Association. *Great Decisions, 1996.* New York: Foreign Policy Association, 1996.

Foreign Policy Association. Headline Series. Published five times yearly. New York: Foreign Policy Association.

Griffiths, Robert J. *Annual Editions: Developing World.* 6th ed. Guilford, Conn.: Dushkin Publishing Group/Brown and Benchmark Publishers, 1995.

Groennings, Sven, and David S. Wiley, eds. *Group Portrait: Internationalizing the Disciplines.* New York: The American Forum, 1990.

Jackson, Robert M., ed. *Annual Editions: Global Issues—95/96.* 11th ed. Guilford, Conn.: Dushkin Publishing Group/Brown and Benchmark Publishers, 1995.

Kegley, Charles W., and Eugene R. Wittikopf. *World Politics: Trend and Transformation.* 4th ed. New York: St. Martin's Press, 1993.

Lutz, Wolfgang. *The Future of World Population.* Washington, D.C.: Population Reference Bureau, 1994.

McFalls, Joseph A., Jr. *Population: A Lively Introduction.* 2nd ed. Washington, D.C.: Population Reference Bureau, 1995.

Olson, William C. *Theory and Practice of International Relations.* 8th ed. Englewood Cliffs, N.J.: Prentice Hall, 1991.

Purkitt, Helen E., ed. *Annual Editions: World Politics—95/96.* 16th ed. Guilford, Conn.: Dushkin Publishing Group/Brown and Benchmark Publishers, 1996.

Rourke, John T., ed. *Taking Sides: Clashing Views on Controversial Issues in World Politics.* 6th ed. Guilford, Conn.: Dushkin Publishing Group/Brown and Benchmark Publishers, 1995.

Russett, Bruce, and Harvey Starr. *World Politics: The Menu for Choice.* 5th ed. New York: W. H. Freeman and Co., 1996.

Segal, Gerald. *The World Affairs Companion.* Rev. ed. New York: Simon and Schuster, 1993.

World Resources Institute. *World Resources 1994–95.* New York: Oxford University Press, 1994.

Global Cultures and World Areas

Anderson, Charlotte C., with Susan K. Nicklas and Agnes R. Crawford. *Global Understandings: A Framework for Teaching and Learning.* Alexandria, Va.: Association for Supervision and Curriculum Development, 1994.

Bennett, Christine L. *Comprehensive Multicultural Education.* Boston: Allyn and Bacon, Inc., 1986.

Collins, H. Thomas, and Frederick R. Czarra. *Global Primer: Skills for a Changing World.* Denver, Colo.: Center for Teaching International Relations, University of Denver, 1986.

Collins, H. Thomas, and Frederick R. Czarra. *Human Rights: Children Count Too!* Arlington, Va.: The American Association of School Administrators, 1993.

Ferguson, Henry. *Manual for Multicultural Education.* Yarmouth, Maine: Intercultural Press, 1987.

Fersh, Seymour. *Learning About Peoples and Cultures.* Evanston, Ill.: McDougal, Littell and Company, 1974.

Fersh, Seymour. *Integrating the Trans-National Cultural Dimension.* Fastback 361. Phi Delta Kappa Educational Foundation, 1993.

Hall, Edward T. *The Silent Language, The Hidden Dimension, The Dance of Life, Beyond Culture.* Garden City, N.Y.: Anchor Press Doubleday, 1983.

Hanvey, Robert G. *An Attainable Global Perspective.* New York: The American Forum for Global Education, 1976.

Hess, J. Daniel. *The Whole World Guide to Culture Learning.* Yarmouth, Maine: Intercultural Press, 1994.

Hoopes, David S. *Intercultural Education.* Fastback 142. Phi Delta Kappa Educational Foundation, 1980.

Hoopes, David S., and Kathleen R. Hoopes, eds. *Guide to International Education in the United States.* New York: Gale Research Inc., 1991.

Kohls, L. Robert. *Survival Kit for Overseas Living.* 2nd ed. Yarmouth, Maine: Intercultural Press, 1984.

Kohls, L. Robert, and John M. Knight. *Developing Intercultural Awareness.* 2nd ed. Yarmouth, Maine: Intercultural Press, 1994.

Parsons, Talcott. *The Social System.* New York: The Free Press, 1951.

Storti, Craig. *The Art of Crossing Cultures.* Yarmouth, Maine: Intercultural Press, 1990.

Trompenaars, Fons. *Riding the Waves of Culture: Understanding Diversity in Global Business.* New York: Irwin Professional Publishing, 1994.

Wilson, Angene. "Bringing the World Closer to Home." In *Georgia Council of the Social Studies Yearbook,* Helen W. Richardson, ed., 1995.

Global Connections: The United States and the World

Alger, Chadwick. *Perceiving, Understanding and Coping with World Relations in Everyday Life.* New York: The American Forum for Global Education, 1993.

Czarra, Frederick R. *Implementing Global Perspectives in Local School Districts.* New York: Global Perspectives in Education, 1982.

Czarra, Frederick R., and David Edwards. *International Dimensions of Education: Documents of State Education Agencies.* Washington, D.C.: Council of Chief State School Officers, 1993. (This contains a listing by state of "Your State and the World," world areas, history, geography, and world language curriculum guides.)

Gilliom, M. Eugene, Richard C. Remy, and Robert B. Wojach. "Using the Community As a Resource for Global Education." *Teaching Political Science* 7 (April 1980): 251–264.

Global Perspectives in Education. *New York and the World.* New York: Global Perspectives in Education, 1985.

Hamilton, John. *Main Street America and the Third World.* Cabin John, Md.: Seven Locks Press, 1988.

Hamilton John. *Entangling Alliances: How the Third World Shapes Our Lives.* Cabin John, Md.: Seven Locks Press, 1990.

Hogan, Michael J., and Thomas G. Paterson. *Explaining the History of American Foreign Relations.* New York: Cambridge University Press, 1992.

Kegley, Charles W., and Eugene R. Willkopf. *World Politics: Trend and Transformation.* 4th ed. New York: St. Martin's Press, 1993.

Rourke, John T. *International Politics on the World Stage.* 4th ed. Guilford, Conn.: Dushkin Publishing Group/Brown and Benchmark Publishers, 1993.

Toma, Peter A. *International Relations: Understanding Global Issues.* Pacific Grove, Ca.: Brooks/Cole Publishing Company, 1991.

Woyach, Robert B. *Making Decisions: Our Global Connection.* Columbus, Ohio: Council on World Affairs, no date.

Woyach, Robert B. "Teaching About the Global Community Using the Local Community." In *Community Study: New Applications for Social Studies.* Washington, D.C.: National Council for the Social Studies, 1986.

Woyach, Robert B., and Janice Love. "Citizenship and World Affairs: The Impact of a Community-Based Approach to Global Education." *Educational Research Quarterly* 7 (1983).

Woyach, Robert B., and Richard C. Remy. "A Community-Based Approach to Global Education." *Theory into Practice* 21 (Summer 1982): 177–183.

The Standards

Center for Civic Education. *The National Standards for Civics and Government.* Calabasas, Calif.: Center for Civic Education, 1994.

Geography Education Standards Project. *Geography for Life: National Geography Standards.* Washington, D.C.: National Geographic Research and Exploration, 1994.

National Center for History in the Schools. *Expanding Children's World in Time and Space, Grades K–4.* Expanded ed. Los Angeles: University of California, Los Angeles, 1994.

National Center for History in the Schools. *Exploring Paths to the Present, Grades 5–12.* Expanded ed. Los Angeles: University of California, Los Angeles, 1994.

National Center for History in the Schools. *Exploring the American Experience.* Los Angeles: University of California, Los Angeles, 1994.

National Council for the Social Studies. *Expectations of Excellence: Curriculum Standards for Social Studies.* Washington, D.C.: National Council for the Social Studies, 1994.

National Standards in Foreign Language Education Project. *Standards for Foreign Language Learning: Preparing for the 21st Century.* Yonkers, N.Y.: National Standards in Foreign Language Education Project, 1996.

Pedagogy for Global Perspectives in Education

STUDIES OF TEACHERS' THINKING AND PRACTICE

Merry M. Merryfield

Abstract

As Americans come to understand the effects of globalization, there is increasing concern that schools today are not adequately preparing students for our interdependent world. Although much has been written about the need to infuse global perspectives in education so that students will understand and benefit from the increasing interconnectedness of the world's cultures, economies, and political relationships, few scholars have studied the actual practice of social studies teachers as they teach global perspectives or tried to understand the contexts of their instructional decisions. In this article multiple perspectives on current classroom practice in global education are examined, including those of master teachers considered the best global educators in their school districts, practicing teachers who have recently completed their first formal instruction in global education, and preservice teachers who are beginning to teach globally oriented social stud-

Reprinted with permission from *Theory and Practice in Social Education,* vol. 26, no. 3 (Summer). © 1998 by the National Council for the Social Studies.

ies as part of their certification programs. Some commonalities of theories and practice across the three groups include teaching students about their own cultures and diverse cultures through multiple perspectives, connecting global knowledge and skills to their students' lives, and making connections across historical time periods and world regions. There are also considerable differences across the three groups of teachers as the master teachers focus much more on global and local inequities, interdisciplinary approaches, higher level thinking, and cross-cultural experiential learning.

As Americans come to understand the effects of globalization in our communities and nation, there is increasing concern that schools today are not adequately preparing students for the challenges of a changing world (Alger, 1974; Anderson, 1990; Bennett, 1995; Boyer, 1983; Council on Learning, 1981; National Governors' Association, 1989). Much has been written about the need to infuse global perspectives in education so that students will understand and benefit from the increasing interconnectedness of the world's cultures, economies, technologies, ecology, and political relationships (Anderson, 1979; Becker, 1979; Goodlad, 1986; Lamy, 1990; Leetsma, 1979; Tye, 1990). Scholars in education, history, and the social sciences have set forth ways in which schools should prepare young people for life in a global age (Alger & Harf, 1986; Gilliom, Remy & Woyach, 1980; Hanvey, 1976; Kniep, 1986a; Lamy, 1987). The National Council for the Social Studies (1982), other professional organizations, and state and local educational agencies have published rationales, goals, methods, and materials for infusing global perspectives into social education. Teacher educators have developed programs, courses, and instructional materials to prepare social studies teachers to integrate global perspectives into their teaching and learning (Begler, 1993; Easterly, 1994; Flournoy, 1994; Gilliom, 1993; Johnson, 1993; Merryfield, 1993a, 1995; Muessig & Gilliom, 1981; Remy, Nathan, Becker & Torney, 1975; Torney-Purta, 1995; Tucker, 1990; Tucker & Cistone, 1991; Tye & Tye, 1992; Wilson, 1997; Wooster, 1993). Commercial publishers, curriculum development centers, and area studies programs have produced a wealth of resources to support changes in state and district curricular mandates and demands of K–12 social studies teachers for globally oriented materials. However, few educators or scholars have studied the actual practice of social studies teachers as they teach global perspectives or tried to understand the contexts of their instructonal decisions.

In this paper I examine multiple perspectives on current classroom practice in global education. Perspectives include those of (1) 16 master teachers considered the best global educators by their school districts, (2) 67 practicing teachers who had recently completed their first formal instruction in global education, and (3) 60 preservice teachers who were beginning to teach globally oriented social studies as part of their certification programs in a professional development school network (PDS) in social studies and global education. At the end of the paper I suggest how the conceptual literature on global education could be informed and strengthened by the perspectives, theories, and practice of the teachers. The goals of the paper are to (1) gain a better understanding of how teachers conceptualize global education as they plan and teach, (2) develop insights into the contextual factors that influence teachers' instructional decisions as they teach about the world and its peoples, (3) examine how teachers' thinking and practice can contribute to the literature conceptualizing global education. An underlying assumption of the paper is that better understanding of teachers' theories and practice can inform the field of global education and improve social studies education.

Contexts of the Studies

Teaching about community, nation and the world from global perspectives differs in several ways from traditional approaches to the study of cultures, world geography, U.S. history, foreign policy, or the history of world civilizations. Scholars in the field have developed both substantive differences and perceptual differences. Substantively, the world is seen as interrelated systems in which technological, ecological, economic, political and development issues can no longer be effectively addressed by individual nations because the issues become global as they spill over borders and regions (Becker, 1979; Hanvey, 1976; Kniep, 1986b). Global perspectives in education focus as much on cultural universals, those things all humans share in common, and perspective consciousness, knowledge and appreciation of other peoples' points of view, as it does on cultural differences (Alger & Harf, 1986; Case, 1991, 1993; Hanvey, 1976; Kniep, 1986a). A fourth element in the scholarly literature on global education is the recognition that each of us makes choices that affect other people around the world, and others make choices that affect us (Anderson, 1979; Alger & Harf, 1986; Hanvey 1976; Lamy, 1987). Because of these interconnections or interdependence between students, their communities and other peoples, global education includes goals of decision-making, participation, and long-term involvement in the larger world beyond our borders as well as in the local community. Scholars have also included other elements, such as global history (Kniep, 1986b), the changing nature of world actors and transactions (Alger & Harf, 1986; Lamy, 1987), persistent global problems and issues (Kniep, 1986b), and cross-cultural experiences (Wilson 1982, 1983, 1993a, 1993b).

In the last decade scholars have conceptualized perceptual dimensions within a global education. Open-mindedness, anticipation of complexity, resistance to stereotyping, empathy and non-chauvinism have been developed by Case (1991), Darling (1995), and Wilson (1994). Pike and Selby (1988, 1995) have conceptualized an inner dimension in which students examine their own perspectives in relation to the perspectives others hold. They include areas of social justice, gender equity, animal rights, health, human rights, and development education (Pike & Selby, 1995). Recognizing a weakness in global education's lack of emphasis on moral education and social justice, Werner (1990) has applied critical pedagogy to global education in order to get at the contradictions of its conflicting goals and interests. Coombs (1989) and Darling (1994, 1995) have further developed relationships between global education and moral education.[1] See Appendix A for a more detailed view of conceptualizations of global education from selected works in the field.

Teacher educators involved in implementing global education in their programs have described their efforts as preparing teachers to (1) make connections across cultures, world regions, and civilizations and across global issues instead of teaching them separately, (2) identify historical antecedents to current world issues, events, and problems, and identify the processes of cultural diffusion and borrowing over time, (3) link global content to the local community, and (4) teach tolerance and appreciation of cultural differences (Merryfield, 1991, 1992).

Although there has been considerable rhetoric about the need for global education, little attention has been paid to how teachers are actually teaching about the world, its peoples, and global issues. There is much conceptual literature that describes the goals, elements, or rationale for global perspectives in education, yet we know very little about what actually happens in globally oriented classrooms or how teachers make instructional decisions as they plan and teach about the world.

Within social studies education scholars have studied teachers as instructional decision-makers and delineated some important contextual factors that relate to how teachers make decisions. Researchers have concluded that teachers vary in how they perceive their overall roles in planning instruction and curriculum (Brown, 1988; Marsh, 1984; Stodolsky, 1988; Thornton, 1985). Although some studies have indicated that teachers are affected by colleagues (Levstik, 1989) and other factors within the school building and community (McNeil, 1986; White, 1985), other studies have found teachers' instructional decisions are influenced by instructional materials, particularly textbooks (Lydecker, 1982; McCutcheon, 1981; also see Kon, 1995 for a contrasting view), concerns over classroom management (Hyland, 1985; Parker & Gehrke, 1986) and perceptions of what instruction is appropriate for their students (Cornbleth, Korth & Dorow, 1983; Kagan, 1993; O'Loughlin, 1995). Other studies have identified teachers' underlying beliefs, values, and experiences as primary influences in shaping instructional decisions (Cornett, 1987, 1990; Shaver, Davis & Helburn, 1980; Thornton & Wenger, 1989; Wilson, 1982, 1983).

In summing up his review of teachers as curricular-instructional gatekeepers, Thornton (1991) called for more qualitative studies of exemplary practice in order to understand the classroom realities of instructional decision-making. These sentiments are echoed by other educators (Cornbleth, 1991; Wilson & Wineburg, 1988) and educational research in general as evidenced in recent paradigm shifts towards interpretive and constructivist theories. Armento (1996), writing in the recent *Handbook of Research on Teacher Education,* noted that the field of social studies needs research that gives greater attention to relationships between teacher education, professional development, and the social contexts of teachers' lives and work.

My inquiry into teacher decision-making and global perspectives grew from this literature and my own experiences and concerns. First, as a professor in a graduate program in social studies and global education, I wanted to learn more about how teachers make instructional decisions as they teach about the world, particularly in courses and school systems that are purported to address global perspectives. How do exemplary teachers conceptualize global education? To what degree do they support and teach the elements of global education as advocated in the scholarly literature? In what ways have teachers developed their own theories of how to prepare young people for their globally interconnected world? Second, I saw a paradox between the social studies literature on teacher thinking that identifies a handful of discrete factors that affect teachers' instructional decisions and the more broadly based literature about teacher thinking that alludes to the complexities of how teachers think about teaching and learning and how they make instructional decisions (Calderhead, 1987; Clark & Peterson, 1986; Connelly & Clandinin, 1988; Elbaz, 1981; McNair, 1978–1979; Shavelson, 1983; Shavelson & Stern, 1981; Yinger & Clark, 1982).

Third, from my own experiences in teaching and in research in classrooms in the U.S. and several African nations, I was convinced that most researchers in social studies and global education don't spend sufficient time in observing practice, in systematic reflection with teachers, and in analyzing data to understand the complexities of global education and teachers' instructional decision-making. From the outset of the studies I wanted to address concerns over the lack of prolonged engagement, persistent observation, and idiographic interpretation (see Lincoln & Guba, 1985) that I perceived as limitations in the extant body of knowledge about teacher decision-making, social studies, and global education.

The overall goal of the three studies is to learn more about how teachers make instructional decisions in globally oriented social studies and what contextual factors influence their decisions. Below I briefly outline the research design of each of the studies and explain how they are connected conceptually. To differentiate the studies I will refer to them as Study 1: focusing on teachers who are considered to be exemplary global educators within their school districts; Study 2: focusing on experienced classroom teachers who have recently studied and begun to teach global perspectives; Study 3: preservice teachers who have studied global education in methods courses and fieldwork within a professional development school network in social studies and global education and plan to make global perspectives an integral part of their teaching and learning.

Study 1: Exemplary Global Educators

The study sought to document how outstanding global educators make decisions about teaching about the world. I selected school districts based upon their commitment to global education as demonstrated through course development, allocation of resources, and staff development. The teachers were selected through recommendations from district and building administrators, their achievements in teaching and curriculum development related to global education, their knowledge of global education and its application to their courses, and their willing-ness to give time each week to the study. Twelve teachers were in the study from 1991–1993, and another four teachers were in the study from 1992–1994. Each of the 16 teachers is considered exemplary by his/her school district and building administrators. Six teachers (two elementary, two middle, and two secondary in each district) were selected from a large urban district. Their classes were pre-dominately working-class African American and white students; most classes had a few immigrants from Asia and the Middle East. Six teachers were selected from a small, very affluent suburban district. While the vast majority of their students were upper middle class white students, all classes had one or more students of color, most frequently Asian Americans. Four teachers were selected from a poorly funded school district that was in a transition from rural to surburban as a nearby city's suburbs expanded towards this small town. The school population was also undergoing significant change as this formerly all-white rural commu-nity was growing from an influx of urban whites fleeing school desegregation and urban African Americans moving to the new suburbs. These four teachers were selected for the study because they were initiating a new program for their district called "World Connections." Based upon the reforms of the Coalition of Essen-tial Schools, this interdisciplinary program for tenth graders integrated social studies, language arts, science, math and art around global themes and issues (see Shapiro & Merryfield, 1995, for a case study of an eight week unit taught by the team on international conflict resolution).

Once a week my graduate research assistants and I observed the teachers as they taught courses in history, geography or world cultures. We recorded what was said by teachers and students during instruction and prepared transcripts of each class period that also included teacher and student actions, the use of instruc-tional materials, and the physical arrangement of the room. Each observation was followed up with an interview, either after class if possible or by telephone on the evening of the observation. The interview questions grew out of the observation notes and most frequently asked the teacher to explain why he or she had made particular instructional decisions.

From the beginning of the study considerable attention was given to having the teachers identify contextual factors—for example, teacher beliefs and experi-ences, mandated courses of study, instructional materials and other resources, student characteristics, team-teaching, parents, state tests, and so forth—that in-fluenced instructional decision-making. The teachers helped improve written con-structions of their perspectives through formal member checks, sessions where the teachers reflected upon and discussed raw data and tentative findings. At regu-lar intervals each teacher examined all the observational and interview data for his or her own case study in order to review and think about decisions, content, strategies, students, and the myriad components of classroom teaching. Teachers were encouraged to help us understand, interpret and articulate their perspectives on teaching and learning. New questions were continuously developed from ob-servational and interview data and from discussions during the member checks.

Literally thousands of questions were asked during the study. Questions encompassed choices of content, time allocations, instructional materials, teaching strategies, and issues related to student motivation, learning, and evaluation. Some questions were posed to all teachers, such as "what were contextual factors affecting the planning of today's lesson?" Other questions were specific to a teacher's instruction, such as "why did you change the group work assignment in the middle of class today?"

Tentative findings grew out of content analysis (as described by Lincoln and Guba 1985, 332–356). Each sentence (or groups of sentences in some cases where meaning might otherwise be lost) was keyed as to teacher and date, then categorized to answer questions related to content, process, contextual factors and several other aspects of instruction. The study produced over 3500 pages of raw data. The teachers and I examined every line (and categorized and recategorized the data) at least six times during the study. I also interviewed the teachers' building principals, school district administrators, and curriculum supervisors in order to understand better the larger contextual factors of school climate, constraints on teacher decision-making, and their perceptions of the impact of parents and the community on teachers' instruction about the world.

These data and findings were used to develop different frameworks for understanding how teachers make instructional decisions as they plan and teach about the world. The last step in data analysis focused on decisions about global content, loosely defined as knowledge, skills or attitudes taught in order that students understand the world and its peoples. All decisions related to global content that were documented in the observations and interviews were analyzed as to (1) the theories underlying the decision and (2) the contextual factors that the teacher identified as influencing the decision. From these analyses a profile of decision-making was developed for each teacher and for teams where teachers planned and taught together. In a final member check, each teacher examined his or her profile and improved its construction. The profiles were organized by (1) the theories underlying the teacher's decisions on global content, (2) the contextual factors that heavily influence each theory, and (3) an example of an instructional decision guided by that theory. See Appendix B for an example of the profiles. The first year of weekly observations was followed by a second year of interviews to examine in what ways the teachers perceived that they changed their teaching, course content, and perspectives on global education from one year to the next.

Study 2: Experienced Classroom Teachers Who Have
Recently Studied and Begun to Teach Global Perspectives

Early on in the study of exemplary global educators I began to notice differences between what I was observing from teachers in my graduate classes on global education and what I was learning from the study. Intrigued by these differences, I began to examine how experienced classroom teachers begin to conceptualize and teach global perspectives. Beginning in 1990, I asked experienced teachers in my graduate seminar, "Infusing Global Perspectives in Education" (see

Appendix C for the conceptual framework for global education that I use in introductory courses), if I could follow up on our coursework and collect data six to nine months later on their application of global education in their teaching. From 1991–1997, I collected data from 67 teachers. The teachers shared these characteristics: (1) at the time that they took the course, they had at least three years teaching experience in social studies in elementary, middle, or high schools, (2) the course they took with me was their first formal study of global education, (3) at the completion of the course they planned to infuse global perspectives into their teaching and learning, and (4) they chose to be included in the study.

Data collection included journals written during the course, structured interviews within six to nine months after the course was completed, and collection of other relevant documents such as lesson plans, new courses of study, and instructional materials developed or adapted by the teachers. The journals captured the teachers' reactions and ideas to different rationales and conceptualizations of global education, their evaluation of instructional materials, and their development of an application project in which they infused global perspectives into lessons, units, courses, or curriculum frameworks. Written as the course progressed over ten weeks, the journals provide insights into the teachers' initial construction of global education and its application to their students and courses. The follow-up interviews included these questions:

1. When you think back to the course, what comes to mind? [Probes to knowledge, skills, experiences, resources, other.]

2. In what ways do you think that the course has made a difference in your thinking, your learning or your teaching? [Probes to get at all three elements.]

3. Could you give me a few illustrations of your teaching of global perspectives over the last six to nine months? [Probes to flesh out illustrations, get at main points and underlying assumptions.]

4. What does global education mean to you at this time? [Probes for conceptualization, any "essential" elements, and areas that may be considered important but do not fit into the teacher's current teaching assignments.]

5. What factors constrain your teaching of global perspectives? What factors support your teaching of global perspectives? [Probe for further elaboration, description, illustrations.]

6. What questions or concerns about global education do you have at this time? What are other issues about global education that you value or have relevance for you?

7. Given your experiences with global education, how would you advise me to improve my introductory course?

Beyond the interview data, I asked the teachers for lesson plans, materials they had developed or used, and any other documents that related to their teaching global perspectives. Most of the teachers provided some documentation of their planning and teaching. All these data—from journals, interviews, and other documents—were analyzed according to the methods described in the first study above. Categories were developed for the elements in the teachers' conceptualizations of global education, their application in their teaching, and the contextual factors that influenced their thinking and practice.

Study 3: Preservice Teachers in a Professional Development School Network (PDS) in Social Studies and Global Education

Along with my research of exemplary teachers and my teaching and learning in my graduate seminar in global education, I was also preparing preservice teachers for comprehensive secondary (grades 7–12) social studies certification. Because of the impact of the exemplary global educators on my own thinking about intersections of teachers' beliefs and experiences, global education, social studies, and teacher education, I began to rethink our B.S. and M.A. teacher preparation programs. One major weakness in our program was the contradiction between what our students learned about global education on campus, and what they learned in their field experiences. Quite frequently they left campus with a foundation in global education and a preliminary resource base and found little or no support in the schools for teaching global perspectives. As I came to know the exemplary global educators over that first year, we often talked about the problems of preservice teacher education and possible ways to improve it.

By 1991, several of the exemplary teachers and I had begun to work collaboratively on improving the preservice program, particularly in the area of global education. In 1992 we implemented a formal restructuring as a Professional Development School (PDS) Network in Social Studies and Global Education that included these components: (1) eight classroom teachers and a college professor team-teaching our methods courses, (2) the collaborative development by the teachers (we began to call them field professors) and the college professor of a new 10 quarter hour PDS methods block, (3) extensive field experience (four clock hours a day) and ten teaching experiences for the preservice teachers during methods, (4) portfolio and performance-based assessment during methods, and (5) similar teacher/professor/doctoral student collaboration during student teaching, a capstone seminar, and final assessments (for more on the global education dimension of the PDS Network, see Dove, Norris & Shinew, 1997; Chase & Merryfield, 1997, 1998).

As we struggled to develop and implement a cohesive collaborative program, the field professors and I also began an inquiry into the preservice teachers' thinking and instruction. From 1992 to 1997, we collected data on the preservice teachers during the six months they were in PDS methods and student teaching. As the preservice teachers learned about global education in seminars, field experiences, and readings, they wrote weekly synthesizing essays to bring together what they were learning and to apply the ideas and experiences to their own teaching. (See our conceptual framework for global education in Appendix B.) They were expected to infuse global perspectives into lessons that they developed and taught during methods. At mid-term and the end of the quarter, we engaged them in further discussion both individually and in focus groups about their conceptualizations and teaching of global perspectives in the social studies. Data also were collected from observations during student teaching, their lessons plans, assessments and their in-flight decisions in the classroom. These data were analyzed as they were collected using content analysis to answer similar questions to those addressed in the two studies described above.

In this paper I focus on findings related to how they conceptualized global education, how they infused global perspectives into their preservice planning and teaching, and their explanations of the contextual factors influencing their decisions. Not all of our preservice teachers from 1992–1997 are in this study. Those 60 selected met these criteria: (1) they purposefully sought ways to integrate global education into their teaching during methods and student teaching, (2) they demonstrated a commitment to their own learning about the world and its peoples, and (3) they chose to become a part of the study. Out of 135 preservice teachers with whom I worked from 1992–1997, the 60 in the study were those who appeared over the six months of methods and student teaching to have the greatest commitment to global education and the best ability to infuse global perspectives into their own teaching and learning.

Although these studies were designed separately, they overlap in their examination of teachers' thinking, their instructional decisions in planning and teaching, and the contexts of those decisions. Together the findings provide insights into the interconnectedness of teachers' lived experience, their theories of teaching and learning in global education, and their practice in teaching about the world and its peoples. The findings are organized by the teachers' explanations of the conceptualizations or theories for infusing global perspectives into their teaching and learning and by the contextual factors they identified as affecting their instructional decisions. The three groups of teachers differed in their teaching experience and backgrounds in global education. However, they all did share knowledge of the scholarly literature and conceptual foundations of global education, and they all had some experience in applying these ideas as they integrated global perspectives into their K–12 courses.

Teachers' Theories and Contextual Factors

Although the teachers phrase them somewhat differently, there are some important similarities in the theories that guide the decision-making of all three groups of teachers in global education and in the contextual factors that the teachers identified as shaping those decisions. There are also some ideas and contextual factors that are unique to each group of teachers and to individual teachers within the groups. The similarities across all groups are discussed first, followed by differences across the groups of teachers and then examples of the ideas unique to individual teachers.

Similarities across the Three Groups

(1) *Guiding theory for preparing students to think with global perspectives: Teach students about their own cultures and diverse cultures through multiple perspectives and comparisons of both similarities and differences so that students understand the complexity of culture and demonstrate tolerance and respect for differences.* A major finding of all three studies is the primacy of the study of culture. These theories include the need to begin the study of culture with an examination of the students' own cultures and their perspectives of what culture means in their daily life. In the study of diverse cultures locally and globally, their students are expected to develop skills in recognizing and analyzing the complexity of peoples' perspectives, and the effects of conflicting perspectives in human relationships. Along with the study of cultures, the teachers include the valuing of tolerance, respect and cooperation.

The guiding theory shared by the most teachers in all three groups was that students need knowledge and appreciation of multiple perspectives, multiple realities, and conflicting viewpoints on issues, events, and people under study. Some teachers phrased multiple perspectives in terms of skills in perspective consciousness, the ability to recognize that other people often have views or perspectives that are different from one's own. The teachers want their students to appreciate the complexity of diverse viewpoints within cultures and examine perspectives different from their own, those of "the powers that be," or those of the U.S. government. Attention to multiple perspectives was brought about through primary sources and conflicting first-hand accounts of events, biography, non-fiction and historical fiction, supplementary materials written by people from other cultures, guest speakers, or the viewpoints of diverse students during class.

Many of the teachers expected their students to make comparisons across cultures for their ways of living, economic and political development, and other cultural characteristics such as beliefs and values related to families, gender roles, religion, and authority. Cultural differences were usually taught as value-neutral. For example, cultural differences in work, technology, religion, gender roles, or daily life were taught as neither good nor bad but simply different. The teachers' knowledge goals focused on students' understanding of why people do or see things differently and how culture is related to history, geography, religion, economics, and exposure to different influences. Similarities across cultures and cultural universals were stressed by the teachers as important linkages across peoples. Cross-cultural understanding was a part of the study of culture for some teachers. That is, they perceived that the purpose of studying other cultures is to bring people together through mutual understanding of beliefs, experiences and the historical contexts of people's lives. Many of the teachers teach about cultural conflict and conflict resolution or management as part of teaching about diverse cultures and cultural universals.

It is difficult to separate the study of culture and multiple perspectives from the teachers' guiding theories of fostering tolerance, respect, and cooperation. Understanding of other cultures was not only an academic matter of facts to be learned. Most of the teachers said they used cooperative learning and collaborative projects to teach students skills in working with people different from themselves. Many of the teachers explained that cross-cultural understanding is more likely to develop if they bring together knowledge of diverse cultures, attitudes of tolerance and respect, and methods that reward cooperation and conflict management. The exemplary global educators called this an "integrative" or "total" or "holistic" approach to cultural understanding fostered by respect for differences and appreciation of commonalities within the classroom, school, and community as well as the larger world. When asked about why they felt the teaching of culture and multiple perspectives was central to global education, a majority of the teachers in each group replied that understanding of one's own and different cultures is the foundation for education to bring about harmony, reduce conflict and prepare students for the realities of many interconnected cultures in their neighborhoods, nation and world.

Contextual factors shaping the study of cultures. There were two major contextual factors shaping these guiding theories. First, many of the teachers in all three groups stated they were personally committed to developing tolerance and respect for views different from one's own. For many teachers this commitment has grown from their own lived experiences, such as observing overt discrimination, growing up in poverty in Appalachia, participating in desegregation, and experiences with students different from themselves in race, class, religion, language or national origin. For the exemplary global educators, appreciation of diverse cultures and multiple perspectives came from cross-cultural experiences in their teaching, travels, or from living in other countries.

Second, no matter what the characteristics of their school population, the teachers see their students as needing to become less ethnocentric and more empathetic with other people. Teachers in relatively homogeneous settings see the school experience as critical in helping their students to overcome their parochialism (see also Zimpher & Ashburn, 1992) and come to understand that not everyone is like them and that difference is not bad or bizarre, it is simply different. Teachers who have classes with diverse racial, ethnic or religious groups also see their influence as critical for the survival and integration of their students into the larger community and American society.

(2) *Guiding theory: Connect global content to students' lives.* Most of the teachers consistently acted upon the premise that global content should be connected to the experiences, knowledge base, and interests of the students. Many teachers decided to spend more time on a topic because their students were very interested or involved in it; or they spent less time when they perceived students as uninterested or unconnected. Many of these teachers made overt attempts in every lesson to relate the content under study to their students' lives.

It is quite remarkable the degree to which students affected instruction in the exemplary group. Most of these teachers were acutely responsive to student interests, abilities, behavior, and concerns. When students were involved and excited about a topic such as an oil spill in the news, the teacher frequently would extend time spent on it at the cost of time for other topics. If a topic related to the background of some students, such as African history for African American students, again that topic received more attention. In one suburban classroom, a question about jewelry in Africa by the only African American student in the sixth grade led to an impromptu unit on African lifestyles and adornment that the teacher developed to build upon student interest about a part of the world her students had never studied.

Contextual factors shaping the connection of content to students' lives. Teachers believe that they increased the motivation of students to succeed in school by connecting content to student interests and experiences. Some saw connections between content and students as a way to increase their students' self-esteem as they learned that they are a part of history and the world today. "Connections to social studies content place my students in the center of history as opposed to leaving them out as some textbooks do," explained one high school teacher. Student characteristics led the teachers to connect their students to the curriculum overtly since it is easier to teach students who see the topics under study as relevant to their lives and who perceive their teachers as caring about their questions and concerns. Some teachers used the connections to students' lives as the basis for community service learning, exhibitions, and other authentic learning and assessments.

(3) *Guiding theory: Have students make connections across time and space.* A third category of guiding theories common to all three groups was a focus on relationships or linkages across time periods and world cultures and regions. The teachers had different ways of articulating this goal. Some referred to their students as "seeing the big picture." Several spoke of students understanding "cause and effect relationships in history," or examining "the ways in which history repeats itself." What these teachers saw as a major goal was student understanding of the dynamic nature of change and the human condition. They wanted their students to see how one event or invention leads to many changes in trade or class distinctions that lead to more and more change in governance or lifestyles. They wanted students to make connections across cultures and throughout history and in their lives today so that the world is seen as an interrelated system that is directly connected to historical antecedents, contemporary decisions, and global issues.

Contextual factors shaping connections across time and space. There were several contextual factors influencing the goal of making connections across historical time periods and across cultures and world regions. Many of the teachers explained that their interest in connections came from their own study of history, geography, economics, comparative political systems, literature, or global education. Some teachers noted that the reason they wanted to teach about the world was because they believed it to be important for students to recognize how today's world was directly related to past events, the acceleration of global interdependence, and the future of the planet. For some teachers, their mandated courses of study (official documents of curriculum content) emphasized making connections across cultures and across historical periods.

The relationship between the official curriculum and the theories of global education in the exemplary group was more extensive. Five of the teachers had written their school districts' courses of study for their classes or grade level and three other teachers were in the process of revising their districts' courses of study. Therefore it is not easy to distinguish between these teacher beliefs and their mandated curricula. In all 17 school districts connected with the three studies, teachers considered the best by the district leaders play a major role in developing the P–12 courses of study in social studies and in choosing texts and other resources for those courses.

Differences across the Three Groups
Each group had, to some extent, theories of global education and contextual factors that were different from the other groups. For example, content analysis of the data from the exemplary group produced several theories underlying their teaching of global education that were rarely touched upon by the teachers in the other groups.

FINDINGS UNIQUE TO THE EXEMPLARY GLOBAL EDUCATORS

(1) *Guiding theory: Teach about the interconnectedness of global and local inequities, the human struggle for rights, self-determination, social justice and a better life.* Recognizing the hegemony of the United States in the world today and the global political and economic power Americans hold, the exemplary global educators sought to help their students understand the relative privilege Americans have compared to other peoples on the planet. Many of their lessons of global interconnectedness taught about global inequities in technology, health care and mortality rates, education, employment opportunities and income, civil and human rights, trade, distribution of capital, and other indicators of peoples' and nations' standard of living. Several activities built off students' interests, such as two activities where students research the global assembly line of how locally sold baseballs and running shoes are made. Students examined the conditions of work and wages paid in other countries as well as the profits taken when they are sold in the United States. Similarities were drawn to circumstances in the United States where workers have been exploited or underpaid and issues such as who benefits from economic integration, the policies of the World Bank or the International Monetary Fund, and bilateral trade agreements.

Another theme developed by some of the teachers was the interconnectedness of European imperialism, colonialization in Africa, the slave trade, contemporary media stereotyping of Africans, and African Americans' fight for rights and respect in the United States. The themes related to inequality and privilege at times integrated economic, political, or cultural factors, such as a fourth grade study of American immigration past and present. The teachers perceived that this attention to global inequity goes hand in hand with the multiple perspectives and understanding of culture described above. In simulations and research projects students were asked to interact from the situations of people who are different from themselves. They explained that "walking in others' shoes" helps students to empathize with children and young people their ages in China or Nigeria or Bolivia who happen to have been born into quite different economic and political circumstances.

Human rights, civil rights, women's rights and children's rights are some other topics that teachers taught about in an effort to help their students understand global inequities and privilege. The genocide of the Holocaust was compared with Pol Pot's reign in Cambodia and the destruction of indigenous peoples of North America. In another lesson, a high school history teacher challenged the conventional wisdom that glorifies the Greeks as the founders of democracy by bringing in supplementary materials on their treatment of women and slaves.

Contextual factors shaping the study of the interconnectedness of global and local inequities. In explaining why they chose content about local and global connections of inequity, the teachers most frequently referred to their own beliefs and the characteristics of their students. The teachers reminded us of commitments they had to improving the lives of peoples in their own community and around the world. When we asked them to identify the contextual factors that led to a lesson about basic human needs, prejudice, or injustice, the teachers often brought up how sheltered or uninformed or parochial their students were about the human condition on the planet or even the way people live in a neighborhood five miles away. At times they explained their instructional choices by relating their concerns that their students did not have either knowledge of or empathy for people different from themselves. After a series of lessons to teach a global perspective of the connections between the economic development of the U.S. and that of several other countries, a high school teacher explained that her students had never been challenged to think about how the things they buy or the jobs their families hold affect and are affected by people around the world. Other lessons that related to political freedoms, refugees, land use, and cultural norms were developed by the teachers to get their students to recognize injustice as a global issue and examine multiple perspectives of how injustice and inequity are linked to their daily lives.

(2) *Guiding theory: Provide cross-cultural experiential learning.* A second commonality across the exemplary global educators was a determination that their students must interact with people different from themselves both within the local community and the global community. Some teachers referred to "cross-cultural competence" as expertise that they wanted their students to develop. Most spoke of skills in working cooperatively with others, listening and trying to understand a person whose English or first language was different from their own, or "cross-cultural communication" skills in interacting across cultures and nationalities.

For several of the exemplary teachers, their cross-cultural experiential learning was grounded in the multicultural nature of the school population or community. Two teachers taught in an international magnet elementary school, two taught in an international magnet middle school, and two taught in a high school that was designated as the district's ESL (English as a Second Language) secondary school. These schools have many nationalities, languages, and cultures within every class. Multicultural perspectives were shared daily in class discussions and activities.

Contextual factors in cross-cultural experiential learning. When the teachers explained why they brought in resource people from other cultures, took a field trip to a mosque or organized cooperative groups that created a positive interdependence of students born in the U.S. with students born in other countries, they spoke of the power of personal experience in bringing about cross-cultural appreciation and understanding. Usually they would compare some experience in their own lives with the experiences they were planning for their students. A summer spent backpacking in Turkey, a childhood in France, a high school exchange in Peru, the adoption of children from another race are examples of the experiences which led to profound changes in the way these teachers viewed themselves and others.

The second contextual factor was the diversity of people in the school or local community which makes it possible for students to have experiences with people different from themselves as a part of each unit of study. Teachers noted that there are many ways to sustain cross-cultural experiences so that they become a part of learning history or geography or the study of current events. All the teachers had contacts in the local community with resource people and organizations and used these networks to enrich their teaching and assessments.

(3) *Guiding theory: Use themes, issues or problems to organize and integrate global content.* The exemplary teachers found ways to bring together different disciplines in their social studies instruction in global education. Some teachers used concepts such as the environment or technology in order to integrate social studies with science, agriculture, or health. Others used themes such as religious conflict, cultural change, or globalization in an integrated multidisciplinary approach. Literature, art, and philosophy were used to enhance history and geography. Teachers explained integration as helping students learn by approaching the topic in many different ways and with different materials. Recurring global issues such as hunger or development or questions such as "how do people resolve conflicts?" served as a constant reminder of goals of a course and helped students organize and use large amounts of information over several weeks, a semester, or even the entire course.

Contextual factors shaping the use of themes, issues or problems. The teachers' expertise, interests, or past experiences were the contextual factors that most heavily influenced planning through themes, issues and problems. These were sometimes selected by a team process or by the entire school as in the case of one of the international magnet schools. Some themes, such as culture, were chosen from the school district's course of study and honed by the interests of the teacher and his/her students. Issues were discarded or received less attention if there were few instructional materials to support them or if the students appeared to be uninterested.

(4) *Guiding theory: Emphasize skills in higher level thinking and research.* One of the most consistent similarities across the exemplary teachers is their commitment to teaching students higher level thinking skills (analysis, synthesis,

evaluation, etc.) and research skills (formulating questions, collecting and analyzing information and writing up findings) as an integral part of global education. From elementary through high school and urban to suburban districts, students were asked higher level questions and expected to find, analyze, evaluate and present answers. Some teachers framed the thinking and research skills within a process of decision-making or problem-solving. Although most teachers were more concerned with the use of information, some teachers highly valued the learning and recall of facts. The teachers integrated thinking and research skills with other skills (reading comprehension, writing, use of statistics and maps, categorization, presentation or debate) into assignments and projects.

Contextual factors shaping the emphasis on skills in higher level thinking and research. Although every course of study includes skills in thinking and research, most teachers explained their decisions based on their own (and, in some cases, their team's) beliefs that these skills were important for their students in order to prepare them for further education or adult life. Elementary teachers spoke of preparing kids for middle school, middle school teachers for high school, and high school teachers for college or adult decision-making. Many teachers explained that they had grown to appreciate these skills or had learned how to teach these skills from colleagues, administrators, or teacher education programs. The ability to integrate higher level thinking skills with globally oriented content is one of the few places where teachers said a teacher education program or course had made a positive difference in their teaching.

(5) *Guiding theory: employ variety of teaching strategies and instructional resources.* The teachers used many different teaching methods, a variety of instructional materials (data bases, primary sources, literature, videos, simulations), resource organizations (university programs, a local council on world affairs) and people (most frequently people from other countries). Most teachers required students to keep up with the news and they linked news stories to the subject under study. Since 1990–1991 was the year of the Gulf War, current events received more attention in the first year of the study than in other years (see also Merryfield, 1993b).

Part of the research design for the exemplary global educators focused on selecting days for observation so that the widest variety of teaching methods could be seen over a school year. Even in April and May teachers were still asking us to come on a particular day because we still had not seen this or that strategy. Most of the teachers purposefully sought out new materials and strategies through their involvement in professional meetings, curriculum development within their school districts, and inservice education or graduate degree programs.

Contextual factors shaping the use of a variety of teaching strategies and resources. The use of a wide variety of materials, resources, and teaching strategies was most frequently explained in terms of increasing student achievement and involvement as in "helping them learn," "getting them involved," or "keeping them thinking." The teachers perceived that diverse strategies were needed to address the range in student abilities and learning styles. Some teachers used a variety of methods to individualize instruction and assessment. Other teachers were concerned about the brevity, shallowness, or biases of textbooks. The teachers used their textbooks as one of many resources. When teachers did use texts, they skipped certain chapters or took them out of order. Their rationale for these decisions was that some topics are more important than others based on their own values, experiences, and education and the characteristics of their students.

In regards to the news as an instructional resource, most of the teachers expressed the view that keeping up with what is going on in the world was an integral part of teaching social studies. Many saw the nightly news as one way to make their subjects relevant to their students' lives. When relatives and teachers began to be called up for the Persian Gulf and the war began, the teachers explained their attention to the news in terms of responding to student fears and questions. As in other guiding theories, it is difficult to separate the teachers' valuing of current events from the teachers' valuing of student concerns and interests.

FINDINGS UNIQUE TO THE EXPERIENCED TEACHERS WHO WERE
BEGINNING TO TEACH GLOBAL PERSPECTIVES

These teachers had taken an introductory, ten-week graduate course in global education and had from six to nine months of experience in beginning to teach global perspectives. Unique to their profiles were these ideas guiding their instructional decision-making.

(1) *Expand curricular focus on less-taught-about parts of the world and global issues.* When asked about how the global education course had made a difference in their teaching, many of the teachers talked about specific parts of the world they had not taught about in the past and global issues that they were now including in their courses. Out of the 67 teachers in the study, 41 said they were now bringing more African, Asian or Latin American history or cultures or current events into their social studies courses. An elementary teacher illustrated her new expertise with a lesson that integrated Vietnamese and Ethiopian experiences into her class's study of immigration and cultural change. A high school teacher had developed a unit on 20th century political and economic globalization for his world history class. Other teachers had changed their teaching by adding comparative dimensions with a country or region of the world that they had not included before, such as comparing political protests in the U.S. and China or the effects of colonization in the U.S. and Mexico. A middle school teacher of social studies and health provided a copy of her new unit on hunger in which she had the students look at food production and distribution globally and locally.

Contextual factors shaping the decision to include more on less-taught-about parts of the world and global issues. According to the teachers, the factors influencing these additions were a new awareness of global change and interdependence and the availability of instructional materials to help them develop lessons. Several teachers mentioned specific books, such as *On Prejudice: A Global Per-*

spective (Gioseffi, 1993), that motivated them to make some changes in the content of their courses. Almost all mentioned publications of instructional materials from curriculum development centers, such as the Stanford Program for Intercultural Education (SPICE), that they said were essential in helping them get started in global education. Several of the teachers made reference to their application projects in the course which helped them begin the process of thinking through how global perspectives could improve their courses. A few teachers spoke of being able for the first time to respond to curriculum mandates in their districts for global history or global geography because now they understood what a global perspective meant and could now see how their students would benefit from global education.

(2) *Bring current global events into social studies instruction.* About half of the teachers responded to the question of how the course had changed their teaching by sharing examples of how they now integrated current global issues and events into their social studies courses. The political changes in South Africa, the break-up of the Soviet Union, elections in Bosnia, the development of Eritrea as a new nation, the Internet, environmental changes in the Amazon Basin, and gene-therapy were among the examples teachers gave of news items that they related to topics in their social studies courses. One middle school teacher had made a game out of his students' abilities to bring in what he called "global news" and make arguments for the economic, political, environmental, historical or cultural connections of the news story to their world cultures course.

Contextual factors shaping the attention to current events. The teachers spoke of their own recognition that they now could better see connections between their course content and contemporary events and issues. One teacher described how he had used some globally oriented time-lines and some of Paul Kennedy's (1993) writings from the class to develop a new emphasis on human problems throughout history that continue to dominate the news today, such as the need for security, peoples' aggression against others, changes in social norms, and the desire of people to better their lives economically. Several teachers referred to the readings in John Maxwell Hamilton's *Entangling Alliances* as critical in their understanding of the complexity of world actors and relationships.

(3) *Recognize one's own biases and those of one's students and the community.* Ten of the teachers brought up their thinking about prejudice or bias in their classrooms and teaching. They expressed concerns about their students' prejudices and ways in which they felt superior to people in other parts of the world. Some spoke of seeing how racism in their schools colored how their students perceived events in Asia or Africa. A handful spoke of confronting their own biases about people different from themselves as they recognized that they held attitudes or beliefs that were constructed from ignorance or stereotypes. Those who brought up their thinking about bias as a result of the course did not provide solutions to these problems. They reflected upon their mental or emotional struggles to accept the recognition that the biases did exist, and they shared their thoughts about the complexity of the problems.

Contextual factors shaping recognition of bias. During the course the teachers worked in pairs and small groups with people from many parts of the world as they discussed readings, evaluated instructional materials and developed projects and presentations. Five out of the ten teachers who brought up their reflection on bias referred to specific times in which a cross-cultural exchange brought about a reflection or "mirroring" of prejudice that they could not ignore. One older teacher spoke of "seeing through Mohammed's eyes the hurtfulness of American prejudice against Muslims." Another recalled how impatient she was with two Indonesian students whose English she had trouble understanding until she had read their "trees of life" (an autobiographical activity where students in the class identify important cultural learning in their lives; see Merryfield, 1993a) and was suddenly humbled by their abilities to overcome poverty and educate themselves. Some of these ten teachers were unable to say what specific activity or reading in the course provoked their reflection upon bias and prejudice beyond their perspective that the course did have that effect.

FINDINGS UNIQUE TO PRESERVICE TEACHERS

The preservice teachers were taking a globally oriented methods course within a professional development school in social studies and global education which requires substantive content (90 quarter hours) about the world in history and two social sciences. They were being mentored in the methods course and in extensive field experiences (four hours a day during methods, all day during student teaching) by eight classroom teachers across six school districts who have expertise and experience in global education. During the six months of methods and student teaching they read conceptual literature in global education, examined and used extensive print and media resources, and they were assessed on their application of global education in their own teaching. The preservice teachers upon whom these findings are based appeared to be committed to the goals of global education and demonstrated some ability to teach global perspectives. The most frequently mentioned conceptualizations are those discussed above that go across all three groups—the teaching of diverse cultures and multiple perspectives, connecting global content to the lives of their students, and making connections across time and space. However, unique to their data was one idea that appeared again and again.

(1) *Integrate multicultural and global education so that students can identify local/global connections and understand how globalization is increasingly bringing diverse peoples closer together economically, politically and culturally.* The preservice teachers looked at global and multicultural education holistically. They perceived the two fields of study as complementing each other in that they both focus on understanding one's own as well as diverse cultures, multiple perspectives, and the nature of human problems and desires. Often they spoke of making connections between issues in the community with global issues, local and national history with global history, and developing ways in which their students could use global knowledge within the local community.

Contextual factors shaping the integration of multicultural and global education. By the time they were completing student teaching, the preservice teachers rarely spoke of multicultural education and global education separately. They were "as two sides of the same coin," or "the way we connect the world to their life here." One young man explained that "it all comes together when I teach because of my students. They are a multilingual and multicultural group who need to see themselves as citizens of Columbus, Ohio and citizens of larger worlds. They need to see where they are on the planet." When asked where these ideas came from, most answered that they had seen them in practice or learned them from the experienced teachers with whom they worked. A few mentioned early readings that had influenced their thinking, such as work by Christine Bennett (1995), Christine Sleeter (1993), Lisa Delpit (1988) and Robert Hanvey (1976).

THE UNIQUE QUALITY OF INDIVIDUAL PROFILES WITHIN EACH STUDY

For all their commonalities, each teacher's theories were to some degree unique. Some teachers had guiding theories that grew out of interests in specific topics or approaches within history or geography. For example, the analysis of decisions across the exemplary teachers revealed that a middle school teacher's first concern was historical chronology. She explained her approach as based on her own undergraduate and graduate work in history which had led her to value chronology. In much the same way, new trends in geography influenced a high school teacher. He focused on the National Geographic Society's five themes of geography as a major factor in his design of his world area studies course and found that they provided entry for global perspectives.

Other teachers' profiles were heavily influenced by their commitment to specific educational goals, philosophies or educational reforms. Two elementary teachers explained their belief that students must develop the ability to work independently from the teacher. This major goal affected their instruction about the world every day. As part of their philosophy in teaming in an informal classroom, the independent work encouraged students to follow up on their own interests in global topics. The independent work habits enriched the curriculum by encouraging students to explore different cultures, individuals, and ideas and then share what they had learned with the rest of the class.

An elementary teacher had guiding theories that he alone followed. As part of his educational background and experiences, he had come to value the process of building a sense of community in the classroom. This was a challenge in that his students were very diverse in race, class, language, and religion. Many of his routines, such as the students developing their own rules, finding time each day for validations (praise for another person), or gathering together in a circle for discussion, were designed to foster a caring environment where students cooperated and helped each other in many ways every day. This sense of community also contributed to his global education goals of developing connections to other peoples, appreciating multiple perspectives and building tolerance and respect.

Some teachers' global content was also influenced by their commitment to a literature-based approach to learning. Their students read the literature of the peoples they studied. They learned about multiple perspectives, cultural diversity, and cultural universals through stories. The contextual factors influencing the literature-based approach were explained as beliefs and experiences, the support of colleagues, and the availability of large numbers of literature books through schools or local libraries.

One teacher who taught social studies within a gifted education program had a unique profile because her course of study mandated skills, not specific knowledge. Because of her knowledge and experience as a gifted education teacher, she focused first on the development of higher level thinking skills. Her attention to teaching global topics stemmed from her own interests and values. Her attention to global education was supported by colleagues and the school district.

Each teacher had his or her own preferences on which topics warrant more or less time and attention. One middle school teacher valued China and a high school teacher valued the Middle Ages and they spent considerable time on those topics. In the same vein, a high school teacher hurried through the Industrial Revolution, and a middle school teacher skipped over much of ancient Africa because they or their students did not value them as much as other topics.

Not surprisingly travel or living overseas did have the effect of increasing attention to that part of the world. Teachers spoke of living in Taiwan, growing up in France, and travel in the Soviet Union as affecting their instructional decision-making. Most of the exemplary global educators had traveled overseas, and all spoke of those experiences as helping them teach about culture and cross-cultural perspectives in general. In reflection they looked at their overseas experiences as major turning points in their motivation to improve their instruction about other peoples and the larger world. The teachers with extensive cross-cultural backgrounds pointed out that these experiences contributed significantly to their commitment to teaching perspective consciousness, recognition of cultural universals, and valuing of cultural diversity.

Conclusions

The teachers agree on the primacy of culture and multiple perspectives, of relating global content to the lives of students, and connecting knowledge across time and space. There appears to be some consensus across all three groups about the theory and practice of teaching global perspectives. Culture is the central component from which other elements in global education develop. The study of culture begins with those of the students in the teacher's class or school and expands to diverse cultures in the local community, the nation and the world. But instead of an expanding environments approach where each is studied separately, the process of making connections between local and global creates constant comparisons and an appreciation of the complexity of cultural borrowing and change. Global approaches do not focus solely on cultural differences. The teachers consistently had students examine cultural universals and explore ways in which the lives of diverse peoples are similar.

Perhaps the most significant difference for these teachers between global education and other ways to teach about culture is the emphasis on multiple perspectives, perspective consciousness, multiple realities and multiple loyalties. These ideas require skills in perspective taking, the ability to look at an event or issue through the eyes of someone different from oneself. Finally, there are attitudinal goals in the teaching of culture. Teachers want their students to develop tolerance and respect for cultural differences that are foreign to or may even conflict with their own. The teachers want students to develop their own ideas and ideals of cultural norms, and they expect their students to recognize other peoples' rights to do the same.

Based on rationales of providing culturally relevant instruction, motivating students to become involved in their own learning and constructivist learning, the teachers made instructional decisions based upon student characteristics. Their choices of topics to include or exclude, amount of time allocated to units and lessons, and their choices of instructional methods were influenced by what teachers perceived as curricular connections to their students' lives, interests and knowledge.

The teachers also focused on teaching the interrelatedness of different time periods in history and different world regions, nations, and peoples. The world is taught about as interconnected and interdependent with attention to the development of a perspective through which students can see their place in the world, and their world as connected to many people, past and present.

There are differences between the exemplary global educators and the practicing and preservice teachers at the initial stages of global education. The exemplary group taught from several guiding theories of global education that were rarely mentioned by the other groups. A major focus was the interconnectedness of global and local inequalities and the human struggle for rights, self-determination, social justice and a better life. In seeing the world as an interrelated system, the teachers went beneath the economic connections and political connections to examine the complexities of power, control, and inequality.

Their emphasis on cross-cultural experiential learning set the exemplary global educators apart from the other teachers also. They planned their instruction so that their students would interact with and learn from people different from themselves in the school, local community and other countries. They brought in resource people, enjoyed on-going relationships with the international community in their city or neighborhoods, and they highly valued their own cross-cultural experiences.

In explaining their planning in global perspectives, the exemplary group demonstrated how they organized units by global themes and concepts. Instead of adding a global component to a lesson or unit as the less experienced teachers did, these teachers began with global content and organized their unit around a global focus. The exemplary teachers also spoke frequently of interdisciplinary knowledge needed for a global perspective and approaches to integrating disciplines around themes and issues. In describing their units and lessons, they frequently connected global education with the teaching of higher level thinking and research skills and the necessity of bringing a variety of methods and resources into their teaching.

The most important contextual factors are teachers' beliefs, values, experiences, their knowledge of globalization and access to resources to teach it, and their perceptions of student characteristics. The studies have focused on major contextual factors (in contrast to all factors) in order to bring some order or priority to the very complex question of how and why instructional decisions are made. In the hundreds of answers to the general question, "What were the contextual factors influencing that decision?" or specific questions such as "Why did you choose to spend more time on China?" there are some factors that the teachers consistently viewed as more important.

Teacher beliefs, values, and experiences were identified as the most important factors in teacher decision-making. In response to question after question the teachers explained their decisions in terms of their own personal values and experiences. Many contextual factors are phrased as "a belief in," "valuing of," "experiences in," or "concern for." Many of these personal values or experiences are natural connections between curriculum and the teachers' own lives. There were some common values and experiences articulated by a majority of the teachers. They valued tolerance, cultural diversity, and cooperation. They recognized the need for diverse people to interact, manage conflicts and find ways to work together.

Second, student characteristics are a major influence on teachers' instructional decisions. Students' backgrounds, their abilities and disabilities, experiences, interests, behaviors, questions and responses are major factors in teachers' instructional decisions. To a much lesser degree, the characteristics of the school system, the mandated courses of study, the goals of magnet schools, common tests, availability of instructional materials, libraries, parents and the local community influence teachers' decisions about global content. However, the teachers in these three studies rarely perceived them as negative influences. For example, parents supported the global education of their children by serving as resources (speaking to the class about Islam in their lives or sharing photos and artifacts from a recent trip to France) and in the cases of the two international magnet schools, by advocating global education within the school district. Perhaps these factors are ranked below the teacher and student characteristics because these school districts are very supportive of global education in general.

Each teacher has some contextual factors that are not shared by most of the teachers. For example some teachers were heavily influenced by their teaming. It was a major factor in how they structured units, lessons, and each day's routine. Current local and international events were a major influence on the instruction of a few teachers. One high school teacher's instruction was influenced considerably by a state-wide proficiency test in citizenship. Time had to be taken away from the regular course content to review and coach the students for a test that they had to pass in order to receive a high school diploma. The relationships between teacher beliefs, student characteristics, and global content are complex and dynamic as teachers, students and the milieu in which they operate are always changing. Events in the community and world also influence what is taught about the world. Undoubtedly content if not the goals of global education is fluid as it is shaped by all these contextual factors over time.

For all of its ambiguity and controversy in curriculum reform, there are some conceptual elements and goals of global education that have been accepted by the teachers in these studies, and they are teaching these across grade levels and school districts. The contextual factors also do indicate that there are a core of beliefs central to teaching global perspectives. Further study is needed to examine relationships between global education and the characteristics and experiences of teachers. The teachers see cultural diversity as positive. They believe in understanding and appreciating the perspectives of people different from themselves. They want their students to connect themselves to people, issues, problems, and events around the world yesterday, today and tomorrow. Are these beliefs prerequisite to the implementation of global education? If they are, then the implications for teacher educators and school leaders involved in global education are immense. Learning to teach global perspectives does not simply depend upon the acquisition of new knowledge or skills, it is grounded in the teacher's own perspectives of cultural diversity and global linkages and is to some degree dependent upon a willingness to tolerate and even appreciate beliefs and behaviors quite different from one's own.

The teachers' theories and practice can inform the scholarly literature. Although there is considerable overlap between the theories and practice of global education in these studies and the conceptual scholarship, there are also some compelling differences. Compare Appendix D: Teachers' theories and practice in global education with Appendix A: Conceptualizations of global education from selected works in the field. First, teachers can inform the field on how to develop a global education that is student-centered. Teachers in all three groups choose and organize global content based upon their students' interests, abilities, and experiences. Global content is used to connect students to their local communities, to people in diverse cultures, and to historical and contemporary issues around the world. Global systems and global interdependence are the basis for most of the conceptual literature as scholars try to demonstrate how a global education is different from the traditional curriculum. Yet these teachers rarely approach global economic, political or environmental systems directly. They place the student in the center and connect the global content to their students so that a study of the global assembly line begins with products or services used by the students or produced by a company where their parents work. They begin with the students' concern about local race relations and connect those experiences to ethnic cleansing in Bosnia and the struggle for human rights in other parts of the world. Goodlad (1986) wrote of "the learner at the world's center." These teachers would rephrase his ideas to place their particular students at the center of their global education. Their goal is to help students see themselves as actors affecting and being affected by an increasingly interconnected world.

Along with student-centeredness, the teachers contribute to the literature by grounding global perspectives in the study of culture as the foundation of a global education. First they want their students to study their own cultures, the role of culture in their daily lives, and the human beliefs and values underlying their cultural heritage and contemporary ways of living. Then, once their students have a foundation of knowledge and multiple perspectives of their own cultures, the teachers connect the students' learning to the study of diverse peoples.

Third, the exemplary teachers are characterized by a commitment to teaching about local and global inequities, subjects rarely mentioned by the American scholars writing about what global education is or should be. For these teachers, one reason for a global education is for students to understand how and why inequities exist within their local community, their nation, and the world at large and to look at alternative solutions to these problems. Students' questions about disparities in local standards of living or access to technology lead to research on access to jobs, education, health care, and political power that compare their community with ones in Japan, Poland or Brazil.

Finally, the exemplary teachers place considerable emphasis on cross-cultural experiential learning. Although the literature is replete with goals of cross-cultural awareness or understanding, the teachers place a much higher value on face to face experiential learning that brings their students together with people of other cultures (see Wilson, 1982, 1983a, 1983b). These four ideas—placing students at the center of global education, beginning with the students' own cultures before other cultures, connecting local and global injustice and inequities, and cross-cultural experiential learning—provide a new vision of education for local/global interconnectedness (Alger, 1974).

APPENDIX A
CONCEPTUALIZATIONS OF GLOBAL EDUCATION
FROM SELECTED WORKS IN THE FIELD

(1) Understanding of humans and the world/planet as dynamic, organic and interdependent systems
state of the planet awareness (Hanvey 1975)
knowledge of global dynamics (Hanvey 1975)
global interdependence is a pervasive reality (Leetsma 1979)
transnational cooperation (Leetsma 1979)
boundaries labeled foreign and domestic as misleading and artificial (Leetsma 1979)
world-centeredness (Becker 1979)
study of humankind, the human species (Becker 1979)
spaceship earth (Muessig & Gilliom 1981)
global procedures and mechanisms (Alger & Harf 1986)

global actors (Alger & Harf 1986)
global transactions (Alger & Harf 1986)
global systems—economic, political, ecological, technological (Kniep 1986a)
the spatial dimension of global education, relational holism (Pike & Selby 1988, 1995)

(2) Understanding of global issues
international human rights (Leetsma 1979; Kniep 1986a)
literacy in global problems and issues (Leetsma 1979)
global issues (Alger & Harf 1986)
global issues and problems, peace and security issues, development issues, environmental issues (Kniep 1986a)
the issues dimension of global education (Pike & Selby 1988, 1995)

(3) Understanding of diverse cultures and multiple perspectives
perspective consciousness (Hanvey 1975)
understanding of diverse cultures and cultural pluralism of the world at large (Leetsma 1979)
understanding of one's own culture and what it means to be human (Anderson & Anderson 1979)
multiple loyalties, diversity of cultures (Muessig & Gilliom 1981)
[human] values (Alger & Harf 1986)
human values and culture, universal values, diverse human values (Kniep 1986a)
multiple perspectives and exploration of world views (Lamy 1987)

(4) Understanding of, skills in and responsibility for making choices and decisions and taking action locally and globally
involvement and decisions within the local community (Alger 1974)
awareness of human choices (Hanvey 1975)
intergenerational responsibility (Leetsma 1979)
exercise of influence (Anderson 1979)
involvement in world system (Anderson 1979)
judgment and decision-making (Anderson 1979)
strategies for participation and involvement (Lamy 1987)
development of analytical and evaluative skills (Lamy 1987)
positive interdependence and cooperation (Johnson & Johnson 1987)

(5) Interconnectedness of humans through time
global history, contact and borrowing and interdependence over time, the ecumene, development of global systems, antecedents to today's world, causes of today's global issues (Kniep 1986a)
the temporal dimension of global education (Pike & Selby 1988, 1995)

(6) Cross-cultural understanding, interactions, and communication
cross-cultural awareness (Hanvey 1975)
cross-cultural experiential learning, cross-cultural effectiveness (Merryfield 1997; Wilson 1982, 1983, 1993)

(7) Perceptual growth for prejudice reduction and moral education within critical contexts
reduction of ethnocentrism, both personal and national (Leetsma 1979)
open-mindedness, anticipation of complexity, resistance to stereotyping, nonchauvinism (Case 1991, 1993; Wilson 1994)
inclination to empathize (Case 1991; Darling 1995)
global education as moral education, moral perspectives (Coomb 1989; Darling 1994, 1995; Werner 1990)

critical pedagogy for global education (Werner 1990)
inner dimension of global education (Pike & Selby 1988, 1995)

APPENDIX B
A PROFILE OF INSTRUCTIONAL DECISION-MAKING IN
GLOBAL PERSPECTIVES

Carl's Profile[1]

Teaming with Robert, Carl taught fourth and fifth graders in an urban elementary international magnet school. He has certification in elementary & special education, an MA in global education and was in his sixth year of teaching at the time of the study.

(1) Guiding principle: Relate global content/interconnections to students' backgrounds and interests.

Contextual factors:
• Carl's beliefs that learning must meet student needs and interests
• Student characteristics: fourth/fifth graders, 9 boys, 17 girls, diversity in class, race, a "u-shaped" ability curve, some students with significant learning or behavioral problems
• Parents who are, in general, supportive and involved
• Conflict with district's competency-based testing
• Problem with "too much going on" in building that takes time away from instruction in his classroom
Example: 4/30 Students plan a garden based on their interests and what they have learned from a unit on agriculture and technology.

(2) Infuse global content through interdisciplinary themes such as conflict, technology, culture, people's contributions to the world past and present.
• Carl's degrees in elementary ed and global ed
• Teaching in an international magnet school
• Carl's teaming partner's experience and materials
Example: In unit on technology, students do scientific experiments, examine the history of the plow, and learn from literature about how technology affects people's lives.

(3) Use current events.
• The conflict in the Persian Gulf
• Carl's interest in the news
• Students' questions, fears, family experiences
• Availability of local and national newspapers, speakers, other resources in community
Example: Carl's first six-week unit focuses on the conflicts in the Middle East and Persian Gulf.

(4) Train students to find and make use of different types, sources, perspectives on global content.
• Carl's belief in teaching "how" to learn
• Carl's valuing of multiple perspectives
• Course of study skills[2]

---

[1] Names of the teachers have been changed.
[2] Course of study refers to the legal document that outlines the content (knowledge, skills and attitudes) mandated by the school district and approved by the state.

• Carl's cross-cultural experiences in Denmark
• Student diversity in race, ethnicity and class
Example: 2/14 Students report on their community poll about people who have made important contributions to the world.

(5) Prepare students to be independent learners who take responsibility for their own actions.
• Carl and his teaming partner's commitment to open classrooms, informal learning, and cooperative learning
• The principal's support
Example: 10/3 Students begin to design a research project to answer their own questions on the Middle East or Persian Gulf conflict.

APPENDIX C

CONCEPTUAL FRAMEWORK USED IN THE COURSES INFUSING GLOBAL PERSPECTIVES IN EDUCATION AND SOCIAL STUDIES METHODS

1. Human values
- one's own values, universal and diverse human values
- perspective consciousness and multiple perspectives
- recognition of the effects of one's own values, culture, and world view in learning about and interacting with people different from oneself

2. Global systems
- economic, political, ecological, technological systems
- knowledge of global dynamics
- local/global interconnectedness
- procedures and mechanisms in global systems
- transactions within and across peoples, nations, regions
- interconnections within different global systems
- state of the planet awareness

3. Global issues and problems
- development issues
- human rights issues
- environmental/natural resource issues
- North-South issues
- issues related to distribution of wealth, technology & information, resources
- issues related to dependency and post-colonialism
- peace and security issues
- issues related to prejudice and discrimination (based on ethnicity, race, class, sex, language, national origin, religion, politics, etc.)

4. Global history
- acceleration of interdependence over time (J-curves)
- antecedents to current issues
- origins and development of cultures
- contact and borrowing among cultures
- evolution of globalization
- changes in globalization and global systems over time

5. Cross-cultural understanding
- recognition of the complexity of cultural diversity
- the role of one's own culture in the world system
- skills and experiences in seeing one's own culture from others' perspectives
- experiences in learning about another culture and the world from another culture's values and world views
- extended experiences with/in other cultures

6. Awareness of human choices
- by individuals, organizations, local communities, nations, regions, economic or political alliances
- past and present actions and future alternatives
- recognition of the complexity of human behavior

7. Development of analytical and evaluative skills
- abilities to collect, analyze, and use information
- critical thinking skills (e.g., ability to detect bias, identify underlying assumptions, etc.)
- recognition of the role of values in inquiry

8. Strategies for participation and involvement
- opportunities for making and implementing decisions
- experience with addressing real-life problems
- attention to learning from experience

This conceptualization of global perspectives in education is based on the work of Chadwick Alger and James Harf (1986), Lee Anderson (1979, 1990), James Becker (1979, 1990), Roland Case (1991), Robert Hanvey (1976), Willard Kniep (1986), Steven Lamy (1987, 1990), and Angene Wilson (1982, 1993).

APPENDIX D
TEACHERS' THEORIES AND PRACTICE IN
GLOBAL EDUCATION

Across all three groups of teachers:
(1) Begin with culture
• first the students' cultures, then diverse cultures
• teach perspective consciousness, multiple perspectives, multiple and conflicting realities, perspective-taking
• teach cultural universals and cultural differences
• teach for understanding of the complexity of cultures
• teach for tolerance and respect

(2) Connect global content to students' backgrounds, daily experiences, interests, and communities

(3) Have students make connections across time (historical periods) and space (world regions/nations/cultures within nations)

Additional theories of the exemplary group
(4) Teach about the interconnectedness of global and local inequities, the human struggle for rights, self-determination, social justice, and a better life

(5) Teach students cultural knowledge and cross-cultural interaction skills through cross-cultural experiential learning and assessment

(6) Use global themes, issues or problems to organize and integrate global content across disciplines

(7) Emphasize skills in higher level thinking and research

(8) Employ a variety of teaching strategies and instructional resources

Additional theories of the experienced teachers
(9) Expand the curricular focus on less taught about parts of the world (usually Africa, Asia and Latin America) and global issues

(10) Bring current global events into social studies instruction

(11) Recognize one's own biases and those of one's students and the community

Additional theories of the preservice teachers
(12) Integrate multicultural and global education so that students can identify local/global connections and understand how globalization is increasingly bringing diverse peoples closer together economically, politically, and culturally

Additional theories unique to individual teachers
(13) Integrate global education with other valued elements of educational philosophy or reform, such as service learning, whole language, interdisciplinary teaming, cooperative learning, authentic assessments, geography standards, constructivism, state/local testing, an alternative school's mission, etc.

(14) Connect global perspectives to teacher or student interest in specific cultures/places (Latin America, Russia, Egyptians, Cuban culture) or global issues (conflict resolution, environmental change, hunger, technology transfer)

(15) Blend global perspectives in with non-global elements such as art, spelling, reading, extracurricular activities

NOTE

1. Most of the conceptual work on perceptual dimensions and moral education has been developed by Canadian and British scholars. Angene Wilson is the only American scholar who has consistently advocated perceptual dimensions and cross-cultural experiential learning as essential components in global education.

REFERENCES

Alger, C. F. (1974). *Your community in the world; the world in your community.* Columbus, Ohio: Mershon Center at The Ohio State University.
Alger, C. F., & Harf, J. E. (1986). Global education: Why? For whom? About what? In R. E. Freeman (Ed.), *Promising practices in global education: A handbook with case studies* (pp. 1–13). New York: The National Council on Foreign Language and International Studies.

Anderson, C. (1990). Global education and the community. In K. A. Tye (Ed.), *Global education from thought to action* (pp. 125–141). Alexandria, Va: Association for Supervision and Curriculum Development.

Anderson, L. (1979). *Schooling for citizenship in a global age: An exploration of the meaning and significance of global education.* Bloomington, Ind.: Social Studies Development Center.

Armento, B. J. (1996). The professional development of social studies educators. In J. Sikula (Ed.), *Handbook of research on teacher education* (pp. 485–502). New York: Macmillan.

Becker, J. M. (Ed.). (1979). *Schooling for a global age.* New York: McGraw-Hill.

Begler, E. (1993, Winter). Spinning wheels and straw: Balancing content, process, and context in global teacher education programs. *Theory Into Practice, 32,* 14–20.

Bennett, C. I. (1995). *Comprehensive multicultural education.* Boston: Allyn & Bacon.

Boyer, E. L. (1983). *High School.* New York: Harper and Row.

Brown, D. S. (1988). Twelve middle-school teachers' planning. *Elementary School Journal, 89,* 69–87.

Calderhead, J. (Ed.). (1987). *Exploring teachers' thinking.* London: Cassell.

Case, R. (1991). *Key elements of a global perspective (EDGE series).* Vancouver, British Columbia: Centre for the Study of Curriculum and Instruction, Faculty of Education, University of British Columbia.

Case, R. (1993). Key elements of a global perspective. *Social Education, 57,* 318–325.

Chase, K. S., & Merryfield, M. M. (1997). Bridging the gap between campus and school. *From The Inside,* 1, 17–19.

Chase, K. S., & Merryfield, M. M. (1998). How do secondary teachers benefit from PDS networks? Lessons from a social studies and global education learning community. *The Clearing House, 71,* 251–254.

Clark, C. M., & Peterson, P. L. (1986). Teachers' thought processes. In M. C. Wittrock (Ed.), *Handbook of research on teaching* (3rd ed., pp. 255–296). New York: Macmillan.

Connelly, F. M., & Clandinin, D. J. (1988). *Teachers as curriculum planners: Narratives of experience.* New York: Teachers College Press, and Toronto: OISE Press/The Ontario Institute for Studies in Education.

Coombs, J. (1989). *Toward a defensible conception of a global perspective.* Vancouver: Research and Development in Global Studies, University of British Columbia.

Cornbleth, C. (1991). Research on context, research in context. In J. P. Shaver (Ed.), *Handbook of research on social studies teaching and learning* (pp. 265–275). New York: Macmillan.

Cornbleth, C., Korth, W., & Dorow, E. B. (1983). *Creating the curriculum: Beginning the year in a middle school.* Paper presented at the annual meeting of the American Educational Research Association, Montreal (ERIC document Reproduction Service No. ED 232 948).

Cornett, J. W. (1987). *Teacher personal practical theories and their influence upon teacher curricular and instructional actions: A case study of a secondary social studies teacher.* Unpublished doctoral dissertation, Ohio State University.

Cornett, J. W. (1990). Teacher thinking about curriculum and instruction: A case study of a secondary social studies teacher. *Theory and Research in Social Education, 18,* 248–273.

Council on Learning. (1981). *Task force statement on education and the world view.* New Rochelle, N.Y.: Author.

Darling, L. (1995). Empathy and the possibilities for a global perspective: A cautionary tale. In R. Fowler & I. Wright (Eds.), *Thinking Globally about Social Studies Education* (pp. 35–50). Vancouver Centre for the Study of Curriculum and Instruction, University of British Columbia.

Darling, L. (1994). *Global education as moral education.* Unpublished doctoral thesis, University of British Columbia.

Delpit, L. (1988). The silenced dialogue: Power and pedagogy in educating other people's children. *Harvard Educational Review,* 58, 280–298.

Dove, T., Norris, J., & Shinew, D. (1997). Teachers' perspectives on school/university collaboration in global education. In M. M. Merryfield, E. Jarchow, & S. Pickert (Eds.), *Preparing teachers to teach global perspectives: A handbook for teacher educators* (pp. 55–71). Thousand Oaks, Calif.: Corwin Press.

Easterly, J. (Ed.). (1994). *Promoting global teacher education.* Reston, Va.: Association of Teacher Educators.

Elbaz, F. (1981). *The teacher's "practical knowledge": A case study.* Unpublished doctoral dissertation, University of Toronto.

Flournoy, M. A. (1994). Educating globally competent teachers. In R. Lambert (Ed.), *Educational exchange and global competence.* New York: Council on International Educational Exchange.

Gilliom, M. E., Remy, R. C., & Woyach, R. (1980). Using the local community as a resource for global education. *Teaching Political Science,* 7, 251–264.

Gilliom, M. E. (1993). Mobilizing teacher educators to support global education in preservice programs. *Theory Into Practice,* 32, 40–46.

Gioseffi, D. (Ed.). (1993). *On prejudice: A global perspective.* New York: Doubleday.

Goodlad, J. I. (1986). The learner at the world's center. *Social Education,* 50, 424–436.

Hanvey, R. G. (1976). *An attainable global perspective.* Denver, Colo.: The Center for Teaching International Relations, The University of Denver [see p. 217, this volume].

Hyland, J. T. (1985). *Teaching about the constitution: Relationships between teachers' subject matter knowledge, pedagogic beliefs, and instructional decision making regarding selection of content, materials and activities.* Unpublished doctoral dissertation, University of California, Los Angeles.

Johnson, R., & Johnson, D. (1987). Cooperation in learning: Ignored by the powerful. In W. Kniep (Ed.), *Next steps in global education: A handbook for curriculum development* (pp. 205–218). New York: Global Perspectives in Education.

Johnson, D. (1993). Academic and intellectual foundations of teacher education in global perspectives. *Theory Into Practice,* 32, 3–13.

Kagan, D. M. (1993). *Laura and Jim and what they taught me about the gap between educational theory and practice.* Albany: State University of New York Press.

Kennedy, P. (1993). *Preparing for the twenty-first century.* New York: Random House.

Kniep, W. M. (1986a). Defining a global education by its content. *Social Education,* 50, 437–466.

Kniep, W. (1986b, November/December). Social studies within a global education. *Social Education,* 50, 536–542.

Kon, J. H. (1995). Teachers' curriculum decision making in response to a new social studies textbook. *Theory and Research in Social Education,* 23, 121–146.

Lamy, S. L. (1987). *The definition of a discipline: The objects and methods of analysis in global education.* New York: Global Perspectives in Education.

Lamy, S. L. (1990). Global education: A conflict of images. In K. A. Tye (Ed.), *Global education from thought to action* (pp. 49–63). Alexandria, Va.: Association for Supervision and Curriculum Development.

Leetsma, R. (1979). Looking ahead: An agenda for action. In J. M. Becker (Ed.), *Schooling for a global age* (pp. 233–243). New York: McGraw-Hill.

Levstik, L. S. (1989). *Subverting reform in the social studies: A fourth grade case study.* Paper presented at the annual meeting of the American Educational Research Association, San Francisco.

Lincoln, Y. S. & Guba, E. G. (1985). *Naturalistic inquiry.* Beverly Hills: Sage.

Lydecker, A. M. R. (1982). *Teacher planning of social studies instructional units: Relationships with selected variables.* Unpublished doctoral dissertation, University of Michigan.

Marsh, C. J. (1984). Teachers' knowledge of and use of social studies curriculum materials in public elementary schools. *Journal of Educational Research, 77,* 237–243.

McCutcheon, G. (1981). Elementary school teachers' planning for social studies and other subjects. *Theory and Research in Social Education, 9,* 45–66.

McNair, K. (1978–1979). Capturing inflight decisions: Thoughts while teaching. *Educational Research Quarterly, 3*(4), 26–42.

McNeil, L. M. (1986). *Contradictions of control: School structure and school knowledge.* New York: Routledge.

Merryfield, M. M. (1991). Preparing American secondary social studies teachers to teach with a global perspective: A status report. *Journal of Teacher Education, 42*(1), 11–20.

Merryfield, M. M. (1992). Preparing social studies teachers for the twenty-first century: Perspectives on program effectiveness from a study of six exemplary programs in the United States. *Theory and Research in Social Education, 20,* 17–46.

Merryfield, M. M. (1993a). Reflective practice in teacher education in global perspectives: Strategies for teacher educators. *Theory Into Practice, 32,* 27–32.

Merryfield, M. M. (1993b). Responding to the Gulf War: A case study of teacher decision-making during the 1990–1991 school year. *Social Education, 57,* 33–41.

Merryfield, M. M. (1994). Shaping the curriculum in global education: The influence of student characteristics on teacher decision-making. *Journal of Curriculum and Instruction, 9,* 233–249.

Merryfield, M. M. (1995). Institutionalizing cross-cultural experiences and international expertise in teacher education: The development and potential of a global education PDS network. *Journal of Teacher Education, 46*(1), 1–9.

Merryfield. M. M. (1997). A framework for teacher education in global perspectives. In M. M. Merryfield, E. Jarchow, & S. Pickert (Eds.), *Preparing teachers to teach global perspectives: A handbook for teacher educators* (pp. 1–24). Thousand Oaks, Calif.: Corwin Press.

Merryfield, M. M., & Remy, R. C. (Eds.). (1995). *Teaching about international conflict and peace.* Albany: State University of New York Press.

Muessig, R. H., & Gilliom, M. E. (Eds.). (1981). *Perspectives of global education: A sourcebook for classroom teachers.* Columbus, Ohio: The College of Education, The Ohio State University.

National Council for the Social Studies. (1982). *Position statement on global education.* Washington D.C.: Author.

National Governors' Association. (1989). *America in transition: The international frontier.* Washington, D.C.: Author.

O'Loughlin, M. (1995). Daring the imagination: Unlocking voices of dissent and possibility in teaching. *Theory Into Practice, 35,* 107–116.

Parker, W. C., & Gehrke, N. J. (1986). Learning activities and teachers' decision making: Some grounded hypotheses. *American Educational Research Journal, 23,* 227–242.

Pike, G., & Selby, D. (1988). *Global teacher, global learner.* London: Hodder & Stoughton.

Pike, G., & Selby, D. (1995). *Reconnecting from national to global curriculum.* Toronto: International Institute for Global Education, University of Toronto.

Remy, R. C., Nathan, J., Becker, J. M., & Torney, J. V. (1975). *International learning and international education in a global age.* Washington D.C.: The National Council for the Social Studies.

Shapiro, S., & Merryfield, M. M. (1995). A case study of unit planning in the context of school reform. In M. M. Merryfield & R. C. Remy (Eds.), *Teaching about international conflict and peace* (pp. 41–123). Albany: State University of New York Press.

Shavelson, R. J. (1983). Review of research on teachers' pedagogical judgments, plans, and decisions. *The Elementary School Journal,* 83, 392–411.

Shavelson, R. J., & Stern, P. (1981). Research on teachers' pedagogical thoughts, judgments, decisions, and behavior. *Review of Educational Research,* 51, 455–498.

Shaver, J. P., Davis, O. L., Jr., & Helburn, S. W. (1980). An interpretive report on the status of precollege social studies education based on three NSF-funded studies. In *What are the needs in precollege science, mathematics, and social science education? View from the field.* Washington, D.C.: National Science Foundation.

Sleeter, C. E. (1993). How white teachers construct race. In C. McCarthy & W. Crichlow (Eds.), *Race, identity and representation in education* (pp. 157–171). New York: Routledge.

Stodolsky, S. S. (1988). *The subject matters: Classroom activity in mathematics and social studies.* Chicago: University of Chicago Press.

Thornton, S. J. (1991). Teacher as curricular-instructional gatekeeper in social studies. In J. P. Shaver (Ed.), *Handbook of research on social studies teaching and learning* (pp. 237–240). New York: Macmillan.

Thornton, S. J. (1985). *Curriculum consonance in United States history classrooms.* Unpublished doctoral dissertation, Stanford University.

Thornton, S. J., & Wenger, R. N. (1989). *Geography in elementary social studies classrooms.* Paper presented at the meeting of the American Educational Research Association, San Francisco.

Torney-Purta, J. (1995). Education in multicultural settings: Perspectives from global and international education programs. In W. Hawley & A. Jackson (Eds.), *Toward a common destiny: Improving race and ethnic relations in America* (pp. 341–377). San Francisco: Jossey-Bass.

Tucker, J. (1990). Global education partnerships between schools and universities. In K. A. Tye (Ed.), *Global education: From thought to action* (pp. 109–124). Alexandria, Va.: Association for Supervision and Curriculum Development.

Tucker, J., & Cistone, P. (1991, Jan-Feb). Global perspectives for teachers: An urgent priority. *Journal of Teacher Education,* 42(1), 3–10.

Tye, K. A. (Ed.). (1990). *Global education: From thought to action.* Alexandria, Va.: The Association for Supervision and Curriculum Development.

Tye, B., & Tye, K. (1992). *Global education: A study of school change.* Albany: State University of New York Press.

Werner, W. (1990). Contradictions in global education. In D. Henley & J. Young (Eds.), *Canadian perspectives on critical pedagogy* (pp. 77–93). Occasional Monograph #1. Winnipeg: The Critical Pedagogy Network and Social Education Researchers in Canada.

White, J. J. (1985). What works for teachers: A review of ethnography research studies as they inform issues of social studies curriculum and instruction. In W. B. Stanley (Ed.), *Review of research in social studies education, 1976–1983* (pp. 215–307). Washington, D.C.: National Council for the Social Studies, and Boulder, Colo.: ERIC Clearinghouse for Social Studies/Social Science Education and Social Science Education Consortium.

Wilson, A. (1983). A case study of two teachers with cross-cultural experience: They know more. *Educational Research Quarterly,* 8(1), 78–85.

Wilson, A. (1982). Cross-cultural experiential learning for teachers. *Theory Into Practice,* 21, 184–192.

Wilson, A. H. (1993a). Conversation partners: Helping students gain a global perspective through cross-cultural experiences. *Theory Into Practice,* 32, 21–26.

Wilson, A. H. (1997). Infusing global perspectives throughout a secondary social studies program. In M. M. Merryfield, E. Jarchow, & S. Pickert (Eds.), *Preparing teachers to teach global perspectives* (pp. 143–167). Thousand Oaks, Calif.: Corwin Press.

Wilson, A. H. (1993b). *The meaning of international experience for schools.* Westport, Conn.: Praeger.

Wilson, A. H. (1994). Teaching toward a global future and the future of global teaching. In M. E. Nelson (Ed.), *The future of the social studies.* Boulder, Colo.: The Social Science Education Consortium.

Wilson, S. M., & Wineburg, S. S. (1988). Peering at history from different lenses: The role of disciplinary perspectives in the teaching of American history. *Teachers College Record,* 89, 525–539.

Wooster, J. (1993, Winter). Authentic assessment: A strategy for preparing teachers to respond to curricular mandates in global education. *Theory Into Practice,* 32, 47–51.

Yinger, R. J., & Clark, C. M. (1982). *Understanding teachers' judgments about instruction: The task, the method, and the meaning* (Research series no. 121). East Lansing: Michigan State University, Institute for Research on Teaching.

Zimpher, N. L., & Ashburn, E. A. (1992). Countering parochialism in teacher candidates. In M. E. Dilworth (Ed.), *Diversity in teacher education* (pp. 40–62). San Francisco: Jossey-Bass.

Part

5

Trends for the Future

In the preceding sections of this book, we have presented articles on the evolution of international studies in higher education and K–12, and on current directions and controversies. The purpose of this section is to look to the future. David E. Albright provides an overview of how changing intellectual perspectives will affect the future of area studies. He maintains that area studies will retain its importance, but he also foresees the need for what he terms "intellectual eclecticism" rather than adherence to rigid theoretical positions.

David M. Trubek draws from his experiences as dean of international studies at the University of Wisconsin–Madison to look at international studies at the century's end and to assess future directions. His vision for the next century is based on the need to preserve existing strengths while developing offerings for new constituencies. Specifically, he focuses on changing student needs, the need to rethink the boundaries of knowledge that have shaped the construction of international programs, and the creation of new partnerships with scholars in different regions of the world, with disciplines and departments, and with external constituencies at state and local levels.

Toby Alice Volkman, a program officer in the Ford Foundation, describes how one foundation is redirecting its resources to assist in the revitalization of area studies, while encouraging higher education institutions to reconsider their ways of thinking about area studies. She provides brief descriptions of nearly a dozen programs, recently funded by the Ford Foundation, that may forecast future trends for area studies.

In his Title VI conference presentation, which he subsequently expanded for publication as the President's Report for the Social Science Research Council, Kenneth Prewitt raises new issues that specific disciplines and area programs will need to take into account in the future. He concludes that American social scientists must engage the world more than ever before and on new terms of collaboration with colleagues abroad who come from different intellectual traditions.

The two chapters we have included from the American Council on Education's report *Educating for Global Competence* advocate a partnership between government, business, and higher education and promote an agenda for action designed to ensure a globally competent work force. Each partner has its roles and responsibilities. Colleges and universities must internationalize the curriculum, encourage higher levels of language proficiency, and reward faculty for being global thinkers. Federal, state, and local governments must provide adequate funds and incentives to sustain the internationalization of U.S. education, as well as utilize the rich resources and expertise that exist. Corporations must work more closely with higher education to strengthen the curricula and help meet the costs of international training and research in business, science and technology, and the professions.

The Future of Area Studies

David E. Albright

Judgments about the future of area studies in the post–Cold War era involve two basic issues. The first is what the nature of the world will be in the coming years. Answers to this question carry with them implications not only for how relevant area studies will be in the future but also for what their intellectual rationale or thrust should be to make them most meaningful. The second issue is how area studies should be organized in light of the global changes that have taken place in the late twentieth century and those that appear likely in the twenty-first century. Answers to this question bear directly upon the structure of area studies programs.

Views within the academic and broader intellectual communities on both of these issues differ. This paper lays out and documents the major positions and trends of thought on the two questions. Then it offers some judgments that flow from an analysis of these.

The World of the Future

Assessments of the key features of the world in the twenty-first century are highly diverse; so too are the implications that flow from them for the future pertinence and rationale of areas studies. Neo-realist scholars of international relations such as Kenneth N. Waltz (1993) and Fouad Ajami (1993) foresee no fundamental changes in the character of the world order in the years ahead. They grant that the

This paper was presented at the Title VI 40th Anniversary Conference, "International Education in American Colleges and Universities: Prospect and Retrospect," Washington, D.C., April 1998.

end of the Cold War has destroyed the bipolarity of the international system that had prevailed since World War II, and they perceive an emerging world dominated by a handful of great powers but replete with troublesome and contentious minor states. Yet they argue that such changes take place constantly in the relations of nation-states, which continue to be the primary actors in international politics. From their perspective, moreover, the basic structure of world politics remains anarchic. Each state must fend for itself, with or without the cooperation of others. To do so, they will rely essentially on a balance-of-power approach.

This view of the future suggests that area studies will retain a high degree of importance during the coming years. Nation-states will serve as the main actors in the global system, and although these will function in accordance with established systemic principles, the precise choices that they make in international affairs will reflect their own particular national preferences. These preferences are rooted in the peculiar experiences, traditions, and perceptions of individual states. Therefore, efforts to understand these experiences, traditions, and perceptions have considerable value.

Such a view also points to a specific emphasis for area studies. If the rationale for looking at the experiences, traditions, and perceptions of individual states derives largely from the impact that these have on the behavior of the states in the global arena, then exploration of the experiences, traditions, and perceptions in this light should have top priority. Examining them from other perspectives is not necessarily worthless, but doing so must be of secondary concern.

International relations specialists of a neo-liberal or structuralist persuasion such as Robert Keohane (1995), Andrew Moravcsik (cited in Long 1995), and Richard Rosecrance (1992) accept some of the basic premises of neo-realists but look forward to more cooperative interaction in the world than neo-realists do. In structuralists' eyes, the chief actors in global affairs will remain nation-states, and they will continue to operate in an environment where agreements cannot be enforced by a higher authority. Structuralists contend, however, that groups of states and even states in general share significant common interests that provide incentives for them to cooperate on at least certain matters. Such interests stem from issues such as growing economic interdependence and mutual security concerns. These interests, structuralists argue, have even increased since the demise of the Cold War and will probably persist in doing so in the years ahead. Cooperation among states with major common interests, structuralists go on to say, has already led to the creation of a number of international institutions or structures, and these will in all likelihood multiply in the future as the scope and character of common interests broaden.

This perspective affords strong justification for area studies, although perhaps not quite as strong as that of the neo-realist outlook. From the structuralist standpoint, not only will the key participants in global affairs remain nation-states, but the behavior of these nation-states will also depend on their assessments of their own interests, which will in turn reflect their particular experiences, traditions, and perceptions. A substantial portion of these interests, however, will not objectively be unique. They will be shared by other states, even by states in other geographic regions.

Like the neo-realist viewpoint, the structuralist perspective implies that area studies should give primary attention to explaining the behavior of nation-states in the world arena. Yet it differs from the neo-realist viewpoint in one major respect in this regard. That is, it anticipates that in some instances individual experiences, traditions, and perceptions will not suffice to account for the choices made by nation-states. In these cases, explanations may require exploration of factors common to two or more states.

More straightforwardly liberal analysts of international relations such as Joseph Nye (1992) advance a picture of the future world with fewer continuities than are evident in the visions of either neo-realists or structuralists. Indeed, liberals hold that the world order after the Cold War is sui generis. In their judgment, there is emerging a world society of peoples as well as states and of an order resting on values and institutions as well as military power. They attribute this development to the rapid growth of transnational communications, migration, and economic interdependence. At the same time, liberals admit that the transition to this new world order is not going smoothly, and they concede that its full realization may require decades and perhaps even centuries.

Inherent in this image of the coming world is a restricted role for area studies. Liberals do not necessarily foresee that nation-states will vanish—certainly not in the near or medium term—but the expanding functions that they assign to international institutions clearly give these institutions primacy in their eyes. Area studies have relatively little to contribute to an understanding of the nature and workings of institutions of this sort, particularly insofar as these entail restrictions on state sovereignty and espouse universal values.

Furthermore, area studies in such a context have utility largely in a negative sense. If the authority of nation-states is decreasing and passing to international institutions, then it is worthwhile to try to gain insight into factors that determine the speed of this process. The experiences, traditions, and perceptions of individual states and peoples can obviously impede the process, so they bear exploring in this light.

Francis Fukuyama (1992) envisions the world in the years ahead in ideological terms. In recent years, and especially with the collapse of communism, he notes, a large measure of consensus has developed throughout the globe on the legitimacy of liberal democracy and a capitalist economy. Thus, he argues, these may constitute the final stage of man's ideological evolution. That is, they may represent the "end of history" in the Hegelian sense. At present, he admits, alternatives to both may still exist in one place or another; moreover, even the most advanced examples today of efforts to realize these ideals have flaws. Nevertheless, he insists, there is a coherent and directional historical process at work ("progress") that will eventually lead the bulk of mankind to seek to attain them.

To a large extent, this conception of the world of the future renders area studies superfluous. It posits the advance of all states and peoples along a common evolutionary path and their arrival at a common destination. To be sure, it does not preclude variations in democratic and capitalist forms even at the end of the evolutionary road, but it does suggest that a high degree of homogeneity will prevail then. The current relevance of area studies in this framework lies chiefly in their capacity to pinpoint obstacles that must be surmounted for the evolutionary process to go forward. Here again, the peculiar experiences, traditions, and perceptions of states and peoples can create obstacles.

Similarly, a limited intellectual focus for area studies flows from the conception. Since the present merit of area studies from its standpoint derives mainly from the role that they can play in identifying and overcoming barriers to the building of liberal democracies and capitalist economies, they should presumably concentrate on these things. Once stable democracies and capitalist economies predominate in the world, of course, the attention of area studies should logically shift to explicating what variations in these exist from country to country. Such a redirection of focus, however, would probably not take place any time soon.

Many observers depict a future world shaped fundamentally by globalization, but their notions of globalization and the precise impact that it will have vary considerably. Analysts such as Kenichi Ohmae (1993, 1995), Klaus Schwab and Claude Smadja (1994), and Andrew Hurrell and Ngaire Woods (1995) regard globalization as a breakdown of the barriers to the flow of industry, investment, individuals, and information across borders. They attribute this breakdown largely to technological developments. They also stress the effects of this process in the economic realm; however, they contend that these economic effects, in turn, have major political ramifications. At this point, important divergences of viewpoint appear.

Ohmae argues that globalization has already rendered the nation-state obsolete in terms of economic activity. As he sees things, globalization has created and will continue to create "regional states." These are natural economic zones that possess, in one combination or another, the essential ingredients for successful participation in the global economy. They are not, he emphasizes, political units. Moreover, they may cut across the borders of existing nation-states or fall within the confines of an established nation-state.

To Ohmae, these regional states are not, and need not be, enemies of central governments. Given suitable autonomy, they can serve as ports of entry to the global economy and become effective engines of prosperity and improved quality of life for peoples of existing nation-states. For Ohmae, then, the key question about the coming years is whether political leaders will adjust to the new economic circumstances or try to stifle the further development of regional states. If they follow the latter course, he concludes, they will wind up presiding over hollow political shells.

Schwab and Smadja maintain that globalization has helped to bring about a worldwide delocalization of industrial production. That is, countries that previously were confined to low-tech, labor-intensive economic activity can now produce, at low cost, goods and services that were once monopolies of the advanced industrial states. Such a development, they say, has created a new strategic economic parity among North America, Western Europe, and East Asia. This result means, in effect, that the world economy is now regionalized and will become increasingly so in the coming years.

In such a context, Schwab and Smadja point out, national and regional economies remain vitally interconnected, but no one state or bloc is in a position to impose its will on the rest of the world. Thus, countries seeking in the future to formulate economic strategies integrating fiscal, monetary, and education and training goals will have to do so in accordance with basic guidelines and rules that can be established only by consensus among the key world trading blocs. This sort of carryover into the political sphere will clearly give political interactions in the international realm a strong regional dimension.

Hurrell and Woods hold that globalization may well yield a world not of progressive enmeshment of states but of coercive socialization of some states by others through a range of external pressures (both state-based and market-based) and a variety of mechanisms linking the external and the domestic. This likely outcome, according to them, reflects the relationship between globalization and inequality. States, the two contend, differ in economic and political capacity to engage in transactions across territorial borders. For example, increases in such transactions are driven at least in part by technological change and growing knowledge, and these tend to develop mainly in large industrialized countries. In addition, what states gain from globalization depends on their ability to absorb and adapt to the new types of transactions—including the domestic political strength of their governments. This ability can vary widely. Such inequalities lead to an unevenness of globalization. Specifically, they tend to bring about an increasingly sharp division between "core" states and "marginalized" states.

Furthermore, Hurrell and Woods declare, this unevenness of globalization coincides with the distribution among states of military and political power and the authority to make international rules. In other words, the rules and institutions that regulate this new interconnectedness are usually drawn up and enforced by the most powerful actors (especially states and firms) in the global political arena.

Neither international institutions nor the expanding economic, political, and social organizations of a non-governmental type, Hurrell and Woods say, will serve to temper the effects of the inequalities. The former are themselves arenas of power and influence, in which the mighty usually make and break the rules. As for the latter, they are of a diverse character and not necessarily representative or politically accountable. They often display negative attributes and pursue their own selfish ends.

Scholars such as Malcolm Waters (1995) treat globalization not in economic but in intellectual and perceptual terms. Waters suggests that we are now entering a third stage of the globalization of human society in which "symbolic exchanges" have become and will remain the key determinant of the degree of globalization. That is, the engine of globalization is no longer capitalism (as it was for

Karl Marx) or the growing interdependence of states (as it is for many contemporary international relations thinkers). Rather, it is the "signs and symbols" of a globalized culture.

From the standpoint of all visions of a globalizing world, linkages and interactions of geographic, political, and cultural entities matter most. Hence, area studies—the examination of particular experiences, traditions, and perceptions—inevitably play a secondary role. Yet this role is by no means inconsequential. Area studies can afford highly illuminating insights into the sources of brakes on the globalization process. Perhaps even more important, they can provide the basis for investigating new "imagined communities" that may arise in the course of globalization. As the conceptualizations propounded by Ohmae, Schwab and Smadja, and Hurrell and Woods indicate, globalization will not necessarily result in a homogeneous world; rather, it may produce some differentiated entities, each with shared perspectives and purposes.

These notions of a globalizing world embody a dual message for the approach of area studies. Insofar as area studies concern themselves with geographic, political, and cultural entities now being displaced in the process of globalization, area studies should look mainly at how these entities' experiences, traditions, and perceptions hold back globalization. At the same time, area studies should identify and subject to detailed examination major new entities that are emerging during the course of globalization. As globalization progresses, the stress in approach should presumably shift gradually toward the new entities and away from the old ones. Indeed, the attention of area studies should eventually be directed entirely toward the new entities.

Paul Kennedy (1993) foresees a world faced with the task of reconciling technological change and economic integration with traditional political structures, national consciousness, old institutional arrangements, and habitual ways of doing things. This task will be complicated, Kennedy believes, by trends which now threaten to exacerbate social relations in numerous ways and may even threaten the long-term existence of humankind itself. According to him, these are (1) the surge in the earth's population and the growing demographic imbalances between rich and poor countries, (2) environmental challenges qualitatively different from those of the past, (3) technology's way of making traditional jobs redundant and replacing them with wholly new systems of production (for example, the biotech revolution in agriculture and robotics in manufacturing), and (4) the global financial and communications revolution.

Kennedy argues that although many individuals and firms seem well positioned to cope with the challenges that the twenty-first century will pose, relatively few nations appear to be. The most likely, he contends, seem to be Japan, Korea, certain other East Asian trading states, Germany, Switzerland, some of the Scandinavian states, and perhaps the European Community as a whole. He goes on to single out three factors as key to any general effort to prepare global society for these challenges. They are education, the place of women, and political leadership.

In Kennedy's world of the future, there would be a significant place for area studies. Although he perceives that the major problems confronting the world in the years ahead will be fundamentally global in character, he doubts that global institutions capable of addressing these will take shape. Thus, he thinks, existing political entities and structures will have to deal with them. Area studies can help to shed light on the capabilities of various of these actors to handle the challenges and the strengths and deficiencies of their approaches to doing so. This view of the world in the coming years, however, suggests a redirection of the thrust of area studies. Rather than focusing on the uniqueness of each country or region, they should explore how and why that country or region approaches the challenges that it shares with other countries or regions. These may, to be sure, reflect elements of its uniqueness, but they will not necessarily result entirely from factors of this sort. Such a focus would permit comparative judgments not only about the merits of individual approaches but also about the chances of success of specific countries or regions in meeting the common challenges.

Benjamin Barber (1995) anticipates a future world with conflicting tendencies. These tendencies he labels "Jihad and McWorld." In his eyes, the first of these holds out the prospect of a balkanization of nation-states, in often bloody fashion, by the pitting of culture against culture, people against people, and tribe against tribe. It entails an attack on every kind of interdependence and social cooperation, on technology and integrated markets, and even on modernity itself in the name of a hundred narrowly conceived faiths. The second tendency leads to integration and uniformity, the pressing of nations into one homogeneous "global theme park" tied together by communications, information, entertainment, and commerce. It stems from onrushing economic, technological, and ecological forces operative around the world. The conflict between these two tendencies, Barber maintains, will take place at two levels. There will be a global aspect to it, but it will rage as well within individual nation-states.

To Barber, Jihad and McWorld have a key feature in common. They both make war on the sovereign nation-state and undermine democratic institutions. Each, above all, is indifferent to civil liberty. Jihad forges communities of blood that slight democracy in favor of tyrannical paternalism or consensual tribalism. McWorld forges global markets that leave to an untrustworthy invisible hand issues of public interest and common good. The outcome of the confrontation between Jihad and McWorld, Barber opines, is uncertain. But whether one triumphs over the other or the confrontation persists, the virtues of the democratic nation could well be lost. Certainly, the nation-state, which enabled peoples to seize sovereign power in the name of liberty and the general good, will be put at risk.

Area studies can contribute much to understanding such a world. Barber envisions that individual nation-states will serve as major arenas for the Jihad–McWorld conflict, and area studies can help to chart the course of the conflict there. They can also provide insights into the challenges that the conflict poses for democratic institutions or the creation of democratic institutions in particular nation-states. They can even clarify the nature of the specific forces of Jihad and McWorld in each nation-state setting.

To render such contributions, area studies would need to concentrate on the interplay of Jihad and McWorld forces in individual nation-states. Doing so would involve analysis in each case of the nature of these forces and the evolution of the conflict between them. Such analyses would then permit comparative examinations of the conflict in different nation-states. On the basis of these comparative undertakings, in turn, it would be possible to arrive at some conclusions regarding the conflict on a global scale.

Samuel Huntington (1993a, 1993b) looks forward to a world that will continue to be characterized by conflict; however, he believes that the fundamental source of conflict will be primarily cultural rather than ideological or economic. Although nation-states, in his perspective, will remain the most powerful actors in world affairs, the main conflicts of global politics will take place between nations and groups of different civilizations. Indeed, the clash of civilizations will dominate global politics, and the dividing lines between civilizations will be the chief battle lines of the future.

According to Huntington, a civilization is the highest cultural grouping of people and the broadest level of cultural identity people have short of that which distinguishes humans from other species. A civilization may include several nation-states or only one. Furthermore, civilizations blend and overlap and may include subcivilizations. No less important, civilizations are dynamic: they rise and fall, divide and merge.

In the coming years, Huntington contends, seven or eight major civilizations will in large measure shape the world. These he identifies as Western, Confucian, Japanese, Islamic, Hindu, Slavic-Orthodox, Latin American, and possibly African civilizations. Nonetheless, he adds, civilization identities will not replace all other identities, nation-states will not disappear, each civilization will not necessarily become a single coherent political entity, and groups within a civilization may conflict with and even fight each other.

Clashes among the seven or eight civilizations, Huntington argues, will occur at two levels. At the micro-level, adjacent groups along the fault lines between civilizations will struggle, often violently, over the control of territory and each other. At the macro-level, states from different civilizations will compete for relative military and economic power, struggle over the control of international institutions and third parties, and competitively promote their particular political and religious values.

This notion of the future world leaves considerable scope for area studies. In their very essence, area studies are explorations of culture and cultural differences. Therefore, they can offer useful input to efforts to understand civilizations and the concrete reasons for clashes between particular civilizations. In addition, they can help to render linkages between nation-states and civilizations comprehensible.

Such a vision of the years ahead, however, does imply a reorientation of area studies. Instead of devoting primary attention to nation-states or even specific geographic regions, they should emphasize groupings of nation-states along cultural lines, or civilizations. To be sure, some treatment of nation-states and perhaps even geographic regions would be critical to lay the proper foundations for explicating and probing civilizations, yet the stress ought to shift to civilizations.

The Future Organization of Area Studies

Although perspectives differ on how area studies should be organized in the years ahead, there is much less diversity of outlook than exists on the nature of the world in the twenty-first century. Only four basic positions have been articulated on the question. Moreover, in certain cases individuals have embraced more than one of these, for not all of the positions are mutually exclusive, even though they involve quite distinct arguments.

Some social scientists, including Robert Bates (1996a, 1996b), insist that the relationship between area studies and the disciplines must be restructured. Critiques of area studies from a disciplinary standpoint, of course, are far from new. In one of the earliest reviews of language and area studies, for example, Richard Lambert (1973) took note of such discipline-based criticisms. Nonetheless, critiques of this sort have intensified since the end of the Cold War, for many discipline-oriented academics believe that area studies came into being as part of the effort to wage the Cold War, and hence have lost much of their rationale.

This group of social scientists express several sources of dissatisfaction with area studies. First, they believe that area studies have failed to generate scientific knowledge. That is, area specialists eschew theory and the development of theory. These specialists focus, instead, on description and interpretivist approaches to scholarship that have more in common with the humanities than with the social sciences. The critics also charge that area specialists are often poorly equipped to undertake scientific investigations. In particular, such specialists have little or no knowledge of statistics and mathematical approaches in the various disciplines. Finally, the critics accuse area specialists of resisting new trends in the social sciences. These specialists are prone to offer principled objections to innovations that they lack the training even to grasp fully.

Although all of these scholars call for a reconstruction of the relationship between area specialists and the disciplines, their precise prescriptions for this reconstruction vary. Some hold that the two should be separated. In this conception, the relationship would be analogous to that of, for example, language specialists and linguists. Area specialists ("language specialists") would provide practical input, while discipline-oriented scholars ("linguists") would function as the scientists. Other academics argue that area specialists and the disciplines should be segregated. They foresee that area specialists would migrate to history departments and simply record the data, from which social scientists residing in other departments would draw scientific inferences. Still other scholars favor "mutual infusion." On the one hand, they contend, the social sciences have recently developed ways of studying in a rigorous fashion unique events of the kind with which area specialists concern themselves; on the other hand, the differentiated responses of states and regions to such phenomena as economic globalization afford opportunities for input from area specialists to comparative analyses within the disciplines.

A substantial number of observers, including Sidney Tarrow and Kent Worcester (1994), have suggested that the traditional geographic divisions of area studies need to be rethought. The classic example to which they point is the way in which the continent of Europe has normally been treated. Europe has been subdivided into Western Europe, Eastern Europe, and (formerly) the Soviet Union or (now) the New Independent States, and these subdivisions have been dealt with as more or less discrete entities. Furthermore, Turkey has been excluded from all of these groupings and relegated to the Middle East. Other illustrations that analysts have cited include the sharp lines drawn between East Asia and Southeast Asia and between Southeast Asia and South Asia; the lumping together of South America, Central America, and the Caribbean as Latin America; and the arbitrary and ethnocentric omission of the United States from all areas for study.

There is by no means complete agreement, however, on exactly how the geographic regions should be redefined. The situation with respect to Europe affords a good illustration. Few scholars quarrel with the notion of eliminating the distinction between Western Europe and Eastern Europe, but exactly what constitutes "Europe" stirs controversy. Some want to stop at the borders of the former Soviet Union (i.e., to leave out not only Russia but also the Baltic states, Belarus, Ukraine, and Moldova); others wish to encompass the Baltic states, Ukraine, Moldova, and perhaps Belarus, but not Russia; still others want to extend the border to the Urals in Russia. Despite Turkey's involvement in NATO, many scholars still have doubts that it belongs to Europe.

Analysts such as Stanley Heginbotham (1994) and Kenneth Prewitt (1996a and 1996b [in this volume], 1996c) maintain that area studies should be redesigned as area-based studies and that they should be internationalized. In making the first point, these scholars note that "areas" today are more porous and less fixed than in the past because of the globalization process. This reality has three major consequences in their eyes. In the conceptual realm, it necessitates a shift toward emphasis on the interplay between global and local (national and/or regional). How are the globalizing aspects of the contemporary world shaped, refracted, altered, and redefined in specific settings which have their own peculiar histories and features? From a research standpoint, these analysts say, the new reality points toward a focus on themes rather than on situations in single countries or regions. How do common problems or issues growing out of globalization manifest themselves in different countries or regions, and how do various countries or regions approach these problems or issues? With respect to training, the group of scholars holds, the new reality dictates that area studies specialists and area studies centers redirect their priorities. That is, they should concern themselves less than in the past with turning out scholars and practitioners with in-depth understanding of the culture, history, and language of one country or region, and more than previously with producing scholars and practitioners who specialize within disciplines but understand how the culture, history, and language of a country or region affect its interaction with global forces. Such a reorientation entails demands for capabilities to serve a larger and more diverse student population, and these demands may require increased reliance on consortial arrangements.

As for internationalization, these analysts call for it for a combination of reasons. To begin with, they observe, area studies emerged as a major scholarly enterprise in an era when the United States enjoyed a virtual monopoly on resources for such undertakings. Thus, area studies in the United States acquired an American-centric character. Area specialists looked to fellow Americans working on different aspects of their country or region as their reference point and audience. Over the years, however, the sources of area scholarship have expanded greatly. In part, this development has reflected the education in the United States of substantial numbers of area specialists from abroad; in part, it has stemmed from the commitment of significant resources to area scholarship by a sizable group of countries aside from the United States. Yet U.S. area studies, according to these analysts, have tended to remain American-centric, for area specialists in the United States have failed to pay adequate attention to area scholarship in most other countries.

In addition, such analysts continue, the area scholarship being produced outside the United States today has a distinctive cast. Even scholars who have been trained in area studies in the United States and then returned home do not consider themselves "area specialists" but historians, sociologists, political scientists, linguists, etc. Therefore, their area scholarship is largely discipline-based, and they tend to address themselves to questions that range across borders and boundaries.

For these analysts, then, internationalization means two things. First, networks of scholars cutting across national lines should be established on the basis of interests in common problems and/or shared norms, standards, and methodologies. Second, efforts should be made to engage in dialogue across national boundaries about conceptual approaches to area scholarship.

Many scholars, including Robert Hubert, Blair Ruble, and Peter Stavrakis (1995), John Creighton Campbell (cited in Shea 1997), Richard Lambert (1996 [in this volume]), Burkhart Holzner and Matthew Harmon (1998), and Peter A. Hall and Sidney Tarrow (1998 [in this volume]), acknowledge that individual area specialists need to share their area expertise more with those working on other areas and to expand their knowledge base in search of processes operating across disciplines and regions, but these analysts counsel that the traditional focus of area studies should be preserved and that care should be taken not to undermine the structures that have grown up in support of them. Members of this group evince acute awareness that globalization has blurred national and regional borders and rendered insularity a great danger for area specialists. Nonetheless, they justify retention of the area studies approach to scholarly undertakings on several grounds. They reject charges that this approach has failed to yield any scientific knowledge, and they cite concrete illustrations that they believe sustain their judgment. In a more philosophical vein, they challenge the deductive method of formulating hypotheses that characterizes many efforts at theory building in the disciplines, especially the social sciences. Much of the theory that emerges from such a method, they say, simply does not accord with reality and hence is not useful in trying to comprehend the real world. They express a preference, instead, for employment of the inductive method to construct theory. In their view, scholars should seek to organize disparate pieces of data into meaningful patterns and then use this organization to extend their research into broader comparative directions.

Finally, these analysts dispute the notion that the value of developing in-depth knowledge of another country or region derived essentially from the Cold War, and that therefore its need has greatly diminished since the Cold War's passing. They believe that there has always been intrinsic merit in trying to understand how people in other countries and regions with whom Americans interact behave and why, and they contend that the increasing interdependence of the world has greatly enhanced this merit.

The concerns of members of this group regarding existing area studies structures arise from a couple of considerations. They fear that attempts to redefine area studies as area-based studies will throw into question the legitimacy of the centers and other institutions that have developed to foster and carry out area studies programs. In short, such attempts will subject these structures to increased challenge from some discipline-based academicians. They point out that challenges from this quarter have already intensified in the post–Cold War era, and they hold that creation of new bases for contesting the worth of area studies in-stitutions might well put such institutions in serious peril. The group also high-lights the budget climate in which area studies structures now operate. Many educational institutions today, they observe, face major financial constraints that require painful cutbacks in activities. A decreased sense of legitimacy of area studies structures and/or proposals to put new stress on consortia can leave area studies structures highly vulnerable to reductions in funding or even abolishment. Suggestions for more reliance on consortia are seen by these scholars as having a particularly high degree of potential for inflicting damage over the long haul.

Conclusions

In light of the diverse positions noted on the value of area studies, their desirable intellectual focus, and their proper organization, what that is meaningful can be said about the future of area studies? Or can anything? Does the wide array of perspectives preclude broad conclusions?

The degree of importance of area studies inherent in the various schools of thought about the world of the twenty-first century does differ considerably, but in no case are area studies wholly inconsequential. Even the schools of thought in which area studies have the least value (that is, the viewpoints of liberal analysts of international relations and of Fukuyama) plainly allow some role for area studies. Thus, it seems safe to say that the utility of area studies will not disappear in the coming years.

To ensure their relevance in the future, however, area studies cannot pursue a rigid intellectual approach; rather, intellectual eclecticism will be essential. It is impossible at this juncture to know which—indeed, if any—of the current visions of the world of the twenty-first century will prove correct. Under such circumstances, singling out a particular area studies focus derived from one of these forecasts makes little sense. Over time, of course, the drawbacks of doing so might diminish as the world of the new century takes clearer shape, but in the interim the situation dictates a course of, to borrow a phrase from Mao Zedong, "letting a hundred flowers bloom."

This sort of eclecticism has special merit because of the large measure of compatibility, often even complementarity, of the approaches to area studies flowing out of the different schools of thought about the world of the twenty-first century. For example, some approaches stress the positive aspects of the experiences, traditions, and perceptions of individual states, while others point up the negative effects of these. Some approaches concentrate on old entities, and others look primarily to new and emerging entities. Some approaches emphasize the elements of uniqueness of states, while others pay attention to commonalities of states, such as shared values and similar ways of handling similar problems. Some approaches confine themselves to the behavior of states in the international arena, and others concern themselves with the internal situations of states or with connections between these internal situations and global conditions.

As for the organization of area studies, two changes seem highly likely in the years ahead. The traditional geographic divisions of area studies will be revised, and area studies will be increasingly internationalized. Few, if any, scholars contest the desirability of either of these changes. In regard to geographic divisions, the only element of real controversy concerns the exact nature of the reconfiguration. Vested institutional interests come into play on this issue, so some accommodation to them may be necessary to resolve it. Yet geographic restructuring of some kind appears inevitable. With respect to internationalization, the pace will depend upon the availability of funding. International networking and cooperation require money, and substantial amounts of it. Technological developments such as the Internet and interactive video may reduce the costs involved, but they cannot substitute for direct, personal contacts. These entail considerable outlays for travel, lodging, cost of living, and the like.

Linkages between area studies and disciplines, particularly the social sciences, seem destined to grow in the future. Many area specialists, especially younger scholars, have already acquired solid grounding in disciplines, and they are now doing research that qualifies as conceptual and theoretical by any standard. Their numbers will in all likelihood rise in the coming years. Furthermore, even the staunchest defenders of area studies have conceded the need for specialists on one area to interact more with specialists on other areas and to look more for processes at work across regions. Such undertakings will inevitably lead area specialists toward deeper involvement in disciplines.

Yet area studies will probably remain separate and distinct from disciplines. This prospect reflects the basic orientation of the two, both of which have scholarly merit. Disciplines look for the universally valid; area studies find worth, particularly in an increasingly interdependent world, in seeking to understand differences in how people in other countries behave and why. In addition, disciplines tend to promote deductive approaches to the building of theory, while area studies favor inductive ones.

Despite resistance from some area specialists, the years ahead will in all likelihood witness a proliferation of certain kinds of "area-based" programs. The demand for business administrators, journalists, lawyers, educators, and other professionals with a broad understanding of a specific country or region, for instance, may well intensify, and this demand will encourage the establishment of joint programs by area studies centers and professional schools. These programs, because of their dual requirements, will almost certainly involve less area work than traditional area studies programs do. It should be underscored, however, that such programs will not replace traditional area studies programs but coexist with them.

Finally, higher education structures for fostering and conducting area studies will probably become more diversified in the future than they have been in the past. At least most existing area studies centers and institutions appear to have sufficient support to remain intact and continue functioning effectively; however, the constraints on funding now present and likely to persist mean that any new programs, whether in smaller schools with no current programs or on areas previously little examined in the United States, will probably take more innovative forms. Consortia arrangements seem to be the most likely of these, even though portions of the area studies community still have reservations about them. The terms of such consortia arrangements might vary. In some cases, most, or even all, of the participating schools might have a piece of the overall program. In others, a central school might have primary responsibility for operating the program, and other schools might participate in it through distance learning methods.

REFERENCES

Ajami, Fouad. 1993. "The Summoning." *Foreign Affairs* 72 (September–October): 2–9.
Barber, Benjamin R. 1995. *Jihad vs. McWorld.* New York: Ballantine Books.
Bates, Robert H. 1996a. "Area Studies and the Discipline." *APSA-CP: Newsletter of the APSA Organized Section in Comparative Politics* 7 (Winter): 1–2.
Bates, Robert H. 1996b. "The Death of Comparative Politics?" *APSA-CP: Newsletter of the APSA Organized Section in Comparative Politics* 7 (Summer): 1–2.
Fukuyama, Francis. 1992. *The End of History and the Last Man.* New York: The Free Press.

Hall, Peter A., and Sidney Tarrow. 1998. "Globalization and Area Studies: When Is Too Broad Too Narrow?" *The Chronicle of Higher Education* (January 23): B4–5.

Heginbotham, Stanley J. 1994. "Rethinking International Scholarship: The Challenge of Transition from the Cold War Era." *Items* [Social Science Research Council] 48 (June–September): 33–40.

Holzner, Burkhart, and Matthew Harmon. 1998. "Intellectual and Organizational Challenges for International Education in the United States: A Knowledge System Perspective." In *International Education in the New Global Era: Proceedings of a National Policy Conference on the Higher Education Act, Title VI, and Fulbright-Hays Programs,* ed. John D. Hawkins et al. Los Angeles: International Studies and Overseas Programs, UCLA.

Hubert, Robert T., Blair A. Ruble, and Peter J. Stavrakis. 1995. "Post–Cold War 'International' Scholarship: A Brave New World or the Triumph of Form over Substance?" *Items* [Social Science Research Council] 49 (March): 30–38.

Huntington, Samuel P. 1993a. "The Clash of Civilizations?" *Foreign Affairs* 72 (Summer): 22–49.

Huntington, Samuel P. 1993b. "If Not Civilizations, What? Paradigms of the Post–Cold War World." *Foreign Affairs* 72 (November–December): 186–94.

Hurrell, Andrew, and Ngaire Woods. 1995. "Globalisation and Inequality." *Millennium: Journal of International Studies* 24 (3): 447–70.

Kennedy, Paul. 1993. *Preparing for the Twenty-First Century.* New York: Random House.

Keohane, Robert O., and Lisa L. Martin. 1995. "The Promise of Institutionalist Theory." *International Security* 20 (Summer): 39–51.

Lambert, Richard D. 1973. *Language and Area Studies Review.* Monograph 17. Philadelphia: American Academy of Political and Social Science. Sponsored by the Social Science Research Council.

Lambert, Richard D. 1996. "Domains and Issues in International Studies." *International Education Forum* 16 (Spring): 1–19.

Long, David. 1995. "The Harvard School of Liberal International Theory: A Case for Closure." *Millennium: Journal of International Studies* 24 (3): 489–505.

Nye, Joseph S., Jr. 1992. "What New World Order?" *Foreign Affairs* 71 (Spring): 83–96.

Ohmae, Kenichi. 1993. "The Rise of the Region State." *Foreign Affairs* 72 (Spring): 78–87.

Ohmae, Kenichi. 1995. *The End of the Nation State: The Rise of Regional Economies.* New York: Free Press Paperbacks, a division of Simon and Schuster.

Prewitt, Kenneth. 1996a. "Presidential Item." *Items* [Social Science Research Council] 50 (March): 15–18.

Prewitt, Kenneth. 1996b. "Presidential Item." *Items* [Social Science Research Council] 50 (June–September): 31–40.

Prewitt, Kenneth. 1996c. "Presidential Item." *Items* [Social Science Research Council] 50 (December): 91–92.

Rosecrance, Richard. 1992. "A New Concert of Powers." *Foreign Affairs* 71 (Spring): 64–80.

Schwab, Klaus, and Claude Smadja. 1994. "Power and Policy: The New Economic World Order." *Harvard Business Review* 72 (November–December): 40–46.

Shea, Christopher. 1997. "Political Scientists Clash over Value of Area Studies." *The Chronicle of Higher Education* (January 10): B4–5.

Tarrow, Sidney, and Kent Worcester. 1994. "European Studies after the Cold War." *The Chronicle of Higher Education* (April 6): B1–2.

Waltz, Kenneth N. 1993. "The Emerging Structure of International Politics." *International Security* 18 (Fall): 44–79.

Waters, Malcolm. 1995. *Globalization.* London: Routledge.

The Future of
International Studies

David M. Trubek

If you wanted to learn about Thailand, the campus of the University of Wisconsin–Madison would be a good place to start. In Dane County, Wisconsin, far from any major port, national capital, or major financial center, you will find experts on Thai history, politics, language, society, and economy. You will find scientists who are working closely with Thai counterparts on basic and applied research. You could meet a number of UW students specializing in Thai studies, most of whom have spent a year or more in Thailand. You can meet and talk to any of the one hundred or so Thai students and visiting scholars currently in residence. Go to the alumni office and they will provide you with information on the active, four hundred-person-strong Wisconsin Alumni Association of Thailand. The library has an excellent collection of Thai materials. UW–Madison faculty visit Thailand regularly, and the chancellor has visited Bangkok twice in the last few years.

This story can be repeated substituting any region of the world, or many countries large and small, for Thailand. Name your country and it is likely that the UW–Madison teaches its languages, studies its history and contemporary affairs, investigates its role in international trade and politics, sends students there

Reprinted with permission from *Proud Traditions and Future Challenges—The University of Wisconsin–Madison Celebrates 150 Years,* ed. by David Ward. Madison, Wis.: Office of the Chancellor, University of Wisconsin–Madison. © 1999 by the Board of Regents of the University of Wisconsin–Madison.

for advanced training, has ties to its universities, and trains some of its future scholars and leaders. We regularly teach forty different languages each year, and offer another twenty on an occasional basis. We have interdisciplinary programs covering all the world's regions and regularly offer our students overseas experiences in thirty countries. We have hundreds of faculty members with in-depth international expertise. We have formal relationships with several hundred universities around the world. Upwards of one thousand scholars from all over the world come to Madison each year to work with our faculty and interact with our students.

International education begins with in-depth knowledge of the countries and regions of the world. But it does not stop there: we also study and teach about issues that transcend countries and even regions. Do you want to learn about commonalities in the literatures of former British colonies? The spread of nationalism and ethnic violence in many parts of the world? The role of the United Nations in peacekeeping? The relationship between African-Americans and Africa? What about the management of global financial markets or the impact of economic globalization on workers and wages? You'll find research groups on the Madison campus working on these questions, and you can enroll in courses that explore these and other contemporary issues.

Look at the student body. Most of our undergraduates develop competence in at least one foreign language. The interdisciplinary undergraduate major in international studies, with close to four hundred students, is one of the largest majors on campus. A large percentage of students in the College of Letters and Science specialize in international topics, major in foreign languages, or spend at least one semester studying overseas. And many do all three. Several hundred graduate students are enrolled in programs in international studies, and many of them are being trained as specialists who will conduct advanced research and train future generations. Increasingly, international studies are becoming *de rigueur* for students in professional schools of business, law, agriculture, engineering, and the health sciences.

Travel around to any of America's research universities and the same story will repeat itself. There is nothing unique about the Wisconsin experience. All of our major universities have made substantial commitments to international education. They have added numerous international specialists to their faculties, incorporated international topics in the curriculum at all levels, provided support for students who wish to develop international skills, built relations with foreign universities, and established linkages with public and private institutions that need knowledge about the world outside the United States.

To this end, they have all made major changes in university structure and organization. During the course of the twentieth century, all the research universities created specialized institutions that are dedicated to developing and transmitting knowledge about the rest of the world and maintaining linkages between the university and institutions here and abroad. Taken together, these institutions constitute the *international education complexes* of the research universities. They organize specialized courses, provide advice for students seeking international learning and careers, support faculty teaching and research, maintain relations with foreign universities, and provide international information to policymakers and the public.

Of course, emphasis varies from one institution to another, as do organizational forms. Some universities stress regional studies while others have focused more on topical issues like arms control and global warming. Some aspire to comprehensive coverage while others have concentrated on specific regions of the world. On some campuses the international complex is highly decentralized and dispersed; on others there are offices, centers, or institutes that serve as central support and coordination mechanisms. But whatever the focus and whatever the form, these complexes have been assembled to build and maintain linkages between the traditional structure of the American university and the sources and consumers of international knowledge. They facilitate both the formation and the dissemination of learning about the world and America's role in the world.

Our university international education complexes are the envy of educators from other countries. Each of our campuses has been able to assemble large numbers of specialists on world regions and global issues. Usually, they have systems of administrative and financial support that enrich scholarly life for faculty and students alike. There are specialized advising services and fellowships for students, and research grants and travel awards for faculty. Colloquia, workshops, and speaker series are available to all. The campuses maintain linkages of one kind or another with universities and research centers around the world. In some cases, they also have connections to domestic policymakers, international organizations, international business, and transnational nongovernmental organizations. Few university campuses elsewhere in the world boast comparable resources and capabilities.

International Studies at Century's End: Turbulence, Debate, and Doubts

This is a time of great turbulence and ferment in international studies at our research universities. Because international education serves as a link between the university and world society, it is susceptible to changes in both. And today, dramatic changes are occurring both in world society and in American universities. The international education community must deal with changed universities, new types of students, and a transformed world scene. It is being forced to rethink both its mission and its methods.

This has led to a great deal of internal debate and no shortage of concern and disquiet. As the community looks ahead to the next century, it is unsure of its future and divided in its counsels. Some predict a decline in the strength and importance of international education on U.S. campuses, while others see the dawn of a new age with great prospects for growth and improvement. Some argue that as a result of globalization and post–Cold War international politics, we need to make radical changes in curriculum and organization. A few go so far as to suggest that we should replace area studies with global studies, and shift our policy focus completely from geopolitics to geoeconomics. Others see "global studies" and similar efforts to respond to a changing world as a passing fad and urge that priority be given to preservation of existing capabilities. Some think that the most pressing need is to strengthen the role of the humanities in international education, while others think social science and professional training should be the top priority.

Behind the debates between optimists and pessimists, regionalists and globalists, traditionalists and reformers, humanists and social scientists, one can detect a shared concern for the fragility of the enterprise and the sustainability of the international education complexes that have grown up on our campuses. These institutions have been built by hard work, sustained by intellectual excitement, and supported by academic leaders and external agencies. Many are flourishing today. But all are being buffeted by forces from on- and off-campus: these forces threaten the foundations on which our contemporary international complexes have been constructed. What seemed like a permanent change on the American campus now looks more evanescent. For the first time in fifty years, international educators fear that the capabilities built up so carefully over many decades may be at risk.

I share these concerns. I am proud of what has been accomplished at Wisconsin and in our sister universities. I am hopeful for the future but I recognize that we face tremendous challenges. I think we have begun to confront these difficulties and are devising imaginative responses to the changes occurring around us. But no one should be complacent: more has to be done at all levels inside and outside the university to ensure the continuity and the growth of international studies in our research universities.

In this chapter I outline the current situation and suggest ways the international education community can overcome the challenges we all face. I draw heavily on my experiences as a faculty member and dean of international studies at the University of Wisconsin–Madison. I will report on some of the efforts underway on the Madison campus, relay information from contacts with other universities in the United States and overseas, and outline the issues common to all large public research universities and to other institutions of higher education at the end of this century.

How We Got Here

International education is nothing new. American universities have been oriented toward the rest of the world and connected to institutions overseas from the beginning. In particular, scholars in the humanities have always been interested in the study of foreign languages, literatures, and the great world civilizations. World War II, however, marked a watershed in the development of international studies in this country and started a shift from an emphasis on humanistic knowledge to one that included development of practical knowledge for policymaking. Changes begun during the war accelerated in the post–World War II period, and they help account for the formation of international studies as we know it today.

During World War II the U.S. national security establishment found itself in a global conflict that involved operations literally in every part of the world. Government recognized the need for trained personnel with language and area knowledge. Although the universities contained people with these skills, their numbers were small, especially relative to the perceived need. Moreover, while there was substantial expertise on Europe, there were relatively few people who studied other parts of the world. Even when experts on places like India, China, Arabia, and Africa existed, many of them were concerned more with ancient civilizations and dead languages than with contemporary speech and immediate social and political issues. While war-inspired crash programs helped fill the immediate need, the American establishment emerged from the war with a sense that our universities were not equipped to produce the international expertise needed for the country's newly found global responsibilities. Voices were heard urging restructuring and expansion of international education for the postwar world.

The Postwar Boom in International Studies

International studies flourished in the postwar period. It was fed by forces internal to the universities and support from outside. Forward-looking educators saw international studies as a promising area for development. Partly inspired by wartime experiences, scholars in the social sciences had awakened to the need both for comparative knowledge and for insights relevant to international policy concerns. Thus they were eager to add experts on world regions to their departments. Historians saw the possibility of expanding beyond the triad of America, Europe, and the Ancient World that dominated curricula in the first half of the century. Similar opportunities were presented to language teachers when universities saw the need for instruction in a whole range of languages that had not been taught at all or were only offered in a few places for advanced specialists. Everyone thrilled to the possibility of constructing knowledge that might be useful to policymakers. The challenges of global security and Third World development offered rich opportunities for policy-oriented social science. Educators at the research universities saw the emergence of a new market for their graduate students as the postwar "internationalization" wave spread quickly throughout the college and university sector, creating a constant demand for trained specialists who could both teach in conventional disciplines and also provide education about all the regions of the world.

The Cold War lent urgency to the project of expanding international studies, stimulated government interest in university developments, and offered a focus for energy. Confronting what they thought would be a protracted global struggle with the Soviet Union, the People's Republic of China, and their allies, the American elite saw the need to institutionalize the temporary relationship between national security and the academy that had been forged on an emergency basis during the hot war. Major foundations like Ford and Rockefeller began to invest heavily in international studies. They were followed by the federal government, which developed programs to support foreign area and language studies in the research universities. These were designed to produce and sustain expertise about the societies, cultures, economies, and languages of all the world's regions. This meant increasing the study of modern languages, especially the languages of potential enemies and possible allies. It meant developing more area expertise within the social sciences. It meant bringing language, cultural, and social studies together to develop a more holistic understanding of events in specific countries and regions.

Universities responded to these opportunities with relative ease. Thanks in part to the GI Bill, the postwar period was one of rapid growth in tertiary education. Public universities like Wisconsin grew dramatically. There were opportunities to hire large numbers of new faculty, thus permitting the universities to expand existing international programs and create many new ones. There was growing student interest in international subjects. World War II had expanded the global awareness of the American public. As a result of the Cold War and the overseas expansion of the U.S. economy, there were more prospects for international careers. The supply of international experts on faculties grew rapidly to meet existing demand and to exploit opportunities to create further demand for their teaching, research, and service.

Even though the boom in international studies was facilitated by national concerns and geopolitical interests, by and large the universities maintained their autonomy from the national security apparatus and often became centers of criticism of U.S. foreign policy. The interest in expanding international studies arose from core concerns of major academic disciplines, and international scholars were supported by core university resources as well as by extramural sources. Traditions of academic freedom encouraged wide-ranging inquiry and vigorous criticism of public policy. So while Cold War concerns had a real impact on the campuses, and external funding affected priorities, the universities never became mere instruments of government policy.

Area Studies Centers and the Emergence of the
International Education Complex

Initially, at least in places like the UW–Madison, attention was focused on the creation of what came to be called "area studies"—an in-depth, holistic, interdisciplinary approach to understanding specific world regions. Of course, many universities had been committed to the study of other parts of the world long before the onset of the Cold War, so that area studies was in some way the continuation, on a much enlarged basis, of earlier traditions. But area studies did not just enlarge the scale of these programs; it also involved a major change in focus. Earlier, humanistic studies were supplemented—if not sometimes replaced—by a focus on contemporary social, economic, and political issues. The postwar area studies movement was based on a belief, then quite strong in the social sciences, in the *interdependence* of knowledge in the social disciplines. That is, people believed that insights in any discipline would depend in part on knowledge to be gleaned from specialists in another. Political scientists believed that breakthroughs in comparative politics could not occur without knowledge of the economies and cultures of the countries under scrutiny; economists thought that economic development involved changes in culture and systems of governance as well as in business behavior. Everyone agreed that a student could not really understand a country without knowing its language, history, and cultural traditions, or without living there.

For those reasons, scholars everywhere supported the creation of new institutions that would foster interdisciplinary communication and cooperation and organize curricula in new ways. These centers would bring specialists from various fields together; organize new curricular offerings that would provide students with comprehensive programs combining language training with studies in the humanistic and social disciplines; and create opportunities for students to spend time in the region of their specialization. Hence the creation of organized "area studies centers," which served to build holistic knowledge of world regions and create organized curricula and new majors, minors, master's programs, and other specialized credentials for area studies students.

Driven by faculty energy and excitement and the support of forward-looking administrators, and heavily supported by extramural funding from foundations and the federal government, these centers flourished on many campuses. In a time of rapid growth of the university, it proved relatively easy to assemble people from many disciplines who wanted to study developments in places like Latin America, the Soviet Union, or Asia, and who were eager to work with others having similar interests. At Madison, and on many other research university campuses, these area studies centers were the nucleus for the emergence of large complexes of specialized centers, programs, and institutes dedicated to international education. These institutional complexes existed in creative tension with traditional departments. They maintained close ties to scholars and institutions in the regions they studied. In some cases they developed linkages to policymakers.

From Area Studies to Global Studies:
The Growth of the International Education Complex

Area studies centers often were the primary nucleus for today's large international education complexes. Over time, however, other major dimensions have been added so that today's typical research university now contains a wide range of specialized international educational offerings, ranging from undergraduate majors to interdisciplinary Ph.D. programs. Most also have large organized interdisciplinary international research enterprises, and many have outreach programs and other service operations.

These varied teaching, research, and service activities, and the institutions that support them, constitute the international education "complexes" that form such a unique feature of research universities like the UW–Madison. In addition to interdisciplinary centers for the study of specific world regions (e.g., Latin American studies, Asian studies, European studies), there are many other types of specialized international units. Most campuses also have interdisciplinary centers organized on a topical rather than a geographic and cultural basis. These include centers on topics like arms control and disarmament, development and economic growth, and human rights. Increasingly, we see the emergence of centers of "global studies," which expand the scale of "area studies" to embrace world society, economy, and politics. Many universities also have units devoted to international issues unique to a given discipline or professional field such as international business, economics, or legal studies: for example, the UW–Madison has a Center for International Business Education and Research, an East Asian Legal Studies Center, and a Law and Globalization program. Some universities have specialized "study abroad" units designed to encourage students to include overseas study and work in their academic programs, as well as offices that provide specialized services for the increasing numbers of international students in all fields enrolled at the research universities. Many campuses have specialized "outreach" offices that disseminate international knowledge to the K–12 system, other colleges and universities, and the general public. And some schools have units whose mission is to provide technical assistance to developing countries.

The International Education Complex and the Traditional Structure of the University

The growth of international education complexes in the postwar period changed the landscape of many campuses throughout the United States. All of a sudden, new majors were defined based on regions (Latin American studies and Asian studies) or around topics (international relations or development). Instead of being limited to majoring in economics, political science, Spanish, or sociology, students could select one of these new sets of offerings in addition to—or instead of—the more traditional fields. And along with these changes in the curriculum came organizational changes as new offices, centers, programs, and institutes that had not existed before were added to manage the new courses, majors, research programs, and service activities. This brought to the fore the issue of the relations between the new structures and the established institutions on campus.

An Alternative Axis

From the point of view of the traditional structure of the American university, this complex of internationally oriented and largely interdisciplinary institutions offers an *alternative axis of organization.* Where the traditional axis is built around disciplinary departments organized into largely autonomous colleges, the international education complex cuts across departmental and college lines. International knowledge requires inputs from many fields, so the area, topical, and global studies centers typically draw people from many colleges and dozens of departments.

Because overseas experiences can enrich almost any field of study, the study-abroad offices usually serve students who are pursuing a wide range of majors and careers, from anthropology and business to water resource management and zoology. Similarly, policy analysis, technical assistance, and outreach usually require holistic knowledge and the services of faculty and staff from several fields. Because so much of international education demands services that combine input from several disciplines, universities built separate international studies structures that complement the historical axis of organization. Some of these structures challenged traditional boundaries.

Different Methods and New Missions
The international education complexes not only represent an alternative axis for the organization of academic services, they also redefine the way the university should fulfill its traditional mission of training students and producing knowledge. Study abroad, for example, exists because educators decided that to acquire a language and understand a culture, long-term residence in another country was superior to simply sitting in a classroom somewhere in the United States. Area studies emerged because people believed in the interdependence of social knowledge and assumed that no single discipline could provide the insights and understandings needed to deal with issues in other countries. Thus it was thought that even if your primary interest was in the Brazilian *economy,* you could not understand it unless you could read and speak Portuguese and had a grasp of the nation's history and politics. More recently, people have also seen the need to supplement interdisciplinary studies of nations and regions with an understanding of broader forces and phenomena, so the study of a subject like the Brazilian economy now also requires an understanding of global capital flows, the emerging world trade regime, and the global shifts in ideas about the role of the state in the economy.

Further, international education represents a significant expansion of the traditional mission of the university. To be sure, the primary role of international studies is to strengthen and expand the university's capacity to produce knowledge and educate students. But the international education complexes also support the direct provision of policy advice; the dissemination of information beyond the campus to the public, K–12 system, and business; the development of universities and other institutions overseas; and similar new missions. This expanded mission had not been contemplated when the UW–Madison was founded 150 years ago, and was only beginning to be recognized when it celebrated its one hundredth anniversary in 1949.

Useful Supplement or Dangerous Rival:
The Traditional Axis and the International Complex
The size of the international complexes varies from university to university. In some cases, they are very large and engage large numbers of students and faculty. At the UW–Madison campus the international education complex is embedded in

separate traditional schools and colleges. However, if all the UW–Madison's international faculty and staff who are now housed in various colleges were to be formally joined together, the resulting "international college" would have hundreds of faculty members, teach thousands of students, and be larger than all but the biggest of the traditional units.

Today the international complexes exist in complex tension with the units that form the older and more traditional axis of university organization. While most educators recognize that the specialized interdisciplinary and cross-college units that make up these complexes are useful if not essential supplements to traditional campus structures, some perceive them as dangerous rivals. Where most see these institutions as enriching disciplines and enhancing the capacities of departments, others see them as competitors for student enrollments, academic prestige, faculty loyalties, and campus resources.

While it is easy to see why conflict might erupt between international studies and traditional units, there was very little tension during the postwar boom. For several reasons, the potential conflict between the disciplinary axis and interdisciplinary international studies was kept under control. Universities favored internationalization and disciplines promoted international study. The social sciences recognized the importance of international knowledge and the interdependence of international studies. Professors sought opportunities to conduct research, teach, and provide advice around the world. First the language departments and then other disciplines recognized the importance of overseas experiences. Few worried about competition for scarce resources because there was no real scarcity: in an era of rapid growth there seemed to be enough to go around for everyone. This was especially true because international education received substantial support from external sources, principally the federal government and the major private foundations. The existence of extramural resources available exclusively for international education made it easier to develop new programs and thus create an alternative axis of campus organization without generating too much conflict with established units.

Challenges at the End of the Century

Two questions face international education on our campuses today. Can the era of good will continue in a different intellectual climate and a period of relative austerity? And can international education change fast enough to meet all the new needs of students and the public? These questions have emerged due to the rapid and unexpected changes—changes both occurring throughout the world that international educators relate to and within the universities they serve. Poised between a world in turbulence and universities undergoing significant changes, international educators are reassessing their missions, reengineering their institutions, and seeking new bases of intellectual and material support. The UW–Madison, like many of its peers, has spent a good part of the last decade reviewing the international education complex, restructuring some units and creating new programs in areas previously underserved.

To understand the new context for international education in universities like the UW–Madison, we have to look closely at three areas of change and turbulence: those occurring in world society; those happening on university campuses; and those affecting the extramural funding sources that have been so vital to international education in the past. The changes in all these areas during the past decade have been rapid and dramatic. We are still struggling to respond to them.

Changes in World Society

At the dawn of the twenty-first century, the world looks very different than it did even a scant twenty years ago. Changes too numerous to mention have taken place, but a few seem to be particularly central to the changing context for international studies. These are the end of the Cold War, globalization of the economy, the communications revolution, cultural conflict and the "clash among civilizations," and the changing role of the United States in world politics and the world economy.

The end of the Cold War created new topics for academic study (like democratization and transitions to a market economy) while rendering others (like the study of communism and nuclear deterrence) less central. It opened up new possibilities for overseas study and research as U.S. universities developed relations with counterparts in places like the former Soviet Union, Eastern Europe, and China. At the same time it seems to have led to declining interest in international affairs in this country and to a reassessment of many government programs, including support for academic exchanges, which had flourished in a period when the U.S. saw itself in an ideological struggle with a major enemy and viewed the universities as allies in this struggle.

The end of the Cold War also coincided with, and facilitated, the most recent wave of economic "globalization." While there has been a world economy for centuries, and although the international economy was highly integrated one hundred years ago, quantitative and qualitative changes in the past twenty years have led many to describe this as a new and different stage of world economic integration. At least four changes mark this era as different: dispersion of manufacturing production from the North to the South and the rise of strong export-oriented economies in many developing countries; a global financial market making capital available throughout the world and constraining national economic policy; the declining importance of nation states in the management and operations of the economy; and the growing importance in the world economy of subnational regions like the American Midwest.

These changes in the world economy and its governance structures have rendered some knowledge bases obsolete and created the need for new knowledge about issues like the operation of the World Trade Organization, the regulation of global financial markets, and the export potential of regions like the Midwest. They have also led to a much greater internationalization of the U.S. economy, as the role of exports and imports in our gross domestic product have soared. This has generated new demands for international knowledge from business and state governments, and for expanded international instruction within professional schools.

A related development is the global communications revolution. The computer, the satellite, and other technical changes have led to better and much cheaper telephonic communications, facilitated the spread of TV, permitted the creation of e-mail, the Internet, and other information technology capacities. The speed and ease with which information and images of all kinds can cross national borders have increased exponentially. This chapter was written in a small and relatively isolated cottage, but while I wrote I kept in contact with people all around the world by e-mail and telephone: these technologies gave me communications capabilities that not even embassies, corporations, or other major institutions could muster fifty years ago when the UW–Madison turned one hundred.

These changes have not only made it possible to link economic actors on a global scale; they also offer tremendous potential for linking individual scholars and universities more generally. E-mail and the Internet have greatly facilitated scholarly exchanges and research, and universities are beginning to share courses by distance education on a global scale. Yet, while the global communications revolution has created a flood of information that can enrich study and research, it also threatens to overwhelm students and professors alike. The sheer volume of information now easily available creates major problems of quality assessment and organization.

Great changes also result from the emergence or reemergence of ethnic, nationalist, and religiously based conflicts that have taken place in many parts of the world. The end of the Cold War unleashed nationalist forces in the former Soviet Union and elsewhere: in many cases these are ethnic conflicts as well. At the same time, the global communications revolution and other changes have made it possible to link cultural groups across national boundaries, thus creating new forms of cleavage and new possibilities for global conflict. Some think a resulting "clash of civilizations" will develop and become the new central axis of world politics.

Finally, the end of the Cold War, globalization of the economy, and other changes have led to major shifts in the position and role of the United States in world society. They help explain the growing interest in economic competitiveness and "geo-economic" concerns, as well as waning interest in traditional issues of national security. They probably help account for what looks like a new wave of isolationism in important segments of American society. As the global ideological, material, and military struggle of the Cold War winds down, Americans seem to want to either withdraw from the world, or redefine our international relations along lines of economic conflict.

The renewal of isolationist tendencies and the new emphasis on U.S. economic competitiveness create tremendous challenges for America's universities. We have to be beacons of international interest and understanding in a time when some in the media and the political elite seem to have lost their interest in world affairs. We have to maintain our commitment to the pursuit of universal knowledge and academic autonomy while at the same time providing assistance to those whose primary concern is with the growth of our national economy.

Changes in Universities

Turbulence in world politics has been matched by turbulence on the campus. There have been fiscal, administrative, and intellectual developments that have challenged the academic traditions and institutional organization of the international education complexes. Some of these represent a critique of existing efforts; others a call for new programs to meet underserved needs.

At the intellectual level, a number of critiques address the way international education was practiced in the post–World War II period. In some circles, there has been a collapse of belief in disciplinary interdependence: as a result, some have suggested that the holistic and interdisciplinary methods pioneered by area studies are inadequate to produce truly scientific knowledge. Others who have not questioned the basic interdisciplinary approach have wondered about the continuing relevance of the regional focus, arguing that a global perspective may be more relevant today. A third type of critique has come from people who view much of U.S. scholarship about the rest of the world as being marked by ethnocentric biases. There also has been criticism of the academy's engagement with policymakers on the grounds that the search for policy relevance can compromise objectivity or result in complicity with dubious policies. Conversely, others have labeled international scholarship as irrelevant "mandarin" studies and called for more applied work of immediate practical use to business and government.

A second shockwave has come from the era of fiscal austerity experienced by all public universities and many private schools. Universities like the UW–Madison have seen their budgets cut and have responded by reducing the size of the faculty and student body. This retrenchment has generated the potential for real tension with traditional academic units as deans and departments look for ways to save money and downsize. The large international education complexes may look to some like tempting targets for cutbacks. International educators find themselves struggling to maintain the range and breadth of curricular offerings established in more affluent times, let alone add new courses needed to equip students with the skills demanded by a rapidly changing world scene.

A third set of challenges comes from changes in campus priorities. The most important of these are the growing interest on the research campuses in undergraduate education and the drift of student interest from liberal arts to professional or preprofessional training. While the international education complexes have always included important elements of undergraduate training, and professional schools like law, business, and public policy have paid attention to international education in the past, the center of gravity in international studies at the UW–Madison (as on many other campuses) has been on graduate education in the humanities and social sciences and particularly on producing Ph.Ds. Now, however, with the Ph.D. "market" at best flat and probably in decline, and with new demands for undergraduate and professional education emerging, international educators have been called upon to revise old programs and develop new ones.

Changes in Extramural Support

One of the most serious challenges facing the international education complexes today comes from changes in their sources of extramural support. Not only has there been an overall decline in the funds available from traditional sources like major foundations and the U.S. government, there is also real uncertainty about what kinds of programs might be funded with the money that remains. This is especially true for the foundations, which have been reassessing the nature and purpose of their support for international education. Some traditional supporters of international studies have announced an end to support for area studies as such but have not articulated a clear vision of what forms of international learning and teaching they hope to support in their place. Others call for major changes in area studies without offering a fully articulated new vision. In such a climate, competition for extramural funding has become very keen, funding search costs have gone up, and it is much harder to make long-run plans for projects that are in whole or part dependent on extramural support.

Impact on International Studies: The Emergence of a Twenty-First-Century Vision

Changes in the world, the universities, and the extramural support system have generated both excitement and anxiety among international educators in recent years. This has been a period both of heated debate and creative ferment. Institutions have been forced to adapt to new circumstances. There have been struggles between those who felt the only priority was to preserve existing courses and academic programs and those who emphasized the need for innovation. For many, the process has been painful, but the struggle is beginning to pay off. International educators have begun to cope with the challenges presented by the new context. They have seized new opportunities made possible by some of the intellectual, political, economic, and technological changes now underway. As the twentieth century comes to an end, a new vision of international studies is beginning to emerge at the UW–Madison and on campuses around the nation.

This vision is based on the need to preserve existing strengths while also developing new offerings for new constituencies. It recognizes that the traditionalists and the reformers were both right. In the new vision, the first goal must be to conserve valuable capabilities. These include both intellectual resources and know-how on ways to develop new knowledge and disseminate it to disparate audiences. The in-depth area knowledge and language capacity fostered by the area centers form the foundation for all other types of international study and education. Existing policy centers not only bring together expertise on important contemporary issues; they also know how to transmit relevant knowledge to policymakers and the public. International relations programs provide essential information on foreign policy and the operation of the interstate system. The specialized administrative staffs that support international education have irreplaceable special knowledge about overseas operations, extramural funding, and interdepartmental cooperation. To the extent possible, these assets must be preserved. But conservation alone is not enough. The emerging vision recognizes that it is equally essential to be innovative. To do that, we must refocus on new needs of our students, reimagine international education, restructure the alliances on which this interdisciplinary enterprise is built, and develop new ideas for a changing world.

Refocusing on Students and Their Changing Needs

The first challenge is to rethink what our students need today and what they will need twenty years from now to operate effectively in the international arena. A much larger percentage of the student body will need to develop international skills in the future than has been the case in the past. As global knowledge and international skills become more important to sectors of U.S. society and the U.S. economy, international educators will have to reach out to a larger and different student constituency. This will not only mean increasing the numbers of students served by our programs, but also changing the programs as well. We are already seeing this process at work in Wisconsin: for example, as exports loom larger in the state economy, government and business have called for new kinds of international education at all levels from K–12 to the doctorate.

While graduate training will continue to be important, and liberal arts will continue to be central to international studies, international educators will have to spend more time with undergraduates and with students in the professional disciplines. Moreover, we will need to provide more general international education, orienting all students to the changing world, and not just train a core of specialists. There will be more demand for courses that deal with business and economic questions in all world regions, as well as new approaches to the study of ethnicity and religion. Demands for language skills will both increase and change in nature as more people seek practical and applied language capacities. Courses on world regions and global issues will continue to be important, but some will have to be tailored to fit into the curricula of the professional schools of business, law, public policy, engineering, and the health sciences. We will need to develop new kinds of overseas experiences to meet the needs of a growing and different student body, finding ways other than the traditional semester or college year abroad to develop global competence. Internships, short-term overseas modules, and similar innovative overseas experiences will be needed. These changes will help us develop capstone experiences and credentials that will facilitate entry into new as well as traditional international careers while preparing the general public for life in a more interdependent world.

Other areas of change include devoting more attention to student information and advising. The larger the student body involved in international studies, the more we will encounter students with little or no prior international background. And the more options for international learning we offer, the more complex the choices facing students become. For these reasons, international educators in the future will need to provide more and better information about students' options and strengthen advising services in general.

Finally, we will need to make changes in programs for graduate students. While we need to preserve the strong Ph.D. capabilities that are vital to the production and dissemination of cutting-edge knowledge, we also have to recognize that the demand for Ph.D.s in international studies is flat at best in this country. So we need to explore other kinds of graduate training, including terminal master's degrees with career potential and degrees offered jointly in international studies and professional schools, e.g., a JD/MA in international affairs.

Rethinking Boundaries

The next thing we need to do is to rethink many of the boundaries that were built into our imagination of the international educational complexes and that have shaped the construction of international programs. The current architecture of international education rests on a series of explicit or implicit distinctions and boundaries that need to be rethought. These include boundaries within the international complexes themselves, as well as between the complexes and other entities.

Within the international complex. Intellectually, we have tended to separate the national sphere from the international system of relations among nation-states. And we have separated the public and the private. As a result, international policy studies tend to look either at the national or the interstate level (or both) but often have left the role of corporations, civil society, religious life, and similar matters to be studied elsewhere, if at all. Yet issues like ethnic and religious conflict or the operation and regulation of global financial markets engage public and private actors at multiple levels. In an era when many issues transcend nations and even regions, when the public and private intersect increasingly, and when policies may involve public and private actors at local, national, regional, and global levels, all these boundaries must be rethought.

The same can be said for boundaries that define the scope and limit of interdisciplinary programs on our campuses. We need to rethink both the formal and informal boundaries that have grown up among the elements of the international education complex. Historically, international education in the liberal arts has been separate from studies of international business, law, agriculture and other professional subjects. There has been a tendency for graduate studies to remain separate from undergraduate programs. Even when programs formally served both undergraduate and graduate students, they sometimes drifted toward a focus on the graduate level. Topical programs in fields like arms control or development often were only weakly linked to area studies. In some cases the separate centers for study of individual world regions had little contact with each other, so that specialists on Southeast Asia had only limited interaction with those who studied East Asia, let alone with those who worked on Russia and Europe.

At the UW–Madison, we have recognized the need to bridge many of these gaps. We have brought all our area and international studies programs together into one International Institute. We have created global studies programs that both deal with comparative cultures, global topics, and cross-regional issues and that straddle the public/private divide. We have created a special initiative that brings scholars from economics, political science, sociology, business, law, and other fields together to study new issues relating to the management of the global economy. And new initiatives focus more attention on undergraduates: a new certificate in global cultures; internationally-oriented residential learning on campus; a revitalized undergraduate major in international studies; and a program to support new and innovative types of overseas learning experiences.

Between the international complex and the rest of the university. Another set of boundaries that must be rethought are those between the international education complexes and the rest of the university. These include boundaries between international studies and the departments and colleges, as well as boundaries between the interdisciplinary international studies programs and other parts of the interdisciplinary axis itself. We need a way to reestablish the sense that international studies are central to the concerns of departments like sociology, political science, and economics; we must renew the belief in the interdependence of knowledge in the social disciplines. We also need to break down the barriers between international studies in the liberal arts departments and those in the professional schools of law, business, agriculture, engineering, education, and public policy. At the same time we need to forge relationships with groups pursuing such interdisciplinary topics as ethnic studies, women's studies, environmental studies, and cultural studies.

Between "our" knowledge and "their" knowledge. Another boundary that must be crossed is that between knowledge produced in the United States and knowledge produced in the regions we study. In the past, area studies in the United States seemed to be a project reserved for Americans and carried out primarily on U.S. campuses with occasional forays to "the field." We would send people out to study "the other," and then transmit the learning developed by these American area specialists to our students. To some extent, this practice was a natural response to objective conditions. In some parts of the world there were no local scholars to work with. In others access to local scholars was cut off. In some parts of the world universities were weak or nonexistent, and the only source of scholarly insight on many parts of the world came from scholars in Western universities. The Cold War meant that U.S. researchers were denied access to many countries and contacts with local academics were limited and tightly controlled. Now, however, as a result of decolonialization, economic development, the strengthening of universities around the world, the end of the Cold War, and the global communication revolution, this is no longer the case. Today it is possible for researchers in this country to work closely with counterparts in most countries around the world.

Wisconsin and its sister research universities are responding to these needs by forming closer ties with universities and research centers around the world and by encouraging our faculty to join with peers in "global research networks" that address broad and widely-shared issues like nationalism and ethnic conflict, the globalization of the media, and the changing role of government in the economy. These networks do not privilege any one center of scholarship but seek to work collaboratively on a global basis. In many cases they are virtual networks that operate primarily through the Internet.

Creating New Partnerships
In addition to challenging and transgressing boundaries, progressive international educators are seeking to develop new partnerships and alliances that will sustain and enrich international studies and programs. These include new partnerships on our own campuses as well as partnerships with other universities in the U.S., with universities overseas, and with the public and private sectors. These alliances form part of the basic architecture of the emerging vision of international education.

Within the interdisciplinary axis. The first set of partnerships are those within the interdisciplinary axis of our own universities. International studies were one of the first elements of the interdisciplinary axis to be institutionalized. They have been followed by many other cross-departmental and cross-college programs. Among them are programs that study specific ethnic groups in this country (e.g., Afro-American studies, Asian-American studies, and Chicano studies), women's studies, environmental studies, and cultural studies. In each case there are natural affinities between these newer members of the interdisciplinary axis and the international studies complexes. Ethnic studies programs look at populations with roots elsewhere in the world and need to understand from whence these communities have come as well as how they have evolved in the United States. Women's studies programs benefit from comparative knowledge of women's roles and conditions around the world as well as from an understanding of transnational advocacy for and international protection of women. Environmental studies programs similarly require knowledge of conditions in other countries and the international arena. And cultural studies is emerging as a global enterprise with interests in the relationship between culture and society worldwide.

While some partnerships have been formed, alliances of this nature have proven more difficult than might be expected. To be sure, some centers of Latin American studies maintain close relations with Chicano studies programs, and some African studies centers work closely with Afro-American studies. But collaborations of this nature are not yet commonplace. The reasons are complex. Some programs may be too busy struggling for survival. Others may be concerned about their relations with departments and disciplines and fearful of too much contact with other interdisciplinary programs that might be looked down on by those wedded to traditional disciplines. At the UW–Madison we have sought to overcome these barriers through joint programs sponsored by the International Institute and units like the Humanities Institute and the Women's Studies Research Center as well as through a growing number of workshops and other activities put on jointly by area and ethnic studies centers.

With disciplines, departments, and professional fields. The second set of alliances are those between the international education complexes and the units that make up the traditional axis of campus organization. Here there is a need both to redefine old relationships and forge new ones. Traditionally, the international complexes have been closely tied to departments of humanities and social science. Some of these relationships have become frayed in recent years, as new trends within the disciplines have challenged extant approaches to international knowledge and pressures to downsize departments have reopened questions about the role and importance of international knowledge within the disciplines. Efforts are being made to clarify and, if necessary, to redefine these traditional relationships. Area and international studies scholars have tried to forge relationships in two ways: by demonstrating that the social sciences have a need for the insights comparative study can produce, and by refining their scholarship to make it more theoretical and employing the latest empirical techniques. At the same time, they are trying to revive older traditions that stressed the interdependence of the social disciplines and counteract what seems to be "go it alone" tendencies in fields like economics, sociology, and political science. At the UW–Madison we have encouraged intellectual innovation and worked closely with leaders of colleges and departments to ensure that the core area and international studies resources embedded in these units are preserved in times of austerity.

Similar issues arise in the relationship with the humanities as cultural studies and post-colonialism become more important in the humanities and require a redefinition of the relationship between area studies and humanities departments. These newer traditions tend to challenge some of the work that has been done by area scholars in U.S. universities. There is a growing critique of "orientalism" or the tendency to construct knowledge of other societies based on assumptions of Western supremacy. This has led to calls to pay closer attention to, and work more in tandem with, scholars from outside American and Western academic traditions. Area studies centers have to deal with these challenges and incorporate these insights or risk appearing insensitive to the critique of "orientalism." On our campus, we are responding to these challenges by creating joint area programs with universities in the regions we study and by fostering global research networks on topics like democratization, ethnic conflict, and the impact of globalization on labor.

Finally, new relationships are needed with language departments as changes in the constituency for international education create pressures for new kinds of language instruction. The spread of international education into professional schools and the heightening of career concerns among liberal arts students have generated a need for more intensive and more pragmatic forms of language instruction—hence the rise of courses in Business French, Technical Japanese, and similar forms of "applied" language instruction. At the same time, budgetary pressures are putting some of the less commonly taught languages at risk. These languages are often essential for the maintenance of area studies capacities, yet the number of students prepared to enroll in languages like Yoruba, Telegu, Thai, Kazakh, or Quechua (all of which are regularly offered at the UW–Madison) are often too small to justify full-time faculty positions in a time of austerity and downsizing. To meet this challenge, the area studies centers and the language departments need to work together in new ways, and language faculty need to take advantage of new technologies to lower the cost of instruction and increase productivity. The UW–Madison, which offers more of these "less commonly taught" languages than most universities in this country, has taken the lead in developing new methods and building consortia with other universities to support innovation and resource sharing in language instruction.

In addition to redefining traditional alliances, international educators are forging new alliances with departments and colleges that reflect changing conditions and the demands of new constituencies. Perhaps the most important of these are the alliances that are growing up between the liberal arts–based international programs and the professional schools of law, business, agriculture, education, and engineering. Largely as a result of economic globalization, the professional schools at all our research universities have recognized the need to expand their international offerings at all levels. We see this in dramatic form at the UW–Madison. Several of our professional schools have created new international degrees or similar specialized programs and have hired additional international specialists. At the same time, they have sought closer relations with the existing area and international studies programs and asked them to provide specialized training for professional students who want to develop language skills, general area knowledge, and competence on selected global issues. This has led some of the area and international studies programs to revise their curricula and develop specialized offerings more suited to the needs of professional school students. These developments have been supported and encouraged by a special initiative on World Affairs and the Global Economy which brings faculty from the liberal arts and the professional schools together in a cross-campus learning community dealing with problems of management of the global economy.

With other universities. In addition to partnerships on campus, international educators are expanding existing ties and forging new relationships with other universities in the United States and overseas. Faced with increasing demands for international knowledge, and often for knowledge of a novel, complex, and specialized nature at a time when resources are shrinking, university leaders have looked for ways to share resources and cooperate more fully. Thus we increasingly see the development of consortia that link two or more universities for all kinds of specialized tasks. These include jointly run area studies centers and overseas programs as well as joint programs for research and graduate training on specialized issues. Consortia are also emerging to facilitate the teaching of less commonly taught languages like Thai, Kazakh, Quechua, or Telegu through summer institutes and distance education. And we are seeking new and deeper relations with individual scholars and research institutions in other countries while also developing global research networks that link our scholars with peers around the world working on similar topics. In the Midwest, the eleven Big Ten universities plus the University of Chicago have worked together in many areas for decades, but only recently have they started to explore cooperation in international studies. In addition to participating in this general consortium, the UW–Madison belongs to many consortia for study abroad, several designed to foster teaching of less commonly taught languages, and some in area and global studies. Recently, we have created a Joint Center for International Studies with the UW–Milwaukee better to serve the UW System and the state. With the University of Minnesota, we jointly manage the Midwest Center for German and European Studies and with Minnesota and Stanford the MacArthur Consortium on International Peace and Cooperation.

While we are working more closely with sister universities in the United States, we are expanding and deepening our relations with scholars and universities overseas. In particular, we have developed a wide range of partnerships to foster exchange of students and faculty and conduct joint research. This is an area that has been materially helped by U.S. government programs, and thus it is one that is at risk as international education budgets in Washington are cut. Given the nature of these relationships, it will be hard to find alternative sources of support should these cuts be deep and permanent.

With external constituencies. Finally, we are strengthening and deepening relationships with existing constituencies outside the university and trying to build new external alliances. International educators in the research universities have lobbied heavily to preserve existing federal programs that are at risk. We have continued our relationships with the K–12 systems and colleges in our states and regions. Many of us are trying to develop relations with the alumni of our programs as well as with alumni of our universities who reside abroad. In recent years, most universities have sought to strengthen relations with the business community. And many state universities like the UW–Madison have sought a much closer partnership with state government, primarily through alliances with state export promotion offices.

The emerging partnership between state business, state export promotion offices, and state universities is the newest and most innovative of the new external alliances being forged in this time of change. As the economies of states as well as whole regions (like the Midwest) become more and more dependent on exports, business and political leaders have seen the need for more international expertise. In some cases, they have turned to the universities to supply the needed knowledge and training. It is too soon to say if this new alliance will prove mutually beneficial and help take up the slack created by the decline in federal support. But it remains a promising area for future exploration. In the past few years the UW–Madison has developed close relations with the State Department of Commerce and the business community. We have offered a pilot program of workshops, conferences, and other programs on international issues relevant to the state's export promotion program and hope to secure long-term funding to continue these activities.

Preserve Knowledge and Develop New Ideas

The most important of all challenges is the need to preserve the great learning of the past and at the same time develop new concepts and ideas to equip students and others to confront a new world. This is, after all, the central responsibility of research universities in all fields. In our domain, we need to use old and new methods to ensure that our students understand other cultures and societies; to refine our understandings of how world society operates in light of recent trends; to seek new insights about, and appreciation of, the great civilizations of the past; to develop new models of an increasingly globalized world economy; to rethink the interdependence of nations and devise new modalities of governance; to listen to new voices in art and literature from around the world; and to otherwise maintain the highest level of excellence in our scholarship and teaching.

Some Recent Breakthroughs

Over the past decade, a new vision of international education has begun to take shape on our campuses. Emerging out of heated debate and no small amount of struggle, this vision is beginning to shape developments here and elsewhere. As a result, we can point to a number of recent breakthroughs on our campus. Thus, for the first time ever, hiring decisions for a cluster of related faculty in several UW departments have been authorized, and this "cluster hiring" plan has been applied to internationalize policy studies. This reflects campus recognition that the interdisciplinary axis needs the same control over hiring that was once the exclusive preserve of departments, as well as a realization that policy studies in the future must be international. The College of Letters and Sciences and College of Agriculture and Life Sciences have joined with the Schools of Business and Law to create a cross-college learning community on the global economy, thus showing they understand that no single college can create needed knowledge in this area on its own. We have joined with universities in Latin America, Asia, and Africa to create a global research network to study the legacies of authoritarian regimes in politics, culture, and individual psyches, showing that our faculty has seen the need to work with colleagues throughout the world. And member programs of the International Institute have started working together on shared projects, demonstrating that they have recognized that the era of splendid isolation is over.

Conclusion

No one can predict what international education will look like on our campus twenty-five or fifty years from now when the UW–Madison celebrates its next major milestones. International studies, like all higher education, is in flux. But the future is hopeful. The structures of international education in this country have been built on five pillars: strong intellectual interest in the disciplines for matters international; support from top campus leadership; creative work and sustained energy among the international educators; mutually supportive relations between the traditional and the interdisciplinary axes; and strong external support for international higher education. On our campus, these pillars remain strong. As a result, the UW–Madison is increasingly recognized as a leader in international education in our region and nationwide. We have confronted the issues of our times and emerged stronger than ever.

Crossing Borders

THE CASE FOR AREA STUDIES

Toby Alice Volkman

Area Studies, an interdisciplinary field born in the United States in the aftermath of World War II, is at a critical turning point as it struggles to respond to dramatic changes in the world. Conceived as an antidote to Americans' lack of understanding of much of the rest of the globe, area studies attracted substantial philanthropic and federal support in its first two decades. From 1951 to 1966, the Ford Foundation granted $270 million to U.S. universities and other institutions to build research and training programs focused on particular regions of the world.

Over the past 50 years, these programs have trained thousands of scholars, expanded students' intellectual horizons, and helped deepen the American public's understanding of distant parts of the world. Today, the need for such knowledge is more compelling than ever, as the speed and intensity of communication and travel create a world that is increasingly interconnected. What was distant a decade ago is no longer so.

In the late 20th century, however, area studies is beset by conceptual debates and programmatic uncertainties. The fluidity and porousness of borders; the unprecedented mobility of people, ideas, information, and capital; the end of the Cold War; the dissolution of old states, and the rise of new identities and new expressions of nationalism—all have forced a radical questioning of conventional ways of viewing the world and of the rationale for area studies. At the same time,

Reprinted with permission from *Ford Foundation Report,* vol. 29, no. 1 (Winter). © 1998 by the Ford Foundation.

shrinking university resources have led to cuts in programs that fall outside mainstream academic disciplines.

By definition interdisciplinary, in practice expensive (requiring years of language training, field research, and specialized library collections), and at times perceived as esoteric, area studies has been particularly vulnerable in recent years. Critiques have been leveled from all directions: Area studies is a product of Cold-War security interests; it is merely descriptive; it is parochial and oblivious to changing global forces.

Perhaps the most interesting critiques have emerged within area studies itself. Many scholars have observed that "areas" of study in the American academy, such as "Africa" or "Latin America," have been generated through a combination of colonial cartography and European ideas of civilization. Debates about the definition of areas are not merely academic quibbles. On the contrary, reformulations of taken-for-granted geographies are key to contested contemporary claims about identity, culture, and territory. Scholars are now asking, "What are the processes through which civilizations, nations, communities, or 'areas' are defined, both historically and in the present? And defined by whom? How do we understand particular societies or cultures, with all the deep knowledge that requires—even as we examine the wider processes—from global capital flows to transnational labor markets—that affect us all?"

Such questions are among those being addressed in a new initiative of the Foundation's Education, Media, Arts, and Culture program. "Crossing Borders: Revitalizing Area Studies" represents a six-year, $25 million commitment that will work on two levels. First, Crossing Borders' grants will reaffirm the importance of in-depth study of particular languages, cultures, and histories, building on the first half-century of work in the field. Second, Crossing Borders will support innovative thinking and practices, through a variety of partnerships and border crossings: geographic, disciplinary, programmatic, institutional, international, and between the academy and the public. In this way, the Foundation hopes to stimulate a revitalized area studies while preserving its intellectual core—the study and analysis of language, history, and culture.

As a first step, the Foundation recently awarded grants of $50,000 each to 30 colleges and universities across the United States, from Maine to Hawaii.

The grantees are among more than 200 institutions that responded to a widely distributed request for proposals sent out by the Foundation last year. The responses were extraordinarily diverse.

Duke University, for example, has focused its program on supplementing the continentally based framework of area studies with a different overlay: one in which the earth's major seas and their shorelines are shifted to the center of vision. Although maritime basins have long been sites of intercontinental trade and travel, seas and waterways have been relegated to the margins of the American academic imagination. When seen at all, these blank blue spaces appear as boundaries, or even barriers, between the territorial blocks where human interaction has been supposedly centered. Historically, however, the world's major seas have done as much to facilitate as to obstruct communication, and maritime basins have witnessed the formation of dynamic communities. Whether in the enclosed Mediterranean or across the vast reaches of the Pacific Ocean, societies on opposite sides of major bodies of water have profoundly affected each other's history for centuries.

Over a 15-month period, Duke's project, "Oceans Connect: Culture, Capital and Commodity Flows Across Basins," will give faculty and students opportunities to focus on transoceanic exchanges across the world's four major seas: the Atlantic, Pacific, and Indian oceans, and the Mediterranean–Black Sea corridor. The university will also create forums where scholars of every world area can debate issues involved in integrating oceanic and continental perspectives. These and other activities will culminate in an international symposium and a book, both of which will help launch a wider discussion in the area studies community about this alternative approach.

The theme of interconnections rather than fixed identities underlies many Crossing Borders projects. Like Duke, the University of Iowa is also working on transoceanic relations in two projects that link Africa and South Asia. "Diaspora and Exchange across the Indian Ocean" involves a faculty-student study group that is exploring the social, artistic, ritual, and economic aspects of exchanges between western India and coastal East Africa over the last 500 years. A second study group, "Indian Films and Filmmakers Beyond the Subcontinent," is examining the dynamics of the world-wide supply and demand for Hindi films, especially in African cities. Such work will require a rethinking of graduate student training as well. One student's research has uncovered a vast penetration of Hindu imagery into ritual practices of the Vodun peoples of coastal East Africa. Although her disciplinary focus is African art history, she is also studying Indian religion and will spend several months in India. A fellow graduate student—researching South Asian immigration and identity in Dar es Salaam, Tanzania—is taking his exams in Indian as well as African history, has traveled in India and Tanzania, and is studying Hindi along with advanced Swahili.

A different approach is being tried by the University of Virginia. There, faculty are developing seminars on such themes as transnational kinship (including cross-border marriage markets, international adoption, and diasporic families) and transnational economic and environmental relations. In an even more experimental mode, graduate students in anthropology are being recruited from the United States and abroad to participate in linked, multisite research projects. One student's study of Indonesia's "green revolution," for example, may be enhanced by another student's research on efforts to spread Western scientific agriculture.

Of the 30 grantees, several chose to focus on particular geographic borders. The University of Texas, El Paso, for example, is implementing an oral history project to explore the 20th-century experiences of several generations of Mexicans on both sides of the U.S.-Mexico border. Others are bringing ethnic and area studies programs together under the umbrella of "diaspora." California State University, Dominguez Hills, is focusing on West African, Mexican, and East Asian diasporas in Southern California. California State University, Los Angeles, is developing a program that will link Asian and Asian-American studies, asking how "homeland" histories and cultures are transformed in Asian America, and how Asian America, in turn, has affected the "homeland."

Among the unusual border crossings represented in this group of grants are those that go beyond the walls of the academy. Hunter College of the City College of New York is developing a Latin America area studies curriculum that includes placing students in internships in human rights organizations. Northern Arizona University is establishing a consortium to promote exchanges among scholars of indigenous studies in New Zealand, Australia, the United States, Canada, and Mexico. And Hamline University in Minnesota has joined with KCTA-TV Public Television and the *Star Tribune Newspaper of the Twin Cities* to formalize an international collaborative that is intended to create links between area studies scholarship and the media.

Ultimately, the revitalization of area studies will depend on the development of worldwide scholarly communities in which there is a far more equal exchange of ideas, perspectives, and fundamental questions than has occurred in the past. Although the field emerged in the United States, it can no longer retain its predominantly U.S. point of departure. To some extent, these goals are a concern of all Crossing Borders' grantees. New York University, for example, is attempting to redefine the field of Middle Eastern studies by involving scholars from the region; the University of Wisconsin (Madison) is building a worldwide network of scholars to investigate "Legacies of Authoritarianism: Cultural Production, Collective Trauma, and Global Justice." A different kind of collaboration is entailed in a University of Hawaii project on the Pacific island of Palau. Scholars from the island, several Asian nations, and the United States are developing a research and teaching program that will study the massive influx of foreign tourists and guest workers to the island, as a way of exploring the intersection of local and global forces in a specific, small place.

International collaborations, nevertheless, are hard to organize and sustain. As one step in addressing that challenge, the Foundation has established the Worldwide Fund for Area Studies. The fund will complement the grant making described above by supporting international collaborations through grants made jointly to academic institutions in the United States and overseas. The Foundation hopes that the impetus for such collaborations will originate largely overseas, so that the historical imbalance—whereby scholars in the West studied the "rest"—may truly begin to shift. Without that change, revitalization of area studies will inevitably be limited.

The Future of International Research

Kenneth Prewitt

In preparing this essay, the readers I have in mind are social scientists and humanists based in American research universities. Three arguments are advanced: the major intellectual issues facing social science scholarship are international and transnational; to address those issues is not the task of a single research community, not even one as robust and sophisticated as that of the US; if the US-based academic community is to play its appropriate role in an international research effort it has to improve its understanding of the constraints under which scholarship elsewhere operates. We start with a quick and superficial tour of a few key substantive questions that face the disciplines.

What We Will Study

Historians

In the coming half-century is social change on a scale and at a pace that is radically transforming? That is, are we "continuists," seeing the present and near-term future as incremental change, as development-by-accumulation, of a piece with the past and consequently implying only gradual modifications of practice

Reprinted with permission from the "President's Report" of the *Social Science Research Council Biennial Report, 1996–98*. © 1998 by the Social Science Research Council.

and beliefs? Or are we "discontinuists," viewing this half-century as one of radical transformation? To borrow from paleontology, is this a moment of punctuated equilibriums—a burst of speciation of new social forms, political alignments, cultural beliefs?

Many view the end of the Cold War, the emergence of a more globally interlocked economy and especially, the enormous changes that new information technologies will allow, as radically transforming. It is asserted that social change is on a scale with the agricultural revolution that carried human beings beyond hunting, gathering and herding to entirely new forms of economic, political and military organization, and with the industrial revolution that exchanged animal for fossil fuel energy and introduced labor technologies that greatly extended musclepower.

If, in fact, the information technologies and the knowledge society do constitute a moment of historical disequilibrium, the ramifications extend far beyond economic matters. Transformations on a scale indicated by the phrase "agricultural revolution" or "industrial revolution" were not only or even primarily about new forms of economic organization. They reordered the division of power on the planet, in the first instance placing the fertile crescent at the center of world history and in the second moving the power center from the Mediterranean to northern Europe and then to the eastern seaboard of the United States. These power shifts were not peaceful, not simple, not controllable.

Even more far-reaching, the revolution that gave humans control over their food supply and then the revolution that transformed the power of mechanical production both penetrated deeply into culture, religion, learning and every aspect of the organization of society. For the discontinuists, the "information revolution" is similarly far-reaching.

The intellectual exchange between the "continuists" and the "discontinuists," much of it carried out in the popular media, cannot be ignored by academic constituencies. And it is in the very nature of the question that it must be framed historically but also internationally. It clearly follows that it will be engaged by scholars whose methodologies and theories, and natural inclinations, lead them beyond the boundaries of the United States. Historians content to dig deeper and deeper into the US economy, political practices and social structure are not wrong to do so—and they will continue to instruct us about our own history. But they will be cut off from the bigger discussion—What kind of world historical moment are we experiencing?—where the "we" number not 270 million but 6 billion and growing.

If the historians have the most encompassing question, we do not conclude that the less encompassing questions facing political science, sociology, anthropology or economics are therefore trivial.

Political Scientists

It is easy to celebrate the triumph of democracy in these closing years of the 20th century—southern Europe in the 1970s, then eastern Europe; still alive in India and Pakistan, gathering momentum in Latin America where Chile and Argentina have been especially successful in setting aside military dictatorships; and hesitant starts across Africa capped by the extraordinary achievement—cross your fingers—of South Africa. But this celebration may be premature.

Democracy is not the absence of demagogues; it is only that the constituencies are small and marginal. There are always "men of destiny" eager to expand those constituencies—a xenophobic right in France and Germany; an Islamic fundamentalism not just in Iran and Algeria but also in Turkey and Morocco; military leaders in power or in the wings across Africa. And we remain deeply uncertain about whether democracy is a likely or even possible outcome in China, its liberalizing economy notwithstanding, or what is in store for central Asia or even Russia.

What social conditions give rise to the return of authoritarian rule? Disorder, uncertainty, anxiety, crime—change that comes too fast, too unpredictably, and leaves large parts of the population without familiar guidelines or anchor points. If we are in a period of "punctuated equilibrium," the security and stability that allow liberal democracy to flourish may be hard to find and harder to sustain. A political science that came of age with liberal constitutional democracy as its project has its work cut out.

And for those political scientists whose arena is security, an old order crumbles and a new one is not yet in sight. The nuclear genie has not been put back in the bottle; if mutual deterrence was the cold war issue, it has now been replaced by proliferation—how many Iraqs are in our future. The well informed speak quietly but anxiously about chemical and biological warfare. In dozens of hot spots around the world, the forces of fragmentation driven by the politics of identity are eager to convert "nations" into "states." These are not likely to be peaceful processes. Should an international community (read that as the big powers) intervene to stop the ethnic strife and even ethnic cleansing that accompanies the drive for nationally homogeneous states? The drive for independence is not the only factor altering the security scene. Few now doubt that environmental and population issues belong on the security agenda. What patterns of violence should we expect as 10 billion people rearrange themselves across the world's surface to get their share of our currently mismanaged eco-systems and energy sources?

For political science, as for history, it is the internationally focused scholars who will be taking on these big questions. Departments that choose to add another rational choice theorist to tease out the next layer of truth in legislative coalition-building, in the process rejecting the area or comparative scholar, will be unlikely to engage these questions in their graduate instruction and research programs.

I more briefly touch upon economics, anthropology, psychology, sociology —and, with apologies, skip altogether geography, demography, law and education. I do not skip these fields because they would reveal a different pattern, but space limitations keep us close to the core social science disciplines.

Economists

There is the broad challenge of deciphering the likely shape and momentum of, cliché notwithstanding, the global economy. There are the already familiar front-page stories: free trade vs. protectionism, the externalities of resource exploitation and energy use, the potential vulnerability of national economies faced with unpredictable movement of finance capital.

As if these issues were not challenge enough for economists, there is the more encompassing question of whether those countries that captured the benefits of the industrial revolution will reproduce their success in the new global economy. Or will those—China or India, for example—that fell behind the last time around now force their way in and perhaps even displace the Atlantic hegemony? That is, will the rich stay rich and the poor stay poor, or will a new economic rank-order emerge in the next half-century? Closely associated is the issue of how much inequality of living standards among nations and within nations is either morally or politically tolerable. A billion people will go to bed hungry tonight. Another billion are living at the margins. Nothing in the new economic order seems likely to reverse this in the near term; it is possible that the two billion will grow not only absolutely but proportionately. About such issues we can only state the obvious. We need economists who are digging into China's economic dynamic, who are asking whether Africa can connect with the global economy and who are turning their powerful econometric tools to the implications of economic inequalities which, if not new, are newly transparent to the worldwide CNN watchers.

Sociologists

The world continues to debate the optimum population size for human habitation on this planet, a debate framed as the carrying capacity of the natural resource system. The technological optimists hold that the pie can continue to expand, suggesting that agronomy will be the wonder-science of the next quarter-century, displacing biology from its favored perch even as biology displaced physics. The pessimists hold that the ecosystem is too fragile to sustain a world population twice what it is today, at least if we assume that an increasing proportion of that population will enjoy the caloric intake now limited to the better-off half of the world's population.

Between these two camps is what one scientist, Joel Cohen, has called the "better manners" school—the belief that we can and should improve the terms under which people interact. If we were successful at doing this, there is ample food supply. The "terms under which people interact," of course, encode all the big sociological questions—how to organize production and distribution, how to allocate across generations, how to balance equity and efficiency, how to plan for not only a larger but a differently structured population.

Sociology, with its sister discipline demography, is at the intersection between, on the one hand, environmental constraints, and on the other, human choices both individual and collective. What organizational forms those choices take has as much to do with answering the "carrying capacity" question as does the gene revolution and new agronomic technologies.

Again and obviously, the sociological question can only be posed internationally and interactively. That is, it is not what one country will do or what each country will do independently. It is about human choices and social organizations that are responsive to what others are doing. Iterative game theory never had a bigger challenge.

Psychologists

There are issues aplenty, not least of which is the renewed interest in "nature vs. nurture" as the implication of the scientific revolution in genetics and biochemistry moves into public policy debates. That these debates are still largely confined to Europe and the United States—the home of bioethics—is true, but only temporarily so. The stakes are too high to expect the issues to remain geographically confined. Are we certain that the world is finished with eugenics? Perhaps it is in liberal democracies, with their traditions of minority rights and open debates. We are less confident when we move to political regimes motivated by ethnic hatred and claims to national superiority.

This issue does not begin to exhaust the questions about which we need a better and bigger psychology. The "Protestant ethic" in its many formulations has been a useful social-psychological master-concept in the effort to make sense of the last century of Euro-American social and economic development. Is there buried in the debate about "Asian values" the functional equivalent for the next phase of economic development? If so, will the entrepreneurial energy to steer the next surge of global economic growth emerge from Asia; or, more unexpectedly, out of the flexibility and resilience of African cultures?

Where will we get the theories and empirical methodologies to think hard about identities? How confident are we that "traditions" from which we get our social "identities" are invented? Is essentialism on the run? Are constructed and imagined identities destined to be multiple, fragmented and strategic? Some have reached these conclusions; other scholars are skeptical. This is vast terrain for social psychology, and it is terrain that is necessarily both international and non-national.

Anthropologists

Anthropology has long been our most international discipline, nurtured in the need to know the exotic other. The exotic other is fast disappearing, and remote groups are at any rate no longer the primary target of anthropology.

What, then, is the anthropological project? Perhaps to help us understand multiculturalism and how to make it work. And this is hardly a project of interest only in this country. Everywhere groups with different diets and dress and beliefs and practices are crammed together, often in very small spaces indeed. With rare exceptions, cities increase in cultural diversity as they increase in size. Certainly you can get a Big Mac anywhere, but so also can you get raw fish, curry, grape leaves and refried beans.

If the issue of multiculturalism must be confronted, so too must the tough ethical question it encodes. Are there moral absolutes, or is it relativity all the way down? Anthropology might want to make an alliance with moral philosophy before drawing firm conclusions on this one. The question of moral absolutes won't go away. John Paul II has planted this seed deep in the soil of official Catholicism. So also have the ayatollahs and the TV evangelists of the Protestant right. Secularists also, especially the international human rights community and the earth-first edge of the environmental movement, are willing to force the issue of moral absolutes.

The complexities of pluralism and its contestants—universalism and relativism—cannot be sorted out by just one country, at least not successfully. It is the moral and cultural question for the world at large.

The intellectual agenda is moving rapidly, and it may be moving out from under us. Why so? Because we are caught up in backward-looking debates about area studies vs. disciplines, about local knowledge vs. abstract theory. I do not mean to make light of these debates. Who gets tenure does make a difference to how well our research universities are positioned to answer the range of questions outlined above. Obviously and thankfully, the questions are being studied, but too much of our scarce intellectual energy is being siphoned away. At just the wrong moment, we risk being preoccupied with local turf battles.

This is not to say that there are not major organizational issues before us. But they have less to do with our immediate, local academic setting than they do with how the US-based scholar will work with academic communities in other parts of the world.

Who Will Investigate the Major International Questions

The array of questions noted above cannot be addressed from the vantage point of any single intellectual community, even one as well-equipped as that in the United States. In the first place, there is the sheer scope and complexity of the questions, and their multiple ramifications in endlessly different settings around the world. The subtlety of how these issues play out in different cultures with their different historical trajectories, speaking different languages, eating different foods and praying to different gods, presents enormous challenges to scholarship. The undertaking is too vast for one country's scholars.

There is a second reason why the research cannot come from the US alone. The public policy issues embedded in the issues raised above will be dealt with in international forums—the World Trade Organization, multilateral banks, UN agencies, treaties and conventions, international nongovernmental organizations —but also and primarily by national and local actors everywhere.

To the extent that the social sciences and humanities have an intelligence relevant to sorting out these challenges, the evidence and interpretations will have to come from a variety of perspectives. For practical policy reasons, knowledge will have to be internationally generated and internationally owned. Consider, for example, the Kyoto climate change agreements on emission controls, introducing tradable permits. A tradable permit regime will not work as policy unless its design and implementation involves economists from Brazil, Nigeria, India, Indonesia, China and more, and not just from the US and Europe.

The examples multiply endlessly, and refer not simply to public policy issues. Whatever intellectual headway is to be made on the questions noted, it will emerge from theories, methods and approaches of historians and social scientists working out of the different settings around the world, a truly international scholarly community.

This cliché falls from the lips all too easily—and we rush off to form international networks, to create university-to-university partnerships, to recruit foreign students to our graduate programs and to send our students abroad, to offer visiting faculty positions to distinguished scholars from overseas, to increase our library holdings of scholarship produced elsewhere and, at least rhetorically, to argue the Internet as the underpinning of new forms of international collaboration. I don't make light of such efforts. The Social Science Research Council is seriously engaged in this range of enterprises, and our new international program focuses on the conditions that will build intellectual linkages internationally.

In such efforts, however, I note a number of missed opportunities, failed efforts, false starts, misunderstandings—and increasingly have come to see these as resulting from an inadequate understanding of what is "out there" and "over there" in the social sciences and humanities.

Scholarship Abroad

What follows is again a quick and superficial tour. It is information familiar to scholars who have worked abroad, but less familiar, I have discovered, even to university administrators charged with "internationalizing" their campuses, let alone to the vast social science and humanistic scholarly enterprise that takes the American experience to be the starting point, and end point, of systematic investigation.

Africa
I start with Africa because it is the continent I know best, and because it illustrates many of the conditions that appear elsewhere as well. A simplified characterization of the working conditions for African-based social science includes: heavily crowded universities, nearly nonexistent library resources, low salaries and therefore the search for multiple sources of income, government hostility toward critical scholarship, infrequent opportunities to cooperate regionally let alone internationally and the ever-present temptation, for the better scholars, to migrate to Europe, North America or the international agencies.

National budgets do not include research funds for social science infrastructure or basic research. Peer-reviewed grant competitions seldom occur, though South Africa is beginning to put them in place. Research funds, then, come most often from international donors, and it is their agenda that drives research priorities. This agenda is largely project-focused, where the African scholar collects data within a framework set in New York, Stockholm or Paris.

Efforts to compensate for these working conditions include the emergence of regional networks which function in Africa less to accelerate information flows (which is how we use them) than to compensate for a weak, thin institutional infrastructure. This gives rise to the worry that innovative networks in Africa might inadvertently further undermine an already weakened university base. Consultancies are, as often as not, the venue for research, and the result is more likely the report to the World Bank or the US foundation than it is an article in a disciplinary journal. Research is instrumental to short-term policy issues.

The internal market for research is largely limited to economists, and then primarily the macro-economists. Micro-economics, and its methodological spin-offs such as game theory and rational choice, is generally absent. In only rare instances is there a commercial market for social science research, though in this South Africa is an exception. Whether economic privatization will create a broader market for research remains to be seen.

Substantively, notwithstanding the pressures to short-term project research just noted, important shifts are taking place. Political economy themes are pursued, especially economic reform under structural adjustment programs, democratization and civil society. Social class is a less central concept than it was only a decade ago, having been replaced, as elsewhere in the world, with attention to identities. Although the colonial legacy remains an issue, it is now sharing space with greater focus on indigenous sources of development, or non-development as the case may be. Bridges linking social and natural sciences are nearly nonexistent, limited work in biodiversity, agronomy and health care being the exception.

African scholars read the international literature in both English and French, though ties between Anglophones and Francophones on the continent are limited. African scholars complain, with cause, that if they publish in local journals their writings are ignored by the international community. The Internet is spottily available, though this is an arena getting the attention of international donors.

With respect to international linkages, African scholars express concern that their links are largely limited to scholars from abroad who study Africa. What they want is not more contact with the American or European or Japanese area study tradition, but more contact with scholars—wherever located—who work on the questions that concern them, be they issues of constitutionalism or ethnic conflict or health system reform.

Former Soviet Union/Eastern Europe

In turning to the Former Soviet Union and Eastern Europe, we see a pattern that in some respects replicates Africa's but with important distinctions.

What most separates social science in the FSU and Eastern Europe from elsewhere is the need to discard and then replace a half-century of scholarship dominated by the official Marxist-Leninist line, a task in which Eastern Europe has a slight head start and where there was, in any event, a more developed counterrhetoric to the central tenets of the orthodoxy. Still, the detoxification project will require energy and effort for at least another generation. Not all who are engaged in this effort welcome the involvement of outsiders, however well-intentioned.

The intellectual content of the social sciences reflects on the one hand an eagerness to raise formerly forbidden or politically sensitive topics, and on the other an agenda that remains close to what the state might need to continue the transition to a market economy and to democracy. That the latter questions are of special interest to international donors, who are funding not just projects but wholesale institutional transformations including new universities and research centers, only complicates the role of independent scholarship.

Structurally, a tug of war is taking place between the scientific institutes of the academies, which are trying to hold onto their research monopolies, and the emerging social science departments in national universities. One outcome is more partnerships between the academies and the universities. Thrown into this mix are the newest type of institutions, those created by foreign assistance—the Central European University, with its bases in Budapest, Warsaw and Prague; the Open University of St. Petersburg; the Higher School of Economics in Moscow. Whether such institutional innovations will survive the eventual withdrawal of external funds is doubted by many close observers of higher education in that part of the world.

There are important differences between the FSU and Eastern Europe, not least in their willingness to embrace the West and its scholarship. The Eastern European social sciences, more literate in English and with access to financial support from the European community, are finding integration both culturally and financially easier. Russian scholars, less fluent in Western languages, are also more suspicious.

Our colleagues in this part of the world, as in Africa, face very low salaries and difficult working conditions, driving them to seek multiple income streams— including consultancies, more than one teaching post and, as available, private sector employment. It is not unusual to find a sociologist in Moscow or an economist in Warsaw with four or five different business cards, to be deployed as conditions warrant. Perhaps the best comparison in the US is to the floating adjunct professor, a point to bear in mind as one speaks easily of forming partnerships with the social sciences in the FSU and Eastern Europe.

East Asia

Employment conditions are far better in East Asia, where the best universities compare with the top institutions in the US and Europe and where intellectuals are venerated as part of the elite class. We are tempted to see professional social science in that part of the world as highly similar to the US variety. But these are countries in which the rewards go to seniority more than talent, in which theoretical creativity and methodological innovation are seldom applauded and in which structures remain, by our standards, fixed and rigid.

Keep in mind as well that English fluency is limited, and that there is sharp stratification between the few, English-speaking, international circuit colleagues and those who work only in local languages. The foreign-educated scholars, with whom we comfortably interact, are a distinct minority when viewed from within Korea, Japan or China. Frequently they are not trusted by their colleagues, who are suspicious of an American or European intellectual hegemony being imported by the foreign-trained.

The East Asian scholar is more likely to consider pathbreaking work as that which falls into the arena of what we call applied research. East Asian social scientists benefit from government funds; science budgets include the social sciences. Moreover, the boundaries between the academy and government, or the academy and private enterprise, are easily crossed. Business and management studies are more central to social science than they are in the US.

In important ways, of course, China differs from its East Asian neighbors. There research remains close to what is ideologically acceptable, even though research funding is not as heavily dependent on government sources as it was before liberalization.

One very large trend underway in East Asia is the growth of privately provided educational services. This phenomenon is not restricted to East Asia; it is occurring even in poorer countries of Africa, across Latin America and elsewhere in Asia. But it is unusually pronounced in East Asia, where it is often commercialized. Open universities now enroll as many as a half-million students. The implications are difficult to sort out, but one possibility—in East Asia and elsewhere—is the progressive separation of research and teaching, with far-reaching consequences for social science training.

Latin America

After Europe and Canada, Latin America is, for US scholars, the best-known world region. Many of us have interacted with Latin American scholars, and found them engaged in projects that we easily recognize on theoretical, methodological, substantive grounds. But we should be careful not to overgeneralize from our interactions with the small subset of the research community that enjoys access to funds, information technologies, library resources, good students and opportunities to travel—especially to the US. These are colleagues who are located in a handful of elite universities, or in one of the rapidly diminishing number of independent academic centers and/or the networks affiliated with FLACSO.

Public universities are poorly funded, burdened with huge enrollments and overly bureaucratic; they are not congenial homes for productive research careers. The expanding ranks of the private universities have not incorporated a research culture. The independent academic centers—the traditional location of quality research—are in precarious shape. Perhaps as many as half are closing their doors as a result of fiscal constraints or the shifting priorities of the international donor community, where interest in Latin America is waning. Funds that are available are, as in Africa, often project-specific evaluation studies closely linked to current policy questions. Private sector research is narrow: market research, political polling and economic consultancies.

Despite these less than optimal working conditions, there are many well-trained and theoretically sophisticated research scholars in Latin America, many of whom work on issues similar to those that occupy our scholars—economic development and inequality; democratization and increasingly the operation of democratic institutions; collective identities and the articulation of citizenship demands through ethnic, gender and racial groups. An earlier interest in revolutionary movements and counterinsurgency is losing favor, replaced in part by a revival of interest in regional integration. Dependency theory has waned, and there is now increased attention to the global economy and Latin America's place in it. Postmodern approaches to cultural studies are popular.

There has been a notable increase in academic freedom in recent years, especially in countries that have discarded military rule—Chile, Paraguay, Guatemala and El Salvador. This favorable development has not, however, resulted in any large-scale return of highly qualified researchers who fled to international organizations or to North American and European universities.

South/Southeast Asia

Here are repeated many of the trends already noted: low salaries and heavy teaching duties, leading to multiple employment; shrinking employment market in the academy, though expanding in the NGO sector and even, for some specialties, in the commercial sector. Research funds are more often project funds from external donors than peer-reviewed grant competitions, and many external donors prefer to fund research by NGOs rather than by university-based scholars. Because university teaching posts are generally civil service positions, there is not much opportunity for career mobility as we know it. Promotion based on research output is rare.

Intellectual themes are undergoing major shifts, as an earlier concern with issues of national development and national integration is now less about social cohesion than it is about social conflict. As in many other parts of the world, social class has given way to social identity as the favored way to frame investigation of social conflict.

There are strong academic communities across South and Southeast Asia, but complications of multiple languages tend to reduce comparative work, even across the region. The flow of scholarly communication is more dense within than across national borders, and often includes the professional class more generally—that is, public intellectuals, government officials, civil servants and NGO leaders. There is more electronic connectivity than one finds in Africa or the FSU, but English fluency limits the number of South and Southeast Asian social scientists who operate internationally. As elsewhere, there is resentment that they are read, if at all, only if their work is translated into English.

Middle East

Many issues already touched upon apply to the Middle East—especially regarding working conditions, limited and project-focused research funds, and few venues for regional or international cooperation. And there is one significant additional factor. In probably no other part of the world does simply being a social scientist carry such political weight. To be a social scientist is to declare oneself a modernist, often a secularist. Issues of intellectual autonomy are prominent in ways hard to imagine in our secular, liberal tradition. To take an unpopular intellectual stand is to take a political stand, and the consequences can be far more severe than loss of research funds or even one's university post.

Conclusion

Across Africa, Asia, the FSU and Eastern Europe, Latin America and the Middle East, new forms of collaboration and colleagueship are required. And they cannot only be with those overseas colleagues we have trained, and thus who look, think and write the way we taught them to. Our challenge is not to conduct joint research with our ex-graduate students (or the functional equivalents thereof), but the much more difficult one of establishing a working relationship with scholars who, for instance:

- inhabit higher education institutions that do not reward research output, and find such rewards as do exist among external donor agencies rather than professional communities.

- have as their "peer group" not professional colleagues, but rather the American foundation officer or the Scandinavian aid official.

- view NGOs as important career opportunities, not as data points for theorizing about civil society.

- learn to write their research results in English so they can publish in the prestige journals but know they thereby risk cutting themselves adrift from their local research cultures.

- fear, when they differ with political authorities, not misunderstanding or indifference but imprisonment or exile.

- have to decide, year in and year out, whether to stick it out in working conditions indifferent to if not destructive of a productive research career, or to pack it in and become another brain drain statistic.

- would think they were on sabbatical if they had our teaching loads.

The research agenda is large, complex and, above all, international. It cannot be advanced based on work that is exclusively conceptualized by any single nation's scholars. Knowledge either will be internationally generated or it will fall short of the intellectual and policy reach that is needed. To generate knowledge internationally requires the institutional engineering that will establish an internationally viable research community. Those who wish to engage this task will want to become familiar with how scholarly conditions vary from one part of the world to another.

The American-based social science does have a strong internationally oriented component—anchored in area studies and comparative research—but the task suggested in this essay is one that should involve a much broader disciplinary base.

Educating for Global Competence

American Council on Education

Higher Education's Role in Developing Human Resources

The challenges of global transformation in national security, foreign policy, competitiveness, the environment, public health, population control, and the eradication of want and misery resulting from famine, natural disasters, or population dislocations call for many more U.S. citizens with in-depth expertise and knowledge of other nations, including their languages, cultures, and political, economic, and social systems.

The human resource implications of this transformed world have begun to surface throughout the public and private sectors:

- American diplomacy and national security depend on access to scholars with advanced training in the languages and cultures of the world. When crises erupt, it is too late to create the expertise that could have forestalled or better managed them. A 1995 survey of foreign language needs at 33 federal agencies concludes that the agencies have more than 34,000 positions that require foreign language proficiency, including more than 20,000 positions in the defense and intelligence community.

Reprinted with permission from the American Council on Education report *Educating for Global Competence*, Chapters 2 and 3. © 1997 by American Council on Education, Commission on International Education.

- Corporations also require global competence to manage production and markets. According to a recent survey, 86 percent of corporations report that they will need managers and employees with greater international knowledge in the decade ahead.[1]

- States and localities are new players in the international arena. Since 1985, most states and many cities have conducted trade missions to foreign countries; several have established permanent offices overseas.

These developments and others point to the need for sustained attention to the human resource requirements of the global village. For reasons of both statecraft and commerce, the United States needs many more people who have much more knowledge in many more disciplines about the international challenges of the new century.

If such knowledge and people are to be found, the nation's institutions of higher education must produce them. The nation's campuses are uniquely positioned to respond to urgent national needs by:

- developing the global literacy of their graduates through the international dimensions of the curriculum;

- creating community outreach programs to help explain global developments to the American people;

- developing experts and leaders through graduate programs;

- conducting research on global issues, world areas, and international business;

- providing first-rate foreign language instruction and research;

- supporting international exchanges of students and faculty; and

- conducting the research that contributes to global well-being and the development of poor nations.

In each of these areas and others, the United States can draw on the world-class resources of its college and university campuses.

A Global Curriculum

By adding international dimensions to their curricula and international experts to their faculties, the nation's colleges and universities have become a major resource for preparing the people of the United States for the global challenges confronting them.

Thematic, multidisciplinary programs, such as environmental studies or conflict resolution, are infusing international dimensions into traditional disciplines. A growing number of universities have established international business programs that require knowledge about the culture and fluency in the language of a particular country or region. In the past few years, several institutions have expanded such programs to engineering and other fields.

Graduates who can function effectively in a global environment can provide direct benefits to businesses, helping them access emerging international markets, supporting the export efforts of small and mid-size companies that have become the greatest source of new jobs in America.

International courses, language training, and experiences in other countries are also vital to teacher training. Teachers with such expertise will better understand the world and the role of the United States in international affairs.

New emphases on the international dimensions of curricula support higher education's public service function, enabling better outreach to primary and secondary schools, the community, the media, and government. In times of diplomatic or military crisis, the media search for academic experts to interpret events as they develop and to explain their significance to an anxious public. During the Persian Gulf War, for example, American universities supported extensive efforts to interpret and explain events to both government personnel and members of the public. One university conducted a workshop for its state's National Guard and made more than 100 presentations to the media. Another institution organized briefings on the complex interplay of culture, politics, and national rivalries in the Middle East for the Federal Bureau of Investigation and the Immigration and Naturalization Service.[2]

Producing Experts and Leaders

Highly specialized graduate programs in the languages and cultures of specific world areas create and maintain the expertise and research base required to support day-to-day American diplomacy and the development of defense and foreign policies in a changing world. University centers in foreign languages, area studies, international studies, and international business and university schools of international affairs are the primary sources of foreign language– and area-trained staff for government agencies, including the Department of Defense, the Department of State, the Central Intelligence Agency, the U.S. Agency for International Development, and the U.S. Information Agency. Graduates of these programs also assume leadership positions in education, journalism and broadcasting, the corporate world, and the non-profit and philanthropic sectors.

These programs are the primary source of national expertise on non-European countries; sometimes they are the *only* source of such training and research. They maintain national expertise in such little-known languages as Tajik, Uzbek, and Kazakh, and in such countries as Uzbekistan and Kazakhstan (a newly independent republic, which is now a global nuclear power). However, recent studies estimate that the number of experts in the pipeline today is not sufficient to replace expected retirements in this decade.[3]

Foreign Language Instruction and Research

The nation's campuses are our national resource for teaching languages of all kinds and for research on language development, teaching methods, and the interrelationships between and among language and culture. Mastery of a second language and cultural sensitivity are crucial for diplomacy, for international business, and in fields as diverse as engineering and medicine.

In Europe, most young people speak a second language (usually English), and many are fluent in a third as well. Although English is the language of commerce around the globe, fluency in a host nation's language is helpful not only in negotiations, but also as a gateway to the culture.

Besides producing language experts, the United States must produce scientists and researchers with language skills that will enable them to collaborate with colleagues in other countries to solve global health, environmental, and other problems. Some colleges and universities have introduced special programs to help students continue their language studies through majors in engineering, business, and other disciplines.

Because it is difficult to predict far in advance what national needs for foreign language expertise will be, the capability for teaching and research in all languages is a significant national resource. The United States must preserve and improve it at the national level, not permitting its erosion in the face of budget pressures.

Exchange Programs

International exchange programs, whether for undergraduates, graduate students, or faculty members, provide Americans with first-hand experience in foreign cultures that often is essential to gaining international competence. They provide foreign students and scholars with a new appreciation of U.S. values and the American way of life.

The personal relationships that develop in such programs contribute to a web of interconnectedness and trust that links our country with the rest of the world. Because exchange programs involve so many people who become leaders in their own countries, they are among our most effective tools for advancing our national interests in foreign affairs.

Exchange programs range from short-term seminars abroad to longer-term study and research. Whatever their length, each provides a unique benefit. Even brief exposure to a different culture may stimulate a lifelong interest in events in that country and its region. A year-long study abroad program allows for immersion in the host country's culture and provides the opportunity to become fluent in its language and functional in its society. Long-term graduate student and faculty research projects and internships in companies abroad develop high-level expertise. They provide the opportunity for deeper understanding of the culture's values and systems and of how its people think and work.

Few diplomatic initiatives can point to the kind of sustained success that international exchange efforts such as the Fulbright program have been able to attain, relatively inexpensively, over the years. Too few Americans have such experiences abroad. Since 1985, study abroad consistently has involved less than 1 percent of total student enrollments. Three-quarters of Americans who study abroad do so for only one quarter, summer, or semester. Most study in England or

THE VALUE OF INTERNATIONAL
EDUCATIONAL EXCHANGE PROGRAMS

- Exchange programs have a multiplier effect for sponsoring governments. A U.S. General Accounting Office study notes that every federal dollar spent on exchange programs attracts $12 in private support.
- Faculty exchanges can directly advance American policy interests. Conferences and exchanges between U.S. academic institutions and the Supreme Court of Pakistan, for example, have helped effect the democratic expansion of the Pakistani judicial system.
- Exchange programs benefit the U.S. balance of trade. One-third of the world's 1.2 million international students study in the United States. Foreign students generated a nearly $7 billion dollar services trade surplus for the United States in 1993.
- Exchange programs support the domestic economy. According to the Department of Commerce, foreign enrollments make U.S. colleges and universities the nation's fifth largest exporter of services and create more than 100,000 American jobs.
- Most of the costs of foreign students in the United States are borne by students and their families. Only about 1 percent of foreign students in the United States receive primary funding from the U.S. government.
- While the majority of U.S. students abroad still go to Europe, the Institute for International Education reports a 15 percent increase in U.S. students in Africa, Asia, and Latin America in the 1990s.
- Since its inception in 1946, many of the more than 200,000 alumni of the Fulbright program have assumed leadership positions in academic, governmental, and private sector organizations throughout the world.
- Foreign Fulbright alumni have assumed important leadership positions in their nations. The president of Brazil and the prime minister, foreign minister, and minister of finance in Poland's new government are all former recipients of Fulbright scholarships who are now building democratic institutions and open, competitive economies.
- American Fulbright scholars contribute to U.S. foreign policy and human rights interests abroad. American Fulbright professors in Albania have established a successful journalism program at the University of Tirana, injecting the concept of freedom of the press into what had been until recently one of the world's most closed societies.

Western Europe. Unlike foreign students in the United States, the vast majority of American undergraduates abroad are not sufficiently fluent in the host country's language to study university-level subjects in that language. Opportunities for internships with foreign companies, among the most useful experiences for building an international career, are extremely limited.

The need for public and private investment in focused study or service abroad is great; the resources currently devoted are insufficient.

Research to Solve Global Problems

Higher education institutions play a key role in cooperative development by working with counterparts around the world to bring a variety of resources and skills to bear on development problems. Partnerships enable U.S. higher education institutions to strengthen their curricula and research, and to provide their students and faculty with opportunities to learn about the issues, systems, and cultures of developing countries. They also help the host nations' universities produce the leaders, officials, managers, scientists, and technicians required to create sustainable economic growth and stable societies.

The continued prosperity of the United States depends increasingly on how other nations manage population growth, improve industrial practice and land and energy use, gain access to international markets, and build stable democratic institutions that are able to advance and defend human rights. Global development in the post–Cold War era needs to be redefined as development cooperation rather than as foreign aid. Such implied mutuality suggests a flow of goods and information to solve common problems.

U.S. higher education institutions work with public and private institutions and organizations in developing countries to create interdisciplinary approaches to complex development problems, such as the environment, health, and agricultural productivity. American colleges and universities also work with corporations and with geneticists, biochemists, and molecular biologists in universities abroad on a range of technological, agricultural, and health issues. The benefits of these efforts help both the United States and the developing world.

The Stakeholders: An Agenda for Action

Higher education, government, and the private sector all have essential roles to play in responding to the need for international awareness. Government at all levels—federal, state, and local—and the private sector must work in partnership with the nation's colleges and universities to increase public awareness of the significance of global changes and to promote new ways of addressing them.

What Higher Education Should Do

Higher education cannot say that it has done all it can to produce globally competent graduates. Colleges and universities must, for example, find new ways to:

- infuse the curriculum with international perspectives and information;

HIGHER EDUCATION COOPERATION ADDRESSES DEVELOPMENT PROBLEMS

- African countries have reduced their dependence on food imports because of agriculturists and social scientists from American universities working with the United States Agency for International Development.
- Many community colleges have provided entrepreneurship training and assistance in the development of technical training programs and institutions in other countries.
- African studies faculty in the United States have worked with the corporate sector, the National Institutes of Health, and colleagues from several African universities on a series of tropical diseases that threaten our own country.
- American researchers used black bean germ plasm from Central America to develop hardy varieties that can be planted and harvested in the United States with fewer losses. American scientists at a major state university are examining newly discovered genetic material from Eastern Europe to see if its ability to diversify and strengthen fruits and vegetables can improve the state's important cherry industry. A parasitic wasp introduced into one U.S. state from Eastern Europe's Carpathian Mountains is helping keep that state's $100 million wheat crop free of cereal leaf beetle damage.

- encourage all students to study languages to a higher level of proficiency and to become knowledgeable about other cultures through study and internships abroad; and

- encourage and reward their faculty for becoming global thinkers in their teaching and research.

Presidential leadership and trustee support—in words and action—are essential if the international agenda of an institution is to be seen as a serious one. Like any institutional priority, internationalization requires the allocation of hard institutional resources to form a solid base, and the use of external funds to supplement and enrich that base. Partnerships with other institutions, community groups, and businesses are important ways to leverage an institution's own investment in international education.

What the Federal Government Should Do
Constitutionally, the federal government has the responsibility to ensure that the nation is prepared to respond to the challenges presented by its relationships with

KEY FEDERAL PROGRAMS
PROMOTE GLOBAL COMPETENCE

U.S. Department of Education
- The Department of Education supports international education through a number of efforts, most funded through Title VI of the Higher Education Act. These programs include: National Resource Centers, Foreign Language and Area Studies Centers, and Centers for International Business Education.
- The department also manages the Fulbright-Hays program, which underwrites the cost of faculty research and dissertation research abroad as well as group projects and seminars abroad for teachers and administrators.
- The department's Fund for the Improvement of Postsecondary Education supports innovative projects in higher education, including many in international studies and foreign languages.

United States Agency for International Development (USAID)
- USAID supports academic involvement in international development projects, training in the United States for technical and professional personnel from developing countries, and linkages with universities in developing nations.

United States Information Agency (USIA)
- USIA administers a variety of international exchange programs, including the Fulbright Program for scholarly, faculty, and student exchanges; the University Affiliations Program, which promotes partnerships between U.S. and foreign institutions of

other nations. National leaders must ensure that America's ability to exercise international leadership continues unimpaired into the next century.

The need for international expertise is growing. The federal government must maintain a stable leadership role in international education because of the clear relevance of global competence to critical national agendas in foreign policy, security, and the economy. To those ends, the federal government should support an international education leadership agenda that:

- adequately funds existing effective international education programs;

- ensures the funding of programs that respond to national needs but that are neither the priorities of individual states nor likely to be met by market forces (these would include programs in less commonly taught languages and educational exchanges);

higher education; the Citizen Exchange Program; and the International Visitors Program, which introduces international leaders to the United States.

Other Departments and Agencies

Many other federal departments and independent agencies also support essential international education activities.

- The Department of Defense supports the National Security Education Program (NSEP), which provides funds for undergraduate and graduate student study abroad in areas less commonly visited by U.S. students. NSEP also supports institutional efforts to develop new international programs.
- The Department of State funds a Russian, Eurasian, and East European Research and Training Program to develop national expertise in these areas.
- The National Endowment for the Humanities supports scholarly work in foreign languages and area studies, as well as the history and literature of many nations.
- The National Science Foundation's Division of International Programs encourages collaborative science and engineering research and education by supporting joint projects of U.S. organizations and institutions and their international counterparts.
- All of these federal efforts are essential. Such international education and exchange activities are not primarily a corporate responsibility, and states and local communities have no reason to support most of them. Universities alone cannot cover the cost of providing instruction in the vast array of foreign languages and area studies needed by the nation.

- uses federal funds efficiently to leverage matching funds from states, corporations, philanthropic organizations, and universities themselves;

- mobilizes the resources and cooperation necessary at all levels of education, government, and the private sector to address national needs for global competence;

- ensures that government agencies at all levels (federal, state, and local) have available the international expertise and knowledge (along with a comprehensive research base) required to respond to international challenges whenever they develop and wherever they occur; and

- recognizes and makes use of the rich international expertise available in our nation's colleges and universities.

What State and Local Governments Should Do

The social and economic well-being of states and communities is increasingly tied to international involvement. Regional interests, often defined by geographic proximity to other regions of the world; the ethnic makeup of communities, cities, and states; state and city relationships with counterparts in other countries; and trade interests abroad or foreign investment at home provide compelling reasons for states to support international education.

We urge state and local government officials and policymakers to:

- provide incentives to colleges and universities to internationalize their curricula and develop the next generation of globally competent teachers;

- collaborate with higher education institutions to produce state and local workforces that are capable of competing in global markets, competent in foreign languages, and aware of the dynamics of international issues;

- provide incentives for collaboration among higher education institutions and K–12 on foreign language instruction and internationalizing the curriculum;

- assess needs and develop appropriate strategies for building global competence, including collaborative activities among institutions of higher education, public and private agencies in the state (and local communities), and academic linkages with institutions abroad;

- call on local colleges and universities for information and expert advice on other cultures when establishing trade missions overseas; and

- support higher education international outreach programs to help the private sector develop emerging markets; help state and local economic development councils attract foreign investment; and improve public understanding of complex foreign policy and development issues through the press and broadcast media.

What Corporations Should Do

While a strength of the private sector in the United States is its emphasis on short-term results, the vast scope and speed of today's global changes also require long-term thinking and strategies. Working with colleges and universities to ensure a globally competent workforce is an important corporate investment.

Some companies in the United States and other countries already engage in such cooperation. For example, many corporations work with universities and community colleges to strengthen international business curricula, while faculty members often serve as consultants on overseas ventures. Other companies provide internship opportunities for U.S. students in their overseas branches, or for foreign students in the United States.

We urge corporate America to:

- partner with higher education institutions to increase public awareness of the growing necessity for global competence and intercultural sensitivity in the workplace;

CORPORATE/HIGHER EDUCATION/ GOVERNMENT PARTNERSHIPS PROMOTE INTERNATIONAL COMPETENCE

- The Coca-Cola Foundation, in cooperation with Michigan State University (MSU), has launched a new Global Fellows Program that will provide grants of up to $2,000 for short-term and up to $5,000 for semester-long study in one of 20 MSU study abroad programs in Africa, Asia, Europe, Latin America, and the Middle East. These scholarships will enable both secondary school foreign language teachers and U.S. university students to acquire international perspectives, promote cross-cultural understanding, and expand their intercultural and language skills.
- In Canada, the Celanese Corporation recently announced the Celanese Canada Internationalist Fellowships. Beginning in spring 1997, between 125 and 150 fellowships of $10,000 each will be awarded over the initial five years. The total value of the program is $1.5 million, and fellowship recipients may study anywhere in the world except Canada and the United States.
- The University of Hartford has hosted more than 30 Russian business entrepreneurs for six months to a year, offering them graduate-level business courses and internships with area companies. They are funded by the area companies.
- The United States–Mexico Chamber of Commerce funds the Buen Vecino Internship Program, under which 40 U.S. and Mexican companies, associations, and state trade agencies provide opportunities for students from the United States and Mexico with an overview of U.S.-Mexico business relations; knowledge about a specific industry by service as unpaid interns in corporate member offices; and exposure to another culture by living with a host family. In 1995 and 1996, 65 students from 15 universities participated in the program. (See web page at http://www. usmcoc.org/bvip.html)
- Sanyo Semiconductor provides support for study abroad for students at Ramapo College, sponsors student interns in the United States, and sponsors students on paid internships in Osaka, Japan, Hong Kong, Singapore, and Hamburg, Germany.
- Jaguar provides co-op placements for students at its corporate headquarters in New Jersey and at its world headquarters in Coventry, England.
- Citicorp funds five Fulbright foreign student grants from five different regions in the business, economic, or international relations sectors.
- In 1997, American, United, Delta, Mexicana, and Aeromexico airlines agreed to provide without cost all travel in both directions for Mexican Fulbright grantees. This program is valued at more than $100,000 a year.
- The Coca-Cola Foundation, partnering with the U.S. Fulbright Association, sponsors the annual J. William Fulbright Prize for International Understanding. The prize, worth $50,000, goes to individuals, groups, or organizations whose contributions "have made a substantial impact in breaking barriers which divide humankind." Coca-Cola also has sponsored Fulbright grantees in such countries as Venezuela and Germany.

- work with higher education institutions to design programs and curricula to address corporations' future employment demands for international competence;

- reaffirm the importance of international education as corporations hire employees who are internationally aware and provide incentives (such as promotions or training opportunities) for employees to expand their global competence;

- help higher education institutions meet the high costs of international training and research programs in business, science and technology, and the professions;

- provide incentives for students, faculty, administrators, and community leaders to participate in international exchange programs; and

- provide incentives for collaboration of higher education institutions and K–12 on curriculum and foreign language instruction.

The Time to Act

This is not the first time the nation's public and private sector leaders have been called on to improve the capacity of the American people and their institutions to meet the nation's international obligations. Nor will it be the last. Yet now is the time to act.

As the nation approaches a new century, all Americans can agree that we seek a more prosperous nation, a healthier and more livable planet, and a safer and freer world. Building such a future will require action from many people on many fronts.

Where America meets the world is where national needs confront international realities. On that frontier, international education is critical. Our higher education institutions are charged with developing a citizenry with the global competence, talent, and skill to create not simply a better and more prosperous America, but a better, safer, and more livable world.

NOTES

1. Coalition for the Advancement of International Studies, *Spanning the Gap: Toward a Better Business and Educational Partnership for International Competence.* Washington, D.C.: Coalition for the Advancement of International Studies, December, 1989, pp. 7–8. See also Clifford Adelman, "What Employers Expect of College Graduates: International Knowledge and Second Language Skills," Research Report, Office of Research and Improvement, U.S. Department of Education, July 1994; and T. K. Bikson and S. A. Law, *Global Preparedness and Human Resources, College and Corporate Perspectives.* Santa Monica, Calif.: RAND, 1994.

2. Coalition for International Education, Testimony on FY97 Appropriations for the Department of Labor, HHS, and Education, House Subcommittee on Labor, HHS and Education Appropriations, 14 May 1996, p. 4.

3. *Prospects for Faculty in Area Studies*, Stanford University, 1991.

6 International Resources

The final section of this book is a selected and partially annotated guide, compiled by Robert Goehlert and Anthony Stamatoplos, to the basic resources currently available, in print as well as on the World Wide Web, for students, faculty, and administrators interested in area studies programs and international studies. These resources range from bibliographies of books, articles, directories, research guides, and journals, to lists of U.S. and international Web sites. They cover such topics as area studies by world region, internationalization of the curriculum, foreign language instruction, global education for K–12, funding sources, and information on international careers.

Guide to Selected International Resources

Robert Goehlert and Anthony Stamatoplos

Introduction

The aim of this guide is to identify basic resources that will best serve the needs of students, faculty, and administrators involved in area studies programs and international education at American colleges and universities. There are five major sections in this guide, each following the same format, with print guides listed first, followed by sources on the World Wide Web. The Web sources are listed by site names and URL.

In the "Bibliography" section, there are three parts. These three parts provide additional references that can be used to supplement the readings in the corresponding Parts 2, 3, and 4 of this volume. Thus the first part of the bibliography focuses on issues in international higher education, the second on the accomplishments and challenges in international programs, and the last on international education and global studies in elementary and secondary schools. Each part of the bibliography includes books, articles, and ERIC documents.

The second section, "Guides to Area Studies," is a survey of the printed guides and Web sites that provide reference materials about area studies resources such as bibliographies, handbooks, guides, journals, etc.

This is a revised version of a bibliography prepared for the Title VI 40th Anniversary Conference, "International Education in American Colleges and Universities: Prospect and Retrospect," Washington, D.C., April 1998.

The third section, "Guides to Language Studies," surveys print guides and World Wide Web sites that are related to the study and teaching of foreign languages. Because the field of foreign language study is enormous, only major reference guides in print and on the Web are given. A number of guides include job and career information for language majors, guides to language learning and teaching, directories of foreign language service organizations, bibliographies on foreign language training and instructional materials, and guides to language associations.

The fourth section, "Guides to International Funding," lists guides to funding sources to support international and area studies programs. For the most part, we have concentrated on identifying current printed guides, as the information tends to go out of date fairly fast. Web sites are becoming increasingly important as more and more funding agencies use the Web as their primary avenue for disseminating information.

The fifth section, "Guides to Overseas Opportunities," provides information regarding overseas careers, study, and internships. This is an area that is growing rapidly. The number of students interested in pursuing careers or studying abroad has increased dramatically.

Section I: Bibliography

The following bibliography focuses on materials that address how to internationalize the classroom experience of students, the curriculum, and foreign language study. It also includes materials that are concerned with increasing our awareness and knowledge of world and foreign affairs. The bibliography draws upon the literatures related to global, comparative, and area studies. While the bibliography does contain some items on study abroad programs and experiences and international students in the U.S., this is not its primary focus. The bibliography includes philosophical items, practical materials, and evaluative studies.

We also have included some materials that are aimed at the general public and public schools at the elementary, middle, and high school levels. The bibliography is not exhaustive, and includes only books, articles, ERIC documents, and Web sites. The Web sites listed range considerably in terms of the audience they address and their content. Many are geared toward public schools. One reason we have included them is that they are of high quality and could be used for outreach purposes. Very few U.S. government documents are included. The bibliography includes only English-language materials.

Keeping up with the literature on international studies is difficult. One problem is that much of the literature is produced as reports by organizations and associations, and not published by commercial presses. Another problem is identifying key words or subject headings. One way to keep current is to check to see if a particular author, organization, or association has published anything new in this field.

The following are a few additional suggestions for updating this bibliography. To find additional monographic literature, use *Books in Print, WorldCat, or*

RLIN. To find ERIC documents and articles in the field of education use *ERIC (Educational Resources).* The best indexes, either in print or electronic form, for finding articles in this area are: *PAIS, Humanities Index, Social Sciences Index, International Political Science Abstracts, Sociological Abstracts,* or *ABC POL SCI.*

Part 1: Issues in International Higher Education

Abeles, Marc. "Political Anthropology: New Challenges, New Aims." *International Social Science Journal* 49 (September 1997): 319–332.

Abraham, Itty, and Ronald Kassimir. "Internationalization of the Social Sciences and Humanities." *Items* [Social Science Research Council] 51 (June–September 1997): 23–30.

Alexandre, Laurien. "Genderizing International Studies: Revisioning Concepts and Curriculum." *International Studies Notes* 14 (Winter 1989): 5–8.

Andreopoulos, George, and Richard Claude, eds. *Human Rights Education for the Twenty-first Century.* Philadelphia: University of Pennsylvania Press, 1997. 636p.

Auletta, Ken. "The Next Corporate Order: American Keiretsu." *New Yorker* (October 20–27, 1997): 225–227.

Axtmann, Roland. "Society, Globalization and the Comparative Method." *History of the Human Sciences* [Great Britain] 6, 2 (1993): 53–74.

Axtmann, Roland, ed. *Globalization and Europe: Theoretical and Empirical Investigations.* London: Pinter, 1998. 214p.

Bates, Robert H. "Area Studies and Political Science: Rupture and Possible Synthesis." *Africa Today* 44 (April–June 1997): 123–131.

Bates, Robert H. "Area Studies and the Discipline." *APSA-CP: Newsletter of the APSA Organized Section in Comparative Politics* 7 (Winter 1996): 1–2.

Bates, Robert H. "Area Studies and the Discipline: A Useful Controversy?" *PS: Political Science & Politics* 30 (June 1997): 166–169 [see p. 51, this volume].

Bates, Robert H. "The Death of Comparative Politics?" *APSA-CP: Newsletter of the APSA Organized Section in Comparative Politics* 7 (Summer 1996): 1–2.

Benavot, Aaron, et al. "Knowledge for the Masses: World Models and National Curricula 1920–1986." *American Sociological Review* 56 (February 1991): 85–100.

Bennett, Christine. *Comprehensive Multicultural Education: Theory and Practice.* 3rd ed. Boston: Allyn and Bacon, 1995. 452p.

Beyer, Peter. "Globalizing Systems, Global Cultural Models and Religion(s)." *International Sociology* 13 (March 1998): 79–94.

Bird, A., et al. "A Conceptual Model of the Effects of Area Studies Training Programs and a Preliminary Investigation of the Model's Hypothesized Relationships." *International Journal of Intercultural Relations* 17, 4 (1993): 415–435.

Blodgett, Steven A. "A Research Agenda for the Internationalization of Higher Education in the United States: Some Thoughts on Next Steps." *International Education Forum* 16 (Spring 1996): 37–41.

Boyce, James K. "Area Studies and the National Security State." *Bulletin of Concerned Asian Scholars* 29 (January–March 1997): 27–29.

Bradshaw, Michael J. "New Regional Geography, Foreign Area Studies and Perestroika." *Area* 22, 4 (1990): 315–322.

Braungart, Richard G. "At Century's End: Globalization, Paradoxes, and a New Political Agenda." *Journal of Political and Military Sociology* 25 (Winter 1997): 343–351.

Brzezinski, Zbigniew. "New Challenges to Human Rights." *Journal of Democracy* 8, 2 (1997): 3–8.

Bugliarello, George. "Telecommunities: The Next Civilization." *Futurist* 31 (September–October 1997): 23–26.

Bulman, Raymond F. "Discerning Major Shifts in the World-System: Some Help from Theology?" *Review* [Fernand Braudel Center] 19, 4 (1996): 383–400.

Buzan, Barry. "The Present as a Historic Turning Point." *Journal of Peace Research* 32, 4 (1995): 385–398.

Carver, Terrell. "Time, Space and Speed: New Dimensions in Political Analysis." *New Political Science* 40 (Summer 1997): 33–44.

Cavusgil, S. Tamer, and Nancy Horn, eds. *Internationalizing Doctoral Education in Business.* East Lansing: Michigan State University Press, 1997. 317p.

Cerny, Philip G. "Globalization and Other Stories: The Search for a New Paradigm for International Relations." *International Journal* 51 (Autumn 1996): 617–637.

Cerny, Philip G. "Paradoxes of the Competition State: The Dynamics of Political Globalization." *Government and Opposition* 32 (Spring 1997): 251–274.

Chege, Michael. "The Social Science Area Studies Controversy from the Continental African Standpoint." *Africa Today* 44 (April–June 1997): 133–142.

Chomsky, Noam, et al. *The Cold War & the University: Toward an Intellectual History of the Postwar Years.* New York: W. W. Norton, 1997. 258p.

Clark, Ian. *Globalization and Fragmentation: International Relations in the Twentieth Century.* New York: Oxford University Press, 1997. 220p.

Clarke, Susan E., and Gary L. Gaile. "Local Politics in a Global Era: Thinking Locally, Acting Globally." *Annals of the American Academy of Political and Social Science* 551 (1997): 28–43.

Cleveland, Harlan. "Ten Keys to World Peace." *Futurist* 28 (July–August 1994): 15–21.

Clinton, William J. "The 21st Century Will Challenge Our Security." *Vital Speeches* 64, 1 (1997): 1–4.

Collins, H. Thomas. *Guidelines for Global and International Studies Education: Challenges, Cultures, Connections.* New York: American Forum for Global Education, 1996. 19p.

Cox, Michael. "Rebels without a Cause? Radical Theorists and the World System after the Cold War." *New Political Economy* 3 (November 1998): 445–461.

Cumings, Bruce. "Boundary Displacement: Area Studies and International Studies during and after the Cold War." *Bulletin of Concerned Asian Scholars* 29 (January–March 1997): 6–26.

Currie, Jan, and Janice Newson, eds. *Universities and Globalization: Critical Perspectives.* Thousand Oaks, Calif.: Sage Publications, 1998. 339p.

Daniels, John, and N. Caroline Daniels. *Global Vision: Building New Models for the Corporation of the Future.* New York: McGraw-Hill, 1993. 197p.

Desmond, Jane C., and Virginia R. Dominguez. "Resituating American Studies in a Critical Internationalism." *American Quarterly* 48 (September 1996): 475–490.

Diamond, Larry. "Is the Third Wave Over?" *Journal of Democracy* 7 (July 1996): 20–37.

Didsbury, Howard F., ed. *Futurevision: Ideas, Insights, and Strategies.* Bethesda, Md.: World Future Society, 1996. 366p.

During, Simon. "Popular Culture on a Global Scale: A Challenge for Cultural Studies?" *Critical Inquiry* 23 (Summer 1997): 808–833.

Elliott, Anthony. "Symptoms of Globalization: Or, Mapping Reflexivity in the Postmodern Age." *Political Psychology* 16 (December 1995): 719–736.

Farmer, Rod. "International Education as a Worldcentric Perspective: Defining International Education." *New England Journal of History* 49 (Winter 1992–1993): 52–55.

Fiero, Gloria. "Global Humanities: Pedagogy or Politics." *Interdisciplinary Humanities* 13 (Winter 1996): 5–11.

Foran, John. "The Future of Revolutions at the Fin-de-Siècle." *Third World Quarterly* 18 (December 1997): 791–820.

Forte, Maximilian C. "Globalization and World-Systems Analysis: Toward New Paradigms of a Geo-Historical Social Anthropology (A Research Review)." *Reviews* 21 (Winter 1998): 29–99.

Fung, C. Victor. "Rationales for Teaching World Musics." *Music Educators* 82 (July 1995): 36–40.

George, Alexander. "The Two Cultures of Academia and Policymaking: Bridging the Gap." *Political Psychology* 15 (March 1994): 143–172.

Gill, Stephen. "Globalization, Market Civilization, and Disciplinary Neoliberalism." *Millennium: Journal of International Studies* 24 (Winter 1995): 399–424.

Giugni, Marco G. "The Other Side of the Coin: Explaining Crossnational Similarities between Social Movements." *Mobilization* 3 (March 1998): 89–105.

Goldsmith, Peter. "Globalization: The European Experience." *Journal of Legal Education* 46 (September 1996): 317–321.

Greenfield, Liah. "Transcending the Nation's Worth." *Daedalus* 122, 31 (1993): 47–61.

Groennings, Sven, and David Wiley, eds. *Group Portrait: Internationalizing the Disciplines.* New York: American Forum, 1990. 468p.

Guyer, Jane I. "Distant Beacons and Immediate Steps: Area Studies, International Studies, and the Disciplines in 1996." *Africa Today* 44 (April–June 1997): 149–156.

Haass, Richard N., and Robert E. Litan. "Globalization and Its Discontents: Navigating the Dangers of a Tangled World." *Foreign Affairs* 77 (May–June 1998): 2–6.

Hall, Peter A., and Sidney Tarrow. "Globalization and Area Studies: When Is Too Broad Too Narrow?" *The Chronicle of Higher Education* (January 23, 1998): B4–5 [see p. 96, this volume].

Halliday, Fred. "International Relations and its Discontents." *International Affairs* 71 (October 1995): 733–746.

Heginbotham, Stanley J. "Rethinking International Scholarship: The Challenge of Transition from the Cold War Era." *Items* [Social Science Research Council] 48 (June–September 1994): 33–40.

Heilbrunn, J. "The News from Everywhere: Does Global Thinking Threaten Local Knowledge (The Social Science Research Council Debates the Future of Area Studies)." *Lingua Franca* 6 (May–June 1996): 48–56.

Hettne, Bjorn. "Development, Security and World Order: A Regionalist Approach." *European Journal of Development Research* 9 (June 1997): 83–106.

Hewitt de Alcantera, Cynthia. "Uses and Abuses of the Concept of Governance." *International Social Science Journal* 50 (March 1998): 105–113.

Heyl, John. "A Research Agenda for the Internationalization of Higher Education in the United States: Comments on Research Categories." *International Education Forum* 16 (Spring 1996): 44–46.

Hicks, David, and Cathie Holden. "Exploring the Future: A Missing Dimension in Environmental Education." *Environmental Education Research* 1 (1995): 185–193.

Hill, Christopher, and Pamela Beshoff, eds. *Two Worlds of International Relations: Academics, Practitioners and the Trade in Ideas.* New York: Routledge, 1994. 233p.

Hoemeke, Thomas. "A Research Agenda for the Internationalization of Higher Education in the United States: Reaction and Comments." *International Education Forum* 16 (Spring 1996): 57–58.

Hood, Christopher. "Emerging Issues in Public Administration." *Public Administration* 73 (Spring 1995): 165–183.

Hounshell, David A. "Pondering the Globalization of R & D: Some New Questions for Business Historians." *Business and Economic History* 25, 2 (1996): 131–143.

Hubert, Robert T., Blair A. Ruble, and Peter J. Stavrakis. "Post–Cold War 'International' Scholarship: A Brave New World or the Triumph of Form over Substance?" *Items* [Social Science Research Council] 49 (March 1995): 30–38.

Hurrell, Andrew, and Ngaire Woods. "Globalization and Inequality." *Millennium: Journal of International Studies* 24 (Winter 1995): 447–470.

Hursh, Heidi, and Jonathan Fore. *Global Issues for the 90s.* Denver, Colo.: Center for Teaching International Relations, 1993. 149p.

Jacobson, Harold K. "International Cooperation in the Twenty-First Century: Familiar Problems and New Challenges." *International Studies Review* 1, 1 (1997): 51–68.

Jameson, Fredric, and Masao Miyoshi, eds. *The Cultures of Globalization.* Durham, N.C.: Duke University Press, 1998. 393p.

Jancar-Webster, Barbara. "Environmental Studies: State of the Discipline." *International Studies Notes* 18 (Fall 1993): 1–4.

Jancar-Webster, Barbara. "An Overview of Area." *International Studies Notes* 19 (Fall 1994): 52–57.

Johnson, Chalmers. "Preconception vs. Observation, or the Contributions of Rational Choice Theory and Area Studies to Contemporary Political Science." *PS: Political Science & Politics* 30 (June 1997): 170–174 [see p. 58, this volume].

Johnson, Donald. "Academic and Intellectual Foundations of Teacher Education in Global Perspectives." *Theory Into Practice* 32 (Winter 1993): 3–13.

Kacowicz, Arie. "Teaching International Relations in a Changing World: Four Approaches." *PS: Political Science & Politics* 26 (March 1993): 76–81.

Karp, Ivan. "Does Theory Travel? Area Studies and Cultural Studies." *Africa Today* 44 (July–September 1997): 281–295.

Keller, William W., and Louis W. Pauly. "Globalization at Bay." *Current History* 96 (November 1997): 370–376.

Kennedy, Paul. "Preparing for the 21st Century: Winners and Losers." *New York Review of Books* (February 11, 1993): 32–44.

Keohane, Robert O., and Lisa L. Martin. "The Promise of Institutionalist Theory." *International Security* 20 (Summer 1995): 39–51.

Kerr, Clark. "International Learning and National Purposes in Higher Education." *American Behavioral Scientist* 35 (September–October 1991): 17–42.

Khosrowpour, Mehdi, and Aren Loch. *Global Information Technology Education: Issues and Trends.* Harrisburg, Pa.: Idea Group, 1993. 517p.

Kilgore, De Witt Douglas. "Undisciplined Multiplicity: The Relevance of an American Cultural Studies." *American Studies* 38 (Summer 1997): 31–41.

King, Anthony D., ed. *Culture, Globalization and the World System.* Minneapolis: University of Minnesota Press, 1997. 186p.

King, Charles. "Post-Sovietology: Area Studies or Social Science?" *International Affairs* 70 (April 1994): 291–298.

Kothari, Rajni. "Globalization: A World Adrift." *Alternatives: Social Transformation and Humane Governance* 22 (April–June 1997): 227–267.

Kress, Gunther. "Internationalization and Globalization: Rethinking a Curriculum of Communication." *Comparative Education* 32 (June 1996): 185–196.

Krombach, Hayo. "International Relations as an Academic Discipline." *Millennium: Journal of International Studies* 21 (Summer 1992): 243–258.

Kushigian, Julia A., and Penny Parsekian, eds. *International Studies in the Next Millennium: Meeting the Challenge of Globalization.* Westport, Conn.: Praeger, 1998. 181p.

Lambert, Richard D. "Blurring the Disciplinary Boundaries: Area Studies in the United States." *American Behavioral Scientist* 33 (July–August 1990): 712–733.

Lambert, Richard D. "Domains and Issues in International Studies." *International Education Forum* 16 (Spring 1996): 1–19 [see p. 30, this volume].

Little, Angela W. "Globalization and Educational Research: Whose Context Counts." *International Journal of Educational Development* 16 (October 1996): 427–438.

Lopez, George A., Jackie G. Smith, and Ron Pagnucco. "The Global Tide." *Bulletin of Atomic Scientists* 51 (July–August 1995): 33–39.

Low, Setha M. "Theorizing the City: Ethnicity, Gender and Globalization." *Critique of Anthropology* 17 (December 1997): 403–409.

Luhmann, Niklas. "Globalization or World Society: How to Conceive of Modern Society?" *International Review of Sociology* 7 (March 1997): 67–79.

McCaughey, Robert. *International Studies and Academic Enterprise: A Chapter in the Enclosure of American Learning.* New York: Columbia University Press, 1985. 301p.

McLaren, Peter. "Education and Globalization: An Environmental Perspective—An Interview with Edgar Gonzalez-Gaudiano." *International Journal of Educational Reform* 4 (January 1995): 72–78.

Marchand, Marianne H. "Reconceptualizing Gender and Development in an Era of Globalization." *Millennium: Journal of International Studies* 25 (Winter 1995): 577–604.

Marden, Peter. "Geographies of Dissent: Globalization, Identity, and the Nation." *Political Geography* 16 (January 1997): 37–64.

Marshall, Don D. "National Development and the Globalization Discourse: Confronting 'Imperative' and 'Convergence' Notions." *Third World Quarterly* 17 (December 1996): 875–901.

Marshall, Don D. "Understanding Late-Twentieth-Century Capitalism: Reassessing the Globalization Theme." *Government and Opposition* 31 (Spring 1996): 193–215.

Martin, Hans-Peter, and Harold Schumann. *The Global Trap: Globalization and the Assault on Prosperity and Democracy.* New York: Zed Books, 1997. 269p.

Martin, William G., and Mark Beittel. "Toward a Global Sociology? Evaluating Current Conceptions, Methods, and Practices." *Sociological Quarterly* 39 (Winter 1998): 139–161.

Mato, D. "On the Theory, Epistemology, and Politics of the Social Construction of Cultural Identities in the Age of Globalization: Introductory Remarks to Ongoing Debates." *Identities: Global Studies in Culture and Power* 3, 1–2 (1996): 61–72.

Mayall, James. "Globalization and International Relations." *Review of International Studies* 24 (April 1998): 239–250.

Mazlish, Bruce. "Psychohistory and the Question of Global Identity." *Psychohistory Review* 25 (Winter 1997): 165–176.

Miller, Morris. "Where Is Globalization Taking Us: Why We Need a New Bretton Woods." *Futures* 27 (March 1995): 125–144.

Mitchell, Michael. "Explaining Third World Democracies." *PS: Political Science & Politics* 28 (March 1995): 83–85.

Mittelman, James H. "Rethinking the New Regionalism in the Context of Globalization." *Global Governance* 2 (May–August 1996): 189–213.

Moisy, Claude. "Myths of the Global Information Village." *Foreign Policy* 107 (Summer 1997): 78–87.

Natoli, Salvatore. "How a Geographer Looks at Globalism." *International Journal of Social Education* 5 (Fall 1990): 22–37.

Nye, Joseph S., Jr. "What New World Order?" *Foreign Affairs* 71 (Spring 1992): 83–96.

Peres, Shimon. "The End of Hunting Season in History." *New Perspectives Quarterly* 12 (Fall 1995): 49–52.

Perez-Baltodano, Andres. "The Study of Public Administration in Times of Global Interpenetration: A Historical Rationale for a Theoretical Model." *Journal of Public Administration Research and Theory* 7 (October 1997): 615–638.

Pieterse, Jan N. "Multiculturalism and Museums: Discourse about Others in the Age of Globalization." *Theory, Culture & Society* 14 (November 1997): 123–146.

Porter, David, ed. *Internet Culture.* New York: Routledge, 1997. 279p.

Prewitt, Kenneth. "Presidential Items." *Items* [Social Science Research Council] 50, 1 (March 1996): 15–18 [see p. 77, this volume].

Prewitt, Kenneth. "Presidential Items." *Items* [Social Science Research Council] 50, 2/3 (June–September 1996): 31–40 [see p. 82, this volume].

Prewitt, Kenneth. "Presidential Items." *Items* [Social Science Research Council] 50, 4 (December 1996): 91–92.

Ratinoff, Luis. "Global Insecurity and Education: The Culture of Globalization." *Prospects* 25 (June 1995): 147–174.

Ray, James L. "Democratic Path to Peace." *Journal of Democracy* 8 (April 1997): 49–64.

Reinicke, Wolfgang H. "Global Public Policy." *Foreign Affairs* 76 (November–December 1997): 127–138.

Rex, John. "Ethnic Identity and the Nation State: The Political Sociology of Multi-Cultural Societies." *Social Identities* 1, 1 (1995): 21–34.

Richards, Huw. "Ageing Crisis Threat to Area Studies." *Times Higher Education Supplement* 1335 (June 5, 1998): 7–13.

Richards, Huw. "Area Studies Lose Their Appeal." *Times Higher Education Supplement* 1103 (December 24, 1993): 2–8.

Robertson, Roland, and Habib-Haque Khondker. "Discourses of Globalization: Preliminary Considerations." *International Sociology* 13 (March 1998): 25–40.

Robinson, William I. "Globalization: 9 Theses on Our Epoch." *Race & Class* 38 (October–December 1996): 13–31.

Robles, Alfredo, Jr. "How 'International' Are International Relations Syllabi?" *PS: Political Science & Politics* 26 (September 1993): 526–528.

Rosecrance, Richard. "A New Concert of Powers." *Foreign Affairs* 71 (Spring 1992): 64–80.

Rosenau, James N. "The Complexities and Contradictions of Globalization." *Current History* 96 (November 1997): 360–364.

Rosenau, James N. "The Dynamics of Globalization: Toward an Operational Formulation." *Security Dialogue* 27 (September 1996): 247–262.

Roseneau, James N. "Governance in the Twenty-First Century." *Global Governance* 1 (Winter 1995): 13–43.

Rossman, Parker. *The Emerging Worldwide Electronic University: Information Age Global Higher Education.* Westport, Conn.: Greenwood Press, 1992. 169p.

Roudometof, Victor. "Preparing for the 21st Century." *Sociological Forum* 12 (December 1997): 661–670.

Sanders, Bernie. "Globalization's the Issue." *Nation* 267 (September 28, 1998): 4–6.

Sassen, Saskia. *Globalization and Its Discontents: Essays on the New Mobility of People and Money.* New York: New Press, 1998. 253p.

Schneider, Ann, and Llewellyn Howell. "The Discipline of International Studies." *International Studies Notes* 16–17 (Fall 1991–Winter 1992): 1–3.

Schott, Thomas. "World Science: Globalization of Institutions and Participation." *Science Technology & Human Values* 18 (Spring 1993): 196–208.

Scott, Peter, ed. *The Globalization of Higher Education.* Philadelphia: Open University Press, 1998.

Shaw, Martin. "Global Society and Global Responsibility: The Theoretical, Historical and Political Limits of 'International Society.'" *Millennium: Journal of International Studies* 21 (Winter 1992): 421–434.

Shaw, Martin. "The State of Globalization: Towards a Theory of State Transformation." *Review of International Political Economy* 4 (Autumn 1997): 497–513.

Shea, Christopher. "Political Scientists Clash over Value of Area Studies." *The Chronicle of Higher Education* 43 (January 10, 1997): B4–5.

Sideri, Sandro. "Globalization and Regional Integration." *European Journal of Development Research* 9 (June 1997): 38–82.

Sjolander, Claire T. "The Rhetoric of Globalization: What's in a Wor(l)d." *International Journal* 51 (Autumn 1996): 603–616.

Smart, Barry. "Sociology, Globalization and Postmodernity: Comments on the Sociology for One World Thesis." *International Sociology* 9 (June 1994): 149–159.

Smelser, Neil. "Internationization of Social Science Knowledge." *American Behavioral Scientist* 35 (September–October 1991): 65–91.

Smist, Frank, Jr. "International Education in an Age of Transition." *International Studies Notes* 16–17 (Fall 1991–Winter 1992): 43–46.

Smith, Hazel. "The Silence of the Academics: International Social Theory, Historical Materialism, and Political Values." *Review of International Studies* 22 (April 1996): 191–212.

Smouts, Marie Claude. "The Proper Use of Governance in International Relations." *International Social Science Journal* 50 (March 1998): 81–89.

Snarr, Michael T., and D. Neil Snarr, eds. *Introducing Global Issues.* Boulder, Colo.: Lynne Rienner Publishers, 1998. 293p.

Spark, Alasdair. "Wrestling with America: Media National Images and the Global Village." *Journal of Popular Culture* 29 (Spring 1996): 83–98.

Spybey, Tony. *Globalization and World Society.* Cambridge, Mass.: Polity Press, 1996. 187p.

Stewart, F. "Globalization and Education." *International Journal of Educational Development* 16, 4 (1996): 327–333.

Stone, Priscilla M. "The Remaking of African Studies." *Africa Today* 44 (April–June 1997): 179–186.

Sweeting, Anthony. "The Globalization of Learning: Paradigm or Paradox." *International Journal of Educational Development* 16 (October 1996): 379–391.

Sylvester, Christine. "Feminist Theory and Gender Studies in International Relations." *International Studies Notes* 16–17 (Fall 1991–Winter 1992): 32–38.

Tabb, W. K. "Globalization Is an Issue, the Power of Capital Is the Issue." *Monthly Review: An Independent Socialist Magazine* 49, 2 (1997): 20–30.

Talbott, S. "Globalization and Diplomacy: A Practitioner's Perspective." *Foreign Policy* 108 (1997): 69–83.

Tarrow, Sidney, and Kent Worcester. "European Studies after the Cold War." *The Chronicle of Higher Education* (April 6, 1994): B1–2.

Tessler, Mark, Jodi Nachtwey, and Anne Banda. "Introduction: The Area Studies Controversy." In *Area Studies and Social Science: Strategies for Understanding Middle East Politics.* Bloomington: Indiana University Press, 1999, pp. 1–7 [see p. 67, this volume].

Thullen, Manfred. "A Research Agenda for the Internationalization of Higher Education in the United States: Comments, Observations, Suggestions." *International Education Forum* 16, 1 (Spring 1996): 47–50.

Tomikura, Masaya. "Problems of Designing Global Simulation/Games." *Simulation & Gaming* 29 (December 1998): 456–472.

Tonelson, Alan. "Globalization: The Great American Non-Debate." *Current History* 96 (November 1997): 353–359.

Turner, Bryan S. "Citizenship Studies: A General Theory." *Citizenship Studies* 1 (February 1997): 5–18.

Van Elteren, Mel. "Conceptualizing the Impact of US Popular Culture Globally." *Journal of Popular Culture* 30 (Summer 1996): 47–89.

Vanbergeijk, Peter A. G., and Nico W. Mensink. "Measuring Globalization." *Journal of World Trade* 31 (June 1997): 159–168.

Vestal, Theodore. *International Education: Its History and Promise for Today.* Westport, Conn.: Praeger, 1994. 229p.

Wallerstein, Immanuel. "The Rise and Future Demise of World-Systems Analysis." *Review* 21 (Winter 1998): 103–112.

Waltz, Kenneth N. "The Emerging Structure of International Politics." *International Security* 18 (Fall 1993): 44–79.

Ward, Robert, and Bryce Wood. "Foreign Area Studies and the Social Science Research Council." *Items* [Social Science Research Council] 28 (December 1974): 53–58.

Waters, Malcolm. *Globalization.* London: Routledge, 1995. 185p.

Watts, Michael. "African Studies at the Fin de Siècle: Is It Really the Fin?" *Africa Today* 44 (April–June 1997): 185–192.

Williamson, J. G. "Globalization, Convergence, and History." *Journal of Economic History* 56 (June 1996): 277–306.

Woods, Ngaire. "Globalization: Definitions, Debates and Implications." *Oxford Development Studies* 26 (February 1998): 5–13.

Part 2: Accomplishments and Challenges
in International Programs

Allaway, William. "The Future of International Educational Exchange." *American Behavioral Scientist* 35 (September–October 1991): 55–63.

Ambrose, David, and Louis Pol. "The International Research Experience: Executive MBA Distinctiveness." *Journal of Teaching in International Business* 7, 1 (1995): 1–18.

American Council on Education. *Educating for Global Competence.* Washington, D.C.: American Council on Education, 1997. 21p [see p. 337, this volume].

American Council on Education. *Educating Americans for a World in Flux: Ten Ground Rules for Internationalizing Higher Education.* Washington, D.C.: American Council on Education, 1995. 16p.

American Forum for Global Education. *The New Resource Book.* New York: American Forum for Global Education, 1992. 246p.

Andrews, Bill. "Global Warming: Understanding and Teaching the Forecast." *Interaction* 7 (January–February 1995): 7–13.

Aronson, David. "Beyond Borders: Geography Offers Students a New Perspective on Our Changing World." *Teaching Tolerance* 5 (Spring 1996): 48–50.

Arpan, Jeffrey, William Folks, and Chuck Rwok. *International Business Education in the 1990s: A Global Survey.* St. Louis: American Academy of Collegiate Schools of Business, 1993. 309p.

Association Liaison Office for University Cooperation in Development. *Serving the World: International Activities of American Colleges and Universities.* Washington, D.C.: Association Liaison Office for University Cooperation in Development, 1993.

Backman, Earl. "Internationalizing the Campus: A Strategy for the '80s." *International Studies Notes* 10 (Spring 1983): 1–6.

Bailey, Martha. "USENET Discussion Groups in Political Science Courses." *PS: Political Science & Politics* 28 (December 1995): 721–722.

Ball, William. "Using the Internet as a Teaching Tool: Why Wait Any Longer?" *PS: Political Science & Politics* 28 (December 1995): 718–720.

Barrow, Clyde. "The Strategy of Selective Excellence: Redesigning Higher Education for Global Competition in a Postindustrial Society." *Higher Education* 31 (June 1996): 447–469.

Beck, John, et al. "Internationalising the Business Student." *Journal of Teaching in International Business* 7, 4 (1996): 91–105.

Beekhan, Anel, and Kamban Naidoo. *Human Rights and Democracy: An Education for the Future.* Durban, South Africa: Independent Projects Trust, 1994. 87p.

Begler, Elsie. "Spinning Wheels and Straw: Balancing Content, Process, and Context in Global Teacher Education Programs." *Theory Into Practice* 32 (Winter 1993): 14–20.

Berman, Sheldon, and Phyllis La Farge, eds. *Promising Practices in Teaching Social Responsibility.* Albany: State University of New York Press, 1993. 267p.

Bermudez, Pedro, and Barbara Cruz. *Latin America and the Caribbean from a Global Perspective: A Resource Guide for Teachers.* University Park: Latin American and Caribbean Center, Florida International University, 1991. 176p.

Bikson, Tora. "Educating a Globally Prepared Workforce: New Research on College and Corporate Perspectives." *Liberal Education* 82 (Spring 1996): 12–19.

Bikson, Tora. *Global Preparedness and Human Resources: College and Corporate Prospects.* Santa Monica, Calif.: RAND, 1994. 84p.

Black, Robert, ed. *Education for a Global Century: Handbook of Exemplary International Programs.* New Rochelle, N.Y.: Change, 1981. 157p.

Black, Robert, and George Bonham. "The Council on Learning Project on Undergraduate Education: Education and the World View." *Annals of the American Academy of Political and Social Science* 449 (May 1980): 102–113.

Boehrer, John. "On Teaching a Case." *International Studies Notes* 19 (Spring 1994):14–20.

Budd, Gregory, and Don Curry. "Problem Solving in Las Vegas: Students Are Building Skills and a Global Network." *EPA Journal* 21 (Spring 1995): 18–19.

Burn, Barbara B. "Study Abroad and Foreign Language Programs." *International Education Forum* 16 (Spring 1996): 20–30 [see p. 178, this volume].

Burns, Jane, and Belverd Needles, eds. *Accounting Education for the 21st Century: The Global Challenges.* Elmsford, N.Y.: Pergamon Press, 1994. 499p.

Callahan, William, Jr., and Ronald Banaszak, eds. *Citizenship for the 21st Century.* San Francisco: Foundation for Teaching Economics, Constitutional Rights Foundation, 1990. 354p.

Calleja, James, Dumitru Chitoran, and Ake Bjerstedt, eds. *International Education and the University.* Paris: UNESCO, 1995. 262p.

Carey-Webb, Allen, and Stephen Benz, eds. *Teaching and Testimony: Rigoberta Menchu and the North American Classroom.* Albany: State University of New York Press, 1996. 391p.

Carman, John, and Steven Hopkins, eds. *Tracing Common Themes: Comparative Courses in the Study of Religion.* Atlanta, Ga.: Scholars Press, 1991. 318p.

Chapman, Marilyn, and James Anderson, eds. *Thinking Globally about Language Education.* Vancouver: University of British Columbia, 1995. 200p.

Chase, Audree, and James Mahoney, eds. *Global Awareness in Community College: A Report of a National Survey.* Washington, D.C.: Community College Press, 1996. 103p.

Chinkin, Christine, and Romana Sadurska. "Learning about International Law through Dispute Resolution." *International and Comparative Law Quarterly* 40 (July 1991): 529–550.

College Placement Foundation. *Developing the Global Work Force: Insights for Colleges and Corporations—How American Colleges and Companies View the New Global Economy and Its Impact upon the Human Resources Function.* Bethlehem, Pa.: College Placement Foundation, 1994. 96p.

Collins, Edward, Jr., and Martin Rogoff. "The Use of an Interscholastic Moot Court Competition in the Teaching of International Law." *PS: Political Science and Politics* 24 (September 1991): 516–520.

Conklin, John. "Integrating Ecology into International Relations: A System Approach." *International Studies Notes* 18 (Fall 1993): 8–14.

Cowton, Christopher, and Thomas Dunfee. "Internationalizing the Business Ethics Curriculum: A Survey." *Journal of Business Ethics* 14 (May 1995): 331–338.

Crouse, Gale, ed. *Broadening the Frontiers of Foreign Language Education: Selected Papers from the 1995 Central States Conference.* Lincolnwood, Ill.: National Textbook Company, 1995. 174p.

Davis, James. *Interdisciplinary Courses and Team Teaching: New Arrangements for Learning.* Phoenix, Ariz.: Oryx Press, 1995. 271p.

Davis, O. L., Jr., ed. *NCSS in Retrospect.* Washington, D.C.: National Council for the Social Studies, 1996. 118p.

Dawson, Leslie. "Population and Development: Perspective on a Teaching Challenge." *Clearing* 87 (January–February 1995): 14–17.

Diaz, Carlos, ed. *Multicultural Education for the 21st Century.* Washington, D.C.: NEA Professional Library, National Education Association, 1992. 223p.

Donato, Richard, and Robert Terry, eds. *Foreign Language Learning: The Journey of a Lifetime*. Lincolnwood, Ill.: National Textbook Company, 1995. 194p.

Dore, Isaak. "The International Law Program at Saint Louis University." *Journal of Legal Education* 46 (September 1996): 336–341.

Dorman, Susan. "Teaching Portfolios: Moving from Ought to Is in Academia." *International Studies Notes* 18 (Fall 1993): 30–35.

Dyer, Brenda. "Write the Vision: Teaching Multicultural Literature from a Global Perspective (Global Issues)." *English Journal* 84 (December 1995): 78–81.

Eagan, David, and David Orr, eds. *The Campus and Environmental Responsibility*. San Francisco: Jossey-Bass, 1992. 133p.

Fersh, Seymour. *Integrating the Trans-National/Cultural Dimension*. Bloomington, Ind.: Phi Delta Kappa Educational Foundation, 1993. 39p.

Focseneanu, Veronica. "Walls, Sovereignty, and Nature: Ecological Security in an Interdependent World Teaching Strategy." *Update on Law-Related Education* 17 (Fall 1993): 81–84.

Fonte, John, and Andre Ryerson. *Education for America's Role in World Affairs*. Lanham, Md.: University Press of America, 1994. 199p.

Fountain, Susan. *Education for Development: A Teacher's Resource for Global Learning*. Portsmouth, N.H.: Heinemann, 1995. 318p.

Fowler, Robert, and Ian Wright, eds. *Thinking Globally about Social Education*. Vancouver: University of British Columbia, 1995. 124p.

Frantzich, Stephen. "Press Briefings Exercise." *PS: Political Science & Politics* 28 (December 1995): 728–730.

Fratantuono, Michael. "Evaluating the Case Method." *International Studies Notes* 19 (Spring 1994): 34–44.

Freysinger, Robert. "Toward Total Internationalization: Comprehensive Institutional Reform and Global Studies—The Case of Bradford College." *Journal of General Education* 42, 3 (1993): 178–190.

Gerner, Deborah. "Foreign Policy Analysis: Exhilarating Eclecticism, Intriguing Enigmas." *International Studies Notes* 16–17 (Fall–Winter 1991–1992): 4–19.

Goddard, C. Roe. "Seizing the Opportunity: International Political Economy and the End of the Cold War." *International Studies* 18 (Fall 1993): 15–20.

Goodenow, Ronald. "The Cyberspace Challenge: Modernity, Post-modernity and Reflections on International Networking Policy." *Comparative Education* 32 (June 1996): 197–216.

Goodman, Louis, ed. *Undergraduate International Studies on the Eve of the 21st Century*. Washington, D.C.: Association of Professional Schools of International Affairs, 1994. 119p (ED382134).

Groennings, Sven. "The Changing Need for an International Perspective: The Global Economy and Undergraduate Education." *International Studies Notes* 13 (Fall 1987): 64–68.

Groennings, Sven. "The Global Economy and Higher Education." *Atlantic Community Quarterly* 25 (Winter 1987–1988): 470–478.

Groennings, Sven. *The Impact of Economic Globalization on Higher Education*. Boston: New England Board of Higher Education, 1987. 97p.

Gunterman, Gail, ed. *Developing Language Teachers for a Changing World*. Lincolnwood, Ill.: National Textbook Company, 1993. 244p.

Hall, Barbara. "Electronic Newsgroups in the Liberal Arts Classroom." *International Studies Notes* 20 (Winter 1995): 9–15.

Harris, Ian. "From World Peace to Peace in the 'Hood: Peace Education in the Modern World." *Journal for a Just and Caring Education* 2 (October 1996): 378–395.

Hawkins, John N., Carlos Manuel Haro, Miriam A. Kazanjian, Gilbert W. Merkx, and David Wiley, eds. *International Education in the New Global Era: Proceedings of a*

National Policy Conference on the Higher Education Act, Title VI, and Fulbright-Hays Programs. Los Angeles, Calif.: International Studies and Overseas Programs, UCLA, 1998. 250p.

Henderson, Sandra, Steven Holman, and Lynn Mortensen, eds. *Global Climates—Past, Present, and Future: Activities for Integrated Science Education.* Washington, D.C.: U.S. Environmental Protection Agency, Office of Research and Development, 1993. 108p.

Hoft, Nancy. "A Curriculum for the Research and Practice of International Technical Communication." *Technical Communication: Journal of the Society for Technical Communication* 42 (November 1995): 650–652.

Holsti, Ole. "Case Teaching: Transforming Foreign Policy Courses with Cases." *International Studies Notes* 19 (Spring 1994): 7–13.

hooks, bell. *Teaching to Transgress: Education as the Practice of Freedom.* New York: Routledge, 1994. 216p.

Johnston, Marilyn, and Anna Ochoa. "Teacher Education for Global Perspectives: A Research Agenda." *Theory Into Practice* 32 (Winter 1993): 64–68.

Kameoka, Yu. "The Internationalisation of Higher Education." *OECD Observer* 202 (October–November 1996): 34–36.

Karp, Basil. "Teaching the Global Perspective in American National Government: A Selected Resource Guide." *PS: Political Science & Politics* 25 (December 1992): 703–705.

Kaufmann, Norman, et al. *Students Abroad, Strangers at Home: Education for a Global Society.* Yarmouth, Maine: Intercultural Press, 1992. 194p.

Kelder, Richard, ed. *Interdisciplinary Curricula, General Education, and Liberal Learning: Selected Papers from the Third Annual Conference of the Institute for the Study of Postsecondary Pedagogy.* New Paltz, N.Y.: The Institute, 1994. 206p.

King, Arthur, Jr. "The Pacific Circle Consortium: A Case of International Educational Consortium." *International Journal of Social Education* 9 (Fall–Winter 1994–1995): 94–106.

Klare, Michael, ed. *Peace and World Security Studies: A Curriculum Guide.* Boulder, Colo.: L. Rienner Publishers, 1994. 425p.

Klass, Gary. "Bringing the World into the Classroom: POS 302-L—The Race and Ethnicity Seminar Discussion List." *PS: Political Science & Politics* 28 (December 1995): 723–725.

Klesner, Joseph. "Narrowing the Focus of Introductory Comparative Politics Courses." *PS: Political Science & Politics* 28 (March 1995): 85–86.

Klinger, Janeen. "The Use of History in Teaching International Politics." *International Studies Notes* 17 (Spring 1992): 39–44.

Kozma, Tamas, ed. *Ethnocentrism in Education.* New York: Peter Lang, 1992. 288p.

Kronenwetter, Michael. *Taking a Stand against Human Rights Abuses.* New York: F. Watts, 1990. 157p.

Kwok, Chuck, et al. "A Global Survey of International Business Education in the 1990s." *Journal of International Business Studies* 25, 3 (1994): 605–623.

Lambert, Richard. "Foreign Language Use among International Business Graduates." *Annals of the American Academy of Political and Social Science* 511 (September 1990): 47–59.

Lantis, Jeffrey. "Simulation as Teaching Tools: Designing the Global Problems Summit." *International Studies Notes* 21 (Winter 1996): 30–38.

Lappe, Frances, and Paul DuBois. "Educating Real-World Problem Solvers." *National Civic Review* 83 (Summer–Fall 1994): 240–258.

Lim, Gill-Chin, ed. *Strategy for a Global University: Model International Department Experiment.* East Lansing: International Studies and Programs, Michigan State University, 1995. 192p.

Long, William. "The Pew Initiative: Case Teaching in International Affairs." *International Studies Notes* 18 (Fall 1993): 36–40.

Lopez, George. *Challenges to Curriculum Development in the Post–Cold War Era.* Notre Dame, Ind.: Joan B. Kroc Institute for International Peace Studies, 1994. 20p.

Lopez, George. "A University Peace Studies Curriculum for the 1990s." *Journal of Peace Research* 22, 2 (1985): 117–128.

Lopez, George, ed. "Peace Studies: Past and Future." *Annals of the American Academy of Political and Social Science* 504 (July 1989): 1–127.

Lyman, Richard. "Overview." In *International Challenges to American Colleges and Universities.* Phoenix, Ariz.: American Council on Education and Oryx Press, 1995, pp. 1–17.

Lynch, James, Celia Modgil, and Sohan Modgil, eds. *Education and Development: Tradition and Innovation.* London: Cassell, 1997. 5 vols.

McCabe, Lester. "The Development of a Global Perspective during Participation in Semester at Sea: A Comparative Global Education Program." *Educational Review* 46, 3 (1994): 275–286.

McGowan, Patrick. "Teaching IR after World War II." *International Studies Notes* 18 (Fall 1993): 21–29.

Mauch, James, and Seth Spaulding. "The Internationalization of Higher Education: Who Should be Taught What and How?" *Journal of General Education* 41 (1992): 111–129 [see p. 190, this volume, for revised version].

Merkur'ev, Stanislav. "Implications of Internationalization for the University." *American Behavioral Scientist* 35 (September–October 1991): 43–54.

Merryfield, Merry, and Richard Remy, eds. *Teaching about International Conflict and Peace.* Albany: State University of New York Press, 1995. 374p.

Milbrath, Lester. "The World Learns about the Environment." *International Studies Notes* 16 (Winter 1991): 13, 16, 30.

Mingst, Karen. "Cases and the Interactive Classroom." *International Studies Notes* 19 (Spring 1994): 1–6.

Mingst, Karen, and Katsuhiko Mori. *Teaching International Affairs with Cases.* Boulder, Colo.: Westview Press, 1997. 227p.

Mische, Patricia. "Toward a Pedagogy of Ecological Responsibility: Learning to Reinhabit the Earth." *Convergence* 25, 2 (1992): 9–25.

Morsy, Zaghloul, and Philip Altbach, eds. *Higher Education in International Perspective: Critical Issues.* Geneva: International Bureau of Education, 1996. 212p (ED393330).

Mortenson, Lynn. *Global Change Education Resource Guide.* Silver Spring, Md.: U.S. Dept. of Commerce, National Oceanic and Atmospheric Administration, 1996.

Myerson, Marilyn, and Susan Northcutt. "The Question of Gender: An Examination of Selected Textbooks in International Relations." *International Studies Notes* 19 (Winter 1994): 19–25.

National Geographic Society, Geography Education Standards Project. *Geography for Life: National Geography Standards 1994.* Washington, D.C.: National Geographic Research and Exploration, 1994. 272p.

Nelson, David, George Joseph, and Julian Williams. *Multicultural Mathematics.* New York: Oxford University Press, 1993. 228p.

Newell, Barbara. "Education with a World Perspective: A Necessity for America's Political and Economic Defense." *Annals of the American Academy of Political and Social Science* 491 (May 1987): 134–139.

Oliver, Arnold. "Enhancing International Studies with Undergraduate Academic Conferences." *International Studies Notes* 20 (Winter 1995): 16–20.

Onuf, Nicolas, and James Taulbee. "Bringing Law to Bear on International Relations Theory Courses." *PS: Political Science & Politics* 26 (June 1993): 249–254.

Organisation for Economic Co-operation and Development. *Internationalisation for*

Higher Education. Paris: Organisation for Economic Co-operation and Development, 1996. 135p.

Ortmayer, Louis. "Decisions and Dilemmas: Writing Case Studies in International Affairs." *International Studies Notes* 19 (Spring 1994): 28–33.

Osler, Audrey, ed. *Development Education: Global Perspectives in the Curriculum*. London: Cassell, 1994. 278p.

Paldy, Lester. "Environmental Science: A Foundation for the Future." *Journal of College Science Teaching* 26 (November 1996): 85–87.

Pappas, James, ed. *The University's Role in Economic Development: From Research to Outreach*. San Francisco: Jossey-Bass Publishers, 1997. 106p.

Parnell, Dale. *Dateline 2000: The New Higher Education Agenda*. Washington, D.C.: American Association of Community and Junior Colleges, 1990. 303p.

Perkins, James. "Report of the President's Commission on Foreign Language and International Studies." *Foreign Language Annals* 12 (December 1979): 457–464.

Perry, Theresa, and James Fraser, eds. *Freedom's Plow: Teaching in the Multicultural Classroom*. New York: Routledge, 1993. 309p.

Peterson, Sophia, and Virgil Peterson, eds. *Agenda for the 21st Century: Global Cooperation*. Morgantown: West Virginia University, 1991. 167p.

Phillips, Mary, and John Muldoon, Jr. "The Model United Nations: A Strategy for Enhancing Global Business Education." *Journal of Education for Business* 61 (January–February 1996): 142–146.

Pickert, Sarah, and Barbara Turlington. *Internationalizing the Undergraduate Curriculum: A Handbook for Campus Leaders*. Washington, D.C.: American Council on Education, 1992. 143p.

Purvis, Nigel. "Critical Legal Studies in Public International Law." *Harvard International Law Journal* 32 (Winter 1991): 81–127.

Rallo, Joseph. "The Challenge to Internationalize the Engineering Curriculum." *International Studies Notes* 16 (Spring 1991): 45–49.

Ray, Douglas, et al. *Education for Human Rights: An International Perspective*. Paris: UNESCO International Bureau of Education, 1994. 304p.

Ray, Russ. "Internationalizing the Business School Curriculum." *International Studies Notes* 15 (Fall 1990): 83–84.

Raymond, Gregory. "Foreign Policy Evaluation: Adding Civicism to International Education." *International Studies Notes* 17 (Fall 1992): 17–21.

Reardon, Betty. *Educating for Human Dignity: Learning about Rights and Responsibilities*. Philadelphia: University of Pennsylvania Press, 1995. 238p.

Reardon, Betty. *Women and Peace: Feminist Visions of Global Security*. Albany: State University of New York Press, 1993. 209p.

Reardon, Betty, and Eva Nordland, eds. *Learning Peace: The Promise of Ecological and Cooperative Education*. Albany: State University of New York Press, 1994. 234p.

Reed-Scott, Jutta. "Research Libraries in a Global Context." In *Scholarship, Research Libraries, and Global Publishing*. Washington, D.C.: Association of Research Librarians, 1996, pp. 3–15.

Reisman, W. Michael. "Designing Law Curricula for a Transnational Industrial and Science Based Civilization." *Journal of Legal Education* 46 (September 1996): 322–328.

Rose, William, Gerry Tyler, and George Lopez. "Teaching about the Future of US-Soviet Relations." *International Studies Notes* 16 (Spring 1991): 45–49.

Rugman, Alan, and W. T. Stanbury, eds. *Global Perspective: Internationalizing Management Education*. Vancouver: Centre for International Business Studies, University of British Columbia, 1992. 360p.

Ryan, Richard. "Teaching International Development Administration: Experiential Techniques and Interdisciplinary Tools." *Teaching Political Science* 13 (Winter 1985–1986): 92–96.

Sassen, Saskia. "Cities and Communities in the Global Economy." *American Behavioral Scientist* 39 (March–April 1996): 629–639.

Savitt, William, ed. *Teaching Global Development: A Curriculum Guide.* Notre Dame, Ind.: University of Notre Dame Press, 1993. 357p.

Sawicki, Gloria. *Teaching Foreign Languages in a Multicultural Setting: A Ford Foundation Diversity Initiative Project. Instructor's Reference Manual.* Flushing, N.Y.: Queens Collection Department of Romance Languages, City University of New York, 1992. 48p (ED360853).

Schneider, Ann. "International Education and the Undergraduate." *International Studies Notes* 18 (Winter 1993): 21–24.

Scott, Robert A. "Campus Developments in Response to the Challenges of Internationalization: The Case of Ramapo College of New Jersey (U.S.A.)." *Higher Education Management* 6 (March 1994): 71–89 [see p. 158, this volume].

Sexton, John. "The Global Law School Program at New York University." *Journal of Legal Education* 46 (September 1996): 329–335.

Shannon, J. Richard, et al. "Preparation of Careers in International Marketing: An Empirical Investigation of Students' Attitudes and Perceptions." *Journal of Teaching in International Business* 7, 3 (1995): 17–32.

Shao, Lawrence. "Techniques for Improving Student Performance in International Finance." *Journal of Teaching in International Business* 7, 3 (1995): 33–44.

Shennan, Margaret. *Teaching about Europe.* New York: Cassell Publishers, 1991. 281p.

Simon, Paul. *The Tongue-Tied American: Confronting the Foreign Language Crisis.* New York: Continuum, 1980. 214p.

Skidmore, David. "Group Projects and Teaching International Relations." *International Studies Notes* 18 (Fall 1993): 49–53.

Skidmore, David. "Teaching about the Post Cold War World: Four Future Scenarios." *International Studies Notes* 20 (Winter 1995): 1–8.

Skolnikoff, Eugene. "Knowledge without Borders? Internationalization of the Research Universities." *Daedalus* 122 (Fall 1993): 225–252.

Skutnabb-Kangas, Tove, and Robert Phillipson, eds. *Linguistic Human Rights: Overcoming Linguistic Discrimination.* New York: M. de Gruyter, 1994. 478p.

Slater, Frances. *Learning through Geography.* Indiana, Pa.: National Council for Geographic Education, 1993. 227p.

Smith, Gregory. *Education and the Environment: Learning to Live with Limits.* Albany: State University of New York Press, 1992. 185p.

Soroos, Marvin. "Adding Green to the International Studies Curriculum." *International Studies Notes* 16 (Winter 1991): 37–42.

Starkey, Hugh, ed. *The Challenge of Human Rights Education.* London: Cassell, 1991. 264p.

Takala, Annika. "Feminist Perspectives on Peace Education." *Journal of Peace Research* 28 (May 1991): 231–235.

Taulbee, James. "Images of International Law: What Do Students Learn from International Relations Textbooks?" *Teaching Political Science* 15 (Winter 1988): 74–79.

Teschner, Richard, ed. *Assessing Foreign Language Proficiency of Undergraduates.* Boston: Heinle and Heinle, 1991. 236p.

Thomas, Daniel, and Michael Kane, eds. *Peace and World Order Studies: A Curriculum Guide.* Boulder, Colo.: Westview Press, 1994. 425p.

Thorne, Bonnie, ed. *Model for Infusing a Global Perspective into the Curriculum.* Annual Meeting of the Center for Critical Thinking, 1992. 28p (ED367575).

Varis, Tapio. "The Role of Peace Education and the Media in the Prevention of Violence: Global Perspective." *Thresholds in Education* 21 (May 1995): 5–10.

Vogelson, Jay. "A Practitioner Looks at Globalization: II." *Journal of Legal Education* 46 (September 1996): 315–316.

Wakeland, Howard. "International Education for Engineers: A Working Model." *Annals of the American Academy of Political and Social Science* 511 (September 1990): 122–133.

Waterbury, Ronald. "World Studies at Queens College, CUNY." *Social Studies* 84 (March–April 1993): 54–57.

Waterstone, Marvin. *Water in the Global Environment.* Indiana, Pa.: National Council for Geographic Education, 1992. 57p.

Weil, Pierre. *The Art of Living in Peace: Towards a New Peace Consciousness.* Paris: UNESCO, 1990. 93p.

Werner, Walt. "Considering New Guidelines for Multicultural Curricula." *Canadian Social Studies* 27 (Summer 1993): 154–155.

Wilson, Angene. *International Student Speaker Programs: Someone from Another World.* Washington, D.C.: NAFSA: Association of International Educators, 1992. 32p (ED356746).

Wollitzer, Peter. "Introduction: Global Change and the Internationalization of Higher Education." *American Behavioral Scientist* 35 (September–October 1991): 5–16.

Wood, Richard. "Toward Cultural Empathy: A Framework for Global Education." *Educational Record* 72 (Fall 1991): 10–13.

Woodhouse, Tom, ed. *Peacemaking in a Troubled World.* New York: St. Martin's Press, 1991. 368p.

Woyach, Robert, and Richard Remy, eds. *Approaches to World Studies: A Handbook for Curriculum Planners.* Boston: Allyn and Bacon, 1989. 272p.

Wrage, Stephen. "Best Case Analysis: What Makes a Good Case and Where to Find the One You Need." *International Studies Notes* 19 (Spring 1994): 21–27.

Part 3: International and Global Studies in Elementary and Secondary Schools

American Forum for Global Education. *The New Global Resource Book.* New York: American Forum for Global Education, 1992. 246p.

Anderson, Charlotte, Susan Nicklas, and Agnes Crawford. *Global Understandings: Framework for Teaching and Learning.* Alexandria, Va.: Association for Supervision and Curriculum Development, 1994. 120p.

Andrews, Ian. "The UN and the Environment." *Green Teacher* 43 (June–September 1995): 22–24.

Ashford, Mary. "Peace Education after the Cold War." *Canadian Social Studies* 30 (Summer 1996): 178–179, 182.

Association for Childhood Education International. *Activities for the Classroom and Beyond.* Olney, Md.: Association for Childhood Education International, 1998. 61p.

Baker, Ralph. "An Academy for Future Diplomats: A New York–Based Program Prepares African American and Latino High School Students for International Careers." *Focus* 23 (May 1995): 5–6.

Bebbington, John, et al. "What Makes a Good Peacekeeper?" *Green Teacher* 43 (June–September 1995): 18–21.

Bednarz, Robert, and James Petersen. "The Reform Movement in Geographic Education: A View from the Summit." *Journal of Geography* 93 (January–February 1994): 61–64.

Berg, Marlowe, and Elsie Begler. "Changing Global Realities: Implications for the Classroom." *Social Studies Review* 31 (Spring 1992): 9–13.

Black, Susan. "A World of Learning." *Executive Educator* 16 (November 1994): 35–38.

Bliven, Arlene. *Learning and Teaching about Japan in Indiana Schools: Program and*

368 **ROBERT GOEHLERT AND ANTHONY STAMATOPLOS**

Resource Guide. Richmond, Ind.: Institute for Education on Japan, 1991. 381p (ED353166).

Boone, William, et al. "Teachers' Attitudes toward Distance Learning Technology in a Science/Society Global Issues Course." *Journal of Computers in Mathematics and Science Teaching* 14, 3 (1995): 305–323.

Brown, Jeffrey. *A Sustainable Development Curriculum Framework for World History and Cultures.* Montclair, N.J.: Global Learning, Inc., 1991. 296p (ED389656).

Brown, Jeffrey, ed. *Sustaining the Future: Activities for Environmental Education in U.S. History.* Union, N.J.: Global Learning Inc., 1995. 266p (ED389654).

Buell, Frederick. "World Studies for a Multicultural Era." *Social Studies* 84 (March–April 1993): 58–62.

Burleigh, Judith. "What Works: A Study of Multicultural Education in an International School Setting." *International Schools Journal* 27 (Spring 1994): 46–52.

Butt, Mahomood, ed. *Helping Students Teach in a Diverse World: A Rationale and Course.* Chicago: American Association of Colleges for Teacher Education, 1996. 33p (ED394917).

Cangemi, JoAnn, and Linda Aucoin. "Global Thematic Units Are Passports to Learning." *Social Education* 60 (February 1996): 80–81.

Case, Roland. "Promoting 'Global' Attitudes." *Canadian Social Studies* 30 (Summer 1996): 174–177.

Caudell, Lee, ed. *The Global Classroom, Special Report: Online for Learning.* Portland, Oreg.: Northwest Regional Educational Lab, 1994. 14p (ED369385).

Collins, H. Thomas, Frederick R. Czarra, and Andrew F. Smith. "Guidelines for Global and International Studies Education: Challenges, Cultures, and Connections." *Social Education* 62 (Summer 1998): 311–317 [see p. 226, this volume].

Copen, Peter. "Connecting Classrooms through Telecommunications." *Educational Leadership* 53 (October 1995): 44–47.

Cortes, Carlos. "Multiethnic and Global Education: Partners for the Eighties?" *Phi Delta Kappan* 64 (April 1983): 568–617.

Cottom, Carolyn. "A Bold Experiment in Teaching Values." *Educational Leadership* 53 (May 1996): 54–58.

Culturgrams: The Nations around Us. Volume I: *The Americas and Europe;* Volume II: *Africa, Asia, and Oceania.* Provo, Utah: Brigham Young University, David M. Kennedy Center for International Studies, 1991. 2v.

Cummins, Jim, and Dennis Sayers. *Brave New Schools: Challenging Cultural Illiteracy through Global Learning Networks.* New York: St. Martin's Press, 1995. 374p.

Cushner, Kenneth. "Creating Cross-Cultural Understanding through Internationally Co-operative Story Writing." *Social Education* 56 (January 1992): 43–46.

Darling, Linda. "Deepening Our Global Perspectives: The Moral Matters in Trickster Tales." *Canadian Social Studies* 30 (Summer 1994): 180–182.

DeCou-Landberg, Michelle. *The Global Classroom: A Thematic Multicultural Model for the K–6 and ESL Classroom.* Reading, Mass.: Addison-Wesley, 1995. 2v.

Dhand, Harry. "Global Doers: A Creative and Challenging Strategy." *Canadian Social Studies* 29 (Fall 1994): 26–33.

Dhand, Harry. "Selected Cooperative Learning Strategies in the Global Context." *Canadian Social Studies* 26 (Winter 1991): 78–83.

Diaz, Carlos. *Global Perspectives for Educators.* Boston: Allyn and Bacon, 1998. 227p.

Donato, Richard, and Robert Terry, eds. *Foreign Language Learning: The Journey of a Lifetime.* Lincolnwood, Ill.: National Textbook Company, 1995. 194p.

Drum, Jan. *Global Winners: 74 Learning Activities for Inside and Outside the Classroom.* Yarmouth, Maine: Intercultural Press, 1994. 209p.

Dunbar, Terry. "Acting Locally: On Site Science." *Green Teacher* 39 (June–September 1994): 18–19.

Easterly, Jean, ed. *Promoting Global Teacher Education: Seven Reports.* Reston, Va.: Association of Teacher Educators, 1994. 74p.

Fernekes, William. "Children's Rights in the Social Studies Curriculum: A Critical Imperative." *Social Education* 56 (April–May 1992): 203–204.

Fountain, Susan. *Education for Development: A Teacher's Resource for Global Learning.* Portsmouth, N.H.: Heinemann, 1995. 318p.

Fox-Genovese, Elizabeth. "The Crisis of Our Culture and the Teaching of History." *The History Teacher* 13 (November 1979): 89–101.

Garcia, Jesus, and Sharon Pugh. "Multicultural Education in Teacher Preparation Programs: A Political or an Educational Concept?" *Phi Delta Kappan* 74 (November 1992): 214–219.

Gaudiani, Claire. "For a New World, a New Curriculum." *Educational Record* 75 (Winter 1994): 20–29.

Gaudiani, Claire. "Global Social Development: Higher Education's Next Moral Commitment." *Educational Record* 76 (Winter 1995): 6–13.

Gaudiani, Claire. "In Pursuit of Global Civic Virtues: Multiculturalism in the Curriculum." *Liberal Education* 77 (May–June 1991): 12–15.

Gibson, Susan. "What's Worth Reading." *Canadian Social Studies* 30 (Summer 1996): 193–194.

Gilliom, M. Eugene. "Mobilizing Teacher Educators to Support Global Education in Preservice Programs." *Theory Into Practice* 32 (Winter 1993): 40–46.

Girard, Suzanne. "Celebrating the UN's 50th in Primary Grades." *Green Teacher* 43 (June–September 1995): 15–17.

Global Education Associates. *Information Packet for Religion and World Order Program Project Global 2000.* New York: Global Education Associates, 1994. 23p (ED396995).

Gutek, Gerald. *American Education in a Global Society: Internationalizing Teacher Education.* White Plains, N.Y.: Longman, 1993. 276p (ED373021).

Hampson, Tom, and Loretta Whalen. *Tales of the Heart: Affective Approaches to Global Education.* New York: Friendship Press, 1991. 244p.

Hanvey, Robert G. "An Attainable Global Perspective." *Theory Into Practice* 21 (Summer 1982): 162–167 [see p. 217, this volume].

Harik, Ramsay. *Thinking about Our Future: War, Society, and the Environment—A Series of Lesson Plans.* Bloomington: Indiana Center on Global Change and World Peace, 1993. 130p (ED360252).

Harris, Judith B. "Information Is Forever in Formation, Knowledge Is the Knower: Global Connectivity in K–12 Classrooms." *Computers in the Schools* 12, 1–2 (1996): 11–22.

Hartoonian, H. Michael, and Hilary Stock. *A Guide to Curriculum Planning in Global Studies.* Madison: Wisconsin Dept. of Public Instruction, Division for Instructional Services, Bureau for School Improvement, Program Development Section, 1992. 180p.

Hatch, Virginia. *Human Rights for Children: A Curriculum for Teaching Human Rights to Children Age 3–12.* Tacoma, Wash.: Amnesty International, 1992. 160p (ED395869).

Hatfield, William, ed. *Visions and Realities in Foreign Language Teaching, Where We Are, Where We Are Going: Selected Papers from the 1993 Central States Conference.* Lincolnwood, Ill.: National Textbook Company, 1993. 149p.

Hirschberg, Stuart. *One World, Many Cultures.* Newark, N.J.: Rutgers: State University of New Jersey, 1992. 704p.

Iowa Peace Institute. *Fostering Peace: A Comparison of Conflict Resolution Approaches for Students (K–12).* Grinnell, Iowa: Iowa Peace Institute, 1994. 35p (ED368993).

Jacobsen, Judith. *Population Growth: Understanding Global Change—Earth Science and Human Impacts—Global Change Instruction Program.* Boulder, Colo.: National Center for Atmospheric Research, 1993. 32p (ED379141).

Kobus, Doni. "Multicultural/Global Education: An Educational Agenda for the Rights of the Child." *Social Education* 56 (April–May 1992): 224–227.

Koller, Mary, and Margaret Legowski, eds. *The World Map Project*. Washington, D.C.: Peace Corps, Office of World Wise Schools, 1995. 74p.

Lang, Edward, and Caryn White, eds. *Geography and the Environment: International Perspectives—Teacher's Resource Guide*. Storrs: Connecticut Geographic Alliance, 1993. 104p (ED368633).

Luderer, William, ed. *Making Global Connections in the Middle School: Lessons on the Environment, Development and Equity*. Union, N.J.: Global Learning, Inc. 1994. 94p (ED389655).

Lundeberg, Mary Anna, et al. "Wandering around the World: Building Multicultural Perspectives through K–12 Telecommunications Projects." *Journal of Technology and Teacher Education* 3, 4 (1995): 301–321.

Lynch, James, Celia Modgil, and Sohan Modgil, eds. *Cultural Diversity and the Schools*. Washington, D.C.: Falmer, 1992. 4 vols.

MacRae-Campbell, Linda, and Micki McKisson. *Our Troubled Skies*. Tucson, Ariz.: Zephyr Press, 1990. 105p.

MacRae-Campbell, Linda, and Micki McKisson. *War: The Global Battlefield*. Tucson, Ariz.: Zephyr Press, 1990. 106p.

MacRae-Campbell, Linda, Micki McKisson, and Bruce Campbell. *The Ocean Crisis*. Tucson, Ariz.: Zephyr Press, 1990. 108p.

McDaniel, Rick, and Jim Petrie, eds. *A Two-Way Approach to Understanding: Issues in Global Education*. 2nd ed. Fredericton, New Brunswick: Global Education Centre, 1992. 189p (ED381346).

McFadden, Jon, Merry Merryfield, and Keith Barron. *Multicultural & Global/International Education: Guidelines for Programs in Teacher Education*. Washington, D.C.: AACTE Publications, 1997. 24p.

McIsaac, Marina. *The Global Classroom: An International Perspective*. New Orleans: Proceedings of Selected Research and Development Presentations at the Convention of the Association for Educational Communications and Technology, 1993. 12p (ED362186).

McNergney, Robert. "Videocases: A Way to Foster a Global Perspective on Multicultural Education." *Phi Delta Kappan* 76 (December 1994): 296–299.

Mason, Robin. *Globalising Education: Trends and Applications*. New York: Routledge, 1998. 167p.

Meagher, Laura. *Teaching Children about Global Awareness: A Guide for Parents and Teachers*. New York: Crossroad, 1991. 144p.

Merryfield, Merry. *In the Global Classroom: Teacher Decision-Making and Global Perspectives in Education*. New Orleans: American Educational Research Association, 1994. 32p (ED401249).

Merryfield, Merry. "Pedagogy for Global Perspectives in Education: Studies of Teachers' Thinking and Practice." *Theory and Research in Social Education* 26 (Summer 1998): 342–379 [see p. 244, this volume].

Merryfield, Merry. "Reflective Practice in Global Education Strategies for Teacher Educators." *Theory Into Practice* 32 (Winter 1993): 27–32.

Merryfield, Merry. "Responding to the Gulf War: A Case Study of Instructional Decision Making." *Social Education* 57 (January 1993): 33–41.

Merryfield, Merry. "Shaping the Curriculum in Global Education: The Influence of Student Characteristics on Teacher Decision Making." *Journal of Curriculum and Supervision* 9 (Spring 1994): 233–249.

Merryfield, Merry. *Teaching about the World: Teacher Education Programs with a Global Perspective*. Columbus: Mershon Center, Ohio State University, 1990. 115p (ED339623).

Merryfield, Merry, ed. *Lessons from Africa: A Supplement to Middle School Courses in World Cultures, Global Studies, and World Geography.* Bloomington: Social Studies Development Center, Indiana University, 1989. 99p.

Merryfield, Merry, ed. *Making Connections between Multicultural and Global Education: Teacher Educators and Teacher Education Programs.* Washington, D.C.: American Association of Colleges for Teacher Education, 1996. 262p.

Merryfield, Merry, and Jay Harris. "Getting Started in Global Education: Essential Literature, Essential Linkages for Teacher Educators." *School of Education Review* 4 (Spring 1992): 56–66.

Merryfield, Merry, and Josiah Tlou. "The Process of Africanizing the Social Studies." *Social Studies* 86 (November–December 1995): 260–269.

Merryfield, Merry, Elaine Jarchow, and Sarah Pichert, eds. *Preparing Teachers to Teach Global Perspectives: A Handbook for Teacher Educators.* Thousand Oaks, Calif.: Corwin Press, 1997. 269p.

Mills, Thomas, and Jean Campbell. *Educational Use of Foreign Students and Americans Returned from Study Abroad: A Project to Improve Global Education.* Eugene, Oreg.: Office of International Education and Exchange, 1994. 92p (ED416807).

Milord, Susan. *Hands around the World: 365 Creative Ways to Build Cultural Awareness and Global Respect.* Charlotte, Vt.: Williamson, 1992. 158p.

Mounkhall, Thomas. "Teaching Global Studies through Architecture." *Social Science Record* 31 (Fall 1994): 37–40.

Moyles, Janet, and Linda Hargreaves, eds. *The Primary Curriculum: Learning from International Perspectives.* New York: Routledge, 1998. 226p.

Nelson, Jennifer. "A Note on Teaching about Australia." *Canadian Social Studies* 30 (Winter 1996): 76–77.

Nelson, Murry, ed. *The Future of the Social Studies.* Boulder, Colo.: Social Science Education Consortium, 1994. 88p.

Nelson, Olga, et al., eds. *Practical Classroom Applications of Language Experience: Looking Back, Looking Forward.* Boston: Allyn and Bacon, 1999. 280p.

Nsirimovu, Anyakwee. *Human Rights Education Techniques in Schools: Building Attitudes and Skills.* Port Harcourt: Nawa Publishers, 1994. 43p.

O'Brien, Anthony, and Annabelle Sreberny-Mohammadi. "Engendering World Studies." *Social Studies* 84 (March–April 1993): 74–77.

Ochoa, Anna, and Shinichi Suzuki. "Globalism and Teacher Education: Summary of a Comparative Joint Research Project." *Peabody Journal of Education* 68 (Summer 1993): 60–75.

Orr, Jeff. "An Historical Example of the Global Economy: James Macbraire and the Newfoundland Cod Trade of 1805: Documents in the Classroom." *Canadian Social Studies* 30 (Summer 1996): 197–200.

Osler, Audrey, and Hugh Starkey. *Teacher Education and Human Rights.* London: D. Fulton Publishers, 1996. 201p.

Paris, Scott, and Henry Wellman, eds. *Global Prospects for Education: Development, Culture, and Schooling.* Washington, D.C.: American Psychological Association, 1998. 407p.

Pesce, Louis. "Addressing Society's Problems in a Global Studies Class." *Social Studies* 87 (March–April 1996): 60–62.

Peters, Richard. *Environments: The Context of Our Lives: A Social Studies Schema for Grades 7–12.* Corpus Christi, Tex.: Global Horizons, Center for Applied Ecosocial Studies, 1994. 34p (ED374048).

Pugh, Sharon, et al. "Multicultural Tradebooks in the Social Studies Classroom." *Social Studies* 85 (March–April 1994): 62–65.

Pyke, Thomas, Jr. "GLOBE Partnership Launched: Kids and Scientists Are Collaborating Worldwide." *EPA Journal* 21 (Spring 1995): 14–15.

Ramsey, Patricia. *Teaching and Learning in a Diverse World: Multicultural Education for Young Children.* New York: Teacher's College Press, 1986. 224p.

Risinger, C. Frederick. "Global Education and the Social: An ERIC/ChESS Sampler." *Canadian Social Studies* 30 (Summer 1996): 190–191.

Scapp, Ron. "Feeling the Weight of the World (Studies) on My Shoulders." *Social Studies* 84 (March–April 1993): 67–70.

Schukar, Ron. "Controversy in Global Education: Lessons for Teacher Educators." *Theory Into Practice* 32 (Winter 1993): 52–27.

Seelye, Ned. *Teaching Culture: Strategies for International Communication.* Yarmouth, Maine: Intercultural Press, 1984. 316p.

Siegle, Candace. *Education around the World: Snapshots from the Global Village.* Arlington, Va.: American Association of School Administrators, 1995. 65p.

Simmons, John, and Lawrence Baines, eds. *Language Study in Middle School, High School, and Beyond.* Newark, Del.: International Reading Association, 1998. 229p.

Singletary, Ted, and Richard Jordan. "Exploring the Globe: Collecting and Sharing Data to Make a Difference." *Science Teacher* 63 (March 1996): 36–39.

Stanford Program on International and Cross-Cultural Education. *Language: A Theme Guide to K–12 Curricular Resources, Activities, and Processes.* Stanford, Calif.: Stanford University, 1983. 67p (ED351226).

Stanford Program on International and Cross-Cultural Education. *Teaching World Literature in the Global Classroom: A Theme Guide to K–12 Curricular Resources, Activities, and Processes.* Stanford, Calif.: Stanford University, 1983. 114p (ED351227).

Stanford Program on International and Cross-Cultural Education. *World Cultures: A Theme Guide to K–12 Curricular Resources, Activities, and Processes.* Stanford, Calif.: Stanford University, 1984. 109p (ED351225).

Stevens, Jacqueline, et al. "Classroom Tips." *Canadian Social Studies* 27 (Fall 1992): 37–38.

Stomfay-Stitz, Aline. *Peace Education for Children: Historical Perspectives.* New Orleans: American Educational Research Association, 1994. 22p (ED381464).

Stopsky, Fred, and Sharon Shockley. *Social Studies in a Global Society.* Albany, N.Y.: Delmar Publishers, 1994. 464p.

Storti, Craig. *The Art of Crossing Cultures.* Yarmouth, Maine: Intercultural Press, 1990. 121p.

Swiniarski, Louise, et al. *Educating the Global Village: Including the Young Child in the World.* Upper Saddle River, N.J.: Merrill, 1999. 230p.

Taylor, Howard. *Practical Suggestions for Teaching Global Education.* Washington, D.C.: Clearinghouse on Teaching and Teacher Education, 1996. 4p (ED395924).

Terry, Robert, ed. *Dimension '96: Global Access through Languages—Selected Proceedings of the Joint Conference of the Southern Conference on Language Teaching and the Alabama Association of Foreign Language Teachers.* Mobile, Ala.: Southern Conference on Language Teaching, 1996. 106p (ED400676).

Thorne, Bonnie, et al. "Model for Infusing a Global Perspective into the Curriculum." Paper presented at the annual meeting of the Center for Critical Thinking, 1993. 28p (ED367575).

Tucker, Jan L., and Anna M. Evans. "The Challenge of a Global Age." In Byron G. Massialas and Rodney F. Allen, eds., *Critical Issues in Teaching Social Studies K–12.* Boston: Wadsworth Publishing Company, 1996, Chapter 7, pp. 181–217.

Tye, Barbara, and Kenneth Tye. *Global Education: A Study of School Change.* Albany, N.Y.: State University of New York Press, 1992. 273p.

Tye, Kenneth, and Barbara Tye. "The Realities of Schooling: Overcoming Teacher Resistance to Global Education." *Theory Into Practice* 32 (Winter 1993): 58–63.

Vacca, John. "CU on the Net." *Internet World* 6 (October 1995): 80–82.

Wahlstrom, Mary, and Rodney Clarken. *Preparing Teachers for Education That Is Multicultural and Global.* San Francisco: American Educational Research Association, 1992. 22p (ED346033).

Wangen, Roger. *Model Learner Outcomes for International Education.* St. Paul, Minn.: Minnesota State Department of Education, 1991. 119p (ED350199).

Wheeler, Ron. "Post Cold War Studies: Some Ideas for Changing the Way Students Think about the World." *Social Education* 58 (September 1994): 287–289.

Wilson, Angene. "Conversation Partners: Helping Students Gain a Global Perspective through Cross-Cultural Experiences." *Theory Into Practice* 32 (Winter 1993): 21–26.

Wilson, Angene. *The Meaning of International Experience for Schools.* Westport, Conn.: Praeger, 1993. 158p.

Wilson, Angene, ed. *To Live in a Multicultural World.* Washington, D.C.: Youth for Understanding International Exchange, 1992. 65p (ED369668).

Wishnietsky, Dan. *Using Computer Technology to Create a Global Classroom.* Bloomington, Ind.: Phi Delta Kappa Educational Foundation, 1993. 42p.

Wooster, Judith. "Authentic Assessment: A Strategy for Preparing Teachers to Respond to Curricular Mandates in Global Education." *Theory Into Practice* 32 (Winter 1993): 47–51.

Major Web Sites

American Forum for Global Education
http://www.globaled.org

> This organization promotes global and international education by providing educational materials, consultations, and professional development programs. The Web site includes an on-line forum, descriptions of programs for teachers, a catalog of publications, and a list of area studies links.

AskERIC: Education Information with the Personal Touch
http://ericir.syr.edu

> An Internet-based information service provided by Educational Resources Information Center, a federally funded educational information system. Includes the Ask-ERIC Question and Answer Service, and the AskERIC Virtual Library, which provides information resources on various topics. AskERIC Web site and ERIC database can also be searched.

Gateway to World History
http://www.hartford-hwp.com/gateway

> This is a collection of Internet resources on world history. This site provides links to history-related sites, including sites covering various topics, geographic areas, images, electronic documents, history departments and other resources.

Stanford Program on International and Cross-Cultural Education (SPICE)
http://www-iis.stanford.edu/SPICE/index.html

> SPICE continues a 23-year tradition of providing up-to-date curriculum materials on international topics for grades 6–14. Topics covered at this site are contemporary world issues, world geography, world history, and world cultures.

Virtual Global College
http://pgw.org/vgc

> Maintained by the Virtual Global College, this site is a collection of links to sites related to research and study via the Internet. It includes a variety of on-line resources, bookstores, publications, journals, newspapers, and other sites.

World Lecture Hall
http://www.utexas.edu/world/lecture
> This site provides links to Web pages created by faculty using Web-based delivery of class materials. The site includes syllabi, assignments, lecture notes, exams, multimedia textbooks, and other resources. It uses an alphabetically arranged index to subjects covered. Each link is briefly annotated. It also provides general links to other institutions.

World-Wide Web Virtual Library: CEEISAWeb International Affairs Resources—Teaching and Curriculum Development
http://ian.vse.cz/resource/curric.htm
> Maintained by the Central East European Studies Association, this site provides links to resources on teaching curriculum development.

Additional Web Sites

Economic Development Institute of the World Bank: Resources for Teachers and Trainers
http://worldbank.org/wbi/resource.html

Global Education Resources on the World Wide Web
http://www.educ.uvic.ca/faculty/triecken/global2.html

Global Educator's Guide to the Internet
http://www.educ.uvic.ca/faculty/triecken

Global Issues Resource Index
http://www.islandnet.com/vglobe/activity.html

Global Learning, Inc.
http://viconet.com/~schnarr/global.htm

Global Schoolhouse: Linking Kids, Teachers, and Parents around the World
http://www.gsh.org

Globe Program: Global Learning and Observations to Benefit the Environment
http://www.globe.gov

IPENet Electronic Archive of Course Syllabi
http://csf.colorado.edu/ipe/syllabi/index.html

International Simulations: University of Michigan Documents Center
http://www.lib.umich.edu/libhome/Documents.center/intsim.html

KIDLINK: Global Networking for Youth through the Age of 15
http://www.kidlink.org

Political Science Cyberclasses
http://www.psci.unt.edu/kho/cybercls

Programs in International Educational Resources: PIER
http://www.cis.yale.edu/pieris/p_res.html

Social Studies School Service
http://www.socialstudies.com

Vglobe: The Virtual Global Learner Centre
http://www.islandnet.com/vglobe/vglobe.html

World-Wide Virtual Library: Education
http://www.csu.edu.au/education/library.html

World Wise Schools Homepage: Peace Corps
http://www.peacecorps.gov/wws

Web Guides

Barron, Ann E., and Karen S. Ivers. *The Internet and Instruction Activities and Ideas.* Englewood, Colo.: Libraries Unlimited, 1996. 159p.

Branscomb, H. Eric. *Casting Your Net: A Student's Guide to Research on the Internet.* Boston: Allyn and Bacon, 1998. 175p.

Crotchett, Kevin. *A Teacher's Project Guide to the Internet.* Portsmouth, N.H.: Heinemann, 1997. 174p.

Leu, Donald L., Jr., and Deborah Diadiun Leu. *Teaching with the Internet: Lessons from the Classroom.* Norwood, Mass.: Christopher-Gordon, 1997. 214p.

Maxwell, Bruce. *How to Access the Federal Government on the Internet.* Washington, D.C.: Congressional Quarterly, 1995– .

Notess, Greg. *Government Information on the Internet.* Lanham, Md.: Bernan Press, 1997.

Parker, Laura. *Net Lessons: Web-Based Projects for Your Classroom.* Sebastopol, Calif.: Songline Studios, Inc., and O'Reilly and Associates, 1997. 284p.

Provenzo, Eugene F., Jr. *The Educator's Brief Guide to the Internet and the World Wide Web.* Larchmont, N.Y.: Eye on Education, 1998. 182p.

Raese, Robert. *Internet.edu: A Sourcebook for Educators.* Arlington Heights, Ill.: IRI/ SkyLight Training and Publishing, 1997. 215p.

Robin, Bernard, Elissa Keeler, and Robert Miller. *Educator's Guide to the Web.* New York: MIS Press, 1997. 409p.

Ryder, Randall. *Internet for Educators.* 2nd ed. Upper Saddle River, N.J.: Prentice-Hall, 1998. 198p.

Stull, Andrew. *Political Science on the Internet: A Student's Guide.* Upper Saddle River, N.J.: Prentice-Hall, 1997. 58p.

Virginia Space Grant Consortium. *The Educator's Guide to the Internet: A Handbook with Resources and Activities.* 3rd ed. Menlo Park, Calif.: Addison-Wesley, 1997. 236p.

Section II: Guides to Area Studies

There are two significant factors that affect the publishing of guides to area studies resources: the constantly changing world community of nations and the advent of the Internet. New countries are emerging, country names are changing, and geographical boundaries are being redefined. Consequently, it is difficult to publish a guide to area studies that is up to date, at least in a geographical sense.

For each of the world areas included in this section, we have annotated what we consider to be the best print and Web sources, followed by lists of additional guides not annotated. Print guides to area studies are not as easy to find as one might think. The best way to find these guides is to do keyword searches using terms such as "sources," "resources," "bibliography," "guides," and the specific area or region. Unfortunately, there is no single Library of Congress subject heading that is used for such guides.

An important source is the World Bibliographic Series published by ABC-Clio. There are over two hundred volumes available, and more are being published. Each multidisciplinary volume covers all aspects of a single country, including its history, geography, economy, politics, culture, religion, and living conditions. All the volumes are uniform in nature, and the annotated entries include books, articles, maps, documents, newspapers, and dissertations. In addition to country volumes, some volumes cover the principal regions of the world and major cities. Our survey does not attempt to list all printed bibliographies on every area.

The enormous growth of the Internet has given rise to numerous World Wide Web sites for all area studies. The Web sites provide valuable full-text materials, current news, databases, and all sorts of information. Although Web sites are not yet as rich in bibliographic information as print guides, both provide important information for students and researchers.

Perhaps the best way to find other or new Web sites not mentioned in this guide is to start with the mega-sites listed in this section. Using search engines to identify general area studies sites is much more difficult and time-consuming. The World Wide Web Virtual Libraries are excellent Web sites to start with, and provide links to other related Virtual Libraries. Several of them are annotated in this section.

Research Guides

Congressional Quarterly. *International Information Directory*. Washington, D.C.: Congressional Quarterly, 1998–.
  This directory profiles more than 4,000 government, inter-government, and non-profit agencies throughout the world. Arrangement is by type of organization. Each entry includes a brief profile of the organization and contact information, including head, address, telephone and fax numbers, and electronic mail and Web addresses when available. It also contains subject and name indexes.

Europa Publications. *Europa World Year Book*. London: Europa Publications, 1926– .
  This is a standard reference work containing detailed surveys of countries of the world, focusing on political, economic, and commercial information. It is especially useful for its comprehensive listing of over 1,600 international organizations, giving descriptions, brief history, and information on membership, organization, activities, leadership, and publications. Major organizations such as the United Nations and European Union are covered, as well as other international organizations. These are organized by categories such as education, law, science, etc. At the end of the first volume, there also is an index to the organizations, listed alphabetically by main reference.

Gale Research. *Encyclopedia of Associations: International Organizations*. Detroit: Gale, 1989–.
  This directory covers more than 20,800 international organizations from 200 countries. The descriptive entries include contact information such as names, addresses, telephone and fax numbers, electronic mail addresses, and other useful information about budget, conventions and meetings, membership, and publications. The first part is arranged by 15 subject categories, with alphabetical keyword subheadings. Entries are listed alphabetically by organization name. The second part contains three separate indexes: geographic, executive, name and keyword.

Gale Research. *International Research Centers Directory*. Detroit: Gale Research, 1982–.
  This is a directory of more than 8,000 research organizations based outside the United States. It covers government, university, independent non-profit, and com-

mercial research organizations in more than 150 countries. There are five broad categories: life sciences; physical sciences and engineering; private and public policy and affairs; social and cultural studies; and multidisciplinary and coordinating research centers. The directory is divided into 17 subject sections. Entries are listed alphabetically within each section. Each entry includes basic contact information, such as address, telephone and fax numbers, and electronic mail and Web addresses when available. Entries also provide brief descriptions of the organizations, including information on publications, educational programs, and libraries. The work contains subject, country, and master indexes.

International Teleconferencing Association. *Global Conferencing Directory.* Parsipanny, N.J.: American Telephone and Telegraph, 1994–.
This work is a guide to video-conferencing sites, manufacturers, service providers, and other organizations. The first section lists codes and abbreviations. The index section lists conference rooms by country, state or province, and city. There are separate U.S. and international room listings sections, arranged alphabetically by company name. A final section contains advertising, arranged alphabetically by product or service conference.

Kurian, George. *Global Data Locator.* Lanham, Md.: Bernan Press, 1997. 375p.
This volume identifies the most important general, global, and statistical source books available in print. It also identifies statistical source books by subject that are available in print. The volume identifies electronic databases, including CD-ROMs, on-line, and on tape. There is a list of publication by publishers and an index of publications by title.

Levinson, David, and Karen Christensen. *The Global Village Companion: An A-to-Z Guide to Understanding Current World Affairs.* Santa Barbara, Calif.: ABC-Clio, 1996. 438p.
This volume is a good starting place to find information about concepts and terms related to global studies. The volume includes over 400 entries that describe more than 1,000 terms. In addition to individual definitions, the entries give the historical and global significance of concepts. The work includes a detailed subject index, maps, appendixes of countries, major international documents, and a chronology.

Schraepler, Hans-Albrecht. *Directory of International Organizations.* Washington, D.C.: Georgetown University Press, 1996. 424p.
This is a handbook to international organizations. It begins with sections listing abbreviations, and giving a brief chronology of international cooperation through 1995. The main directory is arranged by category into six parts: United Nations system, North American Treaty Organization, relevant regional organizations, relevant economic organizations, the Commonwealth and Commonwealth of Independent States, and other relevant organizations. Each entry includes contact information, purpose, membership, structure, activities, and information and/or publications produced. It includes tables showing membership, by country, of major international groupings.

Union of International Associations. *Yearbook of International Organizations.* New Providence, N.J.: K. G. Saur, 1967–.
This is a comprehensive reference work on international organizations. The first volume contains organization descriptions. Entries are alphabetical, and include a sequence number. Descriptions also include contact information, with electronic mail and Web site addresses, if available, year established or founded, aims, relations with other organizations, structure, languages, staff, finances, activities, events, publications, information services, and a list of members. The second volume lists the organizations by country or territory, giving principal contact, address, and a cross-refer-

ence to the description in the first volume. The third volume lists the organizations by subject category, then alphabetically by organization name containing key words of that subject. Contact information also is provided. The third volume contains indexes to the first three volumes. The fourth volume is "International Organization Bibliography and Resources." This is also available on CD-ROM.

Additional Research Guides

Almanac Publishing. *Washington Almanac of International Trade and Business.* 4th ed. Washington, D.C.: Almanac Publishing, 1998. 800p.

Appiah, Kwame, and Henry Louis Gates, eds. *The Dictionary of Global Culture.* New York: Knopf, 1997. 717p.

Baratta, Joseph. *United Nations System.* New Brunswick, N.J.: Transaction Publishers, 1995. 511p.

Beckel, Lothar, ed. *Global Change: The Atlas of Global Change.* New York: Macmillan Library Reference USA, 1998. 164p.

California Institute of Public Affairs. *World Directory of Environmental Organizations.* Claremont, Calif.: Public Affairs Clearinghouse, 1989– .

Carroll, Freda, and Barbara Zolynski. *Basic Sources of European Union Information.* Manchester, U.K.: European Information Association, 1996. 95p.

Colas, Bernard, ed. *Global Economic Co-operation: A Guide to Agreements and Organizations.* 2nd ed. Tokyo: United Nations University Press, 1994. 557p.

Deans, Candace, and Shaun Dakin. *The Thunderbird Guide to International Business Resources on the World Wide Web.* New York: John Wiley, 1997. 142p.

Economist. *Economist Guide to Global Economic Indicators.* New York: Wiley, 1994. 216p.

Europa Publications. *International Relations Research Directory.* London: Europa, 1995– .

Fisher, Julie. *Non-Governments: NGOs and the Political Development of the Third World.* West Hartford, Conn.: Kumarian Press, 1997. 256p.

Flemming, Michael, and Joseph Nellis, eds. *Instat: International Statistics Sources—Subject Guide to Sources of International Comparative Statistics.* New York: Routledge, 1995. 876p.

Gale Research. *Guides to International Education in the United States.* Detroit: Gale, 1991– .

George Washington Journal of International Law and Economics. *Guide to International Legal Research.* 3rd ed. Charlottesville, Va.: Lexis Law, 1998. 784p.

Grey House Publishers. *International Business and Trade Directories.* Lakeville, Conn.: Grey House, 1997. 636p.

Hajnal, Peter, ed. *International Information: Documents, Publications, and Electronic Information of International Governmental Organizations.* 2nd ed. Englewood, Colo.: Libraries Unlimited, 1997. 528p.

Harris, Gordon. *Organization of African Unity.* New Brunswick, N.J.: Transaction Publishers, 1994. 139p.

International Council on Archives. *Guide to the Archives of International Organizations.* Paris: UNESCO, 1979– .

Kelleher, Ann, and Laura Klein. *Global Perspectives: A Handbook for Understanding Global Issues.* Upper Saddle River, N.J.: Prentice Hall, 1999.

Kohls, L. Robert, and Lynn Tyler. *A Select Guide to Area Studies Resources.* Rev. ed. Provo, Utah: Brigham Young University, David M. Kennedy Center for International Studies, 1998. 47p.

Lane, Jan-Erik, David McKay, and Kenneth Newton, eds. *Political Data Handbook: OECD Countries.* 2nd ed. Oxford: Oxford University Press, 1997. 357p.

Levy-Livermore, Amnon, ed. *Handbook on the Globalization of the World Economy.* Northampton, Mass.: Edward Elgar, 1998. 748p.

Mitchell, Bruce, and Robert Salsbury. *Multicultural Education: An International Guide to Research, Policies, and Programs.* Westport, Conn.: Greenwood Press, 1996. 383p.

Moran, Robert, and David Braaten, eds. *International Directory of Multicultural Resources.* Houston, Tex.: Gulf Publishing Company, 1996. 160p.

Organisation for Economic Co-operation and Development. *Directory of Non-Governmental Organisations Active in Sustainable Development.* Paris: Development Centre of OECD, 1996– .

Owen, Richard. *The Times Guide to World Organizations: Their Role and Reach in the New World Order.* London: Times Books, 1996. 254p.

Oyen, Else, S. M. Miller, and Syed Abdus, eds. *Poverty: A Global Review: Handbook on International Poverty Research.* Cambridge, Mass.: Scandinavian University Press, 1996. 620p.

Pagell, Ruth. *International Business Information: How to Find It, How to Use It.* 2nd ed. Phoenix, Ariz.: Oryx Press, 1997. 371p.

Salda, Anne C. M. *The International Monetary Fund.* New Brunswick, N.J.: Transaction Publishers, 1992. 295p.

Salda, Anne C. M. *World Bank.* New Brunswick, N.J.: Transaction Publishers, 1995. 306p.

Savitt, William, and Paula Bottorf. *Global Development: A Reference Handbook.* Santa Barbara, Calif.: ABC-Clio, 1995. 369p.

Schorr, Alan. *Refugee and Immigrant Resource Directory.* 3rd ed. Juneau, Alaska: Denali Press, 1994. 256p.

Schreiber, Mae. *International Trade Sources: A Research Guide.* New York: Garland, 1997. 327p.

Schwartz, Richard. *The Cold War Reference Guide: A General History and Annotated Chronology with Selected Biographies.* Jefferson, N.C.: McFarland, 1997. 321p.

Shaaban, Marian, ed. *Guide to Country Information in International Governmental Organization Publications.* Bethesda, Md.: Congressional Information Service, 1996. 343p.

Sheinin, David. *Organization of American States.* Santa Barbara, Calif.: ABC-Clio, 1995. 209p.

UNESCO. *World Directory of Human Rights Research and Training Institutions.* 3rd rev. ed. Paris: UNESCO, 1995. 178p.

UNESCO. *World Directory of Peace Research and Training Institutions.* 8th rev. ed. Oxford: UNESCO, 1995. 256p.

UNESCO. Social and Human Sciences Documentation Centre. *World Directory of Research and Training Institutions in International Law.* 3rd ed. Cambridge, Mass.: Basil Blackwell, 1994. 245p.

United States. Department of Commerce. *Foreign Science and Technology Information Sources in the Federal Government and Select Private Sector Organizations.* Washington, D.C.: U.S. Department of Commerce, Office of Technology Policy, 1996. 228p.

Williams, Phil. *North Atlantic Treaty Organization.* New Brunswick, N.J.: Transaction Publishers, 1994. 283p.

Web Sites

INTERNATIONAL AFFAIRS

Area Studies, Comparative Politics
http://www.psr.keele.ac.uk/area.htm
The page is a gateway to information on countries, and has links to sub-pages on each country included. Links on sub-pages include relevant government, commercial, organizational, and educational sites, and appropriate Yahoo! categories. There also are links to standard reference sites, such as the *Perry-Castañeda Library Map*

Collection, and CIA publications such as the *World Factbook.* Along with the alphabetical country listing, the main page has links to other government and political sites.

CIIA Links to Other Sites on International Relations
http://www.ciia.org/links.htm
This extensive set of links to Internet sites on international relations is maintained by the Canadian Institute of International Affairs (CIIA). It includes links to sites related to conferences and meetings, electronic publications, educational programs, and other institutes and organizations.

Columbia International Affairs Online: CIAO
http://www.ciaonet.org
This site is an on-line source of scholarly publications on international affairs. Seventy-two selected institutions contribute papers to CIAO. CIAO includes working papers, conference proceedings, journal abstracts, books, a schedule of events, policy briefs and economic indicators, and maps and country data. There also is a selected list of links to other international affairs sites. CIAO updates the material on this site regularly. Full access is through institution subscription.

Global Resources Web Project
http://www.duke.edu/~frykholm/global3.htm
This new site, part of a project by the Association of Research Libraries and Association of American Universities, is the beginning of an inventory of the best Web sites on all regions of the world. The site is meant to be a clearinghouse to provide links to on-line resources and identify institutions abroad that offer access to global sources. This is an excellent listing of sites for anyone interested in area studies programs.

International and Area Studies
http://www.mnsfld.edu/depts/lib/country.html
This site is an excellent starting point for identifying sites related to area studies and international affairs, including topics such as human rights, peace studies, and political affairs. These pages include links to the major international organizations and news sources as well.

International Relations Internet Sites
http://www.library.ubc.ca/poli/international.html
This site is maintained by the University of British Columbia Library. It provides links to Internet sites related to international relations, conflict and peace studies, international economic development, and international and supranational organizations.

Library of Congress Country Studies
http://lcweb2.loc.gov/frd/cs/cshome.html
This on-line series includes 85 countries that are part of the printed Country Studies/Area Handbook published by the Department of the Army. They are excellent sources for economic, political, and cultural information on specific countries. This site is easy to use, very reliable, and an excellent starting point for undergraduates and researchers.

Online Intelligence Project: International Affairs Resources
http://www.icg.org/intelweb/resource.html
This site provides access to on-line foreign affairs information. It includes links to sites of the Department of State, intelligence community, foreign affairs, news sources, and other resources.

Thunderbird IBIC Links
http://www.t-bird.edu/research/ibic/links
> This site is part of the Web site of the American Graduate School of International Management (Thunderbird). Maintained by Thunderbird's International Business Information Centre (IBIC), it provides various information resources appropriate for international research and education, particularly related to business. It includes links to related Internet sites.

University of Texas International Network Information System
http://menic.utexas.edu/
> This is the site of the International Network Information Systems, a joint project of four network information centers at the University of Texas: Asian Network Information Center (ASNIC); Latin American Network Information Center (LANIC); Middle East Network Information Center (MENIC); and Russian and East European Network Information Center (REENIC). The main page has links to each of the centers. Each center maintains its own page, and the content and organization vary. Each has extensive sets of links to other Internet resources related to that center.

Weatherhead Center for International Affairs: Links to Related Web Sites
http://data.fas.harvard.edu/cfia/links/
> This site is part of the Web site of Harvard University's Weatherhead Center for International Affairs. It presents an extensive list of on-line international affairs resources, including government and nongovernment, educational, organizations, and news sites.

World Bank Group
http://www.worldbank.org
> This site contains information about the World Bank, including publications and pages about various aspects of development, and selected links to other sites. It also includes news releases, speeches, and indexes. This site is searchable by keyword.

Yale Library Selected Internet Resources: International Affairs
http://www.library.yale.edu/ia-resources/resource.htm
> This is a Web site of international affairs links selected by librarians at the Yale University Library. It includes a variety of resources: subject guides; discussion groups, mailing lists, and e-mail lists; electronic publications and news sources; organizations and research institutions; libraries; data; reference tools; and teaching resources and Web sites. The links are arranged by subject and region.

INTERNATIONAL ORGANIZATIONS

International Monetary Fund Home Page
http://www.imf.org
> This is the Web site of the International Monetary Fund (IMF). It includes IMF information, news, publications, and links to other related sites.

International Non-Governmental Organization Sites
http://www1.umn.edu/humanrts/links/ngolinks.html
> This site presents a selective list of links to non-governmental organization sites. The site includes a list of on-line information resources and documents. All entries are annotated, include the URL, and have live links to the sites.

International Organization Network: IONet
http://csf.Colorado.EDU/isa/sections/io
> This site is sponsored by the International Organization Section of the International

Studies Association. It contains information and news about the section, and links to on-line resources on a variety of topics and different geographic areas.

NGO Global Network
http://www.ngo.org
This site provides information for non-governmental organizations working with and interested in the United Nations. It has links to selected UN and NGO sites.

OECD Online
http://www.oecd.org
This is the Web site of the Organisation for Economic Co-Operation and Development. It contains information and news about OECD, as well as publications and documents.

United Nations and Other International Organizations
http://www.undcp.org/unlinks.html
This site is maintained by the UN's International Drug Control Programme (UNDCP). It contains links to UN agency and office sites, and to sites for related non-UN resources arranged by subject.

United Nations Home Page
http://www.un.org
This page is the searchable site of the United Nations. It contains information and news related to the UN, its members, and activities. The site provides links to resources, publications, and related sites.

United Nations Scholars' Workstation Home Page at Yale University
http://www.library.yale.edu/un
This site was developed by the Yale University Library and the Social Science Statistical Laboratory. It provides links to UN-related pages, resources, and research tools at Yale, and can be searched by keyword. Some links are to proprietary resources and may be accessible.

World Health Organization
http://www.who.org
This site contains information, news, and publications of WHO. It includes links to WHO offices and related NGOs. The site is searchable by keywords.

Yahoo!—Government: International Organizations
http://dir.yahoo.com/government/international_organizations
This is the Yahoo! directory of selected international organizations. It is searchable, using Yahoo!

African Studies

MAJOR GUIDES

McIlwaine, John. *Africa: A Guide to Reference Material.* London: Hans Zell Publishers, 1993. 507p.
This volume provides detailed annotated entries to over 1,800 reference sources, other than bibliographies, on Africa south of the Sahara. The author includes encyclopedias, dictionaries, directories, handbooks, gazetteers, almanacs, bibliographical sources, and statistical compilations. The volume is arranged by country and includes an author and subject index.

Zell, Hans, and Cecile Lomer. *The African Studies Companion: A Resource Guide and Directory.* London: Hans Zell Publishers, 1997. 276p.

This concise volume provides quick and easy access to information in the field of African Studies. All the entries are annotated and cross-referenced. The volume covers bibliographies, yearbooks, dictionaries, directories, biographical sources, guides to film and video, guides to the Internet, guides to archives and libraries, guides to statistics, and handbooks and encyclopedias. The book identifies important journals and magazines, libraries and documentation centers, publishers, dealers and distributors, African associations and societies, foundations and prizes. The work includes an author and title index.

ADDITIONAL GUIDES

Barker, Philip. *International Directory of African Studies Research.* 3rd ed. New York: Hans Zell Publishers, 1994. 319p.
Gosebrink, Jean E. Meeh. *African Studies Information Resources Directory.* Oxford: Hans Zell Publishers, 1986. 572p.

MAJOR WEB SITES

African Studies World Wide Web: University of Pennsylvania
http://www.sas.upenn.edu/African_Studies/AS.html
    This site, established at the University of Pennsylvania, includes information about African Studies programs and resources, teaching and learning resources, multimedia information, government documents, and funding sources. There are excellent country-specific pages, which are consistent in style and format. This is a very comprehensive and easy-to-use site which is useful to both scholars and students.

African Studies: World Wide Web Virtual Library
http://www.columbia.edu/cu/libraries/indiv/area/Africa/
    This site contains links to African Studies programs, Africa-related organizations, and related home pages and links. The page also includes links to historically Black colleges and universities in the United States. As a Virtual Library site, this is a good starting point for all categories of users.

ADDITIONAL WEB SITES

Africa South of the Sahara: Selected Internet Resources
http://www-sul.stanford.edu/depts/ssrg/africa/guide.html

African Links on the Internet: Yale University
http://www.cis.yale.edu/swahili/afrilink.html

African Studies Center: UCLA James S. Coleman African Studies Center
http://www.isop.ucla.edu/jscasc

African Studies Program of the University of Wisconsin–Madison
http://polyglot.lss.wisc.edu/afrst/asphome.html

Africana Collection: University of Florida
http://www.uflib.ufl.edu/cm/africana

Africanet
http://www.africanet.com

Center for African Studies: University of Illinois at Urbana–Champaign
http://wsi.cso.uiuc.edu/CAS/index1.html

Joint Center for African Studies: University of California at Berkeley–Stanford University
http://socrates.berkeley.edu/~africa2

Asian Studies

Major Guide

Dalby, Andrew. *South East Asia: A Guide to Reference Material.* New York: Hall Zell Publishers, 1993. 302p.
>   This fully annotated guide to reference sources on Southeast Asia provides information about encyclopedias, directories, handbooks, government documents, gazetteers, almanacs, biographical and statistical sources, language directories, and atlases. The volume contains an author, title, and subject index.

Additional Guide

International House of Japan Library. *A Guide to Reference Books for Japanese Studies.* Rev. ed. Tokyo: International House of Japan Library, 1997. 447p.

Major Web Sites

Asian Studies Network Information Center at the University of Texas
http://asnic.utexas.edu/asnic.html
>   The main objective of this site is to assist scholars and students in finding information on the Internet about Asia and Asian Studies programs. In addition to individual countries, one can find information by regions, institutions, and topics. This is a very easy-to-use site that is good for students and non-specialists alike.

Asian Studies World Wide Web Virtual Library
http://coombs.anu.edu.au/WWWVL-AsianStudies.html
>   Started in 1994 and supported by the Australian National Library, this is a well-organized and comprehensive Web site on all of Asia. It is an excellent place to find data, news sources, electronic journals, and subject-oriented materials. The site is very content-rich. It also contains virtual libraries for specific regions and individual countries in Asia. The regional virtual libraries include South Asia, Southeast Asia, East Asia, Central Asia, and the Asian continent.

Orientation: Asia's Web Directory
http://as.orientation.com
>   This multilingual commercial site is especially strong for business and financial news. It contains a great deal of interdisciplinary material as well, including the arts and activities, business and trade, events past and present, facts and information, ideas and institutions, people and cultures, science and technology, and travel and exploration. The areas are searchable by category, country, word, or phrase. This site is not as valuable as the Asian Studies Virtual Library's site, but it is current and multilingual.

Additional Web Sites

AccessAsia Crossroads
http://www.accessasia.com/xroad/mainmenu.html

AsiaOne
http://www.asia1.com

Association for Asian Studies
http://www.aasianst.org

Center for Southeast Asian Studies: University of Hawaii at Manoa
http://www.hawaii.edu/cseas

Center for Southeast Asian Studies: University of Wisconsin–Madison
http://www.wisc.edu/ctrseasia

East Asian Institute: Columbia University
http://www.columbia.edu/cu/sipa/REGIONAL/EAI

East Asian Libraries Cooperative World-Wide Web
http://pears.lib.ohio-state.edu

Electronic Resources on Chinese Regions
http://www.columbia.edu/cu/libraries/indiv/eastasian/china.html

J Guide: Stanford Guide to Japan Information Resources
http://fuji.stanford.edu/jguide

Japan Information Network
http://www.jinjapan.org

South Asia Resource Access on the Internet —SARAI
http://www.columbia.edu/cu/libraries/indiv/area/sarai

Southeast Asian Studies World Wide Web Virtual Library
http://iias.leidenuniv.nl/wwwvl/southeast.html

Canadian Studies

MAJOR GUIDE

Bond, Mary, and Martine Caron, eds. *Canadian Reference Sources: An Annotated Bibliography.* Vancouver, B.C.: UBC Press, 1996. 1076p.
This comprehensive guide to Canadian reference sources is an excellent work for anyone interested in Canadian Studies. The volume includes entries to general reference works, history and related works, the humanities, languages and literature, performing arts, philosophy, and religion. The annotations for each entry are in English and French. The work includes a name index, title index, English subject index, and French subject index.

ADDITIONAL GUIDE

Ryder, Dorothy E. *Canadian Reference Sources: A Selective Guide.* 2nd ed. Ottawa: Canadian Library Association, 1981. 311p.

MAJOR WEB SITES

Canada Internet Resources: University of California–Berkeley Library Web
http://www.lib.berkeley.edu/Collections/Romance/canada.html
This site provides easy access to links on Canadian news, statistics, government services, politics, history, culture, education, and research. It is an excellent site that provides numerous links to Canadian Studies. The site is well designed and easy to use.

Canadian Studies Connections: World Wide Web Resources for Canadian Studies
http://www.er.uqam.ca/nobel/c1015/connections/e_index.htm
This site provides the best access to Canadian Studies programs, research centers, journals, scholarly societies and associations, other Canadian sites and links of interest, and Canadian Studies internationally.

ADDITIONAL WEB SITES

American Studies Web
http://www.georgetown.edu/crossroads/asw

Canadian Information by Subject: National Library of Canada
http://www.nlc-bnc.ca/caninfo/ecaninfo.htm

Canadian Studies Center: The Henry M. Jackson School of International Studies
http://jsis.artsci.washington.edu/programs/canada/canada.html

North American Studies at Duke University
http://www.duke.edu/web/northamer

European Studies

MAJOR GUIDES

Carroll, Freda, and Barbara Zolynski. *Basic Sources of European Union Information.*
Manchester: European Information Association, 1996. 95p.
This is a basic bibliography and guide to sources of information about various aspects of the European Union. The work covers law, activities of European Union official institutions, current awareness services, policy areas, reference works, bibliographical sources, and electronic sources of information. It includes an appendix of publishers' addresses.

Loughlin, John, ed. *Southern European Studies Guide.* London: Bowker-Saur, 1993.
233p.
This edited area studies guide includes eleven chapters by specialists in the field who discuss the current monographic literature on Portugal, Spain, Italy, Greece, Cyprus, Malta, Economic Development, Immigration, Tourism, and the European Community and Southern Europe. The work includes an author and title index.

ADDITIONAL GUIDES

Commission of the European Communities. *Infoguide: Guide to Sources of Information on European Community Research.* 2nd ed. Luxembourg: Commission of the European Communities, 1993. 89p.
European Commission Delegation to the U.S. *The European Union: A Guide.* Rev. ed. Luxembourg: Commission of the European Communities, 1993. 89p.

MAJOR WEB SITES

Europa
http://www.europa.eu.int
This multilingual site is a convenient guide to the European Union. The site is organized into four sections: news, institutions, policies, and the ABCs of the European Union. There are links to other European Union organizations. It has links to World Wide Web servers in European Union offices around the world, EU governments, individuals, and academics. This site is easy to use, authoritative, and updated frequently. It is searchable by keyword or phrase.

Western European Specialists Section: Association of College and Research Libraries
http://www.lib.virginia.edu/wess
This site provides specialists on Europe with information. The site includes links to regional resources, news services, legal sources, on-line texts, library resources, and book reviews. The site is easy to use and reliable. It also is the home page for the Western European Specialists Section of the Association of College and Research Libraries. Consequently, it is a good introduction to sites that provide information supporting the research and teaching of Western European Studies.

World Wide Web Virtual Library: West European Studies Research Resources
http://www.pitt.edu/~wwwes
This site contains references to Internet resources on Western Europe. The focus is

on Europe since 1945. The site is a comprehensive and interdisciplinary guide to World Wide Web sites in the social sciences. The site is co-sponsored by the University Library and the Center for West European Studies at the University of Pittsburgh.

ADDITIONAL WEB SITES

Center for West European Studies: University of Washington
http://jsis-artsci-washington.edu/programs/cwesuw/index.html

Council for European Studies Homepage
http://www.columbia.edu/cu/ces

European Documentation Centre at the University of North London
http://www.unl.ac.uk/edc

European Union in the United States
http://www.eurunion.org

European Union Internet Resources: University of California–Berkeley Library Web
http://www.lib.berkeley.edu/GSSI/eu.html

University of North Carolina Center for European Studies
http://www.unc.edu/depts/europe

Latin American Studies

MAJOR GUIDES

Covington, Paula, et al. *Latin America and the Caribbean: A Critical Guide to Research Sources.* New York: Greenwood Press, 1992. 924p.
This interdisciplinary guide to reference and bibliographic sources is arranged by subjects, including anthropology, art and architecture, databases, economics, education, geography, history, literature, performing arts, philosophy, politics, religion, sociology, and women's studies. Each section includes an essay and bibliography.

McNeil, Robert, ed. *Latin American Studies: A Basic Guide to Sources.* 2nd ed. Metuchen, N.J.: Scarecrow Press, 1990. 458p.
This introductory guide to research on Latin American Studies includes a discussion of libraries and their use, bibliographies, encyclopedias, handbooks, guides, directories, maps and atlases, official documents, and periodicals. The book also covers non-print materials, including databases, microforms, sound recordings, and visual materials. Also discussed are specialized information sources such as census materials, statistics, biographies, law and legislation, and pressure groups. There is a subject index and a reference source index, including authors and titles.

ADDITIONAL GUIDE

Fenton, Thomas, and Mary Heffron. *Latin America and Caribbean: A Directory of Response.* Maryknoll, N.Y.: Orbis Books, 1986. 142p.

MAJOR WEB SITES

Latin American Network Information Center: LANIC
http://info.lanic.utexas.edu
This site is maintained by the Institute of Latin American Studies at the University of Texas. The main purpose of the site is to provide access to Internet sources for schol-

ars and researchers. It includes a country index and an extensive subject index. The site is easy to use, well designed, and very comprehensive. It is one of the best Web sites for students and researchers interested in Latin America.

Library of Congress: Handbook of Latin American Studies: HLAS Online
http://lcweb2.loc.gov/hlas
    The Library of Congress has put this standard reference tool on the Web for greater availability. Each handbook contains approximately 5,000 entries, including books, articles, conference papers, and chapters in books. It covers art, economics, geography, anthropology, government and politics, history, international relations, music, literature, sociology, and philosophy. This site is a great guide to the research and scholarship on Latin America.

Political Database of the Americas
http://www.georgetown.edu/pdba
    The Latin American Political Database is the joint project between Georgetown University's Resource Unit on Democratic Governability at the Center for Latin American Studies, the Unit for the Promotion of Democracy of the Organization of American States, and the Canadian Foundation for the Americas. This site provides documentary and statistical information about Latin America, including constitutions, electoral laws, legislative and executive branch information, and election data. It includes information on political parties, international affairs, and current affairs. It has keyword searching and links to other sites on the Americas.

ADDITIONAL WEB SITES

Center for Latin American Studies: University of Kansas
http://www.ukans.edu/~latamst

Internet Resources for Latin America: New Mexico State University Library
http://lib.nmsu.edu/subject/bord/laguia

Latin America Data Base: A News and Educational Service on Latin America
http://www.ladb.unm.edu

Latin World: A Directory of Internet Resources on Latin America and the Caribbean
http://www.latinworld.com

Stanford University Center for Latin American Studies
http://www.stanford.edu/group/las

Middle Eastern Studies

MAJOR GUIDE

Dorr, Steven. *Scholars' Guide to Washington, D.C., for Middle Eastern Studies: Egypt, Sudan, Jordan, Lebanon, Syria, Iraq, the Arabian Peninsula, Israel, Turkey, Iran.* Washington, D.C.: Smithsonian Institution Press, 1981. 540p.
    This volume identifies collections and organizations related to the study of the Middle East in the Washington, D.C. area. The work describes libraries, archives, museums, music and map collections, film collections, and data banks. The types of organizations annotated include research centers, academic programs, government agencies, associations, cultural exchange programs, religious organizations, and publications and media organizations. The guide includes an oral history and personal papers index, library subject-strength index, name index, and subject index.

ADDITIONAL GUIDES

Auchterlonie, Paul, ed. *Introductory Guide to Middle Eastern and Islamic Bibliography.*
Oxford: Middle East Libraries Committee, 1990. 84p.

Silverburg, Sanford. *Middle East Bibliography.* Metuchen, N.J.: Scarecrow Press, 1992.
564p.

Sluglett, Peter, and Marion Farouk-Sluglett, eds. *The Times Guide to the Middle East: The
Arab World and Its Neighbours.* 3rd ed. London: Times Books, 1996. 349p.

MAJOR WEB SITES

ArabNet: The Online Resource for the Arab World in the Middle East and North America
http://www.arab.net
This site emphasizes news and commercial and cultural information. The site is organized by country and other Web sites, including a Middle East Internet directory.
This site is more useful for students or faculty interested in current events than for
historical research. The site is an excellent starting point for finding other Web resources.

Middle East Network Information Center: The World Wide Web Virtual Library
http://link.lanic.utexas.edu/menic
This site, maintained by the Center for Middle Eastern Studies at the University of
Texas, is perhaps the single best site for Middle Eastern Studies. It links to other centers and institutes. The site is well designed and easy to use. The site is divided into
three major categories: countries, broad categories, and related research resources,
including libraries, outreach, organizations and associations, reference, and conferences. The subject categories include arts and culture, business and economics, government, travel and geography, news, religion, and natural resources and oil.

ADDITIONAL WEB SITES

Center for Middle Eastern and North African Studies: University of Michigan
http://www.umich.edu/~iinet/cmenas

CiAS Front Page
http://i-cias.com

iGuide: Your Guide to Israeli Internet
http://www.iguide.co.il

Shamish: The Jewish Internet Consortium
http://www.shamash.org

University of Utah: Middle East Center
http://www.utah.edu/mec

Oceania and Pacific Studies

MAJOR GUIDE

Kepars, I. *Australia.* 2nd ed. Santa Barbara, Calif.: ABC-Clio Press, 1994. 260p.
The volume includes over 1,000 annotated entries on all aspects of Australia. Subjects covered include geography, natural history, history, politics and law, public administration, foreign affairs and defense, the economy, religion, labor, science and
technology, ethnic studies, and literature, as well as many other topics in the humanities and social sciences. The volume includes an author, subject, and title index.

ADDITIONAL GUIDES

Fry, Gerald, and Rufino Mauricio. *Pacific Basin and Oceania.* Santa Barbara, Calif.: Clio Press, 1987. 468p.

Mills, J. J., and J. Richardson. *Information Resources and Services in Australia.* Wagga Wagga, N.S.W.: Centre for Information Studies, Charles Stuart University, 1992. 505p.

MAJOR WEB SITES

Australia: World Wide Web Virtual Library
http://www.austudies.org/vl
> This site is one of the very best for Australian Studies. It provides links to news sources, academic resources, government information, education, business, and general information and reference. It includes easy access to related World Wide Web Virtual Library sites as well as the Australian Studies Network.

Pacific Studies: World Wide Web Virtual Library
http://coombs.anu.edu.au/WWWVL-PacificStudies.html
> This site covers the Asia-Pacific region as a whole and the Pacific Ocean. There is a menu system that allows one to select a region or country. Also included are search engines that search a database of Asia-Pacific Studies Internet resources.

ADDITIONAL WEB SITES

Australian Studies Network
http://austudies.org

New Zealand: World Wide Web Virtual Library
http://austudies.org/nzvl

Pacific Islanders' Cultural Association: PICA
http://www.pica-org.org

South Pacific Information Network: SPIN
http://sunsite.anu.edu.au/spin

Russian and East European Studies

MAJOR GUIDES

Batalden, Stephen, and Sandra Batalden. *The Newly Independent States of Eurasia: Handbook of Former Soviet Republics.* 2nd ed. Phoenix, Ariz.: Oryx Press, 1997. 233p.
> This volume provides a concise introduction to the newly independent states of Eurasia. For each country the authors provide a short bibliography, statistical profile, history, description, and essay on contemporary issues. There is an author and subject index. While this volume is not a guide to reference sources per se, it is a basic introduction to the new countries that constituted the former Soviet Union.

Burger, Robert, and Helen Sullivan. *Eastern Europe: A Bibliographic Guide to English Language Publications, 1986–1993.* Englewood, Colo.: Libraries Unlimited, 1995. 254p.
> This work continues an earlier volume by Stephen Horak entitled *Russia, the USSR and Eastern Europe.* This volume covers Albania, Bulgaria, Czechoslovakia, the German Democratic Republic, Hungary, Poland, Romania, and Yugoslavia. Each chapter identifies general reference works and bibliographies, as well as monographs on history, government and politics, society, language and literature, the economy, and other topics. The volume includes an author and subject index.

Burger, Robert, and Helen Sullivan. *Russia and the Former Soviet Union: A Bibliographic Guide to English Language Publications, 1986–1991.* Englewood, Colo.: Libraries Unlimited, 1994. 380p.

This volume continues and expands the work of Stephan Horak entitled *Russia, the USSR and Eastern Europe.* The authors identify general reference works, bibliographies, handbooks, encyclopedias, libraries, and archives on a number of specific themes. Those themes include the arts, the economy, education and culture, geography, government and the state, diplomacy and foreign relations, history, military affairs, Russian language and literature, philosophy and political theory, religion, science and technology, social conditions, and minorities. All the entries are annotated, and the volume includes an author and subject index.

ADDITIONAL GUIDES

Bugajski, Janusz. *Ethnic Politics in Eastern Europe: A Guide to Nationality Policies, Organizations and Parties.* Armonk, N.Y.: M. E. Sharpe, 1994. 493p.

Croucher, Murlin. *Slavic Studies: A Guide to Bibliographies, Encyclopedias, and Handbooks.* Wilmington, Del.: Scholarly Resources, 1993. 2 vols.

Gyeszly, Suzanne. *Eastern Europe: A Resource Guide: A Selected Bibliography on Social Sciences and Humanities.* San Bernardino, Calif.: Borgo Press, 1994. 242p.

Ruffin, M. Holt, Joan McCarter, and Richard Upjohn. *The Post-Soviet Handbook: A Guide to Grassroots Organizations and Internet Resources in the Newly Independent States.* Seattle: University of Washington Press, 1996. 391p.

MAJOR WEB SITES

REESWeb at the University of Pittsburgh: World Wide Web Virtual Library
http://www.ucis.pitt.edu/reesweb

The site includes links to subject areas such as government, economics, history, media, and Internet resources by type. It also includes links to national home pages, archives, and related World Wide Web Virtual Libraries.

University of Texas at Austin: Russian and East European Network Information Center
http://reenic.utexas.edu/reenic.html

This is one of the best sites for Russian and East European Studies. It is organized by country and Web resources. The latter section includes current news, libraries and archives, databases, information servers, publications, and subject access. It includes a search engine. It is well designed and easy to use.

ADDITIONAL WEB SITES

Central and East European Legal, Political, Business and Economics World Wide Web Resources
http://law.gonzaga.edu/library/ceeurope.htm

Information about Russia and the Former USSR
http://www.friends-partners.org/oldfriends/mes/russia.html

Links to Russian and FSU Web Resources
http://users.aimnet.com/~ksyrah/ekskurs/russlink.html

Russian and East European Institute: Indiana University
http://www.indiana.edu/~reeiweb

Russian Far East World Wide Web Virtual Library
http://src-home.slav.hokudai.ac.jp/eng/Russia/feast-e.html

Section III. Guides to Language Studies

In this section we list guides and Web sites that are related to the study and teaching of foreign languages. The printed guides are listed first. We have annotated some of the major reference sources and listed them in alphabetical order by author. Additional unannotated guides follow in alphabetical order by author. We have included guides to job and career information for language majors, guides to language learning and teaching, directories of foreign language service organizations, bibliographies on foreign language training and instructional materials, and guides to language associations.

The major Web sites are annotated and arranged in alphabetical order by the name of the site. We have included sites that provide information about the nationally funded resource centers for language study, foreign language learning resources, and language materials and teaching resources. All of the national foreign Language Resource Centers funded under Title VI are listed in the major Web sites section.

MAJOR GUIDE

DeGalan, Julie, and Stephen Lambert. *Great Jobs for Foreign Language Majors.* Lincolnwood, Ill.: VGM Career Horizons, 1994. 242p.
> This invaluable volume discusses all aspects of the job search, including self-assessment, researching careers, writing resumes, networking, interviewing, and graduate school choice. It also discusses a variety of career paths. The authors examine numerous paths, including teaching, translating and interpreting, government work, and educational administration, as well as opportunities in business, industry, and commerce.

ADDITIONAL GUIDES

Byram, Michael, and Veronica Esarte-Sarries. *Investigating Cultural Studies in Foreign Language Teaching: A Book for Teachers.* Philadelphia: Multilingual Matters, 1991. 219p.

Harner, James, ed. *MLA Directory of Scholarly Presses in Language and Literature.* 2nd ed. New York: Modern Language Association of America, 1996. 294p.

Kuber, Cornelius, et al. *NFLC Guide for Basic Chinese Language Programs.* Baltimore: National Foreign Language Center at Johns Hopkins University, 1997. 224p.

Lombardo, Maria, ed. *A Resource Guide to Studying in Italy: Courses in Italian Language and Culture for Foreigners.* Rome: Italy Magazine, 1995. 252p.

United States. Department of Education. *Standards for Foreign Language Learning: Preparing for the 21st Century.* Lawrence, Kans.: Allen Press, 1996. 109p.

Wertsman, Vladimir. *Career Opportunities for Bilinguals and Multilinguals: A Directory of Resources in Education, Employment, and Business.* 2nd ed. Metuchen, N.J.: Scarecrow Press, 1994. 333p.

Woodbridge, Hensley. *Guide to Reference Works for the Study of the Spanish Language and Literature.* 2nd ed. New York: Modern Language Association of America, 1997. 236p.

MAJOR WEB SITES

Center for Advanced Research on Language Acquisition: CARLA, University of Minnesota
http://carla.acad.umn.edu
> Foreign language learning resources and links, especially related to authentic mate-

rials (such as foreign language newspapers) and less commonly taught languages (LCTLs), are collected here for foreign language teachers and learners. The site, a national Language Resource Center, includes references to multimedia language programs, instructional materials, teachers' workshops, multilingual browsing information, and goals in foreign language education.

Center for Applied Linguistics: CAL
http://www.cal.org
> This is the Web site of the Center for Applied Linguistics, a private organization focusing on language research, education, and information. It provides information about the organization, and links to CAL-related projects, directories, publications and products, centers and clearinghouses, and other resources.

Center for Language Education and Research: CLEAR, Michigan State University
http://clear.msu.edu
> A national Language Resource Center, CLEAR's emphasis is on promoting collaborative research in foreign languages and teacher education. Their Web pages describe five groups of activities at the center, including their Web-based journal, *Language Learning & Technology,* and summer institutes on the use of the Internet in foreign language instruction, teaching materials for LCTLs, and other topics.

Computer Assisted Language Instruction Consortium: CALICO
http://calico.org
> This is the Web site of the Computer Assisted Language Instruction Consortium, a membership organization and clearinghouse for modern language teaching and learning. It provides information about the organization, publications, and links to related sites.

CSEES at Duke University
http://www.duke.edu/web/CSEEES/index.html
> This is the Center for Slavic, Eurasian, and East European Studies, a language and area studies National Resource Center as well as a national Language Resource Center.

ERIC Clearinghouse on Languages and Linguistics: ERIC/CLL
http://www.cal.org/ericcll
> This is the Web site of the ERIC (Educational Resources Information Center) Clearinghouse on Languages and Linguistics ERIC/CLL, one of 16 ERIC Clearinghouses. It provides services and materials for language educators, including ERIC Digests, bibliographies, the ERIC/CLL newsletter, and other publications.

Ethnologue: Languages of the World
http://www.sil.org/ethnologue
> Ethnologue, of the Summer Institute of Linguistics, is a major site for checking information about the world's more than 6,000 languages. Now in its 13th edition, it contains more than 100 language maps, overviews of language situations by country, a large list of bibliographic references, 6,700 language descriptions, a language and dialect name index, a language family index and family trees, and a searchable database.

Foreign Language Links
http://monroe.k12.la.us/mcs/hot_list/foreign_lang.html
> Sponsored by the Monroe City Schools, the Foreign Language Section of their Online Resources lists links to a wide variety of foreign language Web pages, including the Global Village French Quarter, the Foreign Language Teaching Forum, e-mail international penpals, and the ZIA Kids Foreign Language Page.

Foreign Language Resources on the Web
http://www.itp.berkeley.edu/~thorne/HumanResources.html
>This is a selective index of Web sites related to foreign (non-English) language and culture. It includes links to sites on various languages, and foreign language learning resources and home pages.

Less Commonly Taught Languages (LCTL) Organizations
http://carla.acad.umn.edu/lctl/orgs.html
>This is the Web site of the LCTL Project at the Center for Advanced Research on Language Acquisition (CARLA), a national Language Resource Center at the University of Minnesota. This list of LCTL organizations is organized into general and specific language groups. Links are provided to some of the organizations.

National African Language Resource Center: University of Wisconsin–Madison
http://african.lss.wisc.edu/nalrc/
>This national Language Resource Center focuses on providing and coordinating U.S. resources and training to enhance the teaching and learning of African languages.

National Capital Language Resource Center
http://www.cal.org/nclrc
>The National Capital Language Resource Center is one of nine federally funded Language Resource Centers, and is a joint project of Georgetown University, George Washington University, and the Center for Applied Linguistics. Its current focus is on effective teaching strategies and foreign language performance tests. Its Web pages provide access to NCLRC research, materials development, and publications.

National Foreign Language Center
http://www.nflc.org
>The National Foreign Language Center (NFLC) at The Johns Hopkins University is a nonprofit research and policy institute dedicated to developing and implementing policies and programs that make the language learning system more responsive to the national interest. The vision that guides the Center's mission, goals, and activities is the recognition that U.S. competence in languages other than English is an issue of national concern.

National Foreign Language Center in Hawaii: University of Hawaii
http://www.lll.hawaii.edu/nflrc
>This national Language Resource Center in Hawaii focuses on research and materials development. These pages link to summer institutes, newsletters and recent publications, as well as to the Foreign Language Multimedia Evaluation Project.

National Foreign Language Resource Center: Ohio State University
http://flc.ohio-state.edu/nflrc/cycle_ii
>At this national Language Resource Center site, users are given access to pathways for research, program evaluation, teacher training, networked materials, and media. Additional resources include materials on teaching the less commonly taught languages (LCTLs) and the *Foreign Languages in the Global Economy* newsletter. A Web-based course for teachers is described, and a "gateway" to language sites is provided.

National K–12 Foreign Language Resource Center: Iowa State University
http://www.educ.iastate.edu/nflrc
>This national Language Resource Center supports professional development for K–12 language teachers, and lists their summer institutes, projects, and publications. There is a particular focus on assessing programs and a new emphasis on technology in the classroom.

Oxford University Language Centre
http://info.ox.ac.uk/departments/langcentre
> This is the home page of the Oxford University Language Centre, its courses, services, and projects. It provides links to Web resources on languages and linguistics.

San Diego State University: Language Acquisition Resource Center: LARC
http://larcnet.sdsu.edu
> One of nine national Language Resource Centers, LARC focuses on innovative technology to improve foreign language skills and language testing. There are links to their multimedia database project, multimedia projects, instructional materials, and summer institutes.

SCOLA: Satellite Communications for Learning
http://www.scola.org
> This is the Web site of SCOLA, a non-profit organization that transmits international television programs in the original language for educational use. SCOLA covers more than 40 countries. The site includes information about SCOLA, its services, program schedules, and links to related sites.

UCLA Language Materials Database
http://www.lmp.ucla.edu
> This Web site provides bibliographic information about teaching materials for the less commonly taught languages. This site also identifies institutions where instruction in these languages can be obtained, and gives profiles that provide sociolinguistic and geographical information.

Virginia Commonwealth University Trail Guide to International Sites and Language Resources
http://www.fln.vcu.edu
> This site is a rich source of foreign language pages that also encourages users to add related sites. It includes a technologically sophisticated and very useful "trail guide" to creating Web pages for teaching foreign languages, and a guide to learning disabilities for foreign language teachers.

World Wide Web Virtual Library Applied Linguistics
http://alt.venus.co.uk/VL/AppLingBBK
> This is the applied linguistics site of the World Wide Web Virtual Library. It provides links to a variety of Web sites related to applied linguistics, and includes conferences, courses, electronic journals, jobs, organizations, people, print journals, and publishers.

World Wide Web Virtual Library Linguistics
http://www.emich.edu/~linguist/www-vl.html
> This is the linguistics site of the World Wide Web Virtual Library. It provides links to various on-line linguistics and language resources.

Yamada Language Guides
http://babel.uoregon.edu/yamada/guides.html
> This page provides a font archive with 112 fonts for 40 languages, as well as a comprehensive list of links to pages about 115 languages.

ADDITIONAL WEB SITES

American Association of Teachers of Slavic and East European Languages
http://clover.slavic.pitt.edu/~aatseel

Center for the Advancement of Language Learning: CALL, Michigan State University
http://call.lingnet.org

Digital Education Network's English Language Teaching and Learning Section
http://www.edunet.com/elt

Foreign Language Instructional Technology Interest Group
http://www.virginia.edu/~asmedia/flitig.html

Foreign Language Learning Center
http://fllc.smu.edu

Foreign Language Resources: University of South Florida
http://nosferatu.cas.usf.edu/languages/flresource.html

Foreign Language Teaching Forum: FLTeach
http://www.cortland.edu/www_root/flteach/flteach.html

General Language Learning Resources: CALL
http://call.lingnet.org/resource/general.htm

Human-Languages Page
http://www.june29.com/HLP

International Clearing House for Endangered Languages
http://www.tooyoo.L.u-tokyo.ac.jp/ichel.html

International Language Development
http://www.ild.com

Language Learning and Technology—Electronic Journal
http://llt.msu.edu/

Language-Learning.net
http://www.language-learning.net

Language Links: A New World of Understanding
http://polyglot.lss.wisc.edu/lss/lang/langlink.html

Languages across the Curriculum: LAC
http://www.language.brown.edu/LAC/Home_Page.html

Rhodes Foreign Language Resource: General Foreign Language Sources
http://www.rhodes.edu/forlanghtmls/genlang.html

Romance Languages Resource Page
http://humanities.uchicago.edu/romance/resources

Voice of the Shuttle: Literatures (Other than English) Page
http://vos.ucsb.edu/

World Language Resource
http://www.geocities.com/Athens/Acropolis/5349

Yahoo!—Linguistics and Human Languages
http://dir.yahoo.com/social_science/linguistics_and_human_languages

Section IV: Guides to International Funding

One of the most critical problems for international and area studies programs is
funding. In this section we have identified guides and Web sites that provide in-

formation about sources of funding. Again, printed sources tend to go out of date quickly, so we have sought to identify current or continuing publications. Printed sources still are extremely useful, as many contain information about past grants. Many of the printed guides also have Web sites that provide additional and up-to-date information. The most important information sources about funding are annotated and listed in alphabetical order by author. Following these entries are additional directories, listed in alphabetical order. Following the directories, major funding Web sites are annotated and arranged in alphabetical order. Additional non-annotated Web sites to a few selected specific funding agencies are then listed in alphabetical order.

DIRECTORIES

Citizens Democracy Corps. *Compendium: U.S. Nonprofit Assistance to Central and Eastern Europe and the Commonwealth of Independent States.* Washington, D.C.: The Corps, 1992– .
This is a directory of organizations providing assistance to Central and Eastern Europe and the Commonwealth of Independent States. It gives profiles of organizations, including brief descriptions, contact information, and types of assistance. The first two volumes contain the profile listings. The third volume contains country sector indexes and various appendices and resource lists.

Klepper, Anne. *Global Contributions of the U.S. Corporations.* New York: Conference Board, 1993. 16p.
This is a report on global giving of U.S. companies, issued by the Conference Board. Based on the Board's annual surveys of corporate contributions, the report includes an executive summary, statistical overview, and six brief case studies of international giving programs of leading companies.

Marquis Academic Media. *Annual Register of Grant Support.* Chicago: Marquis Who's Who, 1969– .
This work includes details about governmental, public, private, and corporate grant programs. Descriptions of each program list addresses, areas of interest, types of grants awarded, eligibility, application procedures, and contact names. The guide is organized by broad disciplinary areas, including international affairs and area studies. Entries are also indexed by subject, organization and program, geography, and personnel.

Rich, Elizabeth, ed. *Guide to Funding for International and Foreign Programs.* 4th ed. New York: Foundation Center, 1996. 397p.
This is a detailed descriptive directory of funding sources with a history of supporting international and foreign programs. Information provided in the entries includes fields and countries of interest, grantmaker type, and limitations. The descriptions are organized by state, with indexes by donor, officer, trustee, geographic location, subject, grantmaker, and type of support, as well as a selected bibliography and a glossary of relevant terms.

ADDITIONAL DIRECTORIES

Bauer, David. *The Complete Grants Sourcebook for Higher Education.* 3rd ed. Phoenix, Ariz.: Oryx Press, 1996. 340p.
Council on International and Public Affairs. *International Studies Funding and Resource Book.* New York: Council on International and Public Affairs, 1990– .

Directory of International Funding Organisations: A Guide for the Non-Profit Sector. West Malling, Kent, U.K.: Charities Aid Foundation, 1997. 273p.

Fogarty, John E., ed. *Directory of International Grants and Fellowships in the Health Sciences.* Bethesda, Md.: National Institutes of Health, 1999. 107p.

Grants to Study in the UK: A Guide for Overseas Students. London: Directory of Social Change, 1998. 20p.

Logan, David. *Transnational Giving: An Introduction to the Corporate Citizenship Activity of International Companies Operating in Europe.* London: Directory of Social Change for Corporate Community Investment in Europe, 1993. 124p.

National Council for Languages and International Studies. *Federal Funding Guide for Language and International Education.* Lincolnwood, Ill.: National Textbook Company, 1995. 36p.

Petrik, John F. *Academic Opportunities: Scholarships, Fellowships, International Study, Undergraduate Research, Postbaccalaureate Education, and Experimental Learning—What They Are, How to Find Them, How to Pursue Them, and What to Do Once You Have Got Them.* West Hartford, Conn.: Graduate Group, 1997. 96p.

United States Information Agency. *USIA Fulbright Program.* New York: The Institute, 1998.

World Bank. *Guide to International Business Opportunities in Projects Funded by the World Bank.* 3rd ed. rev. Washington, D.C.: World Bank, 1995. 32p.

MAJOR WEB SITES

Faculty Grants Directory
http://www.ats.edu/faculty/fgdir.htm
> This site provides information on over 750 funding sources relevant to theology or religion. It is arranged by subjects, sponsors, and grants. This Web site provides links to hundreds of grant organizations.

Federal Money Retriever
http://www.idimagic.com
> This is an inexpensive database program with current information about over 1,300 federal funding programs and more than one trillion dollars in grants and loans. The site is highly informative and provides sample searches.

Federal Register
http://www.access.gpo.gov/su_docs/aces/aces140.html
> Grant announcements from U.S. government agencies are listed at this site. It also includes a searchable database of announcements from previous years.

Foundation Center Online
http://fdncenter.org
> The Foundation Center's Web site provides an on-line library of nonprofit grant resources. The site has many useful resources for grantseekers and grantmakers, as well as information about the Foundation Center.

Grant Advisor Plus
http://www.grantadvisor.com
> This subscription service includes a monthly electronic newsletter for grant opportunities, including international grants and lists of grant and fellowship opportunities. This site is intended for grantseekers at U.S. colleges and universities.

Grants and Related Resources
http://www.lib.msu.edu/dbases/kw/grants.htm
> This is an extensive site developed by Michigan State University. It provides links

and information to funding agencies, descriptions of foundations' funding priorities, bibliographies of published guides, and other useful information for grantseekers.

Grants Database Online
http://www.oryxpress.com/grnton.htm
> This subscription service provides information on more than 8,500 funding programs. It is searchable by title, sponsoring organization, keyword, program type, or any combination. It is also available as a CD-ROM subscription.

GrantsWeb
http://sra.rams.com/cws/sra/resource.htm
> The Society for Research Administrators sponsors this on-line resource. It includes a wide range of public and private sources, agency policies, forms, electronic journals, and legislation.

NonProfit Gateway: A Network of Links to Federal Government Information and Services
http://www.nonprofit.gov
> This Web site presents links to all the major government funding agencies. It also provides links to the *Federal Register* and other important government Web sites. The site is an important place to find out about new laws, regulations, partnerships, and volunteering possibilities.

Sources of Funding in International Affairs
http://www.ned.org/resource/funding/fundmain.html
> Among the resources of the National Endowment for Democracy site are links to foundations that fund international activities. It is arranged alphabetically by name of organization.

URL List for Grant Seekers
http://wsrv.clas.virginia.edu/~ebf9q/url_list.html
> This is a comprehensive annotated list of links to resources, organizations, and agencies for grantseekers. It also provides links to sites for basic Web resources and skills.

ADDITIONAL WEB SITES

The following Web sites are some of the major funding organizations for international and area studies. This is not a comprehensive list. If a funding organization or agency has been identified using a printed directory or another Web site, be sure to check whether that particular organization or agency has its own Web site.

American Council of Learned Societies/Social Science Research Council
http://www.ssrc.org/fcom5.htm

Council of American Overseas Research Centers
http://www.caorc.org

Ford Foundation
http://www.fordfound.org

International Research and Exchanges Board
http://www.irex.org

MacArthur Foundation
http://www.macfdn.org

Mellon Foundation
http://www.mellon.org

National Endowment for Democracy
http://www.ned.org

National Science Foundation
http://www.nsf.gov

Rockefeller Foundation
http://www.rockfound.org

United States Institute of Peace—Grant Program
http://www.usip.org/grants.html

Section V: Guides to Overseas Opportunities

The number of guides and Web sites to international opportunities for jobs, study, and internships is growing each year. We have tried to identify current directories and the best Web sites that provide both information and additional links. Most libraries maintain reference collections devoted to career and study opportunities. Search engines on the Web are useful for finding information about international opportunities as well. As career, study, and other international experiences are not mutually exclusive, some of the directories and Web sites in the career section include information about opportunities for study and internships. Likewise, many of the guides and Web sites in the study section also contain information about career tracks.

Careers

DIRECTORIES

Bell, Arthur. *Great Jobs Abroad.* New York: McGraw-Hill Publishers, 1997. 378p.
   This is a how-to guide and directory containing 1,000 company names and addresses in more than 70 countries. This book also lists Internet job sites, residency requirements, and job descriptions. It includes appendices and a subject index.

Carland, Maria, and Michael Trucano, eds. *Careers in International Affairs.* 6th ed. Washington, D.C.: Georgetown University Press, 1997. 282p.
   Organized by field and type of organization, this guide is an overview of a wide variety of international employment possibilities. It offers descriptions and contact information, a bibliography index, and a separate chapter on the Internet job search.

Griffith, Susan. *Teaching English Abroad.* 3rd ed. Princeton, N.J.: Peterson's Guides, 1997. 415p.
   This is a useful guide about teaching English abroad that also provides information about TEFL/TESOL training. It covers finding a position, preparation, and problems at work and in living in a foreign culture. The second part is a country-by-country guide that includes regulations, placement organizations, and schools. Appendices include a currency conversion chart and a list of consulates in London and Washington.

Griffith, Susan. *Work Your Way around the World.* Oxford: Vacation Work, 1991– .
   This is a comprehensive and informative guide to the preparation and paperwork involved in finding opportunities for working one's way around the world. Individual

chapters are devoted to working a passage by sea, land, or air; running a business; tourism, agriculture, and other industries. Separate chapters address working in the European Union in general, in 14 Western and Northern European countries and in Eastern Europe. This guide also provides information about working in the rest of the world. The appendices include sample itineraries, useful phrases in six European languages, currency conversion charts, and lists of addresses of consulates and organizations. This guide is published biennially.

Halloran, Edward. *Careers in International Business*. Lincolnwood, Ill.: VGM Career Horizon, 1996. 97p.
A primer on preparing for an international business career, this book focuses on identifying the necessary education and knowledge, to evaluate the foreign job market and international entrepreneurship. The appendices include a foreign service exam, a speech by former Secretary of Labor Robert B. Reich, and an interview with a senior executive of an Asian company on hiring Americans.

Hubbs, Clayton. *Work Abroad: The Complete Guide to Finding a Job Overseas*. Amherst, Mass.: Transitions Abroad, 1997. 221p.
This comprehensive guide on working overseas contains five sections: Short-Term Jobs, Teaching Abroad, Teaching English Abroad, Volunteering Abroad, and International Careers. Each section contains a directory of employers or programs in that area. In addition, a selection of key resources on work abroad is provided.

Lay, David, and Benedict A. Leerburger. *Jobs Worldwide*. Manassas Park, Va.: Impact Publications, 1996. 380p.
Those interested in landing international jobs as well as learning helpful planning hints and tips for living abroad will find this guide useful. It provides an extensive breakdown of individual countries, including geographic, economic, and demographic statistics, along with a listing of company names and addresses within those countries. One unique feature of this guide is the section in which one can test one's own overseas employment aptitude.

ADDITIONAL DIRECTORIES

American Society of International Law. *The 1997 International Law Career Guide: A Guide to Career Paths and Internships in International Law*. Washington, D.C.: American Society of International Law, 1997. 170p.

Benjamin, Medea, and Miya Rodolfo-Sioson. *The Peace Corps and More: 175 Ways to Work, Study, and Travel at Home and Abroad*. San Francisco: Global Exchange, 1997. 126p.

Camenson, Blythe. *Opportunities in Overseas Careers*. Lincolnwood, Ill.: NTC Contemporary Publishing Company, 1998. 160p.

WEB SITES

Career Resource Center
http://www.careers.org
This site identifies links to jobs, employers, business opportunities, education indices and associations, and career service professionals. Resources are cross-referenced geographically and alphabetically.

Chronicle of Higher Education: Career Network
http://chronicle.com/jobs
This site provides job postings from both inside and outside higher education. It includes international education programs and services.

Duke University: International Job Resources
http://www.duke.edu/~lpmaskel/intl_jobs.html
> This Web page consists of a list of useful links to job listings, information banks, and organizations.

International Career and Employment Network Job Search Resources
http://www.indiana.edu/~intlcent/icen
> Maintained by the International Center at Indiana University, Bloomington, this site posts international career information on a searchable database. Job postings are listed, and users may also post openings.

International Career Employment Center
http://www.internationaljobs.org
> This site contains information on membership in the International Career Employment Center. Services provided for members include: profiles of major employers of international program professionals; a weekly listing of more than 500 current job vacancies; and opportunities to post one's credentials in their database of international professionals. General information about the organization is provided in addition to membership application information.

Monster Job Search
http://international.monster.com
> At this site, one can browse job listings by international location or career type, receive information about a particular company, and post a resume. Questions about international employment opportunities may be posted to a message board with replies promised "within two days to a week."

Overseas Jobs Web
http://www.overseasjobs.com
> This Web site provides an International Jobs Database that can be searched by keyword or browsed. It includes listings of overseas jobs posted every two weeks, job search resources, and information about traveling abroad.

Peterson's Education and Career Center
http://www.petersons.com
> This site duplicates much of the printed Peterson's guides. It contains information about studying abroad, and provides links to many other useful Web sites.

Purdue University International Career Center
http://www.cco.purdue.edu/student/picc
> This Web site contains access to information sources about international jobs for U.S. and international students. It includes an International Job Search and an Electronic International Career Pathfinder for finding employment opportunities and job listings.

U.S. News Colleges and Careers Center
http://www.usnews.com/usnews/edu/careers/cchome.htm
> This site serves as a location for the *U.S. News and World Report* college and career material on the Web. It includes rankings of graduate schools, hot career tracks, and best values. It is an excellent overall site for study and career opportunities.

Study and Internships Abroad

Major Directories

Cassidy, Daniel. *Dan Cassidy's Worldwide Graduate Scholarship Directory.* 4th ed. Franklin Lakes, N.J.: Career Press, 1995. 249p.

A listing of private financial aid sources, this index is organized by field of study. A "Quick Find" index organizes the information by eligibility requirements. The volume includes a list of helpful publications, a directory of organizations that can provide career information, and an alphabetical index.

Council on International Educational Exchange. *Work, Study, Travel Abroad*. New York: St. Martin's, 1979– .
This guide contains useful information on studying abroad, including sections on study abroad options, selecting a study abroad program, scholarships, loans, and fellowships. It also provides an extensive directory of educational institutions offering yearly, semester, summer, or short-term study abroad programs, which is organized by country.

Higham, Matthew, and Hilary Berkey, eds. *The ACCESS Guide to International Affairs Internships: Washington, D.C.* 5th ed. Washington, D.C.: Access, 1997. 141p.
This directory lists names, addresses, and information for more than 200 organizations that offer international affairs internships. It also provides a bibliography, organization indexes by topic and type of organization, a list of paid internships, and an index of application deadlines.

International Schools Services. *ISS Directory of Overseas Schools*. Princeton, N.J.: International Schools Services, 1981– .
This is an annual directory of kindergarten through twelfth-grade schools abroad with an English language curriculum. The schools themselves provide the information including addresses, data on teaching staff and students, tuition, and curriculum. The entries are organized by country.

Peterson's Guides. *Peterson's Learning Adventures around the World*. Princeton, N.J.: Peterson's, 1997– .
This guide to international learning vacations provides information on destinations, dates, programs, accommodations, and costs. The types of programs include archaeological tours, environmental expeditions, cultural tours, language programs, and outdoor adventures. This guide is indexed by program type, programs offering college credit, and program sponsors.

Peterson's Guides. *Peterson's Study Abroad*. Princeton, N.J.: Peterson's, 1994– .
This is a comprehensive guide to study abroad. This directory lists programs by country and provides short essays on transferring credit, costs, visas, nontraditional destinations, international internships, volunteering abroad, health issues, and opportunities for people with disabilities. This guide is indexed by field of study, program sponsors, host institutions, and internship programs.

Schlacter, Gail, and David Weber, eds. *Financial Aid for Study and Training Abroad*. San Carlos, CA: Reference Service Press, 1992– .
A comprehensive guide, this edition provides information about more than 1,000 funding possibilities for courses, degree programs, internships, seminars, and independent study opportunities abroad. Entries are grouped by eligibility of recipients: high school students, undergraduates, graduates, post-doctorates, and professionals. Entries also are indexed by title, organization, geography, subject, and deadline dates. There also is an annotated bibliography of general financial aids.

Tannen, Greg, and Charles Winkler. *The Student's Guide to the Best Study Abroad Programs*. New York: Pocket Books, 1996. 336p.
This is a guide to study abroad based on surveys of recent alumni. The descriptions are colloquial and subjective. The appendix lists programs by country.

Transitions Abroad. *Alternative Travel Directory.* Amherst, Mass.: Transitions Abroad Publishing, 1995– .
   This is a directory of opportunities in "non-touristic travel." It is an annual compilation of information by *Transitions Abroad* magazine. Listings are divided into "Life-Seeing Travel," "Learning Abroad," and "Working Abroad." Appendices list travel, study and work abroad, publishers and organizations, and a geographic index.

United Nations Educational, Scientific and Cultural Organization. *Study Abroad.* Paris: UNESCO, 1948– .
   This book contains almost 3,000 entries about post-secondary education and training in more than 100 countries. The first part lists international scholarships and courses. The second part lists national scholarships and courses by country. This book includes indexes of international organizations, national institutions, and subjects of study in English, French, and Spanish.

ADDITIONAL DIRECTORIES

Council on Standards for International Educational Travel. *Advisory List of International Educational Travel and Exchange Programs.* Reston, Va.: Council on Standards for International Educational Travel, 1985– .
Fogarty, John. *Directory of International Grants and Fellowships in the Health Sciences.* Bethesda, Md.: U.S. Dept. of Health and Human Services, Public Health Service, National Institutes of Health, 1995– .
Hess, John D. *Studying Abroad/Learning Abroad: An Abridged Edition of the Whole World Guide to Culture Learning.* Yarmouth, Maine: Intercultural Press, 1997. 147p.
Institute for International Education. *Academic Year Abroad.* New York: Institute of International Education, 1988– .
Krannich, Ronald L., and Caryl Rae Krannich. *Jobs for People Who Love Travel: Opportunities at Home and Abroad.* 2nd ed. Manassas Park, Va.: Impact Publications, 1995. 294p.
National Association of Foreign Student Affairs. *Directory of Institutions and Individuals in International Educational Exchange.* Washington, D.C.: National Association for Foreign Student Affairs, 1983– .
Petrik, John. *Academic Opportunities: Scholarships, Fellowships, International Study.* West Hartford, Conn.: Graduate Group, 1997. 96p.

WEB SITES

American Institute for Foreign Study
http://www.aifs.org
   This site provides information about study abroad for college students, educational travel programs for high school students, and study programs in the United States for foreign students. The site provides a wealth of information about cultural exchange programs throughout the world.

Best Bets for Internships Abroad: University of California at Irvine
http://www.cie.uci.edu/~cie/iop/internsh.html
   This site is maintained by the University of California at Irvine International Opportunities Program. It provides links to Web sites related to internships abroad, and has a list of links to sites of major international internship programs.

CCIS: College Consortium for International Studies
http://www.ccisabroad.org
   This site is maintained by the College Consortium for International Studies, a consortium of over 170 colleges and universities, which offers more than 40 study abroad programs in 28 countries. It provides links to descriptions of CCIS programs,

listed by country and subject area. The site also has a course database that is searchable by subject category and program name.

Digital Education Network Study Abroad Index
http://www.edunet.com/couridx.cfm
> This site allows one to select a country and category, such as language school, and search the database for international jobs. It covers all kinds of career opportunities, including language, business, education, tourism, and many more.

Institute of International Education Online: IIE Online
http://www.iie.org
> This site provides information about educational exchange and training opportunities, including fellowships for U.S. and international students. The site includes reference materials and resources for statistical and policy research.

jobNET: Internships Web site
http://www.westga.edu/~coop
> This page is the jobNET Web site at the State University of West Georgia. It presents a collection of links to Web sites that post job-related resources. It includes international opportunities.

Mobility International USA
http://www.miusa.org
> This unique site provides information about volunteering overseas, exchange opportunities, and financial aid for individuals with disabilities. It also has a selected set of links to useful sites.

Nonprofit Internships Search Engine
http://www.idealist.org/IS/intern_search.html
> This site includes a search engine allowing one to search for internships by location, skills, or areas of interest. Users also may subscribe to daily mailings of nonprofit jobs and internships.

Online Study Abroad Directory: OSAD
http://www.istc.umn.edu/osad
> A non-profit student organization at the University of Minnesota maintains this searchable database of study abroad programs and scholarships for foreign study. Users can search by field of study, region, and type of program.

People to People International: Overseas Internship Programs
http://www.ptpi.org/studyabroad
> This site, maintained by People to People International, provides information about their overseas internships. PTPI internships are available in a variety of fields and geographic locations. The site lists programs in more than a dozen countries, and gives basic descriptions and information on costs, dates, language requirements, and application procedures.

Study Abroad Programs Directory
http://www.studyabroad.com
> The Study Abroad Programs Directory lists thousands of programs a user can search by country, semester, or subject. It also includes a list of internships, summer law programs, a discussion forum, tips, and a consumer information page.

UNESCO Education Information Service
http://www.education.unesco.org
> This site provides links and contact information for Ministries of Education, National Education Commissions, multi-regional higher education associations, non-governmental organizations, and other resources.

United Nations Volunteers
http://www.unv.org

> This site contains information about overseas volunteer opportunities with the United Nations.

Worldwide Classroom: Library of International Programs
http://www.worldwide.edu

> This site provides information on international study opportunities in more than 100 countries. It is searchable by country and category. The site includes information to help students prepare for travel and study abroad. It also provides a section of comments from past participants, organized by country and school name.

CONTRIBUTORS*

David E. Albright is Research Associate of the Center for the Study of Global Change at Indiana University and a visiting scholar of the Russian and East European Institute.

The American Council on Education (ACE) is the nation's co-ordinating higher education association. Its offices are in Washington, D.C.

Anne Banda is an administrator in the School of Nursing at the University of Wisconsin–Milwaukee and previously served as Assistant Director of the Center for International Studies.

Robert H. Bates is Eaton Professor of Science and Politics, and Fellow of the Institute for International Development at Harvard University.

Richard D. Brecht is Director of the National Foreign Language Center at The Johns Hopkins University.

Mollie Brown is working in Panama as an adviser for the Free Market Development Advisers Program, sponsored by USAID.

Barbara B. Burn is Associate Provost for International Programs at the University of Massachusetts, Amherst.

H. Thomas Collins is Director of Project LINKS at the Elliot School of International Affairs, George Washington University.

Frederick R. Czarra is a former Executive Editor of *The Social Studies,* and is a consultant in social studies and interdisciplinary learning for the Council of the Chief State School Officers in Washington, D.C.

*Wherever possible, biographical notes have been updated from those that appeared in the originally published sources.

Christoffer M. Escher is Operations Manager for Northwest Radiation Therapy Products, Seattle. He previously worked for the Center for International Business Education and Research (CI-BER), University of Washington.

Robert Goehlert is the librarian for economics, political science, and criminal justice at Indiana University–Bloomington and library liaison to the Center for the Study of Global Change.

Peter A. Hall is Professor of Government in the Department of Government and Senior Associate at the Center of European Studies, Harvard University.

Robert G. Hanvey is a writer and educator with a special interest in global education. He resides in the Bloomington, Indiana area.

Ralph Hines is Director of the International Education and Graduate Programs Office, U.S. Department of Education.

Chalmers Johnson is President of the Japan Policy Research Institute. For more than thirty years, he taught Asian politics at the Berkeley and San Diego campuses of the University of California.

Richard D. Lambert is former Director of the National Foreign Language Center at The Johns Hopkins University.

Lin Lin is Research Associate in the Department of Administrative and Policy Studies, School of Education, University of Pittsburgh.

James Mauch is Professor of Higher Education in the Department of Administrative and Policy Studies, and associate faculty in the Center for Latin American Studies, University of Pittsburgh.

Merry M. Merryfield is Associate Professor in the College of Education at The Ohio State University.

John D. Metzler is Assistant Professor of African Studies and International and Comparative Education at Michigan State University, and coordinator of outreach activities for the African Studies Center.

Walter F. Mondale was Vice President of the United States under Jimmy Carter from 1977 to 1981, and served as U.S. Ambassador to Japan under President Clinton from 1993 to 1996.

Richard W. Moxon is Associate Professor of Management and Organization at the University of Washington, Seattle.

Jodi Nachtwey is a doctoral candidate in political science at the University of Wisconsin–Milwaukee.

Elizabeth A. C. O'Shea is Managing Director of the University of Washington's Center for International Business Education and Research (CIBER).

Kenneth Prewitt is Director of the U.S. Census Bureau. Formerly he was President of the Social Science Research Council in New York.

Robert A. Scott is the President of Ramapo College of New Jersey.

Andrew F. Smith is President of the American Forum for Global Education.

Seth Spaulding is Professor of International and Development Education in the Department of Administrative and Policy Studies at the University of Pittsburgh.

Anthony Stamatoplos is an instructional librarian at the University Library of Indiana University–Purdue University, Indianapolis.

Sidney Tarrow is Maxwell M. Upson Professor of Government at Cornell University.

Mark Tessler is Professor of Political Science at the University of Arizona, and Director of the Center for Middle Eastern Studies.

David M. Trubek is Dean of International Studies, University of Wisconsin–Madison.

Toby Alice Volkman is Program Officer in the Ford Foundation's Education Media, Arts, and Culture Program, and oversees the Crossing Borders initiative.

A. Ronald Walton was an Associate Professor of Chinese Language and Linguistics at the University of Maryland, College Park, and Deputy Director of the National Foreign Language Center at The Johns Hopkins University.

David Wiley is Professor of Sociology and Director of the African Studies Center at Michigan State University. He co-chairs the Council for Title VI National Resource Center Directors and co-directs the National Consortium for Study in Africa.

INDEX

AACRAO. *See* American Association of College Registrars and Admission Officers

AASCU. *See* American Association of State Colleges and Universities

Achen, Christopher, 74

ACLS. *See* American Council of Learned Societies

Africa, 20; bibliographic guides on, 382–383; social science scholarship in, 330–331; Web sites on, 382–383

AIEA. *See* Association of International Education Administrators

Aiken, George, 13

Ajami, Fouad, 283

ALO. *See* Association Liaison Office for University Cooperation in Development

Altbach, P. G., 205

American Association of College Registrars and Admission Officers (AACRAO), 202, 207

American Association of State Colleges and Universities (AASCU), on global education, 205

American Council of Learned Societies (ACLS), 13, 47, 77, 78, 81–83

American Council on Education (ACE), globally competent workforce, 337–348

American Forum for Global Education, The, 173

American Overseas Research Centers (AORC), 9, 16, 18

American Political Science Association, 97

Anderson, Benedict, 72, 99

Anderson, Martin, 59, 75

anthropology, future in international research, 328–329

AORC. *See* American Overseas Research Centers

area studies: accomplishments of, 77–78; bibliographic guides on, 375–379; centers, challenges of globalization for, 293; conflicts with rational choice theory/

disciplinary social science, 49, 51–57, 58–65, 67–76, 293–294; development of "area-based programs," 296; emergence of centers at University of Wisconsin–Madison, 303–304; funding decrease for, 32–34; funding during Cold War, 74; future of, 283–297; history of, 6–10; methodology of, in contrast to globalization studies, 306, 314; "orientalism," 70, 316; response to globalization by SSRC, 78–95; revitalization of, 71; revitalization of, by Ford Foundation grants, 320–323; rigidity of "areas," 35; U.S. parochialism in, 79–81, 86–87, 293, 314; value during Cold War, 70, 294; versus disciplines, 51–57, 58–65, 67–76, 87–88, 329; versus globalization, 96–100; versus transnational studies, 35–37; Web sites, 379–381. *See also* Title VI of the Higher Education Act (HEA)

area-based knowledge. *See* globalization

arms control, 229

Army Specialized Training Program, 13

Asia: Pacific Rim countries, 165; bibliographic guides on, 384; Web sites on, 384–385

Asian Power and Politics: The Cultural Dimensions of Authority (Pye), 63

Association Liaison Office for University Cooperation in Development (ALO), 205–206

Association of International Education Administrators (AIEA), study abroad programs, 187–188, 189

Australia, recruiting foreign students, 43, 198–199

Barber, Benjamin, "Jihad and McWorld," 289–290

Bates, Robert, 72–73, 97; on area studies and social science disciplines, 51–57, 291; critique of, by Johnson, 58–66

belief systems, in global education curriculum, 230